IHS
DE CONTROVERSIIS
CHRISTIANAE FIDEI
ADVERSUS HUIUS TEMPORIS
HAERETICOS
ON THE CONTROVERSIES OF
THE CHRISTIAN FAITH
AGAINST THE HERETICS
OF THIS TIME
ST. ROBERT BELLARMINE
OF THE SOCIETY OF JESUS
DOCTOR OF THE CHURCH
TRANSLATED FROM
THE ORIGINAL LATIN BY
RYAN GRANT
MEDIATRIX PRESS

IHS
Roberti
Bellarmini
S.R.E.

DE CONTROVERSIIS

ON THE CHURCH

VOL. I:
ON COUNCILS
ON THE CHURCH MILITANT
ON THE MARKS OF THE CHURCH

by

ST. ROBERT BELLARMINE, S.J.

Doctor of the Church

TRANSLATED FROM THE LATIN BY

RYAN GRANT

MEDIATRIX PRESS

MMXVII

On the Church
St. Robert Bellarmine

Translated from:
De Controversiis de fidei Christianae adversus hujus temporis haereticos; Tomus II, De Conciliis, De Ecclesia Militante, De Notis Ecclesiae
Tri-Adelphorum, Paris, 1614

ISBN-13: 978-0692903513
ISBN-10: 0692903518

Mediatrix Press
607 E. 6th Ave
Post Falls, ID 83854
www.mediatrixpress.com

Table of Contents

Translator's Preface

ANYONE familiar with our other translations will already be used to the style and model followed there. We have, however, made some changes for this edition that will be reflected in future translations of the Controversies.

I have had the benefit of feedback from Academics and lay theologians, as well as priests, as to the format and rendering of certain terms, which will be reflected in this volume on the Church. The first is in the way of references. In the past, I footnoted the sources which Bellarmine provides no matter how dizzying the number of notes on a given page. In this volume, which incorporates three books previously published separately, this change is reflected in the work on *Councils*, but not in the other two treatises.

A second change, is, whenever possible, we have adjusted how we render the names of the authors that Bellarmine cites to be in accord with how they are typically cited rather than using their Latinized names. This is also reflected in *On the Church Militant* and *On the Marks of the Church.*

Next, we should look to the question of the relevance of this particular work. How accurate was Bellarmine? Interestingly, what historians relate today about ancient councils are largely the same as what Bellarmine relates, although the former know very little of the latter. Bellarmine's analysis is based in primary sources, scripture and the Fathers, resulting in a powerful argument grounded in Catholic tradition. Certainly not every individual thing will be cutting edge for us today as historical scholarship continues and does not remain ossified in any century, no matter how brilliant the intellects; nevertheless, the theological import of Bellarmine's argumentation is not only valid for us today, but entirely needed for a return to the sources and acts of individual Councils. Likewise, Bellarmine's work on the Church Militant is foundational for every text on Ecclesiology until and even including the Second Vatican Council.

What is particularly important here, is that Bellarmine lays down principles that become the fundamental principles of ecclesiology. Then in future books on the Church, such as his work on Clergy, Monks and Laity, all the particular considerations follow logically from the principles laid out here.

Next, in regard to the *Marks of the Church*, Bellarmine does not write on the Marks as given in the Creed: One, Holy, Catholic and Apostolic; rather he continues the work of the theologians of that day in unpacking those four, and developing their consequences in other areas. Thus, in this work, Bellarmine gives 15 Marks of the True Church which can be visibly discerned in history, and uses these to refute Protestant teaching, though they can all be referred back to the aforesaid Four Marks.

Now, a word must be said on the term "Mark." The Latin word is *Nota*, and thus, used to be translated as "Note" by the theologians. *Nota* is from the verb *novisse*, and means "a thing known," or "a thing that something is known by." Yet, since the mid-twentieth century, it has been standard to say the "marks of the Church." Thus we had to resolve a quandary... Do I translate this literally, and in my view, properly, as "note," or more familiarly as "mark?" In fine, "mark" was chosen for the sake of ease for modern readers. Thus my apologies to those who would rather see it as "note."

A word is also in order about Scripture, the Fathers and the Protestants whom Bellarmine quotes. Bellarmine had most of the Bible completely memorized, from an edition that did not have versification. Sometimes, subsequent to the time of the original work, certain verses in Scripture were rendered differently due to reforms of the Vulgate. If this has occurred, I translate what Bellarmine has and note the variation in the footnote. Secondly, where Scripture is concerned, I have made my own translations from the Vulgate, rather than using Bibles based on the Vulgate that are in print now. This is because it is important to understand the Vulgate as Bellarmine did, not as Englishmen half a world away that rendered it for an entirely different purpose. In like manner, I have also rendered the Fathers and other authors, *e.g.* Calvin, from their Latin works. With Calvin this is particularly because I have not found any translations of the *Institutes* coming from the French satisfactory, so I have consulted the 1559 Latin version which seems to be the one Bellarmine used in his own citations, and consequently this is important because it again shows us how Bellarmine understood Calvin.

It is also important to understand the style of argumentation. For Bellarmine, argumentation is made from Scripture and also from the Church Fathers. Though he certainly agreed that individual Fathers could err or go astray, nevertheless, following the principles of all theologians and the Council of Trent, if they were found in a common consensus then the teaching must be infallible. Thus the copious citations of the Fathers which make up this work are necessary to draw a consensus on given points of argument.

Lastly, I have followed the standard English custom of not capitalizing the pronouns for which God is the antecedent, as this is not normally done in scholarly works as it is in devotional books.

As in all my translations, I have endeavored to stay as true to the Latin as possible, even to the point of being slavish in some places, to avoid losing the meaning of a given point, though not so slavish as to retain the endless participle phrases and the "therefore" of every sentence which is such a hallmark of good Latin rhetorical style. Any glosses for clarification are relegated to footnotes, which are simply marked as "-Translator's note."

Next, I would like to especially thank all of those who made this work possible, firstly my wife, whose patience and great sacrifices have allowed me to get this completed. Then, I would like to thank all of those who assisted in the editing of this work, and Dr. Robert Sungenis who graciously has assisted with the Hebrew, sometimes researching and verifying words that the 16th century print got wrong. I would also like to thank Paul Banducci of the Bulldog Pipe and Cigar lounge, who has provided a wonderful and clean establishment for me to smoke, principally because it has furthered this work.

Then, I would like to thank all the benefactors of the Bellarmine translation project, whose donations have allowed me to work on this at all. This project has its goal to have all of the *De Controversiis* translated, but it could never come into being were it not for these great benefactors. I ask the reader to say a prayer for their intentions, and if anyone else should like to assist in this project, they can do so by going to http://www.mediatrixpress.com and going to the Bellarmine project tab.

Post Falls, ID
March 2017

Omnibus benefactoribus laboris S. Roberti Bellarmini votum esse, et praesertim Bryan McCreary atque Erico et Katarinæ Mack, praesidio ejus remoto, hic liber fieri non posset.

Dedicated to all the benefactors of the St. Robert Bellarmine project, and most especially Brian McCreary as well as Eric and Katy Mack, without whose assistance this work would not be possible.

PREFACE

IN this book I am going to defend, with all my strength, the authority of the Sacred Councils, which has always been great in the Church, in opposition to the manifold lies and calumnies of the heretics. Still, before I approach this matter, I have thought a few words must be said on the supreme and incredible subtlety that the supporters of Satan have applied to lessen this authority in our times. For, because the authority of Councils is sacrosanct in the Catholic Church, as is just, it always served to diminish the greatest disturbances of affairs, like a sort of salutary lightening, to shine the light in order to dissipate the darkness of error. As a result, the enemy of the human race reckoned that he could no longer sow discord as well as schism in the Church, and to preserve and propagate heresy, unless he abolished Ecclesiastical judgments and would overturn that chair from which Christ himself speaks and judges through men and settles all controversies and quarrels of faith.

Therefore, he raised up Lutherans, prepared to deceive even as they were prepared to lie, since in the beginning they believed it would never happen that the Supreme Pontiff could be induced to call a general Council. So they began with great contention, even as they grievously accused the Pope at the same time, to appeal to the need for a general Council against the same Pope. They devised this in such a way that they meant to sprinkle each and every one of the crimes and disgraces, although false and unbelievable, freely upon the Pope, and that it would be granted to the Council and all Christian nations to make him guilty of the greatest crimes. These meanwhile, though not yet recognized as enemies of the Church by all (as they really were), were seen as men loving piety and faith, since they were zealous for and recognized the authority of Councils. For that reason, they clearly persuaded many nations with the calumnies and lies that they used to adorn the vicar of Christ, by both word and letter, that he was no Christian prelate at all, but the avowed enemy of Christ even to the point that they said he was truly and properly called Antichrist.

I would most certainly give a lengthy speech were I to review the lies which the heretics of our time most impudently cast onto the Pontiff of the Apostolic See. For the sake of example, I will place one or two. Luther said: (*lib. de Ecclesia*, near the end), "The Pope buried the Sacred Scripture in mud and ash, and nearly blotted out the whole of Christian doctrine." There is also extant a little book titled, *de primatu Papae*, written in the name of the whole Schmalkaldic Council, though I believe the author is actually Melanchthon, whereby that particular Council of the Lutherans commences from this lie: "The Pope arrogates to himself the authority of fashioning laws on worship, to change the Sacraments, doctrine and wants his articles, his decrees, his laws to be accounted equal to divine laws; ... The Pope arrogates to himself divine authority, because he takes for his own the right to change the doctrine of Christ and the worship established by God, and means for his doctrine and worship to be observed as though it were divine."

Yet, what Sacrament, what worship established by God, what article of doctrine has the Pope changed? And who was that Pope who equated his own laws with divine laws? Or do we not see Pontifical laws abrogated on a daily basis, either by the same ones who imposed them, or by their successors, if the occasion demanded it? What divine law is read to have ever been abrogated by any Pope? I refuse to waste any more time on trifles of this sort. I affirm this, that the books of the Lutherans are full of lies of this kind, and that those found therein are not doubtful matters, but are celebrated as most certain maxims in the writing and speech of all. Still, from the beginning, as I was saying, lest it would seem that they were altogether foreign to the Catholic Church, as much as they detract from the authority of the Pope, so much the more do they attribute it to a Council. The provocation of Luther for a general Council is still extant. The Imperial diet of Augsburg, Nuremberg, Spire, Ratisbonne, Worms and several others are extant, in which the Lutherans very often demanded a general Council.

Furthermore, lest it would be tiresome if we labored to expunge these lies in the many different acts of the assemblies they have recited, I would advance to you, O reader, the testimony of their own protestation that is contained in the beginning of their book titled: *Protestatio adversus Concilium Tridentium*, where they say: "We profess and protest that we adhere and have always adhered to the protestation and appeal of the Reverend Doctor, Father Luther, from the most unjust and violent judgment of the Pope and of all the judges of his faction, to a free, Christian, and legitimate Council, gathered in the Holy Spirit. Such protestation proceeded and the appeal was afterwards unanimously and so many times renewed by our Churches, and even in so many of the imperial assemblies approved by all states." These are their words whereby, as you see, they affirm firstly Luther, then their Churches, lastly even the Princes that have been added to them, also very often appealed from the Pope to the judgment of the Council.

But, how long do you think they remained of the opinion that they should await a Council? As long as they hoped there would be no Council. For no sooner did Pope Paul III proclaim a general Council at Trent and lay the foundations for the same Council, and as soon as the beginnings appeared, that straightaway they [the Lutherans] changed their minds, or rather, feigned their support beforehand. Then, when it sprung up, they rejected the Council and not only rebuked the appeal to recent Councils, but even to all the ancient ones as well, and hardly had Trent begun than they labored to oppress it with invective, censure, protestations, calumnies and lies, so that, if it could be done, that Council could be answered by the cleverness of the heretics before the diligence of Catholics could join together.

I say that all are my witnesses that it is so who read the book, *de Conciliis,* written by Luther at that time, and the book of Melanchthon concerning the reasons why Lutherans would not go to the Council (*Protestatio*, XXXIV). Of ministers: The book of Illyricus, *de norma ac praxi Concilii*, then Martin Chemnitz, *examen Tridentini Concilii*; (*Examination of the Council of Trent*), and the counsel of Charles Molina over not being admitted to the same Council; and the *Antidote* of John Calvin, *Against the poison of the same Council.* But it will be worthwhile to propose something from those very authors, whom we have named, so that you might understand from their words and testimony how many Councils of the Church they celebrated, which they had agitated for a little earlier.

Martin Luther, when he became famous, proclaimed a Council; after he seized his pen, he wrote a book and titled it, *de Conciliis.* I believe it was so that he would thank God, congratulate the Church and invite all to the Council. Just the same, the chief point of the book is that there is no need for Councils, since even the most ancient, holy and celebrated Councils erred and each Pastor and schoolmaster can be no less in the Church than each of the greatest and most numerous Councils. It begins without controversy from that very ancient and holy Council which the Apostles celebrated at Jerusalem: in that Council the Apostles decreed that one must abstain from blood and animals that had been suffocated. He returns us to these difficulties, that either we ought to abstain from these foods, or clearly affirm we are free not to obey the greatest and first Council. Next, he shows in earnest what a calamity it would be were we no longer to eat deer, rabbits, stags, hares, geese, thrushes and other small birds as well as certain broths which are seasoned not only with pepper, but even with blood (as he himself says, who is well ignorant of such things) or mixed with liquid, or fat mixed into sausage.

Yet, because it seems that Luther is in no way prepared to undergo such a loss, thus he effects that one need not comply with the Apostolic decree, from which again he so concludes that we are all free to leave behind all other Councils, and thus we are free from all Councils. He is altogether clear: just as we are not held by that law of the Council, which was the only one given in that time, so we are not held by the laws of any other Council.

Therefore, he continues to the First Council of Nicaea, the authority of which has always been the greatest in the Catholic Church. Speaking on the canons of that Council, he says: "All these articles were grass, straw, twigs and stubble ... On those wooden articles the rest shall remain, just as some embers, such as the article on the feast of Easter." This is an example of the honor that Luther has for the most ancient and celebrated Council, that he calls its decrees twigs, grass, straw and stubble. But it would be insufficient, if he were to merely say those canons were not necessary and superfluous, and he would not also contend what is dangerous, impossible and self-contradictory. For, he so rejects the Council, lest they who castrate themselves would be excluded from holy Orders, and at the same time it commands consecrated men not to have any woman in their house apart from mother or sister. Luther says: "Here, altogether I do not recognize the Holy Spirit in this Council. If they are not suitable for Ecclesiastical ministry who castrate themselves to avoid the burning of lust, and again they are not suitable who have wives or marry to conquer the goads of the flesh; in which case, will he not, at length, fall? Or, ought a Bishop, or a preacher sustain the intolerable ardor and heat of illicit love, and not free himself from these dangers by wedlock or castration?" It seems for Luther there was no middle ground between wedlock and castration; but then what do we make of Paul, John, James, the other Apostles, Ambrose, Jerome, Gregory and men without number? What, I say, would we make of so many saints who did not cut off their member but still lived to the end of their lives without a wife? Without a doubt they conquered the glorious struggles with prayers, fasting, and assiduous labor, not by the severing of their members.

But, let us hear with what honor Luther speaks on this same Council of Nicaea at about the end of the passage: "On the other hand, is there no other business for the Holy Spirit in Councils than to burden his ministers with impossible, dangerous and unnecessary laws?" Since that is so, you certainly see, O reader, what Luther makes of the authority of Councils when he does not hesitate to impudently call the decrees of the Council of Nicaea twigs, unnecessary, dangerous, impossible, self contradictory, and at length, straw, grass and stubble, even though in comparison to it not one is praised more by the Fathers. Why he would so diminish all Councils that the industry of Pastors and the authority of schoolmasters would compare with them, he says: "Do you think it is not so light, or narrow, the duty of a Pastor or a schoolmaster that they could not be compared to Councils? I shall say indeed it is more and greater a light of Christian doctrine that comes from a child's Catechism than from *all Councils.* ... And what is necessary for words, if the decrees of all Councils would be sent through a funnel into your body, still you would not be a Christian, because they confer too little." This is rightly an egregious conclusion, and worthy of so serious a theologian who a little before was seen to call for a general Council in earnest. I pass over what he says on the second, third and fourth Councils, since they are similar to the first and I am eager for brevity.

Therefore, I come to those lies which our adversaries babble without any shame to diminish the authority of the Council of Trent. Not including everything, nor even a great many things, for that would be a work without end; rather I will advance a few words from many. Luther says: "These sycophants, who are parasites of the Pope are so demented that they rashly defend this contradiction, that Councils have the power to make new articles of faith and change the old ones" (*liber de Conciliis*). But who are these sycophants? Why is no one named? Where, when, by what witness did they say or write that articles of faith can be changed by Councils?

Matthew Flacius Illyricus, in his book, *de norma ac praxi Concilii Tridentini*, says: "They cry out, that is the Fathers of the Council, the Church, that the Pope with his spiritual powers, is above the Scripture and that the Pope can dispense against the Apostle and the whole Old Testament from the plenitude of his power." But the Council is extant, let it be diligently read; no one will ever discover portents of this sort.

Martin Chemnitz's work, *in examine Concilii Tridentini*, is so rich with lies that in four little sentences, five lies are found: "The Fathers, that is, of the Council, say that the Pope may have a will for rule in these matters that he wishes, that he can change the form of the Sacraments handed down from the Apostles, that he can establish against the epistles of Paul, that he can dispense against the first four Councils and against the words of the Gospel." Who would believe such impudent men could be found, who so boldly lie about the Council of Trent when both the acts themselves are read everywhere and also that many of those who were at the Council themselves are still alive!

But another splendid thing altogether remains, and the lie is more often repeated by our adversaries. For many reasons the Lutherans pursue Cardinal Hosius, a man of eternal memory, with an implacable hatred, particularly because he presided at the Council of Trent as a legate of the Apostolic See; moreover, by his industry and wisdom he conferred upon the same Council no small dignity and benefit. Therefore, that they might at the same time downplay the authority of the Legate and of the Council, these good men took certain words which the Cardinal quoted in the book, *de expresso verbo Dei,* of a heresiarch by the name of Swenckfeld, and disseminated them everywhere with great loathing as if the Cardinal had said them. Cardinal Hosius had only quoted them so that he would show how foul the errors of the Lutheran heresy are, like a poisoned fruit that sprouted forth from a corrupt root; yet we read in the book, *Protestatio XXXIV Ministrorum*: "But now let us hear the words of this glorious governor who was present at the assembly [Trent], how, also following some rule, he and his associates mean to judge and determine on the controversies of the Church and religion; for thus he breaks out into blasphemous words, saying: 'but we will wait for the opinion of God from heaven, and both contending with those affairs for their own, not fearing the judgment of the Scriptures, and we will see the Scriptures go away. It does not behoove us to be expert in the Law or Scripture, but taught by God. The labor which is devoted to Scripture is vain. For the Scripture is created, and in need of a certain element, it is not fitting for a Christian to be too addicted to a creature'." After reciting these words, the Protestants add: "This is the nefarious Cardinal legate of Antichrist, and the impious governor of the assembly, he blasphemes against the living God."

Illyricus, in his book, *On the Norm and Practice of the Council of Trent,* after he repeats these words quoted from the book of the Cardinal, he so prays: "Lord Jesus, stop up with infernal fire these blasphemous mouths of Antichrist and his slaves, and defend your glory from their tyranny." Why does it seem to you, o candid reader, that it is an unheard of crime, and clearly an incredible boldness to lie so clearly and impudently for an atrocious cause? The book is in their hands, there is no obscurity in his words, and if the testimony of the author is required, I have heard the most learned old man himself often saying: "If I so thought, would I write such things? If they were my words, truly I would be worthy of a public burning." Still, it was not one or two, but thirty-four ministers that were pleased to take the words of this great man and so twist them into a foreign sense, which clearly were of Swenckfeld, and they believed were of the Cardinal, to me it seems as though someone would contend that the blasphemous words of the Jews concerning Christ: "Behold a glutton and drinker of wine, this is not a man from God who does not keep the Sabbath; he is worthy of death; take him, take him and crucify him!" and others like it, to say that since these are found in the Gospels, they are not the words of the Jews, but of Matthew or John. Therefore, you see how little account our adversaries reckon Councils, and by how many frauds and calumnies they will try to abolish their authority, who just a few years earlier seemed to desire a general Council as a unique remedy for the present disorder.

On the other hand, someone will perchance say that they indeed wanted it, and they still desire a general Council now, but not of the sort that Trent was. It certainly happens that they desire a general Council, but such as never was. For Philip Melanchthon explains the conditions in a little book which he titled: *de Caussis cur Lutherani ad Concilium non accesserint*,[1] and they are chiefly two.

On the one hand, that all learned men ought to have the right to make a decisive vote, whether they are priests or laity; that is something altogether unheard of in the Church of Christ and such an example cannot be advanced from any Council, especially since when they say learned men, they mean those who, when they speak or write, they will mix in some Greek or Hebrew with the Latin.[2] On the other hand, the condition is that safe conduct be given by the Emperor not only in their persons, but also that their persons would not be punished if they refuse to submit to the Council, as well as that

[1] On the reasons why the Lutherans did not come to the Council.

[2] Translator's note: What Bellarmine means is those who insert Hebrew and Greek to show off their learning as a mark of rhetoric to obscure the points at hand.

neither the faith nor the confession of the Lutherans could be condemned, even if the Lutheran Theologians were unable to defend it; such a condition is clearly opposed with the first one, and is inept and ridiculous in itself. For, if neither their persons nor their opinions can be condemned, then the Council will altogether decide nothing.

Therefore, to what end did it attain to ask that even laymen should have a decisive vote if nothing must be decided in the Council? To what end were so many dangers and labors undertaken so as to gather Council? To what end are Bishops and Doctors troubled from the whole world that they should come to a Council? To what end are so many days consumed in proposed questions of faith, struggles and definitions if after all things have been prepared, yet still each decree of the Council is called back into controversy? Not only does Philip Melanchthon teach this, but Martin Luther taught this before him, as well as John Calvin, John Brenz, Martin Chemnitz, and all Lutherans and Calvinists. Luther says in *artic. 115 ex quingentis articulis*: "This Gospel was consigned neither to the Pope nor to Councils, nor to any man in order that he might conclude something is faith. Therefore, I ought to say you, O Pope, have shut up with Councils, now I have judgment, whether I would accept it or not." Moreover, Calvin says in book four of the *Institutes* (lib. 4, cap. 9, §8): "As often as a decree of some Council is advanced, I would first diligently judge in what time it was held, for what reason it was held, and by what counsel such men were present; next the very matter on which it is treated should be examined precisely according to the Scriptures, in that manner that the definition of the Council may have its weight; the nature of the example; still not the examination, which I said, would impede."

Therefore, Calvin would have it that a judgment of a Council is an example, not of a judgment. Next everyone, especially private men, can and ought to judge in regard to that teaching. Chemnitz, Brenz and all others teach this in similar words. But what else is this than to refuse to let any judgment be made? What else is it but to refuse to ever settle controversies and to refuse peace and concord, but instead to allow wars, schisms, disagreements and quarrels to flourish perpetually? But it stands well unless they were to say another thing, that they would escape notice more easily, for certainly heretics do not conduct themselves so. Moreover, now they so advance themselves, that plainly anyone who would not see them as heretics is blind. For, since heresy is so called from the word "choice", there is no clearer mark, no more certain sign of a heretical man than that he refuses to acquiesce to Ecclesiastical judgment, but instead will follow himself as a judge, and choose his own doctrine. Obedience is the companion of faith and humility a mother. The sister of heresy is contumacy, a proud mother.

Since these things are so, now it will be our part that for the great work, industry, and labor that the enemies of faith put forth to shake Ecclesiastical authority, so much more we must put forth to assert and vindicate the same, and because this is seen especially in the Supreme Pontiff and the Councils of Bishops, we also, now that we have given dissertation on the Pope in five books, we may do so on Councils as best we can in spite of the lack of our own genius, with clarity, and the support and direction of God.

Servo in Xº

Roberto Bellarmini.

BOOK I
ON COUNCILS AND THE CHURCH

CHAPTER I
The Order of Disputation

TO this point we have disputed on the head of the Church militant, now we will dispute on the Church herself. Moreover, because the Church can be considered in two ways, both gathered in Councils and diffused throughout the world, for that reason we will treat first on Councils and then on the Church herself. Furthermore, we propose the disputation on Councils before the disputation on the Church, although the natural order would seem to persuade the contrary, because the disputation on Councils is more connected with the disputation on the Supreme Pontiff that precedes it than the disputation on the Church.

Therefore, the controversy on Councils has been posited over two matters, over the definition of a legitimate Council and over the authority of a legitimate Council. The heretics of our time construct a new form of Councils, and to these they attribute almost no authority. Still, we will add the third to these two parts.

Furthermore, the whole disputation is divided into three parts. In the first we pass over certain matters which might appear as though they were added to the disputation itself; such as who wrote on this matter, what might be a Council, how manifold, how many and which have been celebrated to this point, etc. For we will treat all the matters without contention by a simple manner of narration. In the second we will define what the nature of a properly legitimate Council demands, where we will treat on the matter, form, purpose and efficiency of Councils, and also on those matters which our adversaries require in Councils. In the third part, we will treat on the authority of Councils both absolutely and even in comparison to Scripture, as well as to the authority of the Supreme Pontiff.

CHAPTER II
Those who Wrote on Councils

SO as to begin from the first, the books on the very first Councils treat on this matter but were, nevertheless, carelessly preserved and are swarming with many defects that must be corrected from a reading of the Fathers. Thereupon, there are many things extant from the decrees of Gratian, Ivo, Burchard and Martin of Braga; likewise a few things can be read in St. Hilary in his book on Councils, in St. Isidore (lib. 6 *etymolog.* cap. 16); Bede (in *lib. de sex aetatibus;* in *Constantino IV*); Freculph (*Chronicum*) John Psellus and Photius in his book *de septem Synodis.*

Apart from these older writers, more recent ones can be consulted: Thomas Waldensis (lib. 2 *doctrinal. fide*, cap. 26, et 27]; Juan de Torquemada, (lib. 3 *Summae de Ecclesia*); John Gerson (in various treatises *de potestate Ecclesiae et Conciliorum*); Dennis the Carthusian (in three books *de Conciliis*]; John of Eck, (*in Enchiidio*); Jodocus Clichtovaeus *in defense of the Council of Senonensis*; Iodocus Tiletanus (*in defensione Concilii Tridentini*] John Cochlaeus (*in libro de Conciliis*); John Fisher against article 28 and 29 of Luther. Cajetan in various opiscula; Albert Pighius (lib. 6 *hierarch. Ecclesiasticae*); Cardinal Hosius (*in explanation Symboli*, cap. 24 et lib. 2 *contra prolegomena Brentii*); Pedro de Soto in the defense of his confession against Brenz; John Anthony Delphinus (lib. 2 *de Ecclesia*); Melchior Cano (*de locis Theologicis*, lib. 2); Hugh in a work titled *Synodia Hugonia*; likewise, Jacobatius in a work on Councils, Gaspar Villalpandaeus *in disputationibus novem pro Concilio Tridentino*; Alphonsus a Castro (lib. 4 *de haeresibus*;) William Lindanus, lib. 3 cap. 7, *Panopliae Evangelicae.*

CHAPTER III
On the term "Council" and its Origin

THEREFORE, by the term "Council" the same is meant in the Church as by the term of assemblies in the state; for just as when controversy arises in the state, the leaders or the magistrates of the kingdom agree as one, and they establish what in fact must be done, so also in the Church when some controversy arises in religion, the Prelates of the Churches come together and uniting their opinions at the same time they establish what seems to be good. In this way, we see what was done in Acts 15, where the first Christian Councils began to be celebrated, and thereafter in each age.

Furthermore, although Albert Pighius, in *de coelesti hierarchia*, lib. 6, cap. 1, contends that this origin of Councils was human and devised by natural reason, still it is more probable that the origin is divine. The Council of Chalcedon, in its epistle to Pope Leo, as well as the sixth Council (act 17), and Pope Celestine, in his letter to the Council of Ephesus, and the 3rd Council of Toledo teach that Councils are pointed out by the words of Christ himself in Matthew 18:20, "Where there are two or three gathered in my name, there I am in their midst."

Next, it is believable that the Apostles, who were filled with the Holy Spirit, did not come together in the first Council except at the urging of the Holy Spirit himself. Wherefore, they also say: "It has been seen by the Holy Spirit, as well as us, etc." (Acts 15:8). Besides, even if natural reason would have determined that in doubtful matters the Prince consults learned men, that only Bishops would be called and these would not be counselors, but judges, such does not seem to be an invention of human reason alone. At length, it is certain that the celebration of Councils, which has happened in the Church in every century, descends from Apostolic tradition; but I would certainly not dare to call Apostolic traditions the inventions of men. That is enough on the origin, now on the names in one word.

The Latin term "*Concilium*" is discovered everywhere in the Old Testament as well as the New for gatherings of the Jews, but the Greek term, σύνοδος (*synodos*) is not discovered in the Scriptures, for where we read *concilium* in the Latin, we always find in the Greek text συνέδριον (*synedrion*) or συναγωγη. (*synagogē*). Moreover, the term "Synod" is discovered first in the canons of the Apostles, can. 38, where Bishops are commanded to celebrate Councils twice a year. Next, it is discovered in Eusebius (*hist. ecc.*, lib. 5, cap. 23) and thereafter in all authors.

CHAPTER IV
A two-fold Partition of Councils

THERE are four kinds of Councils: there are some that are general, national, provincial, and some that are diocesan. St. Augustine mentions the first three in *de Baptismo contra Donatistas*, lib. 2, cap. 3, where he says that the Councils of the provinces, or even greater ones, such as of regions, are emended by plenary Councils. He calls to mind the last section of the Council of Toledo, IV, cap. 25.

They are called General in which the Bishops of the whole world can and ought to be present unless they are legitimately impeded, and in which no man rightly presides but the Supreme Pontiff, or another in his name. From there they are called ecumenical; that is, Councils of the whole world.

National Councils are so called, in which Archbishops and Bishops of one kingdom come together, or of a nation in which some Patriarch presides, or a primate, such as many Roman Councils, Spanish and African, on which it must be noted that although they are really distinct from general Councils and provincial ones, still they are often called by both names.

Often Councils are called "universal", as is clear from the Roman Councils under Symmachus, where it is always said: "Symmachus, presiding over the general Council, etc." and still only the Bishops of Italy were present. Thus in the 3rd Council of Toledo, cap. 18, it is said: "This holy and universal Council commands," and still only the Bishops of Spain were present. The same thing is seen in the 4th Council of Carthage, Therefore these are called general or universal, because they are general in that kingdom, but not because they are general absolutely. Moreover, these same are called provincial by Gratian in dist. 3, can. *Porro*, because they are held in certain provinces, but do not pertain to all Christians, just as a truly general Council.

They are called Provincial, in which the bishops of one province come together, in which an Archbishop or Metropolitan presides, and the volumes of Councils are full of a great many of this kind. Concerning these it appears the Seventh Council spoke, when it said that it embraces even the decisions of local Councils (action 3).

Diocesan Councils are those in which only the priests of one Episcopate come together, and a Bishop presides over them. Very few of this sort are extant, and for good reason, for they can hardly be called Councils when in them there is ordinarily no one who has jurisdiction apart from one Bishop.

The second division of Councils embraces four groups: there are some approved by the Apostolic See and received by the universal Church, there are some altogether reprobated, and some partly approved, while partly reprobated, and some neither approved nor reprobated. The last group chiefly has place in particular Councils.

CHAPTER V
Approved General Councils

HITHERTO, there have been 18 approved general Councils.[3] The first is Nicaea, which was celebrated in the year 327-330, held in the 15th year of Pope Sylvester and the 20th of Constantine the Emperor. There, 318 bishops came together, among which were the Patriarchs, Alexander of Alexandria, Eustratius of Antioch and Macarius of Jerusalem, as well as Metrophanes of Constantinople, although these last two were not Patriarchates in that time, receiving that dignity long afterwards. Indeed Metrophanes, not for himself, but through the legate Alexander, who afterward succeeded him in the Episcopate, wished to be present. See Metaphranes in the oration on the deeds in the Council of Nicaea.

Two controversies were especially defined, one on the day of Easter, the other on the divinity of Christ against the Arian heresy; Arius, the chief heretic, died ten years later while using the lavatory and thus died in his own filth.

But, because all these can be called into doubt due to the different opinions of the writers, each must be shown in a few words. 1) There is a marvelous diversity of opinions on the time of the Council, but the truth of our opinion can be confirmed by the following reason: The Council of Nicaea was received in the 20th year of the Emperor Constantine. For, Eusebius writes this (*de vita Constantini*, lib. 3) as well as Socrates (*historiae*, lib. 1, cap. 12), that Constantine began to rule in the year 311.[4] Therefore, it effects that the year 330 A.D. will have been the twentieth of Constantine, and the end of the Council of Nicaea.

Likewise, Socrates in his history, (lib. 1, cap. 9, and 13) and Nicephorus in lib. 8, cap. 26, relate that it was begun while

---

[3] Translator's note: Circa 1588.

[4] *Cf. Chronicus* S. Hieronymi; Gregorius Haloandrus, aliisque Chronologis.

Paulinus and Julian were consuls. Moreover, it endured for three years, as the same sources attest. Hence, Cassiodorus records the consulship of Paulinus and Julian as beginning in the 17th year of Constantine, from which it follows that the Council was ended in his 20th year, hence it began in the year 327 and ended in 330. Onuphrius Panvinus correctly places the beginning of the Council of Nicaea in the year 325, since he places it in the consulate of Paulinus and Julian.

Therefore, the time of the Council fell during the pontificate of Pope Sylvester, not of Sylvester and Julius, as Photius teaches (*de septem synodis*), or of Julius alone, as Sozomen writes in lib. 1, cap. 16, and Calvin from Sozomen (*Instit.* cap. 7, §1) and Joachim Camerarius in his history of the Council of Nicaea, where he affirmed that he was a very diligent reader of ancient writers, as can easily be shown. For, as we said above, in the 20th year of Constantine the Council came to an end, which Camerarius also affirms (*loc. cit.*) Moreover, Sylvester was created Pope in the sixth year of Constantine (*Chronicus Eusebii et Hieronymi*), and was in the Apostolic See for over twenty years, as Damasus, Onuphrius and all writers witness; thus, the 20th year of Constantine necessarily means the Council took place under the Pontificate of Sylvester.

Besides, Milthiades, the predecessor of Sylvester, sat while Constantine was a general, as Optatus (*Contra Parmenianum*, lib. 1), and Augustine (epist. 162 et 165) witness, as well as Constantine himself, quoted by Eusebius in *hist.* lib. 10, cap. 5. So, Sylvester could not have obtained the Apostolic See except after the beginning of Constantine's reign. Therefore, in the twentieth year of Constantine, which was the last of the Council of Nicaea, Sylvester, not Julius, ruled the Apostolic See. This is why many historians (Damasus, *Pontificalis*; Jerome, *Chronicus*; Theodoret, lib. 1, hist. cap. 3, sexta Synodus, act. 18; Concilium Florentium, sess. 3), wrote that the Council of Nicaea occurred in the times of Pope Sylvester.

Opinions seem to vary on the number of Bishops who were present at that Council. Eusebius says that it was more than 250, in *de vita Constantini*, lib. 3, while Athanasius said that there were a little less than 300. (lib. *de sententia Nicaenae Synodi*). Eustachius, (quoted by Theodoret, lib. 1, cap. 8 hist.), says they were numbered over 270, and the historian Sozomen places the number around 310. (lib. 1, cap. 16.) Nevertheless, the true and common opinion is that it was 318. Epiphanius wrote that even in his times the names of each of the bishops were preserved and that it was precisely 318. Hilary and Ambrose (*prafatio liberorum de fidei, mysticum et sacrum*) also say the number of the Fathers of the Council was 318, and was prefigured in the 318 soldiers with whom Abraham brought back victory over the five kings. Next, Jerome, in his *Chronicum*, Sulpitius in lib. 2, *hist.*, Theodoret (lib. 1, cap. 7), and all others constantly posit this number.

Now, there were two reasons for this Council: The question on the date of Easter, and the question on the divinity of Christ, as Eusebius (*de vita Constantini*, lib. 3), Athanasius (*liber de Synodis Arimini et Seleuciae*), and Epiphanius (*Haeresi* 70) make clear.

Next, it is not altogether certain whether the Council of Nicaea was celebrated before the shameful death of Arius. Epiphanius clearly writes that the Council was celebrated after the death of Arius, in *Haeresi* 69, but the historians write to the contrary, such as Ruffinus, in lib. 10, cap. 13, and Socrates (lib. 1, cap. 19 et 25) and the rest, nor can these opinions be reconciled if we were to say there were two men named Arius, as Sulpitius tries to show (*Sacrae Historiae*, liber 2). Even if there were two men named Arius, still there would only be one who perished on the toilet. Moreover, Epiphanius places this very one before the Council, but Ruffinus and the rest place him after the Council, and the historians seem to have sensed this better, especially since it was treated in the fifth Council whether it would be lawful to condemn heretics after their death, because certainly they would not have been able to doubt this if the Council of Nicaea had condemned Arius after he was already dead. Yet, this matter is not of importance, and it would behoove us not to waste any more time on it.

The second Council is that of Constantinople, which was celebrated against the Macedonians who denied the divinity of the Holy Spirit while Theodosius the elder was emperor, and Damasus, the supreme Pontiff. Then, 150 Bishops came together from different provinces, and from the Patriarchs, Nectarius of Constantinople, Timothy of Alexandria, Meletius of Antioch and Cyril of Jerusalem.

Moreover, the time of this second Council was during the consulship of Gratian and Theodosius Augustus, in the year 383 (Prosper of Aquitaine, *Chronicum*), or in the following year as Socrates would have it (lib. 5, *hist.* cap. 8). He writes the Council came together under the Consulship of Syagrius and Eucherius, in the year 384, or if one would follow the reasoning of Onuphrius, in the year 381. Psellus, in his book on the seven Councils, places an interval of 56 years between the first and second Council. Still, if you were to add the number of 56 years to 327, when we said the first Council began, one would make 383, which is the number which Prosper notes down in his Chronicle.

It must also be noticed in this Council that there was no one present from the West. Accordingly, Damasus, the Pope of Rome, compelled a western Council, and also invited Bishops to that place who had come together at Constantinople, that in the same manner the fullest Council would be celebrated at Rome. But, because the Eastern Fathers could not come to Rome for just causes, Damasus received their excuse and the acts of the two Councils were joined, as if they were one and the same. Due to this joining the Council of Constantinople was held to be one of the legitimate Ecumenical Councils. See Theodoret, *hist.*, lib. 5, ca. 9 et 10.

The third Council is Ephesus I, which was compelled by the Emperor Theodosius the younger and Celestine I the Supreme Pontiff. 200 Bishops came together, among which were Cyril of Alexandria, who even obtained the place of the Roman Pontiff, as well as John of Antioch and Juvenal of Jerusalem, although John, because he was still on the way when the decree of the Council was made, began in the beginning to disagree with Cyril, but afterward was reconciled and agreed to the same thing. The reason for the Council was that Nestorius, the Bishop of Constantinople, had coined a new heresy whereby he divided Christ into two persons.

The Council was celebrated while Bassus and Antiochus were consuls, as Prosper witnesses in his *Chronicle*, and Socrates as well (lib. 7, ca. 34), namely in the year 434. Why should Psellus be followed, who places only the interval of forty years between the second and third Council, and Onuphrius, who remarked that this Council was celebrated three years earlier during the thirteenth consulate of Theodosius, and the third of Valentinian, I cannot say, especially when in the second volume of the Council itself, chapter 1, we read the Synod began in the 13th consulate of Theodosius and the third of Valentinian; nor could Onuphrius ignore the fact that the thirteenth of Theodosius and the third of Valentinian were not the same before and after.

Add that Vincent of Lérin, in his book on the profane novelties of speech, about the end, says: "Before nearly three years a Council was celebrated in Asia while the excellent men Bassus and Antiochus were consuls." What could be clearer? Concerning this whole Council see Libertus in his *Breviarium*, cap. 5-8; Socrates, lib. 7, cap. 34; Evagrius, lib. 1, cap. 4, as well as the Council itself, preserved from the Greek in the Latin language, and it is contained in the volumes of Councils.

The fourth Council is Chalcedon, which was gathered against the heresy of Eutyches the Archimandrite, who asserted that there is only one nature in Christ after the incarnation. This Council took place while Leo I was Pope, and Martianus the emperor, during the consulate of the same Martianus, as is clear in the first action. Moreover the consulate of Martianus fell in the year 454, according to the reckoning of Matthew Palmerius and Gregory Haloandrus, or 453 according to Marianus Scotus and Sigebert, or even 452 according to Onuphrius in his book on Roman Pontiffs. Psellus interposes 30 years between the third and fourth Council, but just as he took off ten years in the previous number and placed forty for fifty, so now he added ten years and placed thirty for twenty, unless it is an error of copyists. Next, there were 630 Bishops present among whom were the Patriarchs Dioscorus of Alexandria (who was soon thrown out), Maximus of Antioch, Anatholius of Constantinople, and Juvenal of Jerusalem. One can see Liberatus in his Breviary, ca 11 et seq., and Evagrius, lib. 2 *hist.*, cap. 2-4.

The fifth general Council was not, as many think, the one that was celebrated under Agapetus and Mennas, the four actions of which are contained in the second volume of Councils under the name of the "Fifth Council", for that was a local Council that preceded the fifth, as John Zonaras in the *Vita Justiniani* and Nicephorus in lib. 17, cap. 9, clearly show.

Moreover, the true fifth Council was carried out in Constantinople while Vigilius was Pope and Justinian the elder was Emperor, in the twelfth year after the consulate of Basil, as we read in the beginning of the same Council which is the year 553 or 556 according to Psellus, who would have it that the fifth Council is 102 years later than the fourth. Psellus likewise hands down that 165 Bishops gathered, among whom were the Patriarch of Constantinople Eutychius, Apollinaris of Alexandria, Dominus of Antioch and Eustochius of Jerusalem, although he was not present himself but through legates. Moreover, the Supreme Pontiff was neither present himself nor through Legates. Still, he confirmed this Council, as Nicephorus writes (lib. 17, cap. 27).

This Council was gathered to oppose the heresy of Origen, which was then growing in strength. Therefore, the Council condemned Origen, and at the same time Dydimus and Evagrius his followers. It also condemned the writings of Theodore of Mopsuestia, Theodoret and some epistles of Ibas of Edessa.[5] The historians tell us more on these matters (Zonaras, *loc. cit.*; Nicephorus, lib. 17, cap. 27; St. Gregory the Great, lib. 1 *epist.* 24; Evagrius, lib. 4, cap. 38; Liberatus, *breviarium*, ca. 23 et 24. What Liberatus says must be read very cautiously, either because it was not genuine or he was deceived by a false relation. Certainly what he says does not agree with the narrations of other Catholics.).

The sixth Council was celebrated at Constantinople in the twelfth year of Constantine IV, as Paul the Deacon witnesses in the life of the same emperor, which was the year 681 or 685 according to Psellus, who places 129 years between the fifth and sixth Council. On the other hand, it is generally ascribed to the twenty-eighth year of the same Constantine; this is not an error of the copyists, as Illyricus thinks (Cent. 7, cap. 9). Even if Constantine IV did not rule but seventeen years after the death of his father, nevertheless he ruled with his father for many years, as Zonaras showed, while he said he was crowned by his father before he departed for Sicily. Therefore, the Council numbered the years of Constantine from that first coronation, while Paul the Deacon numbers them from the death of Constantine's father.

Two hundred eighty-nine bishops came together, as Paul the Deacon witnesses, and that number agrees with what is contained in the seventh Council, act 3. Still, Bede, in libro *de sex aetatibus*, Tumginus, (lib. 1), Ado of Vienna, and Freculph only number one hundred fifty fathers. There were two Patriarchs: George of Constantinople and Macarius of Antioch; only legates were present from the Churches of Alexandria

[5] Translator's note: Collectively known as the "Three Chapters".

and Jerusalem. The Supreme Pontiff, Agatho, was present through legates and presided. In that Council they condmened the heresy of those who taught that there was only one will in Christ. On this Council see other cited authors, Albert Pighius *in diatriba*; Francis Turrianum in *Apologia pro VI et VII Conciliis*. Albert contends that the sixth and Seventh Council, in the forms that are extant, have been adulterated and are not genuine. On the other hand, Turrianus teaches that they are true and genuine. What seems more true to us has been related in our treatise *On the Roman Pontiff*. (Book IV, ch. 11).

The seventh Council was gathered in Nicaea in the eighth year of Constantine and Irene, as Paul the Deacon writes in *Rerum Romanarum*, lib. 23, as well as Cedrenus. (*Compendium historiarum*). This was in the year 761 AD if we believe Paul the Deacon, or 786 AD if we believe Cedrenus. Onuphrius places it in the tenth year of Constantine and the year 789 A.D., while Psellus would have it that there were only 60 years between the Sixth and Seventh Council, but this in no way agrees with the truth. Thus some men reckon that it is a mistake of the copyists, and that Psellus himself wrote 100. The same Psellus holds that 350 Bishops were present, and one Tharasius of Constantinople; the rest of the Patriarchs were present only through legates. Pope Adrian presided by legates and together with the rest of the Council condemned those who deprived images of Christ and the saints of all honor. If one wishes to see more about this Council, then look to what we treat on the Council of Frankfurt in the disputation on the cult of images.

The eighth Council is the fourth Council of Constantinople, which was celebrated by Pope Arian II and the Emperor Basil in the third year of that same emperor, as is made clear by that Council in its first act, which was in the year 870 A.D. One Patriarch was present, Photius, and then Ignatius, both of Constantinople, while the rest were present through legates.

In this place we must advert that there were three Councils celebrated at Constantinople on the case of Photius, one, in the time of Pope Nicholas and the Emperor Michael, in which Ignatius was deposed and Photius ordained in his place. Zonaras calls this Council to mind in the life of the Emperor Michael, nor is it doubtful that this was a profane Council, as is clear from the epistles of Nicholas I and Adrian II.

The second Council of this name is that which we have called the *eighth*, which is extant although imperfectly in the tomes of Councils, in which after Photius was deposed, Ignatius was again restored; Zonaras records this in his life of the Emperor Basil.

The third is that which Pope John VIII, the successor of Adrian, celebrated in the time of the same emperor, in which, with Ignatius dead, Photius was again restored and, if what the Greeks said in the Council of Florence, (Sess. 6, cf. Franciscus Turrianus, *libro de actis* VI, VII, et VIII Synodi), is true, the acts of the preceding Council under Adrian were rescinded. It was also stated that the particle *Filioque* was abolished from the Creed, but this does not have the appearance of truth. I am easily persuaded of this, because either all these things were made up, which are said about John VIII, as St. Antoninus teaches (*Summa Historiali*, part 3, tit. 22, c. 13, §10), or certainly it is true that Photius was restored by John VIII through his Legates in the See of Constantinople after the death of Ignatius, but the rest was supposed, adulterated and made up by the Greeks, as Turrianus shows from Manuel Calleca in the book that we cited.

Moreover, I am strengthened in this opinion, because Zonaras, where he calls to mind the restoration of Photius, still says nothing of the abrogation of the eighth Council nor the removal of that particle [*Filioque*] from the creed. Next, the Greeks at the Council of Florence (Sess. 6), did not recognize the Council held under John VIII as an Ecumenical Council, even though it would be a great benefit to them if it were a proper and legitimate Council. Now that is all for the Eastern Councils, so let us briefly add the Western Councils.

The ninth Council is the First Lateran Council, which had 900 Bishops present and was held in the year 1123 against the Saracens for the recovery of the Holy Land, in the time of Calixtus II and Henry V, the Emperor. Platina, as Onuphrius is not extant.

The Tenth is Lateran II. It had a thousand bishops in the year 1139 against Antipopes and for the right of Clergy, in the time of Innocent II and the Emperor Lothaire. Platina. Onuphrius records nothing.

The eleventh Council is Lateran III, which had nearly 300 Bishops for the reform of the Church and against the Waldenses, in the year 1153 in the time of Alexander III and the Emperor Frederick. Platina, Onuphrius, likewise William of Tyre, who was present (lib. 20 *de bello sacro*, cap. 26).

The twelfth Council is Lateran IV, which had 1,283 Fathers, from which there were 473 Bishops in the year 1215, against various heresies and for the Holy Land, in the time of Innocent III and Frederick II. (Mathew Palmerius, Onuphrius, Platina).

The thirteenth Council is the First Council of Lyons, in the year 1245, against the Emperor Frederick and for the Holy Land, in the time of Innocent IV and Frederick II. Mathew Palmerius, Platina, Onuphrius; some decrees of this Council are extant in the Sixth of the decretals.

The fourteenth is the Second Council of Lyons, which had nearly a thousand Fathers, from which nearly 500 were bishops, in the year 1274, against the error of the Greeks in the time of Gregory X and Rudolph the Emperor. (Mathew Palmerius; Platina; Onuphrius). Some things from this Council are extant in the Sixth decretal.

The fifteenth is the Council of Vienne, which had three hundred Bishops in the year 1311, against various heresies, in the time of Clement V and the Emperor Henry VII. (Palmerius;

Platina; Onuphrius). Decrees from this Council are those that are called "Clementine".

The sixteenth is the Council of Florence, (omitting Pisa, Constance,[6] and Basel, on which we will speak later), in the year 1439, which had 141 Fathers that had subscribed, and many others who left before the subscription, that it would be noted in the end of the Council, against the errors of the Greeks, in the time of Eugene IV and the Emperor Albert. (Mathew Palmerius; Platina).

The seventeenth is Lateran V. One hundred-fourteen Fathers were present against schism and for other types of business in the time of Julius II and Leo X, as well as Maximilian the Emperor; it began in the year 1512, and finished in 1518.

The eighteenth is the Council of Trent, begun in the year 1545 and completed in the year 1563, against the heresies of the Lutherans, in the time of Paul III, Julius III, Pius IV as well as the Emperors Charles V and Ferdinand. The number of Fathers is described in these words by Gaspar Villalpandaeus, in his fifth disputation on the Council of Trent. "Six Cardinals, four Legates, three Patriarchs, 32 Archbishops, 228 Bishops, five Abbots, seven minister Generals of religious orders, and a great many procurators of Bishops."

From these Councils, there is not one that was not approved by the Pope or is not received by Catholics; for on the first eight Councils it is certain from the decree, dist. 16, can. *Sancta octo.* On the nine following Councils, they were clearly approved because the Supreme Pontiff was present at all of them. On the last it is clear from the confirmation of Pius IV; the Greeks only receive the first seven Councils, as it was noted in the Council of Florence (sess. 5 &6). The Lutherans

[6] Translator's note: Constance was considered properly to be an ecumenical Council, and St. Robert certainly held it as such, but he will consider that under the section of Councils that were partly approved and partly condemned.

only received the first six, as is clear from the *Centuries of Magdeburg* (*Cent.* 8, c. 9; and cent. 9 cap. 9). The Monophysites, who still are found in Asia, only receive the first three. The Nestorians, who are also found in the East, only receive the first two. The "Trinitarians," who live in Hungary and Poland in our day, receive none.

CHAPTER VI
General Councils that were Condemned

THE first general Council that was condemned is the Council of Antioch held in the year 344, in the fifth year of Constantius, as Socrates the Historian says (lib. 2, cap. 5), as well as Sozomen (lib. 3, cap. 5), in which Athanasius was condemned by the general opinion of the Arians, and the way was open to overturn the first Council of Nicaea.

It must be noted that this Council is confused by the *summa Conciliorum*, with others, since there were six Councils of Antioch. The first and second were against Paul of Samosata in the time of Pope Dionysius, around the year 269 (See Eusebius, lib. 7 *Histor.* c. 23, 24, &25). The third of the Arians, held in the time of Julius I, in the year 345, as we said above. The fourth is of the Macedonians, for their heresy in the year 367, in the time of Pope Liberius (Jerome, *in Chronico*). The fifth was a Catholic provincial Council of thirty Bishops, whose 25 canons are contained in the first volume of Councils. It seems to have been in the time of Jovinian and Liberius (See Sozomen, lib. 6, ca 4). The sixth was inserted in act 14 of the Council of Chalcedon.

The second general Council to be condemned is that of Milan, where more than 300 Bishops were present in the year 354, in the time of the same Constantius in which the Catholic Faith was indirectly condemned. Ruffinus (lib. 10, ca. 20; Socrates, lib. 2, ch. 29).

The third is the Council of Rimini, with 600 Bishops present under the same Constantius in the year 363, as Jerome notes (*in Chronico*), in which the term ὁμοούσιος was abolished from the creed; a certain part of this Council was at Seleucia in the East. (See August., lib. 3, *contra Maximian.*, c. 14; Jerome *contra Luciferianos*; Ambrose, Epist. 32; Ruffinus, lib. 10, c. 21; Socrates lib. 2, cap. 29; Basil, epist. 52 *ad Athanasium*).

The fourth Council to be condemned was the second Council of Ephesus, which was condemned in the time of the Emperor Theodosius the younger, in the year 449, in which St. Flavius, the Bishop of Constantinople, was murdered by the faction of Dioscorus, and the Legates of Pope Leo were put to flight. At length that Council confirmed the Monophysite heresy. This Council was condemned by Leo in his epistle to the clergy and people of Constantinople. Likewise, to the Emperor Theodosius, as well as Pulcheria, the empress, which are numbers 22, 23, 24 and 25 (See the *Breviarium* of Liberatus, c. 12; and Evagrius, lib. 1, c. 9 &10).

The fifth Council to be condemned is the Council of Constantinople held under Leo the Isaurian against sacred images, in the year 730, which was the thirteenth of that Emperor's reign. The Council was condemned, for there was no Patriarch present, with the exception of St. Germanus, who still did not consent, and therefore he was thrown out of his seat of Constantinople.

The sixth is the Council of Constantinople held under Constantine Copronymus, and in the year 755, when 338 Bishops came together, but no Patriarch was present with the exception of a Pseudobishop of Constantinople. This Council defined that images of Christ and the Saints must be abolished. And this Council was condemned by the Seventh Ecumenical Council, act. 6. (See what Paul the Deacon relates on these two Councils of Constantinople, *rerum Romanarum*, lib. 21 and 22, and Zonaras *in annalibus*).

You will also observe that Several people call this Council the third of Ephesus, such as the author of the *Summa Conciliorum*, in the beginning of the seventh Council, as well as Sixtus of Siena (*Bibliotheca Sanctca*, lib. 5, annot. 247). For all the ancients call it of Constantinople, and it is most obvious that it is called this by the Council itself, the insert of which was read in the Second Council of Nicaea, act. 6. The reason for the error seems to have been that Theodosius, the Bishop of Ephesus, presided at this profane Council.

The seventh is the Council of Pisa, gathered in the year 1511 by the Emperor as well as the King of France, and several Cardinals against Julius II, and it was condemned a little after in the fifth Lateran Council, under Julius II (Sess. 1 & 3).

The Council of Wittenberg can be numbered as the eighth, which the Lutherans call a general Council. It had three-hundred pastors over which Luther presided in the year 1536. (See Cochlaeus, *in actis Lutheri*, and Surius, *in commentario rerum in orbe gestarum*, anno 1536).

CHAPTER VII
Councils that were partially confirmed, and partially condemned.

The first general Council to be partly confirmed and partly condemned is that of Sardica, at which 376 Bishops were present in the year 351, in the time of Constantius and Pope Julius I, from which 300 western bishops confirmed the Catholic faith, which Hilary relates in his book on Councils; the remaining 76 Eastern Bishops subscribed to the Arian faith (See Socrates, lib. 2, cap. 16; Sozomen, lib. 3, *histor.* cap. 10 & 11; Theodoret, lib. 2, cap. 7 & 8).

The second is the Council of Sirmium, which was celebrated five years after Sardica, namely in the year 356, while Liberius was the Supreme Pontiff, and Constantius the Emperor. In this Council, two *formulae* of faith dissenting from each other were published. One Marcus Arethusius composed in Greek, who famously endured martyrdom under Julian the Apostate, and it seems to be the case that when Hilary relates the event near the end of his work on Councils, he was a Catholic. Others composed another formula in Latin full of clear blasphemies, which Hilary condemned in his book on Councils, not far from the beginning. Also, in the same Council the Photian heresy was condemned, and such a condemnation all Churches approved (See Socrates, lib. 1, c. 24 et seq.; Sozomen, lib. 4, cap. 5 & 6; also Epiphanius, *haeresi* 71, although he seems to have fallen in that he received Sardica for Sirmium).

The third is the Quini-sext Council,[7] in which the Canons of Trullo are contained. It must be known from the disputation of Tharasius in the seventh Council, act. 4, the sixth Council, which was celebrated in the time of Constantine IV, published no canons, but after so many years in the time of the emperor

---

[7] Translator's note: Also called the Council in Trullo.

Justinian the Bishops returned to Constantinople and the Palace, which is called *in Trullo*, and Theodore Balsamon calls it the *Quinisext Council*, because it is neither the fifth nor the sixth, but added canons to the fifth and sixth Council.

Exactly when this Council was held is not altogether certain. For a certain historian named Theophanes, whom Franciscus Turrianus cites in his book on the sixth Council, teaches that this Council was celebrated 27 years after the dissolution of the true sixth Council, namely, in the second year of the restored Emperor Justinian. But Tharasius in the seventh Council (Act 4), & Epiphanius in the same Council (act. 6, tomus 1), says it was five years after the dissolution of the Council these canons were published, which certainly seems more probable to me; for otherwise I do not see when that erratic Council of Constantinople was held by Justinian in the time of Pope Sergius, and which the same Pope condemned (as Bede witnesses in his book *de Sex Aetatibus*, Paul the Deacon, lib. 6, cap. 4; Otho of Frisia, lib. 5, c. 13; Rhegione, lib. 1, and Ado of Vienna, *in Chronico*). In the twenty-seventh year from the dissolution of the sixth Council, Sergius did not sit, rather, it was Pope Constantine, and certainly Bede and Tharasius are more ancient than this Theophanes, since Bede also lived in the very time in which Pope Sergius sat.

Therefore, we say these canons are partly condemned, because the Supreme Pontiff was present neither in his own person nor through legates when these acts took place. And clearly Pope Sergius, who then sat, condemned the Council as erratic, just as Bede says (*lib. de Sex aetatibus, in Justiniano*). Moreover, it was partly approved because even if these canons have no force of themselves, nevertheless some of them were later approved by the Pope or by other legitimate Councils, such as canon 82 on painting images, which was received by Pope Adrian and the seventh Council, as is clear from the seventh Council itself, act. 1, and 4 (See what we asserted against this Council in *On the Roman Pontiff*, book 2, ch. 18).

The fourth is the Council of Frankfurt, which was celebrated in the year 794, according to Rheginus (*lib.* 2), Pope Arian I, and Charlemagne, King of the Franks, because the Council was confirmed by Adrian, in as much as that part in which Christ was defined to not be the adoptive Son of God, and it was condemned by the same Pope in regard to the other part, in which the error condemned at the seventh Council was present (See what we have said in *On Councils*, book 2, ch. 9).

The fifth Council is the Council of Constance. Nearly a thousand Fathers were present from which over 300 were Bishops. It was begun in the year 1414 under [anti-pope] John 23, and in the year 1418 it was ended by Pope Martin V and Sigismund the Emperor (Platina, Palmerius). This Council was condemned in regard to its first sessions, where it defined a Council was above a Pope both by the Council of Florence and the last Lateran Council, while in regard to its last sessions, all of which were approved by Pope Martin V, it is received by all Catholics.

The sixth is the Council of Basel, begun in the year 1431 and continued at Basel, then later at Lausanne even to the year 1449, in which time Pope Nicholas V put an end to it, as both the Council and [anti]Pope Felix V were created in schism there. See *acta Concilii & Bullam annexam Nicolai V Pontificis.* Nothing was ratified and approved by this Council except certain dispositions in regard to Ecclesiastical Benefices that had been made by the Council, which (for the sake of peace and unity), the aforesaid Nicholas approved. But the Council itself was condemned at the fifth Lateran Council, sess. 11.

CHAPTER VIII
On a Council neither manifestly approved, nor manifestly condemned.

The Council of Pisa seems to be a Council neither approved nor condemned; in 1409 it deposed Gregory XII and Benedict XIII and elected Alexander V. Accordingly, St. Antoninus (*Summa Historalis* 3. part. tit. 22., cap. 5, § 2 & 3) asserts it was an illegitimate Council, and not a true Council of the Church, and the event seems to show the same thing. The Council was convened to abolish schism, and still it did not do that, but increased it. Moreover, without a doubt it was condemned by Alexander VI (who was not the sixth but the fifth), and it is nearly the common opinion that Alexander and those who succeeded him were true Popes. But certainly from the three who then claimed to be Pope, they were venerated as true Popes.

This is enough on General Councils.

On particular Councils, see the volumes of Councils, as well as the Decretals of Gratian, dist. 16, canon *Sexta Synodus*, and dist. 20, canon *de libellis.* Additionally, the *Chronicum* of Onuphrius, and the second book of the *Chronographia* of Genebrardi.

CHAPTER IX
On the utility or even the necessity of celebrating Councils

Therefore, with all of this noted, we must explain in what things legitimate Councils consist, and these can be reduced to four: 1) the end; 2) efficiency; 3) matter and; 4) the form of Councils. Now let us begin with the end, which is the first of the reasons. It will be the first reason that must be briefly explained on account of which Councils are usually celebrated; then from those it will be determined whether a gathering of Councils is necessary or merely useful. Moreover, the particular reasons, on account of which Councils are celebrated, are usually numbered as six.

a) The first reason is a new heresy, *i.e.* something that had never been judged before, which is the very reason the first seven Councils were convened. The Church always so dealt with the danger of new heresies, that she did not think it could be resisted otherwise than if all or certainly a great many leaders of the Churches, once their strength was joined as if it were made into a column of soldiers, would rush upon the enemies of the faith.

b) The second reason is schism among Roman Pontiffs; for a Council in the time of Pope Cornelius was celebrated for this very reason. Likewise, another in the time of Pope Damasus and again in the times of Symmachus, Innocent II and Alexander III, as well as Pisa and Constance in the times of Gregory XII and Benedict XIII, for there is a no more powerful remedy than a Council, as has so often been proved.

c) The third is resistance to a common enemy of the whole Church; in this manner Councils were convened by Urban II, Calixtus II, Eugene III, and other Popes, for war against the Saracens. Likewise, to depose an emperor, Gregory III celebrated Councils against Leo III the Iconoclast, as did

Gregory VII against Henry IV, and Innocent IV against Frederick II.

d) The fourth reason is suspicion of heresy in the Roman Pontiff, if perhaps it might happen, or if he were an incorrigible tyrant; for then a general Council ought to be gathered either to depose the Pope if he should be found to be a heretic, or certainly to admonish him, if he seemed incorrigible in morals. As it is related in the 8th Council, *act. ult. can. 21*, general Councils ought to impose judgment on controversies arising in regard to the Roman Pontiff—albeit not rashly. For this reason we read that the Council of Sinvessano in the case of St. Marcellinus, as well as Roman Councils in the cases of Pope Damasus, Sixtus III, and Symmachus, as well as Leo III and IV, none of whom were condemned by a Council; Marcellinus enjoined penance upon himself in the presence of the Council, and the rest purged themselves (See Platina and the volumes of Councils).

e) The fifth reason is doubt about the election of a Roman Pontiff. For if the cardinals could not or would not create a Pope, or certainly if they all died at the same time, or a true doubt should arise for another reason to whom an election of this sort would pertain, would look to a general Council to discern in regard to the election of a future Pope, although it does not seem to be realistic to expect this would ever happen.

f) The sixth reason is the general reformation of abuses and vices which crept into the Church; for even if the Pope alone can prescribe laws for the whole Church, nevertheless, it is by far more agreeable for matters to be done with the approval of a general Council when the Pope prescribes laws of this sort. Hence, we see nearly all general Councils published canons on reformation (See Juan Torquemada, lib. 3, cap. 9 &10).

CHAPTER X

General Councils are useful and in a certain measure necessary, but not absolutely and simply

FROM these reasons, on account of which Councils are gathered we said it will be easy to judge in what way they might be useful, whether Councils are plainly necessary for preservation of the Church. And indeed I so state on general Councils, convocations of Councils of this kind are very useful, and in a certain measure necessary, still they are not absolutely and simply necessary. I am easily persuaded of it: first for the very reason that in the first three centuries the Church lacked general Councils and yet did not perish. Just the same, in those three hundred years the Church remained unharmed, for without question it could endure another three hundred and again another six-hundred and another thousand, for it was not in want of heresies in that time, and there were many schisms and many vices, and also abuses. Nevertheless, all of which could not overthrow the Catholic Church even if she was destitute of the assistance of general Councils.

Next, it also happens that because none of the reasons for holding a general Council are enumerated it convicts the case. For the first, correction of vices and abuses, (that we might begin from the last reason), it can happen with sufficient suitability, both by laws of the Supreme Pontiff and by decrees of provincial Councils, although it would be more agreeable, as we said, to do it through general Councils.

Furthermore, those reasons cannot be made for the election of the Supreme Pontiff, if we speak morally, not metaphysically, if it ever were to come into use. For who would believe that there is going to be a time when the Cardinals would not or could not create a Pope? But if any of this were to happen there could hardly be a doubt as to whom the election would pertain. For when the Roman Episcopate was carried to the supreme Pontificate of the Church, without a doubt, it fell to those, whose duty it is to choose the Roman Pontiff. Moreover, of those whose task it is to choose the Roman Bishop, there could be no more doubt in the absence of constitutions of Popes, just as it pertains to choose the Bishops of other cities. But this matter must be addressed elsewhere.

It is certain that hitherto a Council has never been called for this purpose. The same can be said about the fourth reason. For on account of suspicions on the doctrine and life of Popes, no Council has been convened apart from provincial or national Councils. Nor does it seem necessary for a greater Council; for while the Pope is truly a Pope, he cannot be judged by any Council, unless perhaps he himself were to grant the power to a Council of examining his case, and it could impose a judgment of Council but not a coercive judgment; consequently, the Pope can equally give power to a particular or general Council.

Indeed, the third reason does not necessarily consider the two-fold name "general Council". In the first place, it is not absolutely necessary to resist a common enemy, such as the Turks. For if the Church could be preserved under the savage persecution of Nero, Domitian, Decius, and Diocletian, why could it not also under the persecution of the Turks? Who does not see even without a general Council war can be declared upon a common enemy, just as it often has been done?

Next, neither the first nor second reason necessarily demands the convocation of a general Council, as past times witness. For, if to extinguish seven heresies seven general Councils were celebrated, more than a hundred heresies, were extinguished by the Apostolic See alone, with the cooperation of particular Councils: and if one schism was abolished by the general Council of Constance, more than fifty-eight schisms were abolished without a general Council.

But on the other hand, St. Augustine, in book 4 *Contra Duas Epistolas Pelagianorum,* ca. 12, affirms that there were very few heresies for which it was necessary to have a general Council of West and East to overcome them. St. Leo also praises Martianus Augustus (epist. 43 ad Martianum) because he demanded a general Council, and he also determined it was necessary.

St. Isidore, in his preface to his book on Councils, writes that before the times of Constantine, the Christian Church was divided into different heresies, because the persecutions of the emperors would not allow the Bishops to celebrate Councils. There it is beyond all doubt that he is speaking about general Councils. For it is certain before the times of Constantine, many particular Councils were celebrated. This is why Isidore seems to mean that general Councils are necessary simply to extirpate heresies.

Likewise, St. Eugenius, the Bishop of Carthage, as Victor is a witness (lib. 2, *de persecutione Vvandalica*), that when it was urged by King Hunericus, that he confer on faith with the Arian Bishops, he responded that the cause of faith is common to the whole Catholic Church, hence it is for the Roman Church to convoke Bishops from all parts of the Church, and especially to define the whole matter, since it is the head of all Churches. But such a response Eugenius meant to explain that a general Council is altogether necessary to explain questions of the faith.

Next, on that ancient question, were those that had been baptized by heretics not to be rebaptized? It could never be defined, until the opinion of a general Council were to be added, even if many decrees of particular Councils as well as of the Apostolic See had preceded it; it seems, therefore, a general Council is necessary simply to put an end to controversies of faith. St. Augustine speaks thus on the matter, "The obscurity of this question, that in earlier ages of the Church, before the schism of Donatus, has caused men of great weight, and even our fathers, the bishops, whose hearts were full of charity, so to dispute and doubt among themselves, saving for peace, that the several statutes of their Councils in their different districts long varied from each other, until at length the most wholesome opinion was established, to the removal of all doubts, by a plenary Council of the whole world, because it was thought very beneficial to be strengthened even from remote doubts" (*De Baptismo contra Donatistas,* lib. 1, ca. 7). In ch. 18 he says: "We piously believe about baptism what the universal Church safeguards from the sacrilege of a remote schism. Nevertheless, if different men still held different opinions on the point, then let them so think, save for peace, until some one clear and simple decree should have been passed by a universal Council, it would have been right for the charity which seeks for unity to throw a veil over the error of human weakness." And in book 2, ch. 4, he says: "Nor should we ourselves dare to assert anything of the kind, were we not supported by the unanimous authority of the whole Church, to which he [Cyprian] himself would unquestionably have yielded, if at that time the truth of this question had been placed beyond dispute by the investigation and decree of a plenary Council."

But to the first testimony of Augustine, it is not overly difficult to respond, since Augustine does not teach that general Councils were ever simply necessary at any time, but only in a certain time, this is, that a more pleasing and agreeable peace were rendered to the Churches. If indeed Augustine wrote in some place that to crush a certain heresy, *i.e.* Arianism, a general Council was necessary, he wrote in the same place about the Pelagian heresy, and several others, saying that it could be crushed without a general Council. Moreover, if you were to ask why did the case of the Arians require a general Council more than that of the Pelagians, Augustine will not respond that the question introduced by the Arians was more obscure than that brought by the Pelagians, since that does not seem to be true, since there are many more clear testimonies in the Scriptures for the divinity of Christ against the Arians, than for original sin against the Pelagians; but God so willed and arranged that the heresy of the Pelagians was condemned in short order by the universal Church, when the Apostolic See at Rome decreed it with peace and consent, as well as Councils of the East in Palestine, and of the West in Africa. The Arian heresy had many Bishops give it patronage in its beginnings, that did not appear to be easily set at rest unless they would be crushed by the supreme authority of the Church. Therefore, a general Council was not necessary to extinguish the Pelagian heresy because it could be suitably and easily subdued by the Apostolic See in cooperation with provincial counsels of different places. The Arian heresy could also have been subdued by the Apostolic See and provincial Councils, but not suitably and easily,

The same answer can be given to the testimony of St. Leo. He judged that the ecumenical Council of Chalcedon was necessary, that by its authority, what had been wrongly done at the second Council of Ephesus could be destroyed by this new Council's authority. This was not an absolute necessity, but precisely something like the clear invalidation of the Council of Ariminium. For the Council of Ariminium was by far more general and populated, as well as more famous, than the second Council of Ephesus, and still it was invalidated by Pope Damasus without the assistance of any general Council. On that businesses, see the epistle of Pope Damasus to the Bishops of Illyricum, as well as epistle 52 of Basil to Athanasius.

In the same mode, we are compelled to explain the testimony of Isidore. For what he says, that before the rule of Constantine the Church was divided into different heresies because the right to gather into Councils, and thereby to teach the people, was not given to Bishops, if it were understood absolutely it is clearly false. For, even before the times of Constantine a great many heresies were altogether abolished and extinguished by Councils of Bishops, and after the times of

Constantine there were not a lack of new heresies which had cause to disturb the Church for the longest time. Certainly the heresies of Nestorian and Monophysite heresies could never be altogether eradicated, and still they arose after the times of Constantine, and still general Councils labored more often in extirpating them. Therefore, Isidore only meant that in the time of Constantine general Councils began to be celebrated, and a very useful thing came into being to crush heresies.

On what St. Eugene meant, the same Victor of Utica explains. For he writes that Eugene made mention of a general Council, and of the Churches beyond the sea, since he was called to confer about the faith with the Arians; not because there were no learned men in Africa, who could safely confer with the Arian bishops, but because he thought the learned men from across the sea, if they came into Africa, would act more freely for the sake of the faith since they were not subjects of the Vandal kings, to whom the Africans were subject. Still, Eugene did not lie when he said that the cause of faith is common, and could not take up that cause without Bishops from across the sea; for even if it were absolutely permitted for him to confer with the Arians about faith, as Catholics in the same region otherwise did with the Donatists, nevertheless, it was not expedient in that time, and hence, it was not lawful without manifest danger. Therefore, Eugene could not truly take up that province without his colleagues from beyond the sea, not because he lacked authority, but because he lacked opportunities; nor was it iniquity, but prudence, to elude the petition of that tyrant with ambiguity of teaching.

The last objection remains, on the baptism of heretics, which is answered in two ways. The first perhaps is not true, which St. Augustine thought, that the question could not be defined before the opinion of a general Council. For the first general Council was celebrated at Nicaea in the time of Constantine. Moreover, St. Jerome writes in his *Dialogue against the Luciferians*, that the Bishops themselves, who decreed with Cyprian that heretics must be rebaptized, later advanced the contrary decree. From which it is gathered that those Bishops, at length, acquiesced to the Roman Pontiff, Stephen, yet who all died before the times of the Council of Nicaea.

Jerome also writes the same thing in his book, on *Ecclesiastical writers*, that Dionysius of Alexandria conceded the teaching of St. Cyprian on rebaptizing, which Eusebius (lib. 7 *historiae*, c. 4) also indicates; still it is certain the same Dionysius changed his teaching a little later, nor did he dare to rebaptize a certain man whom it was certain was baptized by heretics, as Eusebius related (lib. 7 *historiae*, c. 8). Why would even Augustine himself (*epist.* 48 *ad Vincentium*) suspect that Cyprian retracted his teaching? It is probable then that, even before the Council of Nicaea, by the authority of the Apostolic See, that question was settled among all Catholics; but even if the question was not defined even to the determination of a plenary Council, as Augustine says, still, it would not be necessary thence to gather that it could not have been defined. Although the authority of the Apostolic See cooperating with provincial Councils defining that matter was not lacking, still those holy Popes preferred to delay it for a time that was more opportune for an absolute determination of that question which separated so many great men from the Church; because the opportunity of time had not yet advanced itself, in the way that the Council of Nicaea was celebrated, on that account Augustine repeats himself so often, that question was at length defined in a full Council of the whole world.

But, someone will say, Pope Stephen, when a certain particular Council had gathered, commanded that no one be rebaptized and those who did should be excommunicated, as Dionysius of Alexandria writes (witnessed by Eusebius, lib. 7 *hist.* cap. 4, and Augustine in his book on Baptism, chapter 14). Therefore, the Pope wanted to define the question with his particular Council, but could not. Hence general Councils seem altogether necessary.

I respond: Just as I responded to this matter in my treatise *On the Roman Pontiff* (book 4, cap. 7), Stephen indeed commanded that men should not be rebaptized if they were baptized by heretics, and he also thought those that rebaptize should be excommunicated; still, he did not really excommunicate them, which is clearly understood from many ancient authorities. Especially Cyprian himself, who does not say in his epistle to Pompeius that Stephen excommunicated them, but that he thought they should be excommunicated who acted against it: "He thinks those safeguarding the truth of God, Christ and the Church must refrain." And in his letter to Iubaianus, he says that he held his peace, along with those who thought the contrary, but he certainly would not have said this if either Stephen had excommunicated them, or they had excommunicated him: "We, in as much as it is in us, on account of heretics, with our colleagues and fellow-Bishops, do not contend the divine peace with them, and we hold the Lord's peace."

Jerome, in his *Dialogue with the Luciferians*, speaks this way about Cyprian: "He remained in communion with those who thought the contrary." Augustine (lib. 1 *de Baptismo*, c. 7) says that great men and Fathers of the Church, Bishops, *i.e.* Stephan and Cyprian, dissented save for peace and charity. Pacianus (*epis.* 2 *ad Sympronianum*) says: "Cyprian, in concord with all and common peace, suffered in the flock of confessors." St. Vincent of Lérin, in his little book, *Orerum*, says: "A marvelous alteration! The authors of the same opinion are Catholics, but their adherents are judged heretics. The teachers are absolved, the students condemned; the writers of the books will be sons of the kingdom; those asserting their propositions will receive hellfire. For who would doubt that this light of all saints and Bishops, as well as martyrs, Cyprian, will reign with Christ in eternity with the rest of his colleagues? Or who, on the other hand, would be so sacrilegious, that would deny that the Donatists and other plagues, that boasted that they rebaptized on the authority of a Council, are going to burn in eternity with the devil?"

CHAPTER XI
Some Councils of Bishops are simply necessary

Moreover, although general Councils are not absolutely necessary, still, some Councils, whether general or particular, are altogether necessary for the good governance of the Church, and this question can scarcely be called into doubt. For, if "it is necessary that scandals would come," as the Lord says in Matthew 18:7, "and it is necessary that there be heresies," as the Apostle says in 1 Cor. 11:19, certainly it is also necessary that in the Church there be a certain judgment, whereby both scandals could be removed and heresies condemned, otherwise in a short time the universal Church would have been torn into parts and perish, for "every kingdom divided against itself will be despoiled." (Matthew 12:25).

But even if the Supreme Pontiff is the judge, in place of Christ, of all controversies, universal fraternity ought to be submissive, as Cyprian says (lib. 1 epis. 3) and we in our books on the Roman Pontiff have shown in many kinds of arguments; still, the Pope ought not, in judging controversies of faith, either trust in his judgment alone, or to await divine revelation, but to apply diligence, as much as such a matter demands, and the ordinary means, and at length, to await the assistance of the Holy Spirit as well as divine direction.

Hence, the ordinary means, and moreover a necessary one, is a Council, great or small, one or many, exactly as he will judge; this can easily be proven.

First, from the divine promise of Matthew 18:20, "Where two or three are gathered in my name, there I am in their midst." Hence, the Council of Chalcedon understands about Councils (in epist. *ad Leonem et aliae Synodi*) which we shall advance in the following books.

Secondly, from what was done by the Apostles, who could also define controversies by themselves, but still, lest they would appear to neglect the ordinary means, and what was shown by Christ himself, did not wish to define a controversy on the legal matters that arose at Antioch without a Council (Acts 15).

Thirdly, from the custom of the whole Church, and also of all ages. For the Church has always had the custom of holding Councils of Bishops to explain doubtful matters. The Roman Pontiffs themselves never condemned a new heresy without a new Council, as one will be able to gather either from reading the volumes of Councils or the ecclesiastical histories. However, what was always done by all, who will dare to deny it can be called, and really is, ordinary?

We find confirmation from the Fathers. St. Cyprian (lib. 2 epist. 1 ad Stephanum) says: "We had necessity to compel many priests to gather into one place to celebrate a Council." Gelasius, in his tome on the bond of anathema, says: "If the Pope has already given consent, it is taught by some that where it is done, if it celebrated according to the rule of the Church, if it has proceeded from paternal tradition, if it is advanced from the Fathers, if it is produced from competent examination where it must be required without doubt, if it is celebrated in a Council that has been gathered, such as in the reception of a condemned matter and in the warding off of a Catholic, because it is a new case, it becomes most certain."

Lastly, the Council of Toledo, XI, in its very preface, proves by many words the necessity of Councils in the Church. But that is the chief point; if there were no Councils it is necessary that forthwith all things would be filled with vices and errors. Therefore, if God could preserve his Church without Councils by absolute potency, still, according to his ordinary providence, Councils are necessary for the good governance of the Church.

CHAPTER XII
Who gathers Councils?

WE have given exposition to the purpose, now it is fitting that we explain the efficient cause. Therefore, it is suitable between us and our opponents, that Diocesan Councils ought to be convoked by a Bishop, Provincial Councils by an Archbishop, National Councils by a Patriarch or Primates. For all Catholics affirm it to be true with Augustine (epist. 217 *ad Victorinum*). Calvin affirms the same thing in the *Institutes* (lib. 4 c. 7 § 8) and Illyricus (cent. 4 c. 7 col. 534).

But on a general Council there is the greatest controversy; if certain Catholics would have it that the duty of calling a general Council properly pertains to the Roman Pontiff, but in this way another could summon a Council, with the consent of the Pope, that it would also be sufficient if the summoning were made, he later held it ratified and confirmed it; but if neither he nor someone else at his command or consent summons the Council, or he would at least not approve the summoning, it is not a Council, rather perhaps an assembly.

Moreover, the heretics of this time attribute that authority to the Emperor. Luther says it in his book on Councils (pag. 58) where he also says that universal Councils are called because they were compelled by the universal lord and emperor of all. Charles Dumoulin in his *Consilio de Concilio Tridentino non recipiendo*, § 6, thence shows that the Council of Trent must not be received because it was not summoned by the Emperor, but by the Pope. Likewise, the little book of Protestants, in which they render the account as to why they would not come to the Council of Trent. Calvin and the Centuriators teach the same thing (*loc. cit.*); and just the same, Brenz in his *Prolegomena contra Petrum a Soto*, and above all others, Nilos Cabásilas in his book, *de Primatu Papae*.

However, it is really for the Pope, not the Emperor, to gather a general Council; firstly, it can be proven from the

Scripture that a Council of the Church is not legitimate unless it were gathered in the name of Christ, as it is said in Matthew 18, and Calvin admits in the *Institutes* (lib. 4 ca. 9 § 1 and 2) that, to be gathered in the name of Christ, it seems nothing other than to be gathered on the authority of Christ, *i.e.* from him who has the authority from Christ to gather it. For what Calvin says, to be gathered in the name of Christ is to be so gathered as if Christ alone were to preside and have no colleague, but all as subjects. This is not according to the Scriptures, nor is it a sufficient note to discern legitimate Councils; it is not, I say, according to the Scriptures. For in the Scriptures, that, "In the name," wherever it is received for that which is, from authority, as in the last chapter of Mark: "In my name they will cast out demons," and John 5: "I have come in the name of my father," Matthew 7: "Did we not prophecy in your name?", Acts 4: "In what power, or in whose name do you do this?" Nor does any place perhaps occur where someone does something in the name of Christ and it means Christ holds the presidency without a colleague. But whatever the case with this, it is certain that a legitimate Council could not be discerned by this note, for it is indeed true that it is necessary in a legitimate Council for Christ to so preside that there would be no colleague for him, rather all are subjects, but who will judge, who will discern whether Christ so presides when a Council is called, or not? For Christ does not preside in Councils in a visible form.

Calvin responds that one can easily discern it since Christ then presides without a colleague when the whole assembly is guided by the word and its spirit, *i.e.* when the Bishops define nothing by their head, but everything according to the rule of Scripture.

This is ambiguous and obscure, for even our adversaries in their Councils, and Catholics in theirs, affirm they devise nothing from their own head but produce everything from Scripture. Who, therefore, will judge whether they made a true

Council? How, if they are gathered in the name of Christ, is it that Christ holds the presidency, as Calvin explains it? It could not happen that we could discern legitimate Councils from illegitimate ones. Therefore, it remains what we said, to be gathered in the name of Christ is nothing other than to be gathered by one who has the authority from Christ to gather them.

Moreover, Christ, when he ascended into heaven, and withdrew the visible presidency of the Church, did not consign the governance of the Church to the Emperor Tiberius, who reigned at that time, but to Peter the Apostle, to whom he said: "Feed my sheep." Therefore, those who are gathered by him who succeeds Peter are gathered in the name of Christ, but not those who are gathered by those that succeed Tiberius. For this purpose, Peter and those who legitimately succeed Peter, is the Pastor of all the sheep of Christ, hence, even of Kings, Emperors, priests, for he embraces all and excepts none, when he said: "Simon, son of John, feed my sheep." Wherefore, St. Leo (Serm. 3, *on the Anniversary of the Assumption of the Pontificate*) says: "One Peter was chosen from the whole world, who was also put in charge of the calling of all nations, and all the Apostles, of all the Fathers of the Church, that although there might be many priests in the people of God, and many pastors, still Peter properly rules them all, whom Christ principally also rules." But is there anyone who could not discern whether it would be more fitting for the sheep to gather shepherds, or rather more for the shepherd to gather the sheep? Therefore, the Pope is the pastor, the Emperor a sheep, the duty to convoke Episcopal Councils looks not to the Emperor but to the Pope.

Secondly, a general Council ought to be summoned from an authority that can compel everyone; but the Emperor has never had the whole Church as a subject, even in regard to civil actions, as the Pope has in regard to spiritual actions; for the Emperors ruled broadly in the time of St. Leo and St.

Prosper, and still then the Christian world was more subject to the Pope than the Roman world was subject to the Emperor. For So St. Leo Speaks in sermon 1 on Sts. Peter and Paul: "By the sacred seat of Peter Rome, having become the head of the world, presided more broadly in divine religion than by earthly dominion." And Prosper of Aquitaine so sings in his *liber de ingratis*:

> *The seat of Peter at Rome, made head of the world*
> *for pastoral honor, holds by Religion*
> *whatever it did not possess by arms.*

Moreover, now, the Emperor could scarcely compel the Bishops of one province let alone the fact that Italy, Spain and France are not subjects of the Emperor, but have their own kings or temporal princes. What if there were no emperor, nay more, even no Christian prince, would it be the case that Councils could not happen?

Thirdly, provincial Councils are summoned by a Metropolitan, and national ones by a Primate or a Patriarch, as we showed above, even by the testimony of our adversaries. Therefore, general Councils must not be summoned by the Emperor, but by the Supreme Pontiff. For if the Emperor ought to summon general Councils, then a king or duke or a civil Magistrate ought to summon provincial or national Councils. For, as the Emperor of the whole world stands in regard to a general Council, so does a king or duke of one province to a Council of that province or nation. Just the same, since they affirm that provincial Councils are not convoked by a political prince of that province, but by the Ecclesiastical one, why would they not affirm by the same reasoning that general Councils ought not be compelled by a political prince of the whole world, but by the Ecclesiastical one? Moreover, the Roman Pope is the Ecclesiastical Prince of the whole Christian world, as we heard earlier from St. Leo, and we have proven as profusely as possible in the books *On the Roman Pontiff*.

Add that, if the Roman Pontiff were not also a true prince and ecclesiastical monarch, as we teach, but were only the Bishop of the first see, or a *primus inter primarios Patriarchas* as Nilos reckons, still the right to summon general Councils would pertain to him. For, primates do not properly command other bishops, yet because they hold the first place among the bishops of their nation, they can summon national Councils in their own right. For the Metropolitan summons a provincial Council, because he is in charge of the whole province, but the Supreme Pontiff is in charge of the whole world, as is clear from Leo (*Serm. 3 de anniversario die assumptionis suae ad Pontificatum* and *epist. 84 ad Anastasium*).

Fourthly, it is proven from the most ancient canon that Councils cannot be celebrated contrary to the opinion of the Roman Pontiff; for Pope St. Marcellus writes of this apostolic canon in an epistle to the Bishops of the province of Antioch. The first Council of Nicaea renewed the same, as well as the Council of Alexandria witnesses in their epistle to Felix, as well as Julius I in his epistle to the Oriental Bishops, which Socrates calls to mind (lib. 2 cap. 13), Sozomen (lib. 3 cap. 9) and Nicephorus (lib. 9 c. 5). Therefore, if it is not lawful to celebrate Councils without the consent of the Roman Pontiff, it follows he is chiefly the one to convoke them.

Calvin responds, however (*loc. cit.*), that this canon only means that the Roman Pontiff ought to be called to the Council, because he was one from the particular Patriarch. But if that were so, then the canon could also have been made to the effect that Councils could not be compelled contrary to the consent of the Bishop of Alexandria or Antioch, for they were also particular Patriarchs, and they would be equal or greater than the Roman Pontiff according to Calvin.

The *Centuriators* (cent. 4. c 7, col. 533) devised another solution. They say the words of Socrates do not mean Councils ought not be celebrated contrary to the consent of the Roman Pontiff, but Churches ought to be dedicated. For it is held in Greek: Μὴ δεῖν παρὰ γνώμκω τοῦ επισκόπου ρώμης κανονίζειν τας Εκκλησίας. But the Centuriators are deceived, for κανονίζειν τας Εκκλησίας cannot mean to dedicate Churches, but to convoke a canonical body or to summon a Council, just as Pope Marcellus and Julius say, who seem to have written in Latin, and how Socrates and Sozomen render from Latin the Tripartite history of Cassiodorus (lib. 4 c. 9 and 19), as well as how Nicephorus also understood it (*loc. cit.*).

But the whole matter can be very clearly proven from the epistle of Julius I, which Socrates adduces. Accordingly, in that epistle Julius rebukes the Orientals because they celebrated a Council in Antioch without his consent; moreover, wishing to give an account why he so rightly rebuked them, he adduces that canon into the midst. Therefore, either this canon ought to be understood on the celebration of a Council, or it is necessary that Julius was foolish. But who does not see which one is truer? Add, that none of the Fathers mention a canon whereby they are forbidden to dedicate a Church without the consent of the Roman Pontiff: on the contrary, there was never nor is there, in use in the Church such a canon.

Fifthly, it is proven from the Council of Chalcedon, (act. 1) where Dioscorus of Alexandria is bidden not to sit among the Bishops because of the fact that he dared to make a Council without the authority of the Apostolic See: "Which," it says, "was never lawful and has never been done." We have a similar thing in the seventh general Council, act. 6, where what had been decided at a certain Council held at Constantinople was invalidated because it was compelled by the Emperor without the consent of the Roman Pontiff.

Sixthly it is proven from the fourth Roman Council held under Symmachus, during which King Theodoric said he had convoked the Council so that he might judge the case of Pope Symmachus. All the Bishops answered that the Council ought to be called by the Pope and not by the king, even if it were to accuse the Pope. But the king said that he convoked it with the consent of the Pope, but the Bishops did not acquiesce until the King produced the letters of the Pope and the Pope himself when present testified that it was so.

Seventhly, it is proven from the testimony of the ancient Popes. St. Leo (*epistola ad Turbium*, which is 93, c. 17) says, "Having sent letters to our brothers and fellow Bishops, and to others, we have summoned them to a general Council." Pelagius II (in *epist. 1 ad Orientales*): "The authority to convoke a general Council was entrusted to the Apostolic See of Blessed Peter by a singular privilege." Sixtus III, who also preceded Pelagius and Leo, in his epistle to the Orientals, says: "Valentinianus Augustus convoked a Council by our authority." Adrian II, in his letter to the Emperor Basil, which was read in the 8th Council (act 1) said: "We will, by the industry of your piety to convoke a numerous Council at Constantinople."

Add to these Valentinianus the Emperor, who was asked by other Bishops to permit them to celebrate a Council, who responded, as Sozomen relates it: "It is not lawful for me who stands in the lot of the people to investigate such things; it is priests to whom these cares pertain, let them will to gather in some place" (Sozomen lib. 6 c. 7). Lastly, many other canons are added that are held in dist. 17 and many accounts, which Juan Torquemada makes (lib. 3 cap. 6) as well as the Lateran Council held under Pope Leo X, sess. 11, where it is asserted that it is for the Roman Pontiff to summon general Councils. Such a decree was made in the year before the Lutheran heresy arose.

CHAPTER XIII
The arguments of adversaries are answered

IT remains to answer the arguments whereby the truth will also be more confirmed. The arguments of Calvin and the Centuriators are taken from the summons of the first general Councils, which were summoned by the emperors, not by the Popes. Ruffinus says about the first Council of Nicaea (lib. hist. c. 1), "And Constantine convoked a Council in the episcopal city of Nicaea." Theodoret witnesses that the first Council of Constantinople was summoned by Theodosios I (lib. 5 *Historiarum*, c. 9). Evagrius witnesses in lib. 1 cap. 2 *hist.* that at the nod of Theodosius II the first Council of Ephesus was convened. At Chalcedon, as St. Leo witnesses in epistle 43, as well as a few others, a Council was called by the emperor Martianus. Theodoret asserts in lib. 2 cap. 4, that Sardica was also called by the Emperor Constantius.

Nilos Cabásilas confirms this with the testimony of St. Leo I. For he (in epist. 42 ad Theodosius the Emperor) begs the emperor to call a provincial Council in Italy. The Centuriators strengthen the same argument with the testimony of Pope Liberius, who conceded to the emperor the power to convoke Councils (cited by Theodoret, lib. 2 cap. 16). Charles Dumoulin strengthens it again, in the *Consilio de non recipiendis decretis Concilii Tridentini*, § 6, with the testimony of St. Jerome (lib. 2 *Apologiae contra Ruffinum*), where, speaking about a certain Council, Jerome says: "Tell me who is the emperor that commanded this Council to be convoked?" We might add a fourth confirmation, from the fact that general Councils were first compelled at the same time as the emperors began to be Christian, for if they could be celebrated without the emperors, why were none celebrated in the first three hundred years?

I answer these, *firstly*, that we can rightly scorn these arguments, since our adversaries reject efficacious arguments taken up from traditions or the custom of the Church, but only accept them from Scripture, however, these arguments are sought from mere tradition and the ecclesiastical practice without any testimony of Scripture.

Secondly, I say, we can oppose custom to custom: for if emperors summoned four or five Councils, the Popes have summoned more than twelve, as even our adversaries confess. *Thirdly*, I say a general Catholic Council summoned by the Emperor alone is null, *i.e.* without the consent and authority of the Roman Pontiff, and I shall briefly show this from each of them one by one.

Thus, first about Nicaea we read in the sixth Council (act. 18) that Constantine and Sylvester gathered the great Council at Nicaea. And Ruffinus (lib. 10 *histor.* ca. 1) says Constantine summoned the Council by the opinion of priests. From such we do not only have what we want, but even gather in passing that it is false, what Pighius says (lib. 6 cap. 1 *de Ecclesiastica hierarchia*) that the convocation of general Councils is found in Constantine the great, for he did not devise this by himself but followed the opinion of priests.

Theodoret relates about the first Council of Constantinople that Theodosius did not summon it as much as he sent the letters of Pope Damasus, whereby he summoned the Bishops to the Council. In this way the Bishops gathered in that Council wrote to Pope Damasus (cited by Theodoret *hist.* lib. 5 ca. 9): "At your reverence's command in the letters sent to the most holy emperor Theodosius in the previous year, we were prepared to make the journey to Constantinople." Therefore, although Theodosius had summoned the Council, nevertheless, he did so at the command of Apostolic letters. This is why in the sixth Council, act. 18, the Fathers say Theodosius and Damasus opposed Macedonius by means of the second Council, just as it was said a little earlier, that Constantine and Sylvester gathered the first Council to resist Arius.

Prosper of Aquitaine, in his *Chronicle*, indicates on the first Council of Ephesus, that it was summoned by the industry of St. Cyril, and the authority of Pope Celestine. It is also certain from Evagrius (lib. 1 cap. 4) and from the epistle of Celestine to Cyril, which is held among the works of Cyril, and from Photius in his book on the seventh Council, that Cyril set out for the Council as a legate of the Apostolic See, which is a certain argument that the Council was not gathered without the consent of the Pope.

On Chalcedon it is certain from the epistle of the Emperor Martianus to Pope Leo, which is contained before the Council of Chalcedon, in which the Emperor, being about to summon a Council, asked the Pope to come and conduct the Council, or if he refused to come, if he would show by a letter what he willed to be done and in the end concluded that he would write to all the Bishops to come together at a certain place: "And such things are beneficial to the religion of Christians and the Catholic Faith as your holiness has defined according to the Ecclesiastical rules, they [the Bishops] will declare in their arguments." (Epistle 76). There is also extant among the epistles pertaining to the Council of Chalcedon, a certain epistle of the Bishops of lower Moesia to the Emperor Leo, where they say: "In the city of Chalcedon many Bishops came together at the command of Leo the Roman Pontiff, who is truly the head of Bishops."

Lastly, Gelasius, in his epistle to the Bishops of Dardania,[8] says that only the Apostolic See decreed by its authority that Chalcedon would become a Council. Here we must note an error of the Centuriators, since in *Centur.* 5. cap. 7 col. 786 they did not understand what the word "only" (*sola*) excluded and thought it excluded the Emperor, and therefore called Gelasius an impudent liar. But Gelasius, by the word only did not exclude the Emperor, but only other episcopal Sees. For the

[8] Translator's note: Modern Kosovo.

Sees of Alexandria, Antioch or Jerusalem, or even Constantinople, did not will it to become a Council. Rather, only the Roman See, and it really brought that to effect, although not without the assistance of the pious Emperor Martin.

Concerning the Council of Sardica, which was summoned by Pope Julius I, it can be understood from Socrates (lib. 2 ca. 16) where he says that the Oriental Bishops directed the fault of their absence from the Council to Julius the Bishop of Rome, due to the fact that he had commanded it to be held in too short a time. From that it seems clear that the Council was not called by the Emperor alone, but also by Pope Julius, and chiefly by him.

Therefore, we have the first Councils summoned by emperors, but also by the opinion and consent of the Pope. Moreover, the reason why the Pope did not summon them alone, as was done later, was not because the authority of the Council would not be ratified by Christians without the authority of the emperor, as our adversaries dream up, but as St. Athanasius clearly says *in his letter to those leading a solitary life*: "When ever did you hold something to be of the authority of a judgment of the Church from the emperor?" Next, it was on account of many other just causes, the *first* of which was that at that time an ancient Imperial law was in force which forbade all gatherings and frequent assemblies of men without the authority of the emperor for the reason that the Emperors feared sedition would arise from them. See l. 1 *ff. de colegiis illicitis*, and *l. conventicula, c. de Episcopis et Clericis.*

The second reason is because even if that law did not exist, because the emperors ruled the world in a time of great peace a Council could not be held unless it were in some Imperial city, but no reasoning permits that an assembly could be held in some place in the whole world without the license of the master of that place. The manner would be the same if a Council were not held in the Papal States, but in France, Spain or Germany, without a doubt the consent of the one whose city or province it is would be sought.

Third, because in that time general Councils were conducted with public expenses taken up, especially in regard to the journey of Bishops to the place of a Council; for a journey with horses or vehicles of cities, without expense to the Churches, as is certain from book three of the life of Constantine, where Eusebius also adds that all the Bishops lived on expenses of the emperor during the whole time of the Council. The same thing is also clear from Theodoret (lib. 2 cap. 16), where we read that when Liberius sought a general Council, a certain man answered that the public wealth was insufficient to provide for the travel of the Bishops. Likewise, from the epistle of Constantine IV to the Roman Pontiff, which is contained at the beginning of the sixth Council makes plain the same thing.

The *fourth* reason is because in that time, the Pope, even if he was the head of all in spiritual matters, even of emperors, still in temporal matters he was subject to the emperors, and therefore he could not act against the will of the emperor, especially when he ought to seek help from the emperor to convoke a Council, or that he would permit a Council to be convoked. Nevertheless, because he acknowledged him as his temporal lord, he begged that he would command a Council to be convoked. After those times all these causes were changed, for neither was that law in force nor did the emperors rule the whole world, nor were Councils conducted at public expense, nor are there nations that could impede it, and the Pope, who is the head in spiritual matters, is not subject in temporal matters, since even he is the supreme temporal prince of his domains, just as other kings and princes are, which came to pass by divine providence so that the Pope could freely exercise his office.

I respond to the first confirmation from Nilos, whose book Illyricus translated into Latin, that there are two frauds in that testimony of St. Leo which he advances, one of Nilos and the other of Illyricus. For St. Leo, in epist. 24 and 25 to Theodosius seeks a general Council in eloquent words: "that you would bid a general Council to be celebrated in Italy." Nilos, however, referring to this sentence in Greek, placed ἰδικὴν, *i.e.* his own or particular, when he ought to have said οἰκουμενικὴν) And because that word Nilos used, namely ἰδικὴν, could be explained in a good sense, that it would mean a particular Council, that is, gathered for a special cause, Illyricus wanted to eliminate all ambiguity, so he translated ἰδικὴν into *provincialem*, as we are necessarily compelled to understand that St. Leo asked not for a general Council but a particular one.

But this fraud is refuted both from the words of Leo already cited, and also from the epistle of Valentinian to the same Theodosius, which is contained in the preamble to the Council of Chalcedon where Valentinianus says, speaking on the same Council, that St. Leo wanted the Bishops of the whole world to come together in Italy. Lastly, in that very epistle of Leo to Theodosius, wherein he asks for a Council in Italy, he wrote that a provincial Council had already been convoked at Rome, so the inscription has it: "Bishop Leo and the holy Council, which came together in the city of Rome greet the always August Theodosius." Therefore, if Leo had already convoked a provincial Council in Italy, why would he ask for one from the emperor? Rather, he was really asking for a general Council from the emperor, as we already said.

Now I speak to the second confirmation. The Centuriators lie when they say that Liberius conceded the power to the emperor to convoke a Council, that is, to acknowledge that power to be proper to the emperor, as they understand it, for in the whole *Dialog* of Liberius with the emperor, no mention of this question is made, of whose right it is to convoke a Council; rather, Liberius only asks from the emperor, who was all-powerful and an Arian (and hence dangerous to him), that a

Council would be held because he knew it could not be done against the will of the emperor.

To the third confirmation, I say that Jerome says that really then, on account of the aforesaid causes, the emperors were calling Councils, but not without the consent of the Popes.

To the fourth confirmation I say that no general Councils were held before Constantine, not because there was no authority to hold them, but because there was no opportunity: for it was not lawful for Christians from many provinces to gather into one place due to the assiduous persecutions, as Isidore remarks in *liber 6 Egymologiarum*, c. 16.

CHAPTER XIV
Certain doubts are Answered

APART from these arguments of the heretics, Catholics customarily propose certain doubts. *One*, whether or not it is lawful for a Council to be summoned by anyone other than the Pope, when it is necessary for the Church, and still the Pope refuses to summon it. The *second*, whether or not it is lawful for a Council to be summoned by anyone other than the Pope when the Pope should not summon it, for the reason that he is a heretic or a schismatic. The *third* doubt, whether or not it is lawful for a Council to be summoned by someone other than the Pope when the Pope cannot summon one, for the reason that he is captive to infidels, or dead, or became insane or renounced the Papacy.

To the *first*, Torquemada responds (lib. 3 c. 8) that it is scarcely a probable case: for it is not believable that any Pope would be so bad that he would refuse a Council to be celebrated if it were clearly certain that it is necessary for the preservation of the Church, because if he were such of himself, still God, who preserves the Church, without a doubt would either change his mind or remove him from this life. He says secondly, if none of these would happen, he could be held as suspect of heresy, for as it is said in *dist.* 83, can. *Error*, as well as in the others following, one who does not resist a manifest error when he may and must, is thought to approve it.

To *the second* and *third*, I respond that in no cause can a true and perfect Council (such as we make our disputation on here), be convoked without the authority of the Pope, because he has the authority to define questions of faith. For, the particular authority is in the head, in Peter; to whom it was commanded to confirm his brethren, and therefore for whom the Lord himself prayed lest his faith would fail (Luke 22). Still, in those two cases an imperfect Council could be gathered which would suffice to provide for the Church from the head. For the Church, without a doubt, has the authority to provide for itself from the head, although it cannot, without the head, make determinations on many things on which it can with the head, as Cajetan rightly teaches in his little work, *de potestate Papae*, c. 15 and 16, and much earlier on the priests of the Roman Church in their epistle to Cyprian, which is 7 in the second book of the works of Cyprian. Hence, that imperfect Council can happen, if either it is summoned by the college of Cardinals, or the Bishops themselves come together in a place of themselves.

CHAPTER XV
Who are the ones that are called to a Council?

TO this point we have made our dissertation on the final and efficient cause of Councils. Now we must treat on those causes from which Councils are particularly constituted; the material causes, as it were. One, is that the universal Church contains four kinds of men; some are clergy, others lay, and again from the clergy, some are prelates and some are not. Likewise, from the laity, some are princes and some are private citizens. This distinction, although on the one hand, the heretics of this time do not receive it, still on the other they do since they also profess to be certain men dedicated to the ministry of the Word, for whom it is fitting by their office to teach and shepherd the people that call them ministers and again, between those other greater ones, whom they call superintendents, others minors, whom they only call ministers.

The second is, in many Councils on the causes some can be present, others are as judges who are said to have a decisive vote, others that they might examine difficulties in disputation, who are said to have a consultive vote; others, that they would defend the Council and labor that inside and out all will be peaceful. Therefore, the question is, who are the ones from these four kinds of men that must be called to a Council, and for what reasons?

Our adversaries say two things. *First*, some from every kind of man ought to be present who are educated, and all ought to be judges, and also have a decisive vote, whatever might be the other duties. Luther clearly writes in his book on Councils, part 2, pg. 264, where he would have it that, from every place, men learned in sacred Scripture ought to be gathered, up to 300 men. The protestants write the same thing in that book which they titled: *Caussa cur Electores et caeteri*

Confessioni Augustanae addicti, ad Concilium Tridentinum non accedant. For, after they argued for their first reason, namely that the Council was summoned by the Pope, they place a second reason, because nobody will have a vote in it unless they are Cardinals, Bishops, Abbots and Generals of Orders, when all learned men, even if they are lay, ought to have a decisive vote. Charles Dumoulin in his plan for why the *Consilio de Concilio Tridentino non recipiendo*, §28, altogether teaches the same thing. The Centuriators (*Centur.* 1 lib. 2 cap. 9 col. 548) say the same thing, and explain the history of the Council of the Apostles from Acts 15, and say that in that Council, after the opinions were given, votes were conferred upon the whole Church and it was defined by a judgment of all that man is justified by faith alone without works.

Secondly, they say that a Council of the Church is not constituted except from truly pious and chosen men, that clearly Brenz teaches in the *Wirtemberg Confession*, in the chapter on Councils, where, after he had said that Councils ought to yield to the Scriptures, he renders the reason is because we are certain from the Scriptures what is and is not of infallible truth: but on Councils it is not the same, because each body of men is not the true Church, since it is not the faith of all, nor are they all elect; the Confessionists and Calvinists are held to say the same thing, as we will see below, who would have it that only the elect and the saints pertain to the Church, and certainly a Council of the Church is not constituted even if it is from men of the Church.

But the teaching of Catholics is that only greater prelates, that is Bishops, ordinarily have a right to a decisive vote in general and provincial Councils, while from privilege and also custom, even Cardinals, Abbots and the Generals of Orders, even if they are not Bishops. Furthermore, from priests and other lesser clergy only some learned men are called who assist in the disputation, or in other ministries. Princes are called both to defend the Council and to be conscious witnesses to the decrees of a Council, and afterward to punish contumacious transgressors with corporal penalties. Lastly, from private laity, some are only called who seem useful or necessary to some ministry of a Council. This teaching of Catholics is clear both from the persons that were present at the Council of Trent, and from Juan Torquemada (lib. 2 cap. 21 and 15), as well as from other Catholic authors.

Now, we shall constitute the proof of our teaching and the refutation of the contrary. *First*, the second opinion of those we just related does not need refutation; both because it must be refuted in the question on the definition of the Church, and because it is so false that it destroys itself. Really, when it says that a Council is constituted from the elect and the saints, it affirms something to be a Council and nothing to be a Council; for it posits there is a Council, when it explains it is constituted from certain men; no indeed, Brenz presupposes it to so exist that he says the authority of Councils is great, and still when he says it is constituted from the elect, he is compelled to say there is no Council. For to make a Council, it is for men to be joined and cooperate as one, but the elect in this world cannot be joined together since nobody knows who is truly of the elect, because if some of our adversaries do not require the election of true members of the Church, still they require internal faith and piety, and hence they cannot ever show any Council which could certainly be called a Christian Council since nobody can see internal faith and piety.

Moreover, the first opinion must now be refuted, firstly, by reason taken from Sacred Scripture: to define in Councils those things which must be believed or done is the proper office of pastors, for it is properly to shepherd, to teach, and so teach that others would be held to believe. Hence, to teach is to shepherd, as is clear from Jeremiah 3: "I will give you shepherds according to my heart, and they will shepherd you with knowledge and doctrine." Likewise from Ephesians 4: "But some are pastors and teachers." Jerome notes on this verse, as well as Augustine (epist. 59 ad Paulinum) the name of shepherd is joined with the name of teacher, because it is proper for pastors to teach. But laymen are not pastors, nor any Ecclesiastics, but only Bishops; for we so read in Acts 20, "Attend to the whole flock in which the Holy Spirit has placed you as Bishops to rule the Church of God." And the last chapter of John, where it is said to Peter: "Feed my sheep."

If anyone would contend that all Christians are Bishops, and what is said to Peter was said to all Christians, he ought to show who they are that are called sheep in the Church; for if everyone is a pastor, where are the sheep? What if some are pastors, that is, Bishops, and some are sheep, that is laymen, and only pastors ought to come together in Councils to define what are good pastures and what are harmful ones; certainly it follows that Councils are not made up of the laity, but the priests. Add that Melanchthon (*in Locis*, ca. *de numero Sacramentorum*) and Calvin (*Inst.* lib. 4 c. 14 § 20) place the ordination of pastors who are dedicated to shepherd, *i.e.* to teach the people, among the sacraments of the Church. And Calvin clearly says this sacrament is not common to the whole Church but only to certain men who are initiated to it, hence by their confession, the laity are not ordained pastors, but only sheep, therefore it is not suitable for them to teach, especially by the authority that is done in Councils.

Secondly, it is proven from the testimonies of the Fathers. The first Councils in the Church were celebrated in the times of Pope Victor over the question of Easter. Eusebius speaks of these in *hist.* lib. 5 ca. 23: "On account of which assemblies of Bishops and Councils were convoked in each individual province." He says not every educated man you like, but Bishops were gathered into Councils; Cyprian teaches the same thing in the beginning of his letter to Jubianus, and Hilary in his book on Councils, Ambrose (epist. 32), Jerome (lib. 2 *Apologia contra Ruffinum*), Augustine (epist. 119), Leo (epist. 16) and following. Ruffinus, *hist.* lib. 10 cap. 1,

Athanasius in his epistle to those leading a solitary life, and other Fathers, who everywhere assert that Councils are made of Bishops.

Besides, Theodosius II, in his epistle to the Council of Ephesus, which is extant in the first volume of this Council, ch. 32, says: "It is illicit for one who is not in the order of the most holy Bishops to mix in Ecclesiastical tractates." Pulcheria, the empress, in her epistle to the general of Bithynia, which is contained before the Council of Chalcedon, commanded that clergy, monks and laity also be repelled by force from the Council, with the exception of those few whom the Bishops bring with them. In the Council of Chalcedon, act. 1, when it was sent to the Archimandrite Martin that he would subscribe, responded that it was not his place, but for Bishops alone to do so. And in the same Council, when the laity entered on behalf of Dioscorus the monk, the Fathers frequently shouted: "Send the crowd outside, this is a Council of Bishops."

Thirdly, it is proven from the Councils celebrated to this point: the decrees of all the Councils were made by Bishops alone, as is clear from the subscriptions, for everywhere only Bishops are found to have subscribed, with a few general exceptions, in which the Emperor also subscribed, but in a different manner from the Bishops; the Bishops in defining did so as judges while emperors subscribed by confessing, and also a few others, as at Florence, the Lateran Council and the Council of Trent, in which Abbots and the Generals of Orders subscribed: the rest, even if they were the best and learned, were never admitted except to consult, with the exception of the Council of Basel, where priests were admitted to a decisive vote, but in violation of and against all antiquity, nor was that Council legitimate, as we said above.

Fourthly, it is proved from reason. In the first place, the Ecclesiastical and public business must be treated by Ecclesiastical and public persons, as is known, but such are only Bishops. Next, if all learned men ought to be admitted, there would never have been general Councils because all learned men of the whole Church could scarcely be gathered, or if at length they were gathered, it would be impossible to govern such a Council on account of the exceeding multitude; besides then, without a doubt, there would be more inferiors in the Council than superiors and the greater would conquer the better teaching, and superiors in the Church would be ruled by inferiors, not vice versa, which is an absurdity. Likewise, if it were so, then one prince could easily, if a Council were held in his region, define whatever he would want; for could he not easily gather all the most learned men and priests of his province and introduce them into the Council, which other princes who are very far away could not do? Lastly, there is no republic which, by the teaching of natural reason, did not have some order in assemblies, so that no common member of the citizenry would have a place and a vote, but only the princes and heads of the rest.

CHAPTER XVI
The objections of our adversaries are answered

YET, the Protestants object *firstly,* in the little book we have already cited, that the testimony of Luke in Acts 15, where St. Luke speaks about the first Council of the Apostles, says: "The Apostles came together as well as the elders to see about this word." And further on, "Then it pleased the Apostles and the elders with all the Church," where we see that even priests and laity were present in the first Council.

I respond: In that Council the Apostles were present as judges to define, and priests to consult, but the people were not called, but still were present and consented not by defining or disputing, but only by listening and not protesting. That this is so is proven in two ways: 1) from the custom of the Church which is the best interpreter of Scripture; for since in all Councils which were celebrated after Apostolic times, it is certain that this order was observed, namely that only Bishops were judges, although there were man others either clergy or laity present, and we ought to believe the same order was altogether preserved as in the Apostolic Council. For the universal Church would never depart from the examples of the first times, especially from the example of the Apostles.

Then, this same thing can be shown from the very context; that only the Apostles and priests were called is clear from that which is said: "The Apostles and the elders came together to see on this word," where no mention is made of the people. Then, that both the Apostles and the elders spoke, until the controversy was struck, it is gathered from those words ("and that it were done with great inquiry") that after the disputation, in which the Apostles and elders spoke, only the Apostles spoke a definitive opinion. It is clear from the fact that only Peter, Paul, Barnabas and James are introduced as speaking by Luke. The fact that no others gave their opinions, is clear from the continuation of the text, for after the opinion of Peter, it is soon added: "But the whole multitude fell silent and listened to Paul and Barnabas." Then, it is added: "And after they were silent," namely Paul and Barnabas, "James responded saying," and as soon as James finished his speech, it is added: "Then the Apostles were pleased, etc."

Therefore, it is a lie which the Centuriators say, that all who were there gave their opinion because of what follows: "The Apostles and elders were pleased, with all the Church," is understood on the tacit consent, which ought to be given to all things which are in a Council. See the Council of Carthage in the works of Cyprian, for even in that Council many priests, deacons, and laity were present with the Bishops, and still only the Bishops gave their opinions.

Secondly, they object in the same place that a general Council represents the universal Church, therefore, there ought to be there men from every kind, *i.e.* Bishops, priests, princes, private citizens, clergy, laity, etc.

I respond: Something can be represented in many ways, but the best way is in which the people are represented by princes. For just as in general assemblies of many states, consuls or lords of cities are usually gathered, so also in general assemblies of the Church all Bishops are gathered, for each Bishop manages the person of his Church, as is clear from Cyprian (lib. 4 epist. 9) where he says the Church is in the Bishop. Moreover, Eusebius (*de vita Constantini*, lib. 3) calls the Council of 318 Bishops a gathering of the whole world. And St. Augustine (*de Baptismo* lib. 1 c. 18) calls the consent of the same Council the consent of the whole Church.

Thirdly, they object in the same place that common cause must be assisted by common votes and strength, but the cause of faith is common to all Christians, for the faith pertains no less to the laity than to the clergy, therefore, the laity also pertain to Councils.

I respond: The cause of faith pertains to all, but in a different mode; for it pertains to prelates as teachers, to the rest as students, just as in war the cause of victory pertains to the whole army, nevertheless there is a general to command and lead the army, and it is for the rest to fight.

If anyone would object with the words of Nicholas I (*epistola ad Michaelem*, which are held also in *dist.* 96, c. *ubinam*): "Wherever you read that your predecessor emperors were present in conciliar gatherings, unless perhaps in certain ones where it was treated on faith, is it not universal, which is common to all, which is not only for clerics but even for the laity, does it not altogether pertain to Christians?" The response can be made that Nicholas, from that "because faith is common to all," rightly gathered that emperors ought to be present, but not as a judge, but as one to whom it is incumbent to defend the common faith with edicts and laws, and if it were necessary, even with the sword.

Fourthly, the same as well as Charles Demoulin (*loc. cit.*), and Brenz (*Witemberg confession*, c. *de Conciliis*), and Herman Hamelmann (lib. 3 *Prolegomena*, c. 6) object that more often the opinion of one man, even of the laity, was proposed for the opinion of the whole Council, because it was more fortified by the authority of Scripture and without a doubt later must be proposed, therefore even laity and whoever else ought to be called to a Council.

They prove the foregoing: 1) from Gratian (36, q. 2 *can. ult.*) where we read the authority of Jerome was fortified by Sacred Scripture, and was prejudicial to a whole general Council; 2) from Panormitanus, in *cap. Significati, de election* and from John Gerson (par. 1 *de examinatione doctrinarum*) of which he says the opinion of one private man must be put before the opinion of a Pope if the private man is moved by better doctrines or the authorities of the Old and New Testament, for he teaches that every learned man may and must resist a whole Council if he would see it err from malice or ignorance.

This argument is confirmed because the reason why Bishops are especially called is because they are reckoned more learned than others, therefore if many laymen are found more learned than Bishops, or equally learned, why ought they not be called to a Council?

I respond to the first: The opinion of one private man can be placed before the opinion of a general Council before a definition, while a reason is discussed, for in discussion, erudition, not authority of the person, holds the first place; besides, even after a definition, when it is certain that Council was illegitimate, but in no manner after the decision of a legitimate Council.

To that from Gratian, I say: 1) Herman lies when he says that, according to Gratian Jerome was put before a general Council, for Gratian does not speak of a general Council but a particular one. I say: 2) those words which Gratian attributes to Jerome are not found in Jerome's works, nor do they seem to be his words. I say: 3) Gratian made a mistake in that citation, for Jerome and the Council did not fight, as Gratian thought. For Jerome only spoke according to an old law that it was permitted for an abductor to marry a woman that he had abducted if her father would consent. Moreover, the Council stated that not withstanding that old law, which is judicial, it does not obligate Christians, thus it is not lawful for an abductor to marry a woman that he had abducted.

To that from Panormitanus and Gerson, I say: 1) they spoke conditionally, just as the Apostle, when he says: "Even if we or an Angel from heaven would preach a different Gospel, etc." (Galatians 1). Therefore, just as from a conditional sentence of the Apostle it is not permitted to understand that therefore the Apostles and the Angels could preach a gospel that is contrary to the Gospel of Christ, so also, from that which Panormitanus and Gerson say, it is lawful for anyone to resist a Council or a Pope if he sees them err, it is not lawful to gather therefore that Councils and Popes could absolutely err, and therefore private men must be called to Councils. I say: 2) they speak on resistance which can be made to a Council or a Pope, in a time of discussion before a decision or even after when a Council is illegitimate.

I say for confirmation, Bishops indeed ought to be chosen that are the most learned and the best; nevertheless, they have the authority to judge not because they are learned, but because they are public persons, namely princes having ecclesiastical jurisdiction, in the very same way that it is required for secular princes and judges to have jurisprudence and an upright life, but on no account would it be lawful for a private man that is better and more learned to topple the prince or judge from his seat and occupy it.

Fourthly, Herman Hamelmann objects (lib. 3 *Prolegomena*, c. 10) with many old testimonies which were disputed at length on a matter of faith in the presence of the people as a judge. They so argue about Peter and Simon Magus (cited by Clement, lib. 1 and 2, *recognitionum*), Bishop Archelaus and Mani (cited by Epiphanius, *haeresi* 56), Pope Sylvester and the Jews (cited by Zonaras in the life of Constantine), Athanasius and Arius (cited by Bishop Vigilius the Bishop of Trent), Augustine and Maximinus (cited by Augustine lib. 1 cap. 1 *contra Maximinum*), and also in the Council of Nicaea there were many learned and eloquent laymen, as is clear from Nicephorus (lib. 8 cap. 14). Lastly, that the people were a judge, Ambrose clearly says in epistle 32, where he says: "Someone may refuse a case of faith to be carried out in the Church: if anyone trusts, let him come here." And a little after: "That people may judge, who have the divine light and not a human one in their heart; the law was not written with ink, but the spirit of the living God." And further: "But Auxentius is certain that you are not ignorant of the faith, he flees your examination."

Two things must be noted for the answer. 1) There is a twofold judgment, public and private. It is public which is advanced by a public judge with authority, so that the rest would be held to acquiesce to that judge. It is private, that opinion which everyone choses as true, but obliges nobody, in the same way as in the disputations of Theologians and Philosophers, the students are the judges, after hearing each side they choose what they wish, but nobody can compel anyone to think likewise.

2) A public judgment in a cause of faith is never attributed to the people, but a private judgment was sometimes attributed also to pious and holy men, but then only when something else could not be done, for the people are held to follow the judgment of their pastors: nevertheless, when heretics live with Catholics unpunished and seduce many, it is expedient whenever public disputations with them are begun in the presence of the people, to relinquish judgment to the people that it would follow what seems to rest upon better reasons. This is what Elijah did (3 Kings 18) who when he could not otherwise recall the people from the cult of Baal, he instituted a contest with the prophets of Baal, with the people present, and said: "Who will hear through fire, he that is God, if the Lord is God, follow him, if Baal is God, follow him."

With these things being noted, I say to all those citations, that in those disputations private judgment was given to the people, not a public one, and this because it could not be done otherwise. That is what can be understood from the Epistle of Ambrose, for he says: "Let anyone who is present, openly come to the Church, let them hear with the people, not that anyone should reside as a judge, but that each one of his own affect should have an examination, and choose whom he will follow." There you see a public judgment is denied to the people, rather a private one is given. Moreover, the reason that a private one was given, is because then at Milan the emperor favored the Arians, and it could not otherwise be obtained.

This can be said in general to all the cited passages. But in particular, to that about the Council of Nicaea, it must be known that laymen were not called nor were present in the acts of the Council, but came of themselves, that they would dispute with Bishops outside the Council, whom they heard came from the whole world. See Ruffinus (lib. 10, cap. 3).

CHAPTER XVII

How many Bishops are required for a general Council?

BESIDES these arguments of the heretics, Catholics bring up one of their doubts about those who ought to be present in a Council: either all the Bishops of the world are required to make a general Council, or only some; if all, therefore there never was a general Council to this point, nor does it seem there ever will be; if only some, what is that number? For there does not seem to be a better reason for one or another.

I respond: This question cannot be answered better than from the custom of the Church, from those Councils which were general by the consent of all, such as the first four. Moreover, we gather from the custom of the Church four conditions that both suffice and are required for a general Council. 1) The evocation shall be general, so that it is known to all the greater Christian provinces. For it is certain it was always held that even the seventh Council judged that the Council of Constantinople against images was not general because its noise had not gone out to all the earth.

2) That no Bishop would be excluded, no matter from where he would come, provided it is certain he is a Bishop and has not been excommunicated.

3) That the four patriarchs, apart from the Supreme Pontiff, would be present either themselves or through others, namely, that of Constantinople, Alexandria, Antioch, and Jerusalem, because all other bishops are under them; that is clear both from use, and from the seventh Council, act. 6, where it is censed that the Council of Constantinople against images was not a general Council because it did not have the Patriarchs, and in the eighth Council, act. 9, where the vicar of the Patriarch of Alexandria is received with joy, as if without him something would detract from the fullness of the Council. This third is not altogether necessary, but only judged to be

good. The third Council condemned Nestorius of Constantinople without the Patriarch of Antioch, and the Council of Chalcedon concluded nearly everything without the Patriarch of Alexandria, and not because these Patriarchs are not necessary but because they are heretics or certainly schismatics.

4) That some should arrive from at least a greater part of the Christian provinces, and if the Council were in the east, it always seemed to be sufficient if many Bishops from all the provinces of the east would come together, but from the west some would be sent by the Pope who would supply for the place of others. And on the other hand, if it were celebrated in the west, many Bishops come together from all the provinces of the west, but from the east some few would come in the name of others. So in the Council of Nicaea, only two priests from the west were sent from Italy, one Bishop from France and one from Spain, as well as one from Africa. In the second and third Councils, there were no Bishops from the west but still Popes Damasus and Celestine confirmed those Councils in their name as well as that of other Bishops of the West which they gathered in Rome. In the fourth Council, there were only legates for Pope Leo, and besides he sent the consent of the other Bishops of Spain, France and Italy, who, when they had celebrated Councils in their provinces, wrote to Leo that they would follow his opinion in all things. See the volumes of Councils.

On the other hand, to the Councils of the west, such as that of the Lateran under Innocent III, Lyons under Gregory X, Vienne under Clement V, and recently to Trent, numerous Bishops came from the whole west, but from the east merely a certain few. From which it follows, there can be national Councils that are much greater than general ones in regard to the number of Bishops, and still lesser in regard to their authority, for the second Council only had 150 Bishops from different provinces and nations, but the national Council of

Carthage from Africa alone, in the time of St. Augustine, had 217 Bishops, as Prosper of Aquitaine relates in his *Chronicum* for the year 450.

CHAPTER XVIII
In Councils, Bishops are not counselors, but judges.

THE last question follows from the form of Councils, which will be bipartite. *Firstly,* for it occurs it must be explained, whether Councils have a form of judgment or only of inquiry?

Secondly, after this has been defined, that it has a form of judgment, what order ought there to be among the judges, as the form is said to be a form in the body, or the order of all the members in their place of positions, so that in the body of men the form is said to be a certain order in which the one who ought to be in charge is in charge, and the one who ought to be subject is subject. Therefore, this is the first part of the question: Is a Council a true judgment and Bishops true judges, so that their opinions must be so favored because they so favored them, just as the opinion of a judge in political cases; or would it be only a certain inquiry and would a decree of a Council only be valid in as much as its reasoning avails, in the way in which we speak on the decisions of Doctors, which they make either in the schools or in their commentaries?

The heretics of this time nearly all agree on this, that a Council is nothing other than inquiry and that Christ alone and his written word has a decisive vote. Therefore they say the number of those voting must not be attended to, and often one must be more followed who advances the Scripture for himself than the whole rest of the Council. And thence they also deduce that it is lawful for anyone to examine the decrees of a Council and receive or not receive as he wills. Luther teaches this in his assertion of the articles, 29, and cited by Cochlaeus in 500 articles, art. 115. Calvin teaches the same thing (*Instit.* lib. 4 cap. 9 § 8). Brenz writes the same thing in the Wirtemberg Confession, *c. de Scriptura,* and Chemntiz also in his examination of the Council of Trent, 4 sess., where he everywhere rebukes Catholics because they attribute to Bishops judicial authority to judge on controversies.

Lastly, the aforementioned little book of the Protestants, where they explain the reasons why they would not come to the Council, clearly teach that Councils ought not to be convened so that they might define questions by votes, but that someone would be found among so many who shows from the Scripture what must be followed and proposes such a thing to the very numerous Council, even if the number of teachers would convict him. By this opinion the heretics show how little they make of Councils and that they truly desire nothing other than that questions would never be defined.

Therefore, we say that an assembly of Bishops in legitimate Councils is a true assembly of judges, and their decrees and laws must necessarily be followed. Firstly, it is proven from the Scriptures. 1) Deut. 17, where those who have doubts are commanded to have recourse to the Councils of priests, and: "Let those who do not obey their judgments be condemned to death." 2) Matthew 18, "If he will not listen to the Church, let him be to you as a heathen and a publican." This passage, even if it admits different explanations, still, "the Church" can properly be called a Council by the consent of all; this explanation cannot be rejected in any way, whereby we assert the Lord commanded that we should obey the teachings of a legitimate Council. 3) Acts 15 and 16, where Paul, encompassing different cities, commanded them to preserve the dogmas which were decreed by the Apostles in the Council of Jerusalem. On that Council three things must be noted.

First, in that Council it was not from the Scriptures, rather the question was defined by a vote of the Apostles. For the question was not, as our adversaries imagine, whether faith alone would justify, but whether circumcision and the remaining legal ceremonies were necessary for Christians. It is manifestly gathered from the occasion of the Council, from what St. Luke says in Acts 15: "Certain men rose up from the heresy of the Pharisees who believed, saying 'that it was necessary for them to be circumcised, and to command them to preserve the law of Moses.' And the Apostles and the elders came together to see about this word, etc." And from the epistle of the Council, in which nothing is commanded except for abstinence from blood, strangled animals and those immolated to idols, and that the Gentiles would be freed from all other Jewish ceremonies. Certainly none of these are contained in the Scriptures, for where, I ask, was it written that the Gentiles should not keep the laws with the exception of the command on abstinence from blood, suffocated animals and those immolated to idols?

The second thing that must be noted is the teaching of the Apostles was not consigned to the disciples for the examination, rather, they were simply commanded to obey it, as is very clearly constituted from the cited passages of Acts 15 and 16; why do our adversaries, who would have it that the teaching of Councils is examined by any private man, so manifestly oppose the Scripture?

The third is the definition of the Council of the Apostles. It was a true law binding in conscience, on which matter we treated above in the fourth book *On the Roman Pontiff*, and Luke showed it well enough when he calls upon precepts with a mode, decrees with the mode and dogmas.

Secondly, it is proven from the Councils themselves, for all Councils say anathema to those who do not obey; they call their decrees canons or ecclesiastical laws; when the Bishops subscribe, they say: "I N., defining, subscribed." Besides, in the Council of Chalcedon, act. 4, when ten Bishops of Egypt refused to acquiesce, they were held as heretics by the judgment of the greater part, all of which are the clearest arguments that Councils are true judgments.

It is proved *thirdly*, for if votes were not taken in Councils, but merely disputations, it would be done wrongly that only Bishops would impose sentence when the duty to dispute would be of learned men, whether they were bishops or not, the contrary of which we showed above. For in vain are some bishops called unlearned and simpletons, such as some were in the Council of Nicaea as Ruffinus writes (lib. 10 *hist.* c. 3). Add that the Protestants in their little book clearly oppose themselves, for in that book they teach that laity ought also to have a decisive vote with Bishops, and a little later, in the same place, they say that in Councils something ought not to be defined from the multitude of votes, but only by the testimonies of the Scriptures. We will advance many other things later, when we take up the dispute as to whether Councils can err.

But they object with the example of Paphnutius, who is cited by Socrates (lib. 1 c. 8) and Sozomen (lib. 1 cap. 22), that when the whole Council of Nicaea wished to forbid priests the use of a wife, he alone freely resisted and prevailed. Luther (art. 115 from the 500 cited by Cochlaeus, *Septicipite*, c. 34) says: "The matter is insane that Councils mean to conclude and establish what must be believed, when often there is no man there who gets a whiff of the divine Spirit, just as happened in the Council of Nicaea where they treated and wanted to fashion laws on the Ecclesiastical state, that they could not marry, already they were all false, then one Paphnutius advanced, and refuted the whole body and said this is not so, this is not Christian, then the whole Council needed to desist from that conclusion of theirs."

I respond: *Firstly*, this story is uncertain since the more ancient writers, Eusebius, Athanasius, Epiphanius, Ruffinus, etc. make no mention of it. Secondly, if the tale is true, Paphnutius resisted before the definition of a Council, as the authors themselves witness, hence this example is not to the purpose. *Thirdly*, I say Paphnutius does not allege a Scripture, but only contended on his own authority, and for that reason, by the judgment of our adversaries, he ought not to be heard. *Fourthly*, I add, Paphnutius only desired that the use of a wife ought not to be forbidden to those who had them; still, the Council exhorted that it was severely forbidden for priests and Monks to marry after their sacred Ordination or profession, as Socrates and Sozomen witness, from which it is a marvel if the Lutherans are not ashamed, since they marry against the opinion of Paphnutius, even if they were monks and priests.

Some Catholics object *secondly*, if all Bishops are judges, the Pope would be held, who presides in a Council, to follow the decrees made by a greater part of the Bishops; but it is false, since Damasus invalidated the acts of the Council of Armenia, in which a greater part of the Bishops consented, as is clear from the letter of Damasus to the Bishops of Illyria; and Leo invalidated a certain decree of the Council of Chalcedon, to which even a greater part of the Council had consented, as Leo himself witnesses in epistles 53, 54 and 55.

I respond: *firstly*, it perhaps never happened that the Pope followed the lesser part in a Council when they gave their opinions without fraud or deceit. What I say, I say on account of the Councils of Armenia and Chalcedon, which did not lack some deceit, for in the Armenian Council Catholics were deceived by the obscurity of a Greek word, as Ruffinus shows (lib. 10 c. 21). However, in the Council of Chalcedon there was fraud, which is clear from act. 16 of that Council, where the vicars of the Roman Pontiff complained that the decree was fraudulently made while they were absent.

I say *secondly*, the president of a Council, as president, ought to follow in the greater part of the votes in forming a decree; still the Pope, not as president, but as supreme prince of the whole Church can retract that judgment, and consequently, if he were the president of the Council, he can, not as president, but as the supreme Prince, not follow the greater part just as in temporal judgments a president that is constituted by a king ought to follow the greater part of the judges, still the King, as the superior, can invalidate the whole judgment. And this especially holds place in the Pontiff, whose right it is to confirm and direct his brethren, and to have this assistance of the Holy Spirit lest he would err, according to that of Luke 22, "I have prayed for thee, etc." See Juan Torquemada, lib. 3 ca. 63 and 64; Melchior Cano, lib. 5 c. 5 qu. 2.

CHAPTER XIX
Who is to preside at a general Council

The other part of the question is whether someone ought to preside and who it should be. The heretics of our time teach that the emperor ought to be the ordinary president of Councils, or someone sent by him, or if he sends no one, it ought to be constituted by the Council itself. And really, they say that in the ancient Councils the Roman Pontiff was never in charge, but either the Emperor or his deputies, or the older Patriarch, or the bishop of that place, where the Council was held. The Centuriators teach this (*Cent.* 4 cap. 7 col. 536), Calvin (*inst.* lib. 4, cap. 7 § 1 and 2), Charles Demoulin (*consilium de Concilio Tridentino non recipiendo*, § 4) who clearly lies when he says the legates of the Pope always sat behind all the Bishops in Councils, when in no Council are they discovered in the last place. Further, Herman Hamelmann, (lib. 3 *Proleg.* ca. 8) and Brenz (*Proleg. contra Petrum a Soto*).

All Catholics teach that this office is proper to the Supreme Pontiff, to preside over a Council either by himself or by legates, and as the Supreme Judge to moderate all things. Moreover, we say by himself or by legates, because the Supreme Pontiff was never present at the Eastern Councils by himself, nor was it done in a certain case, but for a certain reason, as is clear from epistle 17 of Leo to Theodosius, and 47 to the Council of Chalcedon, where he says he is not coming to the Council because custom does not suffer it; nor did he have any examples on this matter from his predecessors.

Add, that Pope Vigilius was at Constantinople when the fifth general Council was taking place in the city, but he confirmed the acts of the Council through a little book, as Photius writes in his book on the Seven Councils. The emperors themselves, when they summoned Councils, called all other bishops by an edict, but invited the Bishop of Rome that he may deign to come if he pleased, as is clear from the epistle of the Emperor Martian to Pope Leo, which is held before the Council of Chalcedon. Moreover, what would be the reason for this matter is uncertain. Juan Torquemada (lib. 3 cap. 11) posits several reasons, which do not seem to prove much to me.

I suspect that these two were different reasons among others. *One*, because it did not seem to be fitting for the head to follow the members, when rather more the members ought to follow the head; therefore, on that account the Pope was present at the Roman Councils, and certain others which he convoked to himself, *i.e.* to the place where he was, but he did not wish, nor ought, to go to Councils gathered in other places.

The other reason is because in the eastern Councils the Emperor was always present, or some of his legates, and although neither the emperor nor his legates presided over the Council properly as a judge, nevertheless, he presided at least in regard to the material place, and even if the Supreme Pontiff would have been there, still he would have wanted him to preside in some manner, as is clear from the Council of Florence, in the beginning, where the Greeks altogether contended that the Emperor should have the highest place, and the Supreme Pontiff would precede him. But although it would have been tolerable to some extent, as secular princes would sit in the Council before other bishops, still it was in no way fitting before the Supreme Pontiff himself, lest therefore either this would be tolerated or a tumult aroused, he did not go to these Councils, but only sent legates.

But after all these have been omitted, the right of presidency in general Councils pertains to the Supreme Pontiff, and it is proved firstly by reason sought from the Scripture. The Supreme Pontiff is the Pastor and father of the universal Church, even as all Bishops and princes, in respect to the Supreme Pontiff, are called sheep and sons, as is known from that last chapter of John: "Feed my sheep." And it is confirmed from the fact that the Councils call the Pope father, and he sometimes calls Bishops gathered into Councils sons, as is clear from Theodoret (lib. 5 *hist.* c. 10), where Damasus, responding to the Bishops of the second general Council, so begins: "That you would show due reverence to the Apostolic See, it is for you with great honor, most honored sons." Likewise, from the epistle of the Council of Antioch to Pope Julius, which so begins: "To the most blessed and honorable lord and father, Julius, etc." Stephen, the Archbishop of Carthage, so writes with three Councils: "To our most blessed lord and holy father of fathers, Damasus, etc." And the Council of Chalcedon, in the epistle to Leo, said: "We ask that your strength would fulfill by your decrees the honor of our judges, which is fitting." But who, I ask, can be ambiguous as to whether fathers ought to preside over sons, and pastors over sheep, or the other way around?

Secondly, it is proven from the Apostolic Council, in Acts 15, in which Jerome affirms that Peter presided in his epistle to Augustine, which is 11 among the epistles of Augustine and he gathers the same thing from it; that Peter rose first, spoke first, defined the first question, and all, as Jerome said, followed his opinion.

It is proved *thirdly* from the acts of the eight general Councils, for even our adversaries affirm the Roman Pontiff was in charge of others. The first was at Nicaea, on the presidency of this Council there are four opinions. Some would have it that the Emperor presided, such as Brenz. Others that it was Eustathius of Antioch; such as the Centuriators (*loc. cit.*), and Luther (liber *de Conciliis*, parte secunda). Others, that Athanasius presided, such as Calvin (*loc. cit.*). Others that Bishop Hosius of Cordova, and Vitus and Vincentius, priests and legates of the Roman Pontiff.

The first opinion is absolutely false. In the first place, Constantine subscribed after all the Bishops, as the Emperor Basil witnessed at the end of the eighth Council, but the president subscribed in the first place. Then Constantine did not dare to sit except in a lower place than the Bishops, and those assenting to the Bishops, as is gathered from Theodoret (lib. 1 c. 7 *Hist.*) and Eusebius (lib. 3 *de vita Constantini*). Besides, Constantine professed in that very Council that he ought to be judged by the Bishops, and subject to them, not put in charge of them, as Ruffinus writes (lib. 10 cap. 2). Therefore, how could he oppose himself if he meant to preside in episcopal judgment?

Ambrose says to this (epist. 32) that Constantine, at the Council of Nicaea, did not make himself a judge, but left a free judgment to priests. Likewise, Athanasius, in his second *Apologia*, says that he could not be present at the Council in which it was not a Bishop, but a Count that presided. And in his epistle to those leading a solitary life, he forcefully about that Constantius, because he meant to hold the first place in Councils, "If the judgment was of Bishops, what does the Emperor have in common with it?" And Hosius wrote to the same Constantius in which he relates of his predecessor: "So that he would not be a teacher for us in this kind of thing, but rather more learn from us, God consigned to you *imperium*, but he entrusted these matters which are in the Church to us." And not far from the end: "For who, when they saw that he made himself a head of Bishops to make judgments and to preside over ecclesiastical judgments, would they not say rightly, that the very thing is the abomination of desolation, which Daniel foresaw?" There clearly he calls Constantius antichrist, because he dared to preside in Ecclesiastical judgment. Suidas also writes in the life of Leontius, that when Leontius saw Constantius presiding in the Council and speaking, he said to him that he marveled that he would furnish so curious a sight, while neglecting his own affairs, namely wars and other civil business, he was among foreigners, namely Ecclesiastics. But certainly, neither Athanasius, nor Hosius, nor Leontius would have rebuked Constantius for desiring to preside over the Council if his father Constantine would already have presided over the Council of Nicaea.

That Eustathius was not the president is proven, *firstly* because in the subscription he is not found first, nor second, nor even third; rather, he was placed lower. *Secondly*, because when Alexander, the bishop of Alexandria, was in the Council he was greater and more worthy than the patriarch of Antioch, no reason permitted that he should be in charge.

But the Centuriators say, citing Eusebius (*de vita Constantini* lib. 3), we read him who sat first to the right of the Emperor, gave a speech in praise of the Emperor; but he, who gave the speech was certainly Eustathius, from what Theodoret says in his history, lib. 1 cap. 7.

I respond, Eustathius was the first at the right of the order of bishops, as Eusebius says, but still he was not immediately first after the Emperor. It is certain from Athanasius, in his epistle for those leading a solitary life, that Hosius was the chief of this Council, and thence sat before Eustathius.

Therefore (if one may be permitted to conjecture) there were three orders of those sitting in the Council; one from the right, the other from the left, and the third in the head of the whole assembly, and certainly in this third the emperor sat in between the Bishop Hosius, the legates of the Pope, and bishop Alexander of Alexandria; still Vitus and Vincent were likewise Apostolic legates. Then, the first of its order, who was at the right, sat Eustathius, the Bishop of Antioch. The second of that order, who was at the left, was first Macharius, the Bishop of Jerusalem, and by this account the order of the dignity of the primary Patriarchs was preserved, which was certainly very probable that it was preserved in the Council; or certainly, if it was pleasing, we could respond that a worthier place was granted to Eustathius on account of antiquity and the merit of his sanctity, but that he did not, on that account, preside over the Council; for otherwise the Emperor would have presided over the fourth and sixth Council, in which he sat in the lowest place. Therefore, the presidency must not be gathered from the place as much as from the subscription, for often someone sits as first for the sake of honor who really does not hold first place.

But that Athanasius was not the president hardly needs proof, for only Calvin asserts it, and without any reason. Besides, it is certain that Athanasius was only a deacon and went to the Council with his Bishop, Alexander, and did not sit nor subscribe. See Ruffinus (lib. 10, hist. cap. 14) and Sulpitius (lib. 2 *Sacrae Historiae*), Gregory Nazanzien (*Oratio in Athanasius*) and Athanasius himself (*in secunda Apologia*). Moreover, that a deacon would sit, much more preside in a Council of Bishops, even if he held the place of his bishop, is altogether unheard of. But Athanasius did not stand in place of his Bishop, since Bishop Alexander himself was present presiding; lastly among the subscriptions, the subscription of Alexander, the Bishop of Alexandria is found, placed after the subscription of the priests of the Roman Pontiff, but no subscription of Athanasius is found.

Therefore, the fact that Bishop Hosius, as well as the priests Vitus and Vincent, the legates of the Pope, were the presidents is proved, *firstly* from the subscriptions. For these three were the first of all to have subscribed. *Secondly*, from Cedrenus in his *Compendium Historiarum* and Photius in his book *de Septem Synodis*, who say that Sylvester conferred authority on the Council of Nicaea by legates. *Thirdly*, from Athanasius, in his epistle to those living a solitary life, where he says that Hosius was the chief in that Council, and that it was he that composed the Creed which is called Nicene. Moreover, since Hosius was a simple Bishop, and hence was inferior to all the Patriarchs that were present in the Council, without a doubt, he would never have had first place unless in turn he managed it for the Roman Pontiff. Therefore, in the aforesaid Council of Sardica, which is contained in the first volume of Councils, and is perhaps by Dionysius Exiguus, a very learned man, he says precisely that Hosius of Cordova acted as a legate of the Roman Pontiff at the Council of Nicaea. The fact can also be understood from the Greek codex which the Vatican library holds, whose testimony can be seen in the second book on the Council of Nicaea, published by Alphonsus of Pisa of the Society of Jesus, at Cologne in 1581.

The second general Council was the first Council of Constantinople, in which it is certain the Emperor did not preside, but only sent the letters of the Roman pontiff to Bishops, whereby they were called to the Council (Epistle of the Council to Damasus, cited by Theodoret, lib. 5 c. 9). It is also certain that the Roman Pontiff did not preside, rather, Nectarius, the Bishop of Constantinople. The reason for this is because the Roman Pontiff was not present, either himself or through legates. For Pope Damasus called together the Bishops of the East at Constantinople, but later wanted them to come to Rome from there, where he would summon a Council of western Bishops, so that the fullest Council would take place at Rome. The remainder of the eastern Bishops excused themselves on account of just causes, and joined their mind and teachings with the western Bishops, but not their physical presence. See the epistles of Damasus to the Council of Constantinople, and of the Council to Damasus, contained in Theodoret, lib. 5 cap. 9 and 10. Moreover, what if Damasus were present? Without a doubt he would have presided, as is clear from the same epistles, where they acknowledge Damasus as their head, and he calls them sons.

The third Council was the first of Ephesus, in which it is certain that the Emperor did not preside, rather the Roman Pontiff through legates. The fact that the emperor did not preside, nor anyone else in his name, is clear from the epistle of Theodosius the younger to the Council of Ephesus, which is contained in volume 1 of that Council, c. 32, where he says that he sent his constable Candidianus to the Council, not that he would mix in ecclesiastical questions, but for the defense of the Council. See the epistle of Nicholas I to the Emperor Michael. That the Roman Pontiff Celestine presided through his legate St. Cyril, all historians witness (Evagrius, lib. 1 cap. 4; Photius in libro de septem Synodis; Prosper, *Chronicum*; Nicephorus, lib. 14 cap. 34 and Liberatus Abbas in Breviariuo, c. 15; lastly Justinian in his edict and Nicholas I in his epistle to the Emperor Michael, and Celestine himself in his epistle to Cyril which is extant in this Council, tom. 1 c. 16, and among the works of Cyril).

But Calvin responds that Celestine, by some artifice, sought at least the name of the presidency when he could not hold it in fact and therefore sent his own there, to Cyril, who otherwise was going to hold the presidency, to delegate in their place, that he would at least appear to preside through him.

But this is a figment of Calvin, which he advances without any reason and it is easily refuted. *First*, from Prosper, who says that Nestorius especially resisted the industry of Cyril and the authority of Celestine. *Secondly*, from the epistle of Celestine in which we see that authority was entrusted to Cyril in place of the Roman Pontiff; much earlier than the other legates were sent. *Thirdly*, from Nicepherous (*loc. cit.*) who says that the great eastern Bishops confirmed this privilege given to Cyril from Celestine, that later Cyril received a mitre and the name of Pope, and was called judge of the whole world, and these ornaments he also transmitted to his successors.

Fourthly, from the epistle of Cyril to the people of Constantinople, in which he says that if Nestorius did not come back to his senses within the limit set by Pope St. Celestine, he would be deprived of communion with the

Church. *Fifthly*, from the Council itself, which (as Evagrius relates in liber 1, cap. 4) and from the very sentence which is held in volume 2, cap. 10 of this Council, when it meant to pronounce the condemnation against Nestorius, it prefaced the decree with other canons of the Church, and especially the letters of Pope Celestine necessarily compelled to so severe a sentence. Lastly, an epistle is extant from the Council to Celestine, in which they reserve to the judgment of Celestine himself the case of Bishop John of Antioch, as he was of the same opinion. All such are certain arguments that Celestine really was the president and chief in that Council.

The fourth Council is of Chalcedon, in the beginning of which, that is in the first action, the Emperor Martianus was present and sat in the first place, but he did not preside as a judge, and he himself witnesses to the fact in his speech to the Council, which is extant in the first act, where it says that he came to confirm the faith, just as formerly Constantine the Great had done, *i.e.* to not have come to explain the faith and judge controversies, but of this purpose, that the faith should be explained by the Council, and should be constituted firm and safe, defended by the aid and authority of the Emperor. Then, certain secular judges were present in the name of the Emperor in the other actions, who were not judges of controversies of faith, but were only present that everything would be conducted legitimately, without force, fraud or tumults. This is because, in the second Council of Ephesus, the Bishop Dioscorus, after he had introduced troops, compelled the Bishops to subscribe by force. Either the emperor or his vicar were present at this Council to impede the violence. This appears from the whole Council, for they never imposed sentence, never subscribed and they acquiesced in all the teachings of the Bishops.

Moreover, the legates of Pope Leo were really ecclesiastical judges. For they are named first in every action; they sat first, spoke first, subscribed first, and they advanced a definitive sentence against Dioscorus in the name of the Pope and the whole Council in act 3, in these words: "The most holy and blessed Pope, head of the universal Church, through us his legates, with the approval of the Holy Council, provided with the dignity of Peter the Apostle, who is named the foundation and rock of faith as well as porter of the heavenly kingdom, made Dioscorus an exile from Episcopal dignity and every priestly work." Then, blessed Leo and the whole Council affirmed it. Leo so said in epistle 47 to the Council of Chalcedon: "In these brethren, Paschasinus and Lucentsius, Bishops, Boniface and Basil, priests, who have been guided by the Apostolic See, let your fraternity view me as presiding over the Council." The Council of Chalcedon, in a letter to Leo, contained in the third action, (while in certain other copies it is after the end of the Council): "Over whom [the Bishops of the Council] you indeed presided as a head over these members, who hold your order, preferring benevolence. But the Emperors presided to arrange things in a most becoming manner, etc."

Calvin responds that the legates of the Pope presided in the Council because Pope Leo had extorted this privilege from the Emperor. "When the second Council of Ephesus took place Leo did not dare to seek the first seat in the Council, but sent legates and suffered them to be under Dioscorus, the bishop of Alexandria, as president. Since the matter fell out badly, and Dioscorus did not rightly govern the ship, Leo received the occasion and sought from the Emperor that he would permit another Council to be held over which his legates would preside. The emperor, because he saw there were no Bishops in the east suitable for such a burden, permitted the presidency of the Roman legates from a defect of persons."

This history, which Calvin recites without any proof, is full of lies, for in the first place, that Leo did not dare to seek the first seat in the Ephesine Council is a lie. Liberatus writes that the legates of the Roman Pontiff refused to sit in the

Council when they saw Dioscorus preside, and the presidency was not given to the Roman See. (*Breviarium*, c. 12). Hence, Dioscorus extorted that presidency from the Emperor, against what was right, as Zonaras (in *vita Theodosii*) and Evagrius (lib. 1 c. 10) write. Wherefore, Leo also (epist. 24, 25 and 26 to Theodosius and Pulcheria) frequently repeats that Dioscorus claimed the presidency for himself, where he also witnesses that Flavianus, the Bishop of Constantinople, appealed from that Council to the Apostolic See, and handed a petition of appeal to the Roman legates; how, therefore, did Leo not dare to seek the presidency in that Council, from which it was appealed to him as though to a greater person? Then, that Leo sought from the Emperor that his legates would preside in the Council of Chalcedon, and that the Emperor conceded it on account of defect of eastern persons, is the most impudent lie, since nothing of the sort is related by anyone, nay more, we see that Leo absolutely sent legates to preside, and sought consent from no one, still less by favor or permission.

The fifth Council was the second of Constantinople, in that Menas did not preside (as Calvin falsely teaches) for the Council Menas celebrated was a particular Council, not a general one, as we proved above; rather Eutychius, the successor of Menas, who acknowledged and professed that the presidency should go to the Roman Pontiff if he should wish to be present at the Council. Zonaras says in the life of Justinian: "Under this, the fifth Council gathered 165 Bishops, of whom the chief was Vigilius, the Roman Pope." And Eutychius himself, the Patriarch, in his epistle to Vigilius, which is contained in the end of the first conferral of the fifth Council: "We ask to discuss and confer with your Beatitude as our president on the three chapters." Such words of the Patriarch not only refute the lie of Calvin, who wrote that Menas presided in that Council, but also that of Illyricus, who, in *Cent.* 6, c. 9 col. 509 asserted that Pope Vigilius refused to be present at the Council lest he would be compelled to sit near

Eutychius as second. But who could fear this, when Eutychius offered him the presidency?

The sixth Council was the third of Constantinople, in that the legates of the Roman Pontiff, Agatho, Peter and George, priests, and John the deacon. Zonaras affirms this fact in the *Life of Constantine IV*, and besides it is clear from the Council itself where they were named; they spoke and they subscribed first of all in each action. The Emperor Constantine IV was also present at this Council, and although he presided over such famous men, *i.e.* in the first seat, still he was not in any way a judge or formally president, for he imposed no sentence, and subscribed last of all, not defining, but assenting.

The seventh Council is the second of Nicaea, in which legates of Pope Adrian I were presidents without controversy. For these first are named and they were the first to subscribe. The emperor is read to have done nothing in this Council.

The eighth Council is the fourth of Constantinople, in which the legates of Pope Adrian II presided without controversy, namely Donatus and Stephen, Bishops, and Marinus a deacon, who are the first to be named, to have subscribed, and in the first action itself were asked by the Council to show the letters of the Pope, whereby the presidency would be given to them, which they did right away. Lastly, at the end of the Council the first so subscribes: "I, Donatus, Bishop of Ostia, by the grace of God, holding the place of my master, Adrian, universal Pope, presiding over this holy and universal Council, have subscribed and promulgated all the things which are read above." Moreover, the Emperor Basil was present, but at the last part of the Council he clearly witnessed with a long speech that it was not for him, nor of any layman to mix in ecclesiastical judgments, and at length he subscribed after all the Patriarchs, not defining, but receiving and confessing the aforementioned formula. He also ought to have subscribed after all the Bishops, as formerly Constantine, Theodosius and Martianus had done, still he subscribed immediately after the Patriarchs, because the Bishops wanted to move him with such an honor.

Therefore, if we were to add to these the rest of the general Councils, in which the Roman Pontiff presided without any controversy, we will have from the continual custom of the Church, that the office of presidency in general Councils properly pertains to the Roman Pontiff. On the rest, which pertain to the form of Councils, such as their order, on which the rest ought to sit, on the garments of Bishops in a Council, on the mode of procession, etc., see Juan de Torquemada (lib. 3 cap. 26 and 27); Council of Toledo, IV cap. 3; XI c. 1 and the beginning of the Councils of Constance and Basel.

CHAPTER XX
The arguments of our adversaries are answered.

THE arguments of Calvin are taken from the practice of the Church. He puts forth five Councils in which the Roman Pontiff did not preside. Certainly the Council of Nicaea, where he says Athanasius presided; the fifth Council, over which he says Menas presided; the second Council of Ephesus, over which Dioscorus presided; the sixth Council of Carthage, over which Aurelius presided (even if legates of the Pope were present), and Aquileia, over which not Damasus, but Ambrose presided. We have already responded to the first three in the last chapter.

To the *fourth*, I say that it is only necessary for the Roman Pontiff to preside over a general Council, for in provincial or national Councils, of the sort as all the Carthaginian Councils were, we do not doubt that the presidency ought to be given to the Archbishop, or the primate of that place. Hence, the legates of the Roman Pontiff were not sent to the Council to preside, but to treat on a certain matter with that Council in the name of the Roman Church.

To the *fifth* I say, the argument is constituted from two lies of Calvin that are the major and minor proposition, whereby it can be gathered except that it is a lie? The first lie is that the Council of Aquileia was a general Council; firstly, if it were general, it would be the second and hence Constantinople which followed after it would not have been second but third. Then, there were hardly thirty Bishops which certainly does not suffice to make a general Council. Next, in the epistle of this Council to the emperor, the Fathers say it was not necessary to gather a general Council, but it was abundantly sufficient for that purpose for which they were called, especially since those few Bishops were from various provinces of the west. Therefore, the Council was provincial, but assisted by a few legates of certain other provinces.

The second lie is that Ambrose presided. The Bishop, Valerian of Aquileia, was named first, Ambrose of Milan second, which is the argument, that the first place was given to Valerian, nor is it opposed to this that Ambrose disputed nearly alone with heretics, for the office of disputation is not for the president, but is customarily demanded from the most learned Bishop.

Brenz looks to arguments from the Old Testament, in which it is certain that princes or kings were special judges even in spiritual matters, as is clear from Moses, Joshua, David, Solomon, Hezechia, and Josiah. It happened that God consigned custody of the divine law to the princes, as it is said in Romans 13:4, "If you do evil, be afraid; for he does not carry the sword without cause. Therefore, it is for princes to judge concerning the law of God, how it is to be kept and to punish transgressors. But we already answered this argument in the third book *On the Word of God*, and in the first book *On the Roman Pontiff*. Still, because our adversaries are not pained to often repeat the same arguments we will not be at pains to more often also repeat the answers.

Therefore, I respond *firstly*: Moses was not only a prince but also the high priest, as is clear from Psalm 98 (99):6, Moses and Aaron among his priests." Moreover, Joshua, David, Solomon and others were not only kings, but also prophets to whom God entrusted certain things extraordinarily, which otherwise were considered to belong to the priests by their office. In this way, King Solomon removed Abiathar from the priesthood and constituted Sadoc in his place (3 (1) Kings, 2:35), for he did this not as a king but as a prophet by divine inspiration, wherefore the reason is added in the same place, "That the word of the Lord would be fulfilled, which he spoke over the house of Heli in Silo." But on account of this extraordinary law what we read about the general law in

Deuteronomy 17:9 was not blotted out, in which all are commanded when in doubts to have recourse to the priests, nor that of Malachi 2:7, "The lips of the priest will guard knowledge and the they will seek the law from his mouth."

I say *secondly*, other kings of the Synagogue, who were good, never mixed in priestly business, and whenever they did so, they were punished, as is clear from the best king, Josaphat, who in 2 Chronicles 19:11 clearly distinguished offices, and says: "Amarias the priest and Pontiff will preside in all things which pertain to the Lord; hence Zabadius, who is a general in the house of Judah, will devote himself to the matters which pertain to the office of the king." On the other hand, King Hoziah, in 2 Chronicles 26, when he meant to usurp the office of the priest, soon after he was struck by God and became a leper, and this disease remained even to his death.

I say in confirmation, kings are custodians of the divine Law, but not interpreters and hence it pertains tot heir office that they command the faith to be held in their edicts and laws, which the priests teach must be held, and compel heretics to ward off from the Church with temporal penalties, as Augustine teaches in his epistles (48, 50 and 166) and the pious emperors Constantine, Theodosius, Martianus, and others often did, as is clear from *l. Cunctos populos, C. de summa Trinitate et fide Catholica*, and from the whole title on heretics in the same code.

The arguments of Herman are taken from various examples of the Fathers. His first is from a disputation of Athanasius with an Arian, while a judge named Probus presided, a layman and not yet a Christian whom the Emperor Constantine assigned, which is extant in an incomplete work in the works of Athanasius, but is completed in the works of Bishop Vigilius of Trent, who lived around the year 500 A.D.

I respond: Such a disputation was never really held; rather, Vigilius composed it in the manner of a Dialogue, and in that way he wrote against the Arians, as he himself affirms in book

5 against Eutyches, not far from the beginning and besides the matter speaks for itself; for the disputation is held among four men, Sabellius, Arius, Phtinus and Athanasius, then a Bishop, as is clear from the letter of the Emperor which he made up in the beginning of the disputation sent to Probus; but Sabellius died before any of the three are made known to the world, as is clear from Eusebius, book 7, *hist.* cap. 5. Arius also died in the time of Constantine, before Constantius began to reign, as is clear from Socrates (lib. 1 cap. 25), therefore he could not have met Athanasius in the time of Constantine, as he makes up here. Moreover, certain men say there were two Arius's, and Athanasius only disputed with the later one, but it is refuted by Vigilius himself, who in the beginning of his disputation clearly witnesses that he spoke on that Arius, who first devised the Arian heresy.

But someone will say, even if the dialogue were fictitious, still it did not seem absurd to Vigilius if a lay judge would preside in a disputation on religion.

I respond: Vigilius so composed the Dialogue to show how great the force of Catholic truth is, that it could even convict under a non-Christian judge.

The second example is taken from Zonaras in the life of Constantine, where we read that at the petition of Helen, who tried to drag her son Constantine to Judaism, thus Pope Sylvester disputed with the Jews in the presence of certain senators who acted as judges at the Constantine's command.

I respond: This story seems uncertain, for all the Fathers praise Helen as a most Christian woman, and not only Catholics; even the Centuriators mock this story as fabulous (*Cent.* 4 col. 694), and it is gathered from the *Chronicum* of Eusebius for the year 325 that Helen discovered the true Cross, and Marianus Scotus under the year 327 writes that the disputation fell upon the works of Helen, then a persecutor of Christ, which does not make sense in any way.

The third example is taken from Optatus of Miletus and St. Augustine, who writes in many places that the Donatists demanded judges from the Emperor in the case of Caecilianus. But the Emperor gave them the Bishop of Rome, with certain other Bishops, yet they appealed them, and received other judges in Gaul from the Emperor; when they appealed again the Emperor himself gave judgment, therefore, the Emperor is the supreme judge in cases of Bishops.

I respond: It is well that the heretics take their argumentation from the deeds of their elder heretics, for the fact is they acted badly in having recourse to the Emperor as a judge, and again acted worse by appealing to him, as Optatus, Augustine and the Emperor themselves witness. Augustine (epist. 48) says thence rightly the Donatists were rebuked because in the presence of the emperor they accused Caecilianus, when rather more they ought to convict him with Bishops from across the sea. He adds in the same place that the Emperor acted more orderly who remitted the Donatists coming to him to the judgment of Milthiadis the Bishop of Rome.

Optatus (lib. 1 contra Parmenianum) relates that the Emperor so shouted: "O rabid boldness of wrath, they have introduced an appeal just as it is usually done in the cases of the Gentiles." Likewise, Augustine, in epist. 162, says: "In such a matter, just as he detested them, Constantius listened and would that he cause them to cease, that for that reason afterward he judged Bishops would afterward seek pardon from holy bishops, so even these at some time would yield to the truth." There you see Constantius did not take well to an appeal made to himself, and judged that after Bishops should be gathered to either so break the fury of the Donatists, since they saw themselves to be condemned by all others, and besides, Constantius understood that he cannot judge by his own right, but only in that hope that later Bishops would give him pardon, from whom he was going to seek it. That such was the mind of Constantius outside of the points of necessity, is clear from Ruffinus (lib. 10 *Histor.* cap. 2) where he asserted that he ought to be judged by Bishops, not to judge them.

The Fourth example is taken from the Brief Conference with the Donatists, near the beginning, where Augustine so spoke: "When Catholic Bishops and the party of Donatus conducted disputation among themselves in the presence of Marcellinus (the tribune and notary more known by his habits), at the command of the Emperor, he conferred, etc." And at the end of the Brief conference, he asserted that Marcellinus, as a judge, imposed sentence for Catholics against the Donatists.

The fifth example is taken from Sozomen (lib. 4, cap. 5) and from Epiphanius (*haeres.* 71) who writes that Photinus sought and begged judges from the emperor in whose presence he would argue his case.

I respond to the *fourth* example, from the doctrine of Augustine himself, that the conference with the Donatists was extraordinary, and was received from a certain necessity. When the Pelagians wanted works of the emperor to compel Catholics to a conference in the manner in which the Catholics had earlier compelled the Donatists, Augustine responded that the Catholics held that conference with the Donatists in an extraordinary manner born from necessity, to the extent that they infested the whole of Africa, nor could they be otherwise repressed or compelled to a Council except by the temporal powers, and then it was done (lib. 3 *contra Julianum*, ca. 1).

Besides, I say that judge was not such a judge as we are arguing about, for Marcellinus did not so judge that his sentence would oblige the whole Church, but only that he would repress the boldness of the Donatists; for the opinion of Marcellinus was that these Donatists were so refuted by the Catholics, that they had nothing with which they could respond. Just as also when Augustine disputed with Pascentius the Arian, with Laurence on free will, as is clear from epistle

174 and 178, the teaching of Laurentius was not conducted on a matter of faith, but only availed for the confusion of Pascentius, who was pronounced conquered; and the same thing must be said on the disputation of the heretic Photinus, and on similar disputations. For they were never held for legitimate definitions in the Church, such as the decrees of Councils are.

The sixth example is taken from Socrates (lib. 5, c. 10) and Sozomen (lib. 7 c. 12) where we read that the Emperor Theodosius commanded that individual princes of various religions, that is, Catholics, Arians, and Eunomians, should advance for themselves a written formula of their faith, and when it would come to pass, the Emperor zealously prayed to God that he would direct his mind to choosing the true faith, and then at length after having read all the confessions, approved only the Catholic and commanded it to be kept.

I respond: Theodosius did not undertake to define some new controversy, nor to make himself a judge in a case of faith by any means, as is clear: 1) because that question had already been defined in the Council of Nicaea, of which he was so strenuous a follower, that he refused to be baptized by the Bishop of Thessalonika unless he would first understand that he was of the faith of Nicaea, as Socrates cites (lib. 5, c. 7), therefore he could not hesitate as to whether the Arian or Catholic faith were truer.

Secondly, because Ambrose says in his thirty-second epistle, that it is not for emperors to judge in a case of faith, and he proves this from the testimony of Constantine, Valentinian the elder and Theodosius, likewise in the Council of Aquileia, Ambrose says the same thing, the Emperor Theodosius left free judgment to the priests. Therefore, Theodosius judged nothing in a case of faith, but only read the confessions of those following different faiths, that he would acquiesce to them and satisfy them lest it would seem he condemned them unheard without a reason.

Moreover, Socrates writes that Theodosius asked God by prayers that he would direct him in the choosing a faith, I think is false. For when he prayed in secret, as the same Socrates affirms, who could know what he prayed for? And besides, it is certain that he did not so pray because by so praying he would commit the sin of infidelity, by doubting the faith, which he once received; and still made no sin in this deed, but acted in a praiseworthy manner as all affirm. Therefore, he prayed not that he would be directed in the choice of faith, but that he would be directed in that business not to do something imprudently and perhaps asked forgiveness of God that it seemed he occupied someone else's right; and at the same time he prayed lest he would be deceived by reading the confessions of so many heretics.

The *seventh* example is taken from Theodoret (lib. 5, cap. 23) where we read that when the Roman Pontiffs refused Flavianus to be the bishop of Antioch, still Theodosius the emperor judged otherwise and commanded Flavianus to be the Bishop at Antioch.

I respond: this history wonderfully shows the primacy of the Roman Pontiff, and nothing clearly impedes the present case. Therefore, I say the Pope refused by right that Flavianus would be the Bishop, but the Emperor did it from power, not from justice. I prove that because, as Socrates relates (lib. 5 c. 5) when there was a schism in the Church of Antioch, and Meletius and Paulinus sat at the same time, it at length pleased all that they would sit at the same time; but when one of them would die the other would be the sole Bishop, succeeding no dead bishop, and they confirmed it by swearing an oath; just the same, after Meletius died Flavianus succeeded in his place, while Paulinus was still living, against the oath, and hence it was illicit as is known to all. Therefore, why would it be any wonder if Pope Damasus was displeased?

In that regard, St. Ambrose (epist. 78 to Theophilus of Alexandria), speaking on this affair, so said: "Your holiness writes that Flavianus went back on the judgment to an imperial rescript; therefore, the labor of such priests is in vain, to again return to the judgments of this world. ... We think this must rightly be referred to our holy brother, the priest of the Roman Church." Besides, Chrysostom was also at Antioch and was ordained a priest not by Flavianus, but by Evagrius the successor of Paulinus, as is cited by Socrates (lib. 6 c. 3) because he would never suffer to have held Flavianus for a true Bishop. Likewise, Theophilus the Bishop of Alexandria, as Socrates relates (lib. 5 cap. 15) asked the Roman pontiff through his legate to forgive the sin which Flavianus received. And later Chrysostom labored on a similar work with the Pope, as is clear from Sozomen (lib. 8 c. 3). Whereby it is abundantly clear that Flavianus sinned and his judgment was that the Roman Pontiff was superior. Likewise Jerome, in his epistle to Damasus on the name of hypostasis, speaking about the same schism, asks from the Pope with which of these bishops he should communicate, and asserts that he will communicate with the one that the Roman Pontiff communicates with.

Besides, the three best and holiest Popes, Damasus, Syricius and Anastasius, as Theodoret writes (lib. 5 c. 23) freely rebuked the emperor in that case and said that it is enough if he diligently oppresses tyrants who rise up against him, but in those who exercise tyranny against the law of God, to depart with them unpunished. Certainly Popes as holy as these would never have applied so fierce rebuke unless it seemed to them that the emperor gravely erred. Why would the emperor, moved by that rebuke, as Theodoret relates in the same place, not judge the Roman Pontiffs, but twice command Flavianus to sail to Rome so that he would oppose himself in the presence of the Pope?

Lastly, as Theodoret relates in the same place, even if the emperor acted from his power, as we said, he did not from justice, for he willed Flavianus to be a Bishop, still he never put an end to that case, nor did he will the Bishops of the west and of Egypt to communicate with Flavian, until after Evagrius died and the Roman Pontiff forgave the crime of Flavianus and promised to admit his legates to himself, so Flavianus sent the most famous priests and deacons of Antioch in a legation to Rome.

Therefore, we have what is required for a legitimate Council. Now, briefly in the place of an appendix, we will take up what kind of Council the Protestants require in that book which they titled: *Caussae cur Electores, Principes, aliisque addicti Confessioni Augustana ad Concilium Tridentinum non accedant?*[9]

[9] *The reasons why the Electors, Princes and others attached to the Augsburg Confession should not come to the Council of Trent.*

CHAPTER XXI

The conditions, which the Lutherans require to celebrate a Council are refuted

THE Lutherans, who call themselves Protestants, propose eight conditions for celebrating a Council. Since Gaspar Villalpando has made a sufficient dissertation on these, we will briefly refute them here.

Firstly, therefore, they require that before the Council occurs all the acts of the Council of Trent be invalidated. *Secondly*, that the Council be conducted in Germany; for there the canon *Ecclesiasticus*, cited by Cyprian (lib. 1 epist. 3) says that suits should be judged in the places where they arose. *Thirdly*, that the Roman Pontiff should not summon the Council, nor preside in it, but that it should be on the other side of those litigating, just as when someone is accused and no man is at the same time the judge and the accusing party. *Fourthly*, that sentences should be imposed only from the divine Scripture, not from Traditions. *Fifthly*, that the decision should not be made in the power of a plurality of votes, but pronounced according to the norm of the divine word. *Sixthly*, that the Roman Pontiff would absolve all prelates from the oath of fidelity, in which they have been bound. *Seventhly*, that theologians of the principles and statutes of the Augsburg Confession, no less than Bishops in the Council, be permitted decisive opinions and voices. *Eighthly*, that safe conduct be granted by the emperor, not only to persons, but even to those principal cases, *i.e.*, that neither can persons be punished if they refuse to assent to the Council, nor the faith and confession of the Lutherans can be condemned, even if the Lutheran theologians cannot defend it. They say with these conditions that they desire a Council with all their heart, and they call this a truly pious and free Council.

The first condition is unjust because nothing ought to be held invalid unless it is condemned by a legitimate judgment. Moreover, the Council of Trent is accused by heretics but has not been condemned by any legitimate judge. Therefore, just as the second Council of Ephesus was condemned at the Council of Chalcedon, and the Council of Constantinople against images was condemned at the seventh Council, so also the Council of Trent, if it must be condemned, ought to be examined and judged in another Council, but not invalidated before the judgment of another Council.

The second condition is also unjust, for the Lutherans seem to seek the right for themselves that the Council not be conducted in Italy, where Catholics prevail, so Catholics can rightly demand that it not be conducted in Germany, where the Lutherans prevail, and really a better and more suitable place could not have been chosen than Trent, which is on the borders of Germany and Italy, even if this question were relinquished to the judgment of a heathen man.

Moreover, to the canon which is cited by Cyprian, I say that canon is understood on particular cases, *i.e.* on crimes of particular men, which ought to be judged where they are committed, because there witnesses can be discovered more easily; but on cases of faith which pertain to the whole Church, there is another reason. The question on the cessation of the law arose at Antioch, but it was finished in the Council of the Apostles at Jerusalem (Acts 15); the Arian heresy arose at Alexandria in Egypt, but it was judged at Nicaea in Bithynia; the heresy of Nestorius rose at Constantinople, but it was condemned at Ephesus; the Monophysite heresy was born at Constantinople, it was condemned at Chalcedon; the heresy of the Originists, Didymus and Evagrius was judged in the fifth Council at Constantinople, but it hardly arose there; the Monothelyte heresy was born in Alexandria, Cyrus being its author, and was condemned first at Rome in the Council of Pope St. Martin, then at the sixth Council in Constantinople;

lastly, the heresy of the Iconoclasts, which arose at Constantinople, or at least was wonderfully increased and had been strengthened there, was judged and condemned at the second Council of Nicaea in Bithynia, and before also at Rome in a Council.

Add that the Lutherans have also had not a few provincial Councils such as at Cologne, Moguntinus, and others in which they were condemned. Our adversaries should not object if these Councils were made up of Papists, for all heretics could make the same objection. In the Church it has always been preserved that those who were then Bishops would judge controversies, and new Bishops were not created because of new questions.

The third condition is unjust, because the Roman Pontiff cannot be deprived of his right to summon Councils and preside over them, in whose possession this right has already been for 1500 years, unless he were first convicted by the legitimate judgment of a Council and is not the Supreme Pontiff. Moreover, what they say, that the same man ought not be a judge and a party, I say has place in private men, but not in a supreme prince. For the supreme prince, as long as he is not declared or judged to have legitimately been deprived of his rule, is always the supreme judge, even if he litigates with himself as a party.

Therefore, private men, when they litigate with their prince, usually appeal from the prince badly represented, to represent the same better, and it is confirmed from the ancient histories, for when Marcellinus sinned, and on account of it he gathered a Council, all the Bishops said he could not be condemned by anyone, rather he ought to be the judge, and the defendant, as Nicholas I relates in his epistle to the Emperor Michael. Likewise, Sixtus III, when he was accused of adultery, the Emperor gathered a Council with the Pope's consent, but in that Council no man dared to strike up the case of the Pope unless first he would have said that he willed the case to be discussed, even if he would be judged by his own judgment, but not judged. It is clear both from the acts of that Council and from the epistle of the same Sixtus to the Bishops of the east.

Next, in the fourth Roman Council under Symmachus, we read that all the Bishops said the Council could not be summoned by right unless it were by the Pope, even if he were the one that were accused. For this purpose, did not Arius litigate with Alexander on the faith? And still in the Council of Nicaea Alexander sat, because he was a Bishop as a judge. Likewise, in the third Council Cyril presided in episcopal judgment, still it was said on the side of the Nestorians to have the side of those litigating. So also in the fourth Council, legates of Pope Leo presided, although the whole case turned the dispute between Leo and Dioscorus. It happens also that the Pope in a Council is not only the judge, but has many colleagues, that is, all the Bishops who, if they could convict him of heresy, they could also judge and depose him even against his will. Therefore, the heretics have nothing: why would they complain if the Roman Pontiff presides at a Council before he were condemned?

The fourth condition is unjust, because that which was once defined ought not be recalled into doubt, according to the law of the Emperor Maritanus, *l. nemo; c. de summa Trinitate et fide Catholica*. It is certain, however, in the seventh general Council that it was defined that unwritten traditions must not be received. Although, however, that condition is so unjust; still it could be admitted as long as again it were not legitimately defined in a Council that these must be received for the word of God. Hence, the Council of Trent, before it progressed to other things, defined the Scriptures and the Apostolic Traditions received for the word of God.

The fifth condition altogether abolishes the form of Councils that we showed above, and on that account it cannot be done that at some time it would arrive at the end of controversies unless place were given to the greater side of those with a vote, for when both sides advance testimonies of the Scriptures, how can it be understood what the teaching of the Council is unless it is gathered by a vote, and the opinion of the greater would prevail?

The sixth condition is unjust and impertinent. Unjust, because inferiors ought not be free from the obedience to superiors, unless first he were legitimately deposed or declared not to be a superior, just as it would be unjust that as often as imperial assemblies were conducted, the Emperor ought to make the oath of fidelity that all the princes must offer in subjection to him free. Moreover, it is no new or recent thing that Bishops should furnish an oath of obedience to the Pope, as is clear from St. Gregory (lib. 1 epist. 31) and from *cap. Significasti, extra de elect.* Likewise, from the eleventh Council of Toledo (ca. 10). Furthermore, it is impertinent because that oath does not take away the freedom of the Bishops, which is necessary in Councils, for they swear they will be obedient to the supreme Pontiff, which is understood as long as he is Pope, and provided he commands these things which, according to God and the sacred canons he can command; but they do not swear that they are not going to say what they think in the Council, or that they are not going to depose him if they were to clearly prove that he is a heretic.

The seventh condition, if it were understood to be on a properly decisive vote in a form of judgment, it is opposed to the fifth condition, and is against the form of all Councils, as we showed above; if it were understood improperly, and a "decisive voice" were called the divine Scripture in testimony of some teaching brought to the fore, then the condition is most just and was never denied to the Protestants, nay more it was offered to them three times in the Council of Trent, namely in session 13, 15 and 18.

The last condition for the first part, *i.e.* what attains to the safe conduct of persons, was offered to the Protestants, as is clear from the same places of the Council of Trent, namely sessions 13, 15 and 18; for the second part it is altogether inept and ridiculous, for it is as if they were to have clearly said we want the Bishops of the whole Christian world to be troubled, and take up expenses and suffer great labors to come to the Council, and nevertheless, when they come we will refuse anything to be established, nor quarrels ever to be settled.

BOOK II
ON THE AUTHORITY OF COUNCILS

CHAPTER I

The argument and partition of this book.

HITHERTO, we have made our disputation on the definition and causes of a Council, so as to make the beginning brief; the authority remains and because both from those Councils that are extant, and from book 4 of *On the Roman Pontiff* it is certain that Episcopal Councils judge controversies both of faith and morals which arise in the Church at some time. With that question omitted, we will only take up the explanation of this point: whether or not the judgments of Councils are infallible?

Moreover, the disputation on the authority of Councils will be bipartite. For the *first part,* the authority of Councils must be understood absolutely, then compared with other similar principles of faith, *i.e.* with Scripture, and decrees of the Pope.

On the authority considered absolutely there are two questions. One, whether Councils confirmed by the Supreme Pontiff could err. The second, whether Councils that have not yet been confirmed by the supreme Pontiff, but are otherwise altogether legitimate, could err. For on Councils that have been condemned or partly approved and partly condemned, there is nothing which we will say since they erred beyond any doubt, however, on those the judgment is the same as others, which were either confirmed or condemned.

CHAPTER II

It is proven from the Scriptures that general Councils confirmed by the Pope cannot err.

SO that we might begin from the first question, the heretics of this time would have it that there has never been a Council that could not err. Luther asserts this in article 28 and 29, and in his book on Councils. Brenz, in the *Wirtemberg Confession*, in the chapter on Councils; Calvin in the *Institutes*, lib. 4 cap. 9 § 8, and in the *Institutione minore*, cap. 8 § 163 et *seqq.* But all Catholics constantly teach that general Councils confirmed by the Supreme Pontiff cannot err, either in the explication of the faith, or in handing down precepts of morals common to the whole Church. But in regard to particular Councils, it seems there is some dissension among Catholics, for since the whole strength of those sort of Councils nearly depends upon the strength of the Pope, those who say the Pope can err, consequently ought to say that even Councils of this sort can err. To explain it more easily and clearly, we shall constitute two propositions.

The first proposition is: *It must be held with Catholic faith that general Councils confirmed by the Supreme Pontiff can neither err in faith nor morals.* It is proved first, from the testimonies of divine Scripture, which can be reduced to four classes. In the first, there will be proper testimonies; in the second, those which prove the Church cannot err; in the third, those which prove the Pope cannot err; in the fourth, those which prove that all the Bishops and Doctors of the Church cannot err.

The proper testimonies are three: 1) Matthew 18:20, "Where there are two or three gathered in my name, there I am in their midst." Calvin does not make much of this testimony because it seems it can be proven from it that a Council of two men cannot err. Yet, while he does not scorn this testimony, he observes that the argument is not taken simply from these words, but from these words continued from what came a little before, and on that account with added argumentation from the minor to the major. For previously the Lord had said in regard to an incorrigible man: "Say it to the Church, and if he will not listen even to the Church, let him be to you as a heathen and a publican." But lest someone would think that the Church or a gathering of prelates must be condemned, he immediately added: "Amen I say to you, whatever you will have bound upon earth will be bound in heaven also, etc."

And so that no one would be uncertain about the assistance of God, when the Bishops have been gathered to condemn something, or absolve, he added: "For where two or three are gathered in my name, there I am in their midst."

This is the meaning of such words: if two or three are gathered in my name, they always obtain what they ask from God, namely wisdom and light which is sufficient for them to discover what is necessary for them. Thus, how much more will all Bishops gathered in my name obtain what they justly seek, *i.e.*, wisdom and light to judge those things which pertain to the direction of the whole Church?

Therefore, whether few or many, whether private men or Bishops gathered in the name of Christ, all have Christ present, helping, and they obtain what is suitable for them to obtain. But in the gathering of the few and private men Christ is present to help them in small and private matters; in a gathering of Bishops, however, he is present to help them in great and public matters. The Council of Chalcedon explains this passage the same way, and uses this argument in its epistle to Pope Leo, which is after the end of the third action of the same Council. Likewise, the sixth Council, act. 17; the third Council of Toledo, not far from the beginning. Likewise, Pope Innocent, cited by Gratian (*dist.* 20, ca. *de quibus*).

2) John 16:13, "The Spirit of truth will teach you all truth." And lest we would think this is said to the Apostles alone, and not also their successors, in chapter 14 the Lord clearly witnesses that the Holy Spirit is going to remain with the Apostles forever, *i.e.* perpetually with them and their successors. But the Holy Spirit does not teach Bishops standing apart all truth, therefore he will at least teach all Bishops gathered into one, and rightly since in the Church there is no greater seat whereby God shall teach us than that of the Supreme Pontiff, joined with the consent of a general Council. If this chair could also be deceived, although it teaches the universal Church, I do not know how that promise, "He will teach you all truth," would be true.

3) Acts 15:28, where the first Council confidently said: "It has been seen by the Holy Spirit, and us." Moreover, if that Council, from which all other Councils receive their form, asserts its decrees, they are decrees of the Holy Spirit; certainly the other legitimate Councils can assert the same thing, which prescribe rules of belief and action for the universal Church. For the Holy Spirit was present in that Council because it was necessary for the preservation of the Church; but it is and will be no less necessary in other times when new heresies arise.

The second class of testimonies contains all those passages with which it is proved that the Church cannot err either in belief or in teaching, such as these: "Upon this rock I will build my Church; the gates of hell will not prevail against it" (Matt. 16); "I am with you even to the end of the age" (Matt. 28:20); lastly, "The Church of the living God is a column and firmament of truth." (1 Tim. 3:15).

From these passages it is clearly gathered that approved general Councils cannot err, and in two ways: 1) Because formally, the whole authority of the Church is in none but prelates, just as it is seen formally of the whole body, it is only in the head; consequently, it is the same thing that the Church cannot err in defining matters of faith and that the Bishops cannot err. It is otherwise, as we said, if they are individuals for then they can err; therefore, they cannot err when they are gathered into one.

2) Secondly, a general Council represents the universal Church, and so has the consent of the universal Church; this is why if the Church cannot err, neither can a legitimate and approved ecumenical Council err. Thus, the universal Church is represented by a general Council, although Calvin rejects this, it can easily be proved. For in the first place, in 3 Kings 8:22, an assembly of princes is clearly called the whole Church of Israel, which had come together with Solomon, for it cannot happen that all Israel, which took pride in the number of thousands upon thousands of men, would be together in the temple at the same time; and in the beginning of the chapter we read that the priests gathered before the king, and the heads of individual tribes.

Additionally, Athanasius, in epist. *de Synodis Arimin. et Seleuciae*, and in epist. *ad Episcopos Africanos*; Epiphanius in fine *Ancoratus*, Eusebius, lib. 3 *de vita Constantini*; Augustine lib. 1 contra Donatistas, c. 18 and lib. 2 c. 4 c. 6; Gelasius in epist. *ad Episcopos Dardaniae*; Gregorius lib. 1 epist. 24 ad Ioannem Eulogium, and other Patriarchs argue this. Then, the eighth Council, act. 5, calls a general Council a gathering of the whole world, or the consent of the whole Church. Besides, Martin V, at the end of the Council of Constance, bids those suspect of heresy to be questioned whether or not they believe a general Council represents the universal Church. Likewise, St. Cyprian, in lib. 4, epist. 9, when he says the Church is in the Bishop, without a doubt he understands that all Churches are in all Bishops. Lastly, if in each kingdom or republic, that which establishes a senate or assemblies, it is said to be for the whole kingdom or republic, why would the same not be said about Ecclesiastical decrees, which are made with the consent of all the Bishops?

The third class of testimonies contains all those places which prove the Roman Pontiff cannot err in faith: such as that of Luke 22:32, "I have prayed for thee that thy faith would not fail," and if there are some others, they are explained in another place, for from these it is clearly gathered that a Council confirmed by the Pope cannot err. Although there are some Catholics who think the Pope can err, still they say then he can err only when he does not apply all diligence; but when a general Council is convoked, without a doubt he applies all diligence in investigating that matter, for what more can he do? Therefore, at least then, by the consent of all, he will not err.

The fourth class of testimonies contains those passages which teach that Bishops must be held as pastors, listened to as teachers and followed as leaders. In Luke 10:16, "He who hears you, hears me;" and Hebrews 13:17, "Obey those put over you and be subject to them." Likewise, those passages where they are called pastors, Acts 20:28, and Ephesians 4:11, for when they are bid to feed the flock, we are bid to follow them to pasture; especially since the Apostle says they were constituted as pastors for that end in the Church. Likewise, those passages in which they are called doctors, in Matthew 28:19, "Teach all nations;" and 1 Timothy 3:2 as well as Titus 1:9, accordingly by some precept they are bid to teach, in the same we are bid to listen. Likewise, those where they are called watchmen: "I have given you as a watchmen over the house of Israel," (Ezechiel 33:7). Jerome and Gregory explain that this passage refers to Bishops. This is why the eighth Council of Toledo (cap. 4) and Ambrose (lib. *de dignitate sacerdotali* cap. 6) are not wrong when they call Bishops "eyes", and certainly, so if Bishops are commanded as watchmen, and the eyes show us the path, then we are bid to embark on that path which they show us. Lastly, those passages where Bishops are called fathers and the rest are called sons, such as Galatians 4:19 and 1 John 2:1.

From all such places, we can reason that: If we are commanded by God to listen and follow Bishops as overseers, pastors, doctors, watchmen and fathers, then certainly they cannot deceive us or err at some point, and whenever they disagree among themselves that we would not know which of them must be followed; therefore, at least all of them, being gathered at the same time, especially in the name of the Lord, when they teach us unanimously, cannot err.

CHAPTER III
The same is proven from the Fathers

WE add the second testimony, the tradition of the ancient fathers. The Church and the fathers write many things about Councils, from where it is certain that they thought general Councils cannot err. *First*, they affirm that the teaching of a general Council, in a case of faith, is the last judge in the Church, from which one cannot appeal, nor be invalidated or retracted in any way. Hence it most clearly follows that Councils of this sort cannot err, for otherwise it would be very unjust to compel Christians to not appeal from that judgment if it could be erroneous.

Moreover, this first opinion is cited very frequently in the Fathers. Athanasius, in his letter to Epictetus, which Epiphanius also relates in *heresy 77*, marvels how some dared to question matters already defined at the Council of Nicaea, since the decrees of Councils of this sort cannot be changed unless they were in error. Augustine, in *epist. 162*, says the last judgment of the Church is a general Council. Leo, in epistle 50 to Martianus, asks that what was once defined in general Councils would not be retracted. The same Emperor Martianus ratified this with his own law in *l. nemo, c. de sum. Trinit. et fide Catholica*. Leo also teaches the same thing in epist. 61 to the Council of Chalcedon as well as epist. 62 to Maximus the patriarch of Antioch. Likewise, Gelasius in his epistle to the Bishops of Dardania. The same is established in the Council of Ephesus, near the end, and in the Council of Chalcedon, act. 5, can. ult.

Secondly, the fathers and Councils teach that all those who do not acquiesce to plenary Councils are heretics and must be excommunicated. It manifestly follows from this that they thought that Councils could not err, and also that and all general Councils that in particular declare anathema to anyone that would contradict it, as Athanasius witnesses about Nicaea in his letter to the Bishops of Africa, and it is clear from their other acts.

Gregory Nazianzen, because the Apollinarists denied that they were heretics and said that they were received in a certain Catholic Council, said in his first letter to Clidonius: "Let them show this, and we will acquiesce, the particular mark will be if they will assent to right doctrine, for the matter cannot stand otherwise if they do not act accordingly." St. Leo, in epistle 78 to the Emperor Leo, teaches that those who resist Nicaea or the Council of Chalcedon cannot be reckoned as Catholics, and he commands a certain priest named Atticus to either acquiesce to the Council of Chalcedon or be excommunicated. Basil explains the faith in epistle 87, in which he teaches that those suspect of heresy must display the decrees of the Council of Nicaea, thence it will be clear whether they are heretics or Catholics. Besides, Augustine, in *de Baptismo*, book 1 ch. 18, only excuses Cyprian from heresy for this reason, because still in that time a general Council did not exist from which that question on the baptism of heretics could be defined. Likewise, Gregory, in lib. 1 epist. 24, says anathema to those that do not receive the five general Councils, which were the only ones celebrated in that time.

Thirdly, the Fathers teach that the decrees of legitimate general Councils that have been published are divine and from the Holy Spirit. From that it follows that they cannot be guilty of error. So Constantine, in his epistle to the Churches (which is cited by Eusebius, lib. 3 *de vita Constantini*) calls the decrees of the Council of Nicaea heavenly commands. Athanasius, in his epistle to the Bishops of Africa, says: "The word of the Lord remains eternal through the ecumenical Council of Nicaea.

Gregory Nazianzen in his oration on Athanasius, says the Bishops were gathered at the Council of Nicaea by the Holy Spirit. Cyril in book 1 *de Trinitate* calls the decree of the general Council of Nicaea a divine and most holy oracle. Leo in epistle 53 to Anatholius and 54 to the Emperor Martianus, affirms that the canons of the Council of Nicaea were drawn up by the Holy Spirit. And in epist. 37 to the Emperor Leo, he asserts that the Council of Chalcedon was gathered by the Holy Spirit. St. Gregory affirms in book 1, epist. 24, that he venerates the first four Councils like the four Gospels. Nicholas I, in his epistle to the Emperor Michael, calls the decrees of Councils divinely constituted, inspired teachings. Lastly, the Councils themselves affirm that they are gathered in the Holy Spirit.

Fourthly, they teach that it is better to die than to recede from the decrees of the general Councils. Ambrose speaks this way in epistle 32: "I follow the tract of the Council of Nicaea from which neither death nor the sword could separate me." Moreover, Hilary really suffered exile on account of the faith of Nicaea, as he witnesses at the end of his book on Councils. And Victor of Africa in the three books on the Vandal persecution, describes many famous martyrdoms of the saints who died for the faith explicated in a general Council. Jerome, in his book against the Luciferians, while speaking about Athanasius, Hilary, Eusebius and other holy confessors, says: "How could they act against the Council of Nicaea, on account of which they suffered exile?"

CHAPTER IV
The same is shown by arguments lead in from reason

LASTLY we add the argument from natural reason. *First*, if general Councils could err, there would be no firm judgment in the Church from which controversies could be settled and unity in the Church would be preserved, for there is nothing greater than a legitimate and approved general Council.

Secondly, if the judgment of Councils of this sort were not infallible, all condemned heresies could rightly be recalled from doubt. For Arius said the Council of Nicaea erred, Macedonius that Constantinople erred, Nestorius that Ephesus erred, Eutyches that Chalcedon erred.

Thirdly, there would be no certitude on many books of Sacred Scripture; for the epistle to the Hebrews, 2 Peter, 3 John, James, Jude and on the Apocalypse, which books even the Calvinists receive, at length were in doubt until the matter was declared by a Council.

Fourthly, if all Councils could err, it would certainly follow that they would all admit intolerable error, and hence would be worthy of no honor. For it is an intolerable error to propose something to be believed as an article of faith on which it is not certain whether it is true or false; yet particular Councils, such as Nicaea, Constantinople, Ephesus, and Chalcedon published a new creed of faith, or certainly new opinions, which they willed to be held as articles of faith. Moreover, who will dare to say that those four Councils contained intolerable error and were worthy of no honor when we see they are received with honor even by our enemies, and are often adduced in testimony to true doctrine? Therefore, it remains that we ought to believe their judgments are firm and infallible.

CHAPTER V
Particular Councils approved by the Pope cannot err

THE second proposition: *Particular Councils confirmed by the Supreme Pontiff cannot err in faith and morals.* This proposition is not received as equally as the first. Therefore, for that reason, we do not affirm this proposition must be held with Catholic faith since we do not yet see the authors who think the contrary to have been condemned by the Church as heretics. It is also certain from Eusebius (lib. 7 *hist.* ca. 2, 3, et 4). Pope Cornelius, with a national Council of all the Bishops of Italy established that heretics ought not be rebaptized, and the same was later approved by Pope Stephen who commanded that heretics would not be rebaptized. And at the same time it is certain from the same Eusebius, that St. Cyprian thought the contrary and tenaciously defended it, which he declared in his epistle to Pompeianus, where he argued that Pope Stephen was in error, and still Cyprian has always been held in the number of Catholics.

But whatever about this, upon which we spoke in another place when were treating about the Pope, it is certainly temerarious, erroneous and proximate to heresy to think that particular Councils confirmed by the Pope can err. This *first* is proven from those arguments with which we showed above that the Supreme Pontiff in judging affairs which pertain to faith and good morals, cannot err. For if the Supreme Pontiff cannot err, certainly even the scantiest Council approved by him could not err.

Secondly, the same is proved from the fact that if Councils of this sort could err, many heresies which were condemned by particular Councils alone could again be called into doubt, such as that of the Pelagians, Priscillanists, Jovinians and others.

Thirdly, to this point a Council of this sort which erred has never been discovered.

Fourthly, in the seventh Council, act. 3, and the eighth Council, in the last act, can. 1, the fathers say they venerate and receive even the decrees of local Councils; nay more, in the same seventh Council they called decrees of this sort divinely inspired. It remains that we propose the arguments of our adversaries and refute them.

CHAPTER VI
Arguments produced from the Scriptures are answered

OUR adversaries make objections to us with four types of arguments. They seek one from the Scriptures, the other from testimonies of the Fathers, the third from the Councils themselves, which seem to often oppose other Councils or the Scriptures. The fourth is from natural reason. But the first have nearly no force, therefore they will be refuted briefly.

Calvin objects in the *Institutes* (lib. 4 cap. 9 §3) with those passages of the Old Testament wherein pastors and priests, as well as prophets, are rebuked not only for wickedness but even for ignorance and error. One is from Isaiah 56:10, "All his watchmen are blind, and they do not know anything, they are all mute dogs that do not bark but lying down sleep and love dreams, and the shepherds themselves know nothing nor understand." Likewise that of Hosea 9:8, "The watchmen of Ephraim was with my God; the prophet is become a snare of ruin upon all his ways, madness in the house of God." And that of Jeremiah 6:13, "From the prophet even to the priest, everyone follows lies." And chapter 14:14, "The prophet prophecies a lie in my name." Lastly that of Ezechiel 22:25, "The conspiracy of the Prophets in his midst are just as a roaring lion and some take prey, his priests violate my law, and they profane my holy things."

But all of these can be answered in three ways. *First*, it happens very frequently in sacred things that all are rebuked on account of some bad ones, while on account of some good men all are praised, in such a way that both the rebuke and the commendation are more forceful. St. Augustine records in his book *de Unitate Ecclesiae*, cap. 12, that there are many examples from the divine Scriptures, but this one will suffice. The Apostle writes to the Philippians 2:21, "All seek those things which are the things of Jesus Christ." And still, in chapter 1:15, he had already said certain men from contention, certain ones from charity, declare Christ. And in chapter 3:17, he says: "Be imitators of me and observe those who so walk that you have our form, for many walk, whom I have often spoken to you of, but now I say weeping, that they are enemies of the cross of Christ." And which follow. If therefore, certain men announced Christ from charity, and walked according to the form of the Apostle, so that they would also be worthy, whom the Philippians would ımitate and observe; therefore, all do not seek what is their own and still in that mode, *i.e.* by the figure of understanding, all sought what is their own, as the Apostle says. Therefore, the testimonies of the Scripture do not compel that we would understand pastors and priests and prophets of the Old Testament to have all been liars at the same time and that they were wicked, but only a few.

Then, since none of these were said against a Council of priests, but against shepherds and prophets, who deceived the people separately; these testimonies do not seem to affect our argument; another reason is in a Council of pastors gathered by the public authority and who are called in the name of God to diligently examine questions; another reason is of those dispersed and who, while they sit in their own places give way to their own judgment. This is why the same Scripture, which so frequently inveighs against wicked shepherds and warns us to beware of false prophets, sends those who are uncertain about some matter to a Council of priests and commands that they observe that which the priests will have said, "who preside in the place which the Lord has chosen" (Deut. 17:10).

Then, even if we were to have nothing of these, still one may not, thereupon, transfer all those things that are said against Prophets and priests in the Scriptures of the Old Testament to the priests of the New Testament, especially those gathered in a Council. The Church has more certain and greater promises of God than the Synagogue. For, we have never read about the Synagogue what Christ says about the Church in Matthew 16:15, "Upon this rock I will build my Church and the gates of hell will not prevail against it." Nor that which the Apostle says in 1 Timothy 3:15, that it is "a pillar and firmament of truth." Nor was it written about Caiaphas, but Peter: "I have prayed for thee that thy faith shall not fail" (Luke 22:32).

Calvin objects *secondly* (*Ibid.*, §4) with these passages of the new Testament: 2 Peter 2:1, "But there will be pseudo-prophets among the people, just as even among you there will be liars as teachers, who will introduce sects of perdition;" Acts 20:29, "I know that ravenous wolves will enter after my departure among you, not sparing the flock and from you men will arise speaking perverse things so that they would lead away disciples after themselves;" and Matthew 24:24, "Pseudo-Christs and pseudo-prophets will rise and give great signs and wonders, so that, if it could happen, even the elect would be led into error."

But it is a marvel if Calvin, while he proposes these, does not turn his gaze to himself and say: What if I myself am one from the number of these unhappy pseudo-prophets? For, even a blind man can see that Christ, Peter and Paul are describing heretics while using the term of false prophets, who, opposing the doctrine which is preserved in the Church by Bishops in an ordinary succession do not fear to introduce sects and lead away disciples after themselves, and they make a name for themselves on earth such as Lutherans and Calvinists are named. But at length, it is simply not the case that those passages, which warn us to beware of false prophets, should be understood about Councils of Bishops, as it is the other way around; this is the ordinary cause of a Council, that false prophets would be uncovered and refuted so that ravenous wolves would be kept far away from the sheepfold of Christ.

CHAPTER VII
Arguments sought from the testimonies of the Fathers are refuted

IN the second place they advance testimonies of the Fathers, and first off, Calvin brings to the fore St. Gregory Nazianzen, who, in a letter to Procopius, so speaks: "If I must write the truth, I am so minded that I would flee all Councils of Bishops because I have never seen a happy and prosperous end to a Council, nor that it was ever an occasion for the repulsion of wicked men rather than their entrance and increase."

I respond: Nazianzen does not deny legitimate Councils make certain faith, rather, in his time it was a question of whether no Council could be completed that was *legitimate on every side*. That is the truest thing. For in the age of Gregory it happened that in the time between the first and second general Council, numerous Councils were held, which, on account of the multitude of Bishops favoring heretics, had an unfortunate end, such as the Councils of Seleucia, Tyrense, Armenia, Milan, Sirmium, etc. Therefore, since he saw so many bad Councils in his time, and none good, and yet was still called by Procopius in the name of the emperor to a certain Council, he applied two excuses: 1) that he despaired of seeing a legitimate Council in that time; 2) the chief reason, that he was detained by so serious an illness that daily he thought he would die. This response is confirmed by St. Basil, who lived at the same time, *i.e.* after the first Council and before the second. And, writing in epist. 52 to Athanasius, he says it seemed impossible to him that in that time a legitimate Council could be held, and so it was fitting to write to the Roman Pontiff asking him to invalidate the acts of the Council of Armenia by his own authority.

Next, it is abundantly clear what Gregory thought about legitimate Councils, both from his opinions cited above and also from the fact that he was so strenuous a preacher of the Council of Nicaea, that the Church in which he preached at in Constantinople was called αναστασία, [*anastasia*] *i.e.* the Resurrection, because there the faith of Nicaea, which before had been extinguished for a time by the Arians, rose again by the work of Gregory, he relates (*historia Tripartita*, lib. 9 cap. 9) and then, because later he was present in the second general Council as is clear from the subscription and from the sermon he gave to 150 Fathers.

Another testimony is that of Augustine, who says in *Contra Maximinum*, lib. 3, cap. 14: "Neither ought I to advance the Council of Nicaea, nor you that of Armenia, as if to prejudice the matter, nor will I be detained by the authority of the latter, nor you by the former, etc."

I respond: Augustine does not mean that Maximinus was not held in any way by the authority of the Council of Nicaea, but that he is not held *in that disputation*, whereby Augustine promised that, because Maximinus objected to the Council of Nicaea, and the Council of Armenia by Augustine, it seemed to him a waste of time to show the Council of Nicaea was legitimate and that of Armenia not, when he had better arguments from the Scriptures, so he said: "No, neither will I be held by the authority of former Councils nor you of the latter, in other words, I refuse no that we be held by the authority of Councils. Let us omit the Councils and come to the Scriptures." Yet, the fact that Augustine thought otherwise, that the Council of Nicaea was of the greatest authority and that it behooved all to acquiesce to it, is clear from the preceding words, where he so says: "This is the term *homousion*, which was confirmed in the Council of Nicaea against the Arian heretics by Catholic Fathers, by the authority of truth, etc." For what is truth of authority except true and certain authority?

He advances another testimony from Augustine's *de Baptismo*, c. 3, where Augustine says that earlier plenary

Councils are emended by later ones, nor can it be said that he speaks improperly about plenary Councils, *i.e.* of national ones, for a little earlier he said regional Councils, and provincial ones ought to yield to plenary ones, and then adds, among plenary Councils themselves, that they are corrected by later ones. Here, Hermann exults (lib. 3 cap. 16, *Prolegom.*): "For if the earlier most ancient Councils need correction, how many errors bubble out of more recent ones?"

I respond: *Firstly*, perhaps Augustine speaks about illegitimate Councils which are later corrected by legitimate ones, as happened to the second Council of Ephesus, which was corrected at Chalcedon. I say, *secondly*, if he speaks on legitimate Councils, he argues on questions of fact, not of law, since, in such questions there is no doubt a Council can err and certainly Augustine seems to argue on questions of this sort, for the particular question of Catholics with the Donatists was about Caecilianus, whether he should hand the sacred books to the enemies of faith, or not? It can be said *thirdly*, if our adversaries contend that he spoke on all questions, when he said earlier Councils are corrected by later ones, then it was in regard to precepts of morals, but not in regard to dogmas of faith. Precepts are changed according to the changes of times, places and persons, and these changes are called corrections, not for a matter that was bad in the time in which it was established, but because they began to be bad with the change of circumstances. Each answer is sufficiently confirmed from the words of Augustine, who says then Councils are corrected; when what had been closed is opened by some experiment. For by experiment questions of fact are opened, either on morals or when they are not universal questions of law.

Thirdly, Calvin advances Leo the Great, who, in epistle 53 to Anatholius and 54 to Martianus, as well as 55 to Pulcheria, recognizes that the Council of Chalcedon was legitimate, and still does not hesitate to attribute ambition and injudicious temerity to it, therefore he thought that a legitimate Council could err.

I respond: A legitimate Council can err in these matters which are not done legitimately and err on a question of fact, when it is condemned by the Apostolic See; such is that, on which the Council of Chalcedon was rebuked by Pope Leo. For it is clear from the last action of the same Council, and from epist. 61 of the same Leo, which is to the Council of Chalcedon, that decree in which the Bishop of Constantinople is placed ahead of the Patriarch of Alexandria and Antioch, was made while the legates of the Roman See were absent, and not without deceit, and was rebuked by Leo because it was contrary to the constitution of the Council of Nicaea.

To these things, Hermann adds (liber 3 cap. 13, Prolegomena) that Isidore, who asserted with Gratian (distin. 50, *can. Domino Sancto*), that when Councils disagree with themselves, the more ancient and approved must be favored; such a rule is contrary to the earlier rule of St. Augustine who places later Councils ahead of earlier ones, and besides, it is gathered from that rule that at some point Councils oppose themselves and thus some of them can err.

I respond: Isidore speaks on Councils of which the authority is not certain, namely, which have not been expressly confirmed by the Pope; we do not deny that such Councils can oppose themselves and err. Nor is Isidore opposed with Augustine, for Isidore speaks about the doctrine of Faith, whereas Augustine about questions of fact or precepts of morals.

Luther, in his book on Councils (pag. 54) shows Councils oppose themselves from the title of a decree of Gratian, *concordantia discordantiarum*.

I respond: he speaks about apparent disagreements but not true ones, for if they were true disagreements there could be no reconciling.

Some other men add lastly that Gratian, who in dist. 18, can. 2, says that Episcopal Councils are invalid to define and constitute, but not to correct. I respond, Gratian does not call any Council you like an Episcopal Council, but only provincial ones; for those are properly Episcopal in which only Bishops come together, not Archbishops or Patriarchs. Moreover, these Councils are ordinarily not begun to constitute dogmas of faith, for that is proper for general Councils, rather only to restore Ecclesiastical discipline and correct morals. Therefore, of itself, and ordinarily, they are invalid to constitute dogmas of faith, still if by some urgent necessity they were to define something on faith, and their decree were approved by the Apostolic See, nothing stands in the way for them to be valid.

CHAPTER VIII
Arguments from the errors of Councils are answered

LASTLY, our adversaries enumerate errors of Councils, and especially Hermann (lib. 3 cap. 15 and 16 *Prolegomenorum*) as well as the book of the Protestants that we have already cited. But from the great number of the errors, only a third needs some discussion. The errors that our adversaries observe in Councils are only three. Certain errors are true and crass, but only of illegitimate Councils, and were condemned by Popes, such as that of Ariminium, Seleucia and the second Council of Ephesus, which they enumerate in vain, since they cause no harm to our position. See what we said above on condemned Councils, in book 1, ch. 7-8.

Then the other errors are not true errors, but feigned of legitimate and approved Councils; for everything that they do not approve of, they call errors. In this way they say the Council of Chalcedon erred, in which consecrated religious are forbidden to violate a vow of continence, and the fifth Council of Carthage in which it is established that altars may not be raised without relics of the martyrs, but while they say these things, they assume what must be proved.

Next, they observe errors in true and legitimate Councils, which really seem to have some species of error, *i.e.* they seem to contain opinions of this sort which are judged to be erroneous both by us and them, and to this extent we ought to examine and refute them.

1) Calvin brings up the Council of 150 Prophets who all erred while protesting that God had placed a lying spirit in their mouth (3 Kings 22:23). I ask, however, what sort of Council was this? *First*, they were not Prophets of the Lord, for when these 150 Prophets spoke their opinions, we read that King Josaphat sought from King Ahab whether there was some prophet of the Lord through whom the Lord could be

asked? But Ahab answered: "One remains, but I hate him." Thereupon, Councils ought to be made up of priests, not of prophets. Lastly, that Council was gathered by King Ahab, not by the High Priest, hence it will be no wonder if they erred.

Secondly, Calvin and Brenz propose a Council of the Jews, while Caiaphas, the high priest, presided, in which everyone that confessed Jesus was the Christ were excommunicated (John 9) and later, Christ was judged guilty of death in John 11:47 and Mark 14:64.

I respond: Some say the question was of fact, not of law, which that Council judged, namely whether Jesus must be killed, for in judgments of this sort there is no doubt that Councils can err. But that question, even if it were of fact, still involved a most serious question of faith, namely, whether Jesus was the true Messiah and the Son of God, and also the true God. For that reason Caiaphas erred most grievously in faith with a universal Council, since he judged Jesus blasphemed because he called himself the Son of God.

Others say the high priest and the Council erred in as much as it was an error of their own mind, but still not in the opinion which it advanced. For truly Jesus was guilty of death because he received our sins so as to purge them in himself, and truly it was expedient that he die for the people. This is why in John 11:51 it says Caiaphas prophesied. But although they receive the words of Caiaphas in a good sense, not everything that he said about Christ. "He has blasphemed; what need have we of witnesses?" (Matt. 26:15). Then certainly he did not prophesy, but committed blasphemy.

Others say that the Council erred because it did not proceed according to the custom of a legitimate trial, but by a tumultuous conspiracy. After suborning false witnesses, it condemned Christ: that which was not known to all, that even Pilate knew he had been handed over to him by the priests out of envy, as we have it in Matthew 27:18, and this is indeed a probable response. Yet, because it is not for an inferior to judge whether superiors legitimately proceed, unless it was absolutely manifest that he committed an intolerable error, it is also credible that God did not permit that the Councils, over which the High Priest presided, proceeded legitimately. Therefore, we respond that the priests and Councils of the Jews could not err before Christ came, but they could while he was present; nay more, it was foretold that the Jews would err and deny Christ in Isaiah 6:9, Daniel 9:26 and other passages. For just as it was not necessary that the vicar of the Pope could not err when the Pope rules the Church, and defend it from error, so also it was not necessary that the Pontiffs of the Jews would not err when Christ, the supreme Pontiff of the whole Church, was present and he administered the Church by himself.

Thirdly, it seems Luther rebukes the Council of the Apostles that took place in Acts 15, for he says in his assertion of the articles, n. 29, that James changed Peter's judgment. For it is certain that the teaching of Peter, who judged that the gentiles should not be compelled to the laws, was good and true, for Paul upheld it in his whole epistle to the Galatians, therefore the opinion of James, which the whole Council followed, was bad and false, namely which commanded the gentiles to abstain from blood and suffocated animals, which is nothing other than to Judaize. Likewise, Luther in his book on Councils, in the first part, says many things on this law of the Apostles, and although he did not dare to assert it was evil, still from there he tries to show that the Council was of no benefit because that law cannot be defended unless we would say that a Council does not oblige.

I respond: There are not lacking Church fathers who would deny that the Council of the Apostles gave any precept on abstinence from the eating of blood and suffocated animals.

Irenaeus (lib. 3 cap. 12), while bringing up this passage twice always omits suffocated animals and seems to understand homicide for the word blood. Cyprian (lib. 3 to

Quirinus, near the end) clearly says that the Apostles only commanded that they should abstain from idolatry, fornication and the shedding of blood. Chrysostom and Oecumenius understand blood in this passage to mean homicide. Just the same, in all Greek and Latin codices we discover blood and suffocated animals, and it is certain from Tertullian in his *Apologeticus*, ch. 9, and from the Council of Gangrense, can. 2, that this was kept as a precept in the Church for many years, so that Christians would not eat blood or suffocated animals. Besides, there was no reason why the Apostles should forbid homicide, for they only meant to forbid certain things on which the gentiles were uncertain as to whether they were sins; but all confessed that homicide was a sin.

Therefore, we respond that the Apostles especially forbade fornication because this did not seem to be a sin to the gentiles since it was punished by no law; then they commanded abstinence from anything immolated to idols, as well as blood and suffocated animals, not as an observance of the old law but as their own, namely Apostolic precepts. The purpose for this law was to make it easier for the Church to make a unity of the Jews and Gentiles, for in these beginnings the Jews could not have a common society with the Gentiles if they saw them eat meat immolated to idols, or blood or suffocated animals, from which they vehemently recoiled. Later, as the Church rose and the purpose of that law ceased, the law also ceased in itself. St. Augustine speaks on this matter (lib. 32 *contra Faustum*, c. 13): "Then, if the Apostles commanded Christians to abstain from the blood of animals and not to eat the meat of suffocated animals, it seems to me they chose an easy matter for a time, and by no means an onerous observance, in which with the Israelites the Gentiles also on account of that cornerstone, building two walls in themselves, commonly observed something. ... With the passage of time, while these two walls came together, the one from circumcision, the other of the foreskin, although they would build upon the cornerstone, still, they stood out more distinctly from certain properties, and where the Church was so effected of the nations that no fleshly Israelite remained, no Christian feels bound to abstain from thrushes or small birds because their blood has not been poured out, or from rabbits because they are killed by a stroke on the neck without shedding their blood. Any who still are afraid to touch these things are laughed at by the rest."

Thus, neither did the Council err, nor James change the teaching of Peter, but before the matter was defined he thought this precept must be added to Peter's judgment, both at that time and later when it was defined by the common opinion. See Jerome in his letter to Augustine, which is 11 among the epistles of Augustine, where he says that James and all others acquiesced to the teaching of Peter.

Fourthly, they advance the Council of Neo-Caesarea, confirmed by Leo IV (dist. 20, ca. *De libellis*) and received in the Council of Nicaea as it is said in the Council of Florence (sess. 7), for in this Council, can. 7, an explored error is discovered in which second marriages are forbidden: "A priest [says the Council] shall not be a guest at the nuptials of persons contracting a second marriage; for, since the bigamist is worthy of penance, what kind of a priest will he be, who, by being present at the feast, sanctioned the marriage," which still the Apostle concedes in 1 Cor. 7: "If her husband sleeps, she is free to marry whom she will, but in the Lord"?

I respond: The Council speaks on one who has two wives at the same time, as the Gloss correctly explains (31 q. 1 can. *de his qui frequenter*). Or, it can be said secondly, it is not forbidden according to matrimony, but according to the solemnity of matrimony, for such a solemnity is not suited to the name of marriage, as Ambrose witnesses about Abraham (lib. 2 *de Abraham*, cap. 9). Therefore, that canon forbids a priest to be present at the celebration of a second marriage, because he ought to enjoin penance upon them instead, who apply a celebration of this sort in a second marriage against the custom of the Church.

Fifthly, they advance the first Council of Nicaea, about which Luther says he does not see the Holy Spirit in that Council (*de Conciliis*, pars prima). For in one canon it says that those who have been castrated are not suitable to be priests, while in another it forbids priests to have wives, and he concludes at length, on page 92, "Does the Holy Spirit have any other business in Councils than to bind and burden his ministers with impossible and unnecessary laws?"

In the same place, Luther relates an erroneous Canon of the Council of Nicaea that the Paulians must be rebaptized, and a similar one from the Council of Iconium related by Eusebius in book 7 of his *Ecclesiastical History*, ch. 6. Likewise, Luther, Brenz and Hermann assert that military service was condemned in the same Council of Iconium, although it was certain that it is licit from the approval given by John the Baptist in Luke 3:14. Moreover, canon 11 of that Council holds: "Those who truly, by the grace of God, were called to show their faith, by having lain aside their military gear, yet after this return to their own vomit so as to make money and again return to military service shall live for ten years among the penitents, after they have been with the "listeners", that is, the Catechumens, for three years."

I respond: The Council of Nicaea was always held in authority by the Fathers, so it is a wonder if it could come into Luther's mind that he would write something against this Council. But without a doubt, it so behooves the heretics to advance so as to rebuke those things which every Catholic Church always approved. Still, to the matter. Luther is displeased by the law enjoining ecclesiastical men to continence, and therefore he declares the Council erred. But to us it seems that Luther erred both in word and in deed, not the Council, but the disputation on this matter will be established in its proper place.

Still, when he rebukes the canon on rebaptizing the Paulians, he advances his ignorance. The Paulians believed that Christ was a mere man; they publicly rejected the Trinity, and did not baptize in the name of the Trinity. Hence, they do not truly baptize. Moreover, the Council of Iconium was a particular Council, and condemned by the Supreme Pontiff, just as the Council of Carthage celebrated under Cyprian, and we scarcely defend Councils of this kind.

Now with what attains to military service: the Council of Nicaea did not forbid military service except insofar as at one time it was a sign of idolatry. It must be known that at one time the marks of military service were a great honor and also suitable on account of the great privileges conceded to soldiers, and for that reason, those ancient heathen emperors, in the time of persecution, customarily took away these marks to dishonor anyone discovered to be a Christian who refused to deny the faith. This fact is clear from Eusebius (lib. 8 Hist. cap. 10), who also says Licinius, from the beginning of his persecution expelled Christians from the palace and from all military service. Likewise, Ruffinus, who in his history (lib. 10 cap. 32) speaks about Julian the Apostate, that he commanded the marks of military service not to be given except to those that sacrificed to idols. He also says (lib. 11, cap. 2) that Valentinianus received rule from God, because he removed all military garb in the time of Julian for the sake of his faith.

Because then certain Christian soldiers laid aside military honors for the love of the faith, preferring rather more to live without honor than the faith; but then, seduced by the devil, again wore these honors and were prepared to deny the faith, the Council constituted this severe penance against them. That this is so is clear, *firstly*, from Theodore Balsamon and Zonaras, who explained it this way in their commentaries on these canons. *Secondly*, from Ruffinus, who in book 10 of his history, ch. 6, while enumerating the canons of the Council of Nicaea posits: "Who cast off military service for the sake of the confession of faith, etc." *Thirdly*, from the canon itself, since in the whole canon it is argued on those that fell, and first indeed to those who fell on account of fear for their life, or of losing wealth, fell by denying the faith, the Council enjoined a penance of ten years, then on those who took up military service again which they scorned for the faith, he enjoins them a penance of thirteen years, because without a doubt these fell more seriously, for the former simply denied the faith, while the latter, after denying the grace after the confession in which a greater ingratitude toward God is discovered.

In the *sixth* place, Hermann advances the second Council of Arles, where it is said in the second canon: "It is not fitting for someone to be taken up to the priesthood while continuing in the bond of matrimony unless he will have promised to convert." Here, Hermann Hamelmann notes two errors. 1) That it is not lawful for priests to have use of wives since it is against the Council of Gangrense, and in canon 4 of which they are excommunicated that refuse to be present at Mass which is offered by a married priest. Moreover, this Council was received by Leo IV, dist. 20, can. *De libellis*. Nay more, it is also against the Council of Nicaea wherein the opinion of Paphnutius was approved, who thought that Ecclesiastics should not be forbidden their own wives by custom, as is clear from Socrates (lib. 1 cap. 8) from which it necessarily follows that the Council of Arles erred, or else Gangrense and Nicaea did. 2) He notes the error in the word "convert," for we do not convert from something unless it is bad, therefore whoever bids a married man to convert condemns wedlock, which is a heresy condemned in the same Council of Gangrense, can. 1.

I respond: Those Councils are not opposed with themselves nor did any of them err; for the Council of Gangrense published canons against those who thought marriage, as well as the eating of foods, were absolutely evil and from the devil, which was the Manichaean heresy, and later, Eustachius Sebastenus, against whom the Council of

Gangrense was celebrated. Therefore, because these heretics so abhorred marriage that they could not bear priests that had wives, even if they would not have them (at least as wives), that Council also thought this canon must be added. From there, it is so held in the very canon: "Whoever discerns that it is not fitting to partake in the Sacrifice [of Mass] from a priest that had a wife whenever he offers it, *anathema sit*." There you see it is a question of one who had, a wife not who has one.

As for that about the Council of Nicaea above, we answer that the history was not faithfully related by Socrates and, so as to pass over other arguments, it is gathered enough from that Council of Arles, for this Council was celebrated soon after the conclusion of the Council of Nicaea and received all of its canons as is clear from the fact that this Council repeats nearly everything that was in it. Therefore, since we even find this here, without a doubt it was either also in the Council of Nicaea or at least was not contrary to it, for Catholics never opposed the Council of Nicaea.

I say to the last argument that conversion is not only said from a bad state to a good one, but also from a good to a better. This is why Gregory the Great (lib. 2 epist. 100) calls the profession of monastic life a conversion, and there is extant a title in canon law on the conversion of spouses.

In the *seventh* place, Hermann Hamelmann advances the Council of Sirmium, which seems to have been received because the heresy of Photinus was condemned in it, yet, clearly the Airan heresy was confirmed in this Council. The same can be said on Sardica, that it was received by Leo IV (dist. 20 can. *De libellis*). And still, St. Augustine says: "Learn what you do not know, Sardica was a Council of the Arians, etc." (*contra Cresconium*, lib. 3 cap. 34).

I respond: These arguments proceed from ignorance of history. Accordingly, many confessions were published in the Council of Sirmium besides the condemnation of Photinus, some Catholic, others of heretics, as we taught above, and is clear from Hilary in his book on Councils. Moreover, Sardica was soon divided into two parts, one part, being composed of 300 western bishops, with whom there were legates of Pope Julius on the side of the Catholic faith and the restoration of Athanasius. This is clear from Hilary in his book *de Synodis*, as well as from Athanasius in his *Second Apology*, and Leo IV confirmed this party. The other part was of 70 eastern bishops who, coming together separate from the others, condemned the Catholic faith and St. Athanasius. And Augustine speaks about the latter. Moreover, it does not appear that Augustine read anything from the Council of Sardica than that which the eastern bishops sent to Africa to unite themselves with the Donatists.

In the *eighth* place, Hermann Hamelmann advances the Council of Laodicaea, in the first chapter of which it is established that, following an indulgence, communion should be given to those who are joined in a second marriage, from which it seems the Council earlier had taken away communion from those who married a second wife and later condoned sin by restoring it to them; for it signifies it with, "following an indulgence".

I respond: *firstly*, perhaps the Council speaks about those who apply solemnity in a second marriage, as we said on the Council of Neo-Cesarea. *Secondly*, I say the Council did not err, even if it spoke on a second marriage, rather it corrected an error; for it appears in this place that some particular Bishops, from zeal but not according to knowledge, denied communion to someone married twice, which error the Council corrected and commanded those married twice to be restored to communion; therefore in the beginning of the canon it calls second marriages free and legitimate. But that "following an indulgence" is taken from Paul in 1 Cor. 7:6, where he says that he does not command the use of a spouse, but forgives. When he says he forgives the use of a wife, he did not mean that he forgives a sin, but that he concedes a lesser good, although he desired that they would embrace a greater good; so this Council says it forgives second marriages, *i.e.* concedes them as a lesser good, although it would prefer widowhood to be chosen, which is a certain good that is more excellent than wedlock.

In the *ninth* place, Hermann Hamelmann advances the second general Council, in canon 5 in which two errors are discovered opposed with the decrees of other Councils: 1) is that Ecclesiastical Primacy is of the Roman Pontiff. 2) The other is that the Bishop of Constantinople ought to follow immediately after the Roman Pontiff, which was again renewed in the Council of Chalcedon in the last act. The first error is opposed with the Council of Nicaea, in the seventh canon of which it attributes primacy to the Bishop of Jerusalem, and with the third Council of Carthage, ch. 26, where it is discerned that no man ought to be called prince of priests, or supreme priest.

The second error is opposed with the Council of Nicaea, can. 6, where second place is given to Alexandria, third to Antioch, and Pope Leo I frequently cites this canon (epist. 53, 54 &55).

I respond: First it is neither an error nor opposed to any Council. But what Hermann adds from canon 7 of the Council of Nicaea is of no avail, for there some honor is attributed to the Bishop of Jerusalem, but not primacy in every Church; nay more, the See of Jerusalem is not only subjected in that Council to the Roman See, but also to those of Alexandria and Antioch, and even Caesarea which was the Metropolitan See of Palestine, as is clear from canon 6 & 7 of that very Council, and from Leo (*loc. cit.*) as well as from St. Jerome in his epist. to Pammachius on the errors of John of Jerusalem. Still, what he adds from the Council of Carthage is even more impertinent, since that Council was a *national* Council, nor did it impose laws for the universal Church, but only *for the Bishops of Africa*: therefore it neither did nor could forbid the

Roman Pontiff to be called a prince of priests, or supreme priest, but merely lest any Metropolitan of Africa would be so called.

The second error cannot properly be said to be an error; for that decree on the honor of the Sees, just as it was done at the Council of Nicaea, could in like manner be changed by a similar Council; still, because it was changed without a just reason by the Council of Constantinople and later by Chalcedon, the Roman Pontiffs, Damasus and Leo, refused to approve it, and no decree in the times of those popes commanded it to be put into execution, as is clear from the epistle of Pope Leo to Anatholius, where, speaking on the decree of the Council of Constantinople he says: "The consent of certain bishops was advanced in vain, for which the succession of so many years denied the effect." And in epistle 55 to Pulcheria, speaking on the decree of the Council of Chalcedon he said: "We make void the agreement of the Bishops opposed to the rules of the holy canons enacted at Nicaea, by the piety of your faith united with ours, and through the authority of Blessed Peter the Apostle we altogether invalidate it by a general definition."

In the *tenth* place, Hermann Hamelman advances the third Council of Carthage, can. 47, where certain Apocryphal books are numbered in the Canon, such as Tobit, Judith, Baruch, Wisdom, Sirach and Maccabees, against the authority of the last Canon of the Council of Laodicea, where all these books are rejected from the Canon.

I respond: In the *first* place, the Council of Carthage is of greater authority than Laodicea both because it is *later*, and also because it was a national Council of 44 Bishops that was later *confirmed* by Pope Leo IV (dist. 20 can. *De libellis*). But Laodicea was a provincial Council of 22 Bishops and was not confirmed by the Pope. Consequently, here is what Augustine says can have place, that earlier Councils are corrected by later. Nevertheless, I say *secondly* that neither Council erred.

The Council of Laodicea placed in the canon those books on which the Bishops of that Council were certain; they omitted others, however, certainly not denying them to be canonical, but *refusing to define a doubtful matter*; but the Council of Carthage discussed the matter at greater length and defined that which an earlier Council left in doubt.

In the *eleventh* place, he advances the first Council of Toledo, where it is written in its 17th canon that someone that has a concubine can be admitted to communion, provided he were not married; this Council was celebrated at the command of Pope Leo I, as is clear from cap. 21. I respond: In this place a wife is called a concubine, who was married without a dowry and external solemnity, as Gratian correctly noted (dist. 34, can. *Omnibus*); which is in conformity with civil law, as is clear from *Novella* 18 of Justinian. Genesis says the same thing about Hagar (25:6), and Cethura are called the concubines of Abraham who were still true wives, as is clear from Genesis 16:3 about Hagar, and 25:1 about Cethura.

But someone will object that St. Leo, who commanded this Council to take place and approved it in ep. 92 to Rusticus of Narbonne in chapter 4, speaking about a wife and a concubine, says: "A concubine is not truly a wife nor does a union with her make a sacrament or matrimony; and for this reason that woman, who marries a man having a concubine, does not sin as though she wed a married man, because the man having the concubine, is not said to be married. I respond that Leo receives the term concubine in a different sense than the Fathers of this Council received it, for he calls someone a concubine that is taken as a consort to the bed without mutual consent to live together forever; but the Council calls a woman a concubine that is wed with this consent but privately and not by public means.

But someone might say, if Leo was the author of this Council, how did he absolutely deny a wife could be called a concubine? I respond that Leo was not the author of this

Council, but of the last canon. For from the beginning, it is said of the Council that this Council was gathered in the time of the emperors Honorius and Arcadius, Leo was not yet Pope in that time; for he was created in the time of Theodosius the younger, thirty years after the death of Arcadius, as is clear from the *Chronicum* of Prosper. Then in the last canon some explanation of faith is placed, which was made at the command of Pope Leo, which cannot make sense unless we were to say that the Council of Toledo was held before the times of Leo, but later, in his time, that explanation of faith, was finished, and connected to the same Council, because the same Bishops subscribed to this explanation who were in the Council earlier. And certainly there can be a great conjecture of this matter which we shall see, before that explanation of faith the subscriptions of the Bishops were placed, among whom the Council came to an end. Then, again, the other subscriptions of the same after that explanation of faith. Therefore, St. Leo did not confirm this Council except for that last Canon made in his time.

In the *twelfth* place, Hermann Hamelmann advances the Council of Worms, in canon 3 of which an explored error is discovered. It commands that secret thieves be discovered by reception of the Holy Eucharist, which St. Thomas teaches is an error (3 q. 80 ar. 6 ad 3). I respond, the Council was provincial and not confirmed, nay more it is rather more condemned, in regard to that canon, by the Supreme Pontiffs, as St. Thomas shows in that place.

In the *thirteenth* place, he advances Canons of the sixth Council, since these seem to be received, for Adrian I in his epistle to Tharasius, which is in the second action of the seventh Council, says these canons were divinely and legally predicated. Likewise, Nicholas I in his epistle to the Emperor Michael, as well as Innocent III, *cap. A multis, extra de aetate ordinandorum*, and the seventh Council in act. 2, 3, 4 5 and 6 uses these canons. But great errors are discovered in these canons. Canon 2 receives the Council under Cyprian on rebaptizing heretics, which St. Augustine proved was erroneous in his seven books *on Baptism*, likewise, 72 canons are judged to be invalid and dissolve marriages of Catholics with heretics, which is an express error; even if a Catholic sins in marrying a heretic, still the marriage is a sacrament on account of the character of Baptism which heretics retain and therefore such a wedlock cannot be broken.

I respond: Not only these two, but even many other canons are erroneous among these canons, but they were not published by any legitimate and approved Council. For it is certain from Tharasius in the seventh Council, act. 4, that these canons were not published by the sixth Council, which took place in the time of Pope Agatho and the Emperor Constantinus, but many years after under the emperor Justinian II, at which Council the Roman Pontiff was not present either in himself or through legates, and he did not later confirm the Council but clearly condemned it, as Bede witnesses in his book *de sex aetatibus* in Justinian, as well as Paul the Deacon in his life of the same Justinian, and Platina in the life of Sergius.

I respond to the words of Adrian: here he only recites the opinion of Tharasius, nor does he refute it, because that 82nd Canon on pictures was useful in the time for which that question was argued. I respond to Nicholas, that his words were for us, for he says he cited that canon of the Greeks in the way that Paul cited the words of heathen poets. I say to Innocent, there he defined nothing in regard to these canons, but only cited one canon from them; moreover, the fact that he cited them in the name of the sixth Council happened either because they were so-called commonly, although they were not truly from that Council; or because Innocent received them from Gratian, dist. 32, can. *Si quis*. Moreover, Gratian often erred in this regard, attributing a work to those of whom they were not. I say to the seventh Council, these canons were always cited by private men in that Council during disputation, but nothing was defined by the whole Council, for the definition of the Council is contained in act 7 only. There, however, no mention is made of these Canons. See Francis Turrrianus in his book on the *seventh Council*, and those which argued on these canons in book 2 of *On the Roman Pontiff*, ch. 14.

In the *fourteenth* place, Hermann Hamelmann (lib. 3 *Prolegom.* can. ult.), Calvin (*Inst.* lib. 1 cap. 11 § 14 and following), lib. 4 cap. 9 § 9; and even the Centuriators (8 cap. 9) advance the seventh Council, that second of Nicaea, which they say is opposed with two Councils: the one earlier, that is of Constantinople under Constantine Copronymus, the other later, of Frankfurt under Charlemagne, so that one must either follow the rule of St. Augustine in *de Baptismo* book 2, cap. 3, who would have it that earlier Councils are corrected by later ones, or the rule of St. Isidore cited by Gratian, *dist.* 50, can. *Domino sancto*, which teaches the more ancient Councils must be placed ahead of more recent ones, either way it would be necessary to reject this Council of Nicaea.

The fact that Nicaea II is opposed with the earlier Council of Constantinople is clear from Nicaea II, act. 6, where the Fathers in the time of the more recent emperor at the Council of Constantinople defined that images were not to be venerated in any matter, which is opposed with the later Council of Frankfurt, in which even the legates of the Roman Pontiff were present; our adversaries prove: 1) from Ado, Aimonio, the Abbot of Ursberg, Platina and other historians who, when they speak on the times of Charlemagne and Adrian, say that in the Council of Frankfurt the seventh Council of the Greeks was condemned; 2) they show it from four books of Charlemagne which were recently published in the year 1549, and there Charlemagne uses many words against images and opposed the seventh Council, and in the same place we read those books were approved in the Council of Frankfurt.

I respond: Nicaea II is not opposed to any legitimate Council. *First*, what attains to the Council of Constantinople under the emperor Constantine Copronymus, it is certain that it was neither general nor legitimate in any way, since the Roman Pontiff is not found at it in himself or through legates, as John Zonaras and Cedrenus relate in the life of Constantine Copronymus, and the Centuriators affirm the same thing (Cent. 8 cap. 9 col. 551). Yet, without the Roman Pontiff ecumenical Councils cannot be celebrated, as is clear from the rule of the Council of Nicaea which Socrates cites (lib. 2 cap. 13). The fact that the other three patriarchs were not present, namely of Alexandria, Antioch and Jerusalem, as is clear from the same Zonaras, Cedrenus and the Centuriators. Therefore, how can it be called a general Council to which neither the east, nor the west, nor the south consented, but merely a few bishops from the north? Then, as many historians as are extant, both Greek (such as Zonaras, Psellus, Photius, Nicetas, Cedrenus), and Latin (such as Rheginus, Sigebert, Ado, Paul the Deacon, the Abbot of Ursberg) and many others, all either clearly condemn this Council or refuse to number it among the Councils of the Church.

Moreover, on the Council of Frankfurt, which our adversaries especially depend upon, I say three things. *Firstly*, whatever that Council defined, it is not made greater, since there is no question that the second Council of Nicaea must be placed before it, which certainly was more universal, more ancient, and without controversy approved by the Supreme Pontiff. For it is certain from the Council itself, legates of Pope Adrian were present and again that it was approved by Leo III is clear from Ivo of Chartres, 4 part. cap. 147.

I say *secondly*, if it is true what the Centuratiors say (*Cent.* 8 cap. 9 col. 639) this Council does not harm our position. For they say Adrian and his legates did not consent to the Council of Frankfurt but condemned it; but it is certain that a Council which the Roman Pontiff condemns is of no authority, as is clear from Gelasius in his volume on the bond of anathema, as well as from experience. No Council was ever held as legitimate which the Roman Pontiff condemned. What of the fact that this Council of Frankfurt teaches this thing, for that is clear from the Carolingian books, the Council of Frankfurt decreed that the last judgment of controversies pertains to the Roman Pontiff, and especially by this argument tried to refute the seventh Council because it thought that it was celebrated without the authority of the Roman Pontiff; therefore the Council of Frankfurt destroys the position of the Centuriators by its own testimony.

Besides, the Centuriators say in the same place that the Council of Nicaea was confirmed by Adrian, and that the Council of Frankfurt condemned a Council completed without the authority of the Pope, therefore in the judgment of the Centuriators, it is not our Nicaea, but some other which is condemned by that Council. Next, the Centuriators teach in the same place that the Council of Frankfurt did not define that images must be removed from Churches, but that in churches they should remain *but not be worshipped*; therefore, why remove images from Churches? Why break them? Why not preserve the decree of Frankfurt? From all this, the lie of the *Apology* of the English is refuted, since it teaches that in the Council of Frankfurt there was a decree that images be destroyed, while on the other hand, the Council of Frankfurt, by the testimony of the Carolingian Books, Hincmar of Reims and of the Centuriators themselves, anathema was pronounced upon those who would destroy images. Besides, the matter itself shows the same thing; if that Synod established it, why was it not done? For who in the western Church would resist a decree of all Bishops and an all-powerful king? Moreover, the fact that it did not happen is more certain because no historian relates it, nay more, Jonas Aurelianensis relates it as a new thing and a sacrilege that Claudius Taurinensis wanted to destroy images in his diocese.

Thirdly, I say the matter is most uncertain which was established on images in the Council of Frankfurt, for ancient authors have not proven it. In the first place the very decree of this Council, which is cited in the preface of the Carolingian Books witnesses that in the Council of Frankfurt, a Council that had convened at Constantinople and had commanded images to be worshiped was condemned. Since it names Constantinople, it seems to speak about the Council of the heretics against images, but when it says there was a decree that images should be worshipped, it seems to speak about the Council of the Catholics [at Nicaea].

For equal reason, these Carolingian books say in the Council of Frankfurt a Council was condemned that was held in Constantinople in Bithynia without the authority of the Pope, for the adoration of images; after it names Constantinople and says that this Council did not have the authority of the Pope, it seems to speak about a Council of heretics; moreover, since it says in Bithynia the Council was celebrated for images, it seems to speak about our Nicaea. For Nicaea is a great city in Bithynia, but Constantinople is in Thracia.

Indeed, Hincmar of Reims, in cap. 20 of his book against Hincmar of Laon, who lived in nearly the same time, says a Council which convened at Nicaea without the Pope's authority was condemned in the Council of Frankfurt, where he also unites two contrary things, as is clear. Aimonius (lib. 4 cap. 85) on the deeds of the Franks and the Abbot of Ursperg in his *Chronicum* for the year 793, writes that in the Council of Frankfurt the seventh Council of the Greeks was condemned, which had convened at Constantinople under Constantine and Irene. There they also join contrary things between themselves. Moreover, many recent historians say that in the Council of Frankfurt, the Council that abolished images was condemned, which the Greeks call the seventh General Council. So does Platina in the life of Adrian, Blondus, *decadis* 2, lib. 1, Sabellicus lib. 8; Enneadis, 8; Paulus Aemilius lib. 2, *de gestis Francorum.*

On account of this confusion Alanus Copus, in his Dialogue (4 and 5), teaches that in the Council of Frankfurt only the heretical Council of Constantinople was condemned, but not only was Nicaea not condemned, rather it was also confirmed. I would desire such an opinion to be true, nevertheless I suspect it is false.

1) Because these Carolingian books, although they are falsely attributed to Charlemagne, as we will say, were nevertheless written in his times, as is clear from the refutation of the same books which Adrian I published; and they seem to have been written in the Council of Frankfurt, and they also contain the acts of this Council. Hincmar asserts that the author was of this time and the books themselves represent this: moreover, the fact that the Council, which is refuted in these books, is really the Second Council of Nicaea cannot be doubted if either the books themselves, or the response of Adrian were read.

2) Because all ancient authors agree on this, that in the Council of Frankfurt the Seventh Council was condemned which had decreed that images must be adored. So teach Hincmar, Aimonius, Rheginus, Ado and others; but to say that all of them lied or that their books were corrupted, as Copus says, seems to me a little too hard.

3) Because if these authors spoke on the false seventh Council, that is the Council of Constantinople against images, certainly they would also have remembered Nicaea II in their histories, but they do not mention any seventh Council except for this one which they say condemned images. It is also not opposed that the Carolingian books, as Abbot of Ursperg and Aimonius say, condemn the Council held at Constantinople; for the Abbot followed the Carolingian books, as also

Aimonius, but the author of these books either had a lapse of memory or from inexperience placed the name of Constantinople in place of Nicaea; for otherwise when he says a Council celebrated in the province of Bythinia, where Nicaea is, not Constantinople, it seems to show enough that he spoke about Nicaea, and likewise the Abbot and Aimonius when they say a Council celebrated under Constantine and Irene, clearly they show that they are speaking about Nicaea II, even if through an error they named Constantinople.

And it is not opposed that Hincmar and the Carolingian books say the Council was condemned at Frankfurt was convened without the authority of the Pope, which is false about Nicaea and true about Constantinople. For Hincmar followed the Carolingian books, as he shows, for the author of those books fabricated this lie with many others that he would impose upon the Council of Frankfurt, as we will say in a little while.

Lastly, it is not opposed that Platina, Blondus, Sabellicus and Paulus Aemilius say that a Council forbidding images was condemned, for in the first place all of these are more recent. Then, what they say does not oppose the sayings of the old historians since two Councils are condemned in the Council of Frankfurt, namely Constantinople against Images and Nicaea II for images, as is clear from the Carolingian books and from Hincmar, and perhaps this is the reason why some of the ancient historians name Nicaea, some Constantinople, when they say a Council of the Greeks condemned at the Council of Frankfurt.

Therefore, it seems to me that in the Council of Frankfurt Nicaea II was truly condemned, but in error and materially, in the same way as once the Council of Ariminium condemned the term *homoousion*. For the author of the Carolingian books inflicted upon the Council and blocked it up with two lies. One lie was that in the Council of Nicaea it was defined that images should be adored with the cult of *latria*. The other is that the decree was made without the consent of the Roman Pope. Since it held these two lies as true, the Council of Frankfurt condemned, and rightly if these two things were true, the Council of Nicaea as profane and illegitimate.

The fact that these two lies persuaded the Council is clear from he Carolingian books themselves, for the preface clearly says: "A new question has been brought [to the Council's attention] from a Council of the Greeks, which they made at Constantinople concerning the adoration of images, in which it was decreed that those who would not so devote service and adoration of images of the saints deified as the Trinity, will be judged anathema, which moreover, our Fathers refusing to devote service to them, scorned and condemned those consenting to it." Also, in the work, Constantine, the Bishop of Cyprus is introduced at the second Council of Nicaea speaking anathema against anyone that does not adore images with the same cult in which the most Holy Trinity is adored. There you clearly have the first lie.

The same author clearly teaches that judgment of controversies of faith pertains to the Pope, and therefore, that Council would avail nothing for the adoration of images which lacked the authority of the Pope.

Besides, these ancient authors, who say they condemned the false Council which had decreed images must be adored, without a doubt understand "must be adored with *latria*" for "must be adored", for they also teach images must be venerated and still that Council rebuked those that commanded images to be worshiped. Ado, in his *Chronicum* for the year 696, says that at Rome, on the day of the exaltation of the Cross, the Cross was kissed by the whole people, and given customary adoration and even in the same work for the year 717, he calls an image which the heretic Philippicus overturned and the Catholic emperor Theodosius restored something that must be venerated. Rheginus, in book 1 of his *Chronicum*, near the end, recognizes the adoration of the Cross and called the toppling of images by Leo the Iconoclast a crime. John Aventinus (lib. 4, *annalium*) says that at a sign from the Emperor Charlemagne, his image in the Church was venerated by all present. The Abbot of Ursperg, in his *Chronicle*, inveighs against Leo the Isaurian and Constantine Copronymus, on account of the casting out of images and calls them impious and precursors of Antichrist; and on the other hand he praises Pope Gregory and calls him a holy man because he excommunicated the emperor on account of the destruction images of Christ and the Saints.

The fact that these are truly lies, namely that Nicaea II lacked the authority of the Pope and that it decreed images must be adored with the cult of *latria* is most certain. In the Second Council of Nicaea itself, act. 2, they recite the epistles of Pope Adrian favoring images and in all actions the legates of the Pope are the first to subscribe. Then with what attains to cult, in the first act Basil of Ancyra, who was previously a heretic, when he had become reasonable again published a Catholic confession with the attention and approval of the whole Council, said he certainly worships images, but not with the cult of *latria*, since this is due to God alone. The Bishop Constantine of Cyprus spoke likewise in the seventh Council, act. 3. All the rest say the same thing in act. 4 and 7.

And one ought not marvel that the author of the Carolingian books would have blocked up the Council of Frankfurt with such manifest lies about Nicaea II held a little earlier. If today the Centuriators and Calvin dare to write that we worship images with divine honors as gods when so many books of Catholics and a Latin Council celebrated in German lands at Trent all clearly and eloquently declare the contrary, what marvel is it if the same was made up about a Greek Council which was celebrated in the east and few could read?

Yet, what if someone were to say that at least the Council of Frankfurt, which was very well attended and legitimate could err?

I respond: It could err and did err not in a matter of law but on a question of fact, and besides, it would be no wonder if it could err for the Roman legates did not consent, as the Centuriators say. For the Pope not only withheld his consent, but even refuted the decree of Frankfurt, as is clear from the book of Adrian on images to Charlemagne, where all the lies of those Carolingian books are refuted.

Next, the fact that they advance these accounts from those books as though they were of Charlemagne, which serves as the foundation of this case. I say those books are neither of Charlemagne nor can any trust be placed in them.

That they are not of Charlemagne is proved 1) because the book of Pope Adrian I to Charlemagne is extant, in which these books are accurately refuted and it is especially understood that those books were composed by a heretic and sent by Charles to the Pope so that he would respond to them. Moreover, there is this book of Adrian, which is extant in the third volume of Councils, and it can also be understood from Ivo of Chartres, who transfers many things from this book in the name of Adrian in the fourth part of his decree.

2) It is certain from the Greek and Latin historians, Zonaras and Cedrenus in the life of Leo the Isaurian, still Paul the Deacon in the life of the same, that the Roman Pontiffs Gregory III, Adrian I and Leo III defected from the Greek emperors, excommunicated them, forbade taxes to be sent to them from Italy, and consigned themselves to the protection of the Franks, and also at length transferred the empire to them especially for the reason that the Greek Emperors gave patronage to the heresy of Iconoclasm, since conversely, the kings of the Franks were steadfast in the ancient faith. How could it have the appearance of truth that the Emperor Charlemagne labored in the same heresy and favored the error of the Greeks against which the Roman Pontiff wrote? Rather, let us hear the words of Zonaras: "Therefore, Pope Gregory forsook obedience of the emperor on account of the perversity

of his opinion, made peace with the Franks since they had previously often given assistance that he might recall Emperor Leo from hatred of God by letters, and lead him back to the cult of sacred images." And then on the life of Irene: "After the death of Adrian, the Pope of old Rome, Leo was appointed Pope, a revered and honorable man, who, consigned himself to Charles, the king of the Franks, and from that time Rome was in the power of the Franks, and Charles, after being crowned by Pope Leo, was called Emperor of the Romans." For Pope Gregory would have nothing to do with the impious governors of the Church of Constantinople, and made peace with the Franks.

3) John of Arles writes in book 1 *de cultu imaginum* (and he lived in the time of Louis the Pious, the son of Charles), that Claudius Taurinensis, the patron of that heresy for the whole time in which Charlemagne lived, never dared to utter a sound. And in the same place, he calls the Emperor Charlemagne that most pious man, and of holy memory. Therefore, if the Iconoclasts, living at the same time as Charlemagne did not dare to preach their heresy, if the defenders of images venerated Charlemagne as a pious and holy emperor, how impudent is it to attribute these books against images to Charlemagne?

4) Paulus Aemilius writes in book 2 of his history of the Franks, just as Rheginus in his *Chronicus*, in Council compelled by a certain heathen, King Peppin, the father of Charlemagne, confuted the error of the Greeks against sacred images with the legates of the Greek emperor present; from the same Paulus it is certain that not long after Pope Stephen celebrated a Council at Rome against the same error of the Greeks to which Charlemagne sent twelve bishops from particular parts of his kingdom. So what boldness do our adversaries rest upon to transform this most Christian prince into an Iconoclast? Especially when the Centuriators assent on the side of Paulus Aemilius? (Cent. 8, cap. 9 col. 570).

5) It is certain from all historians and from the letters and songs of Charlemagne, nay more even from his deeds, that he was always most united with Pope Adrian. Still, there is an epitaph extant by the Emperor Charlemagne that is no less elegant than it is piously written, cited by Onuphrius in his addition to Platina, which begins in this way:

Hic pater Ecclesiae, Romae decus, inclytus auctor
Adrianus requiem Papa beatus habet.
Vir cui vita Deus, pietas lex, gloria Christus:
Pastor Apostolicus promptus ad omne bonum.
...
Post patrem Carolus lacrymans haec carmina scripsit,
Tu mihi dulcis amor, te modo plango pater.
Tu memor esto mei, sequitur te mens mea semper,
Cum Christo teneas regna beata poli.

This father of the Church, ornament of Rome, the illustrious authority
Blessed Pope Adrian has rest.
A man for whom God was life, law piety and Christ glory;
Apostolic Pastor eager for every good.
...
After a father Charles crying wrote these things,
You are sweet love to me, now I a father mourn you,
Remember me, my mind always follows you,
May you hold the blessed kingdoms of heaven with Christ.

How is it believable then, that Charles was of another religion and faith than Adrian? Or that he wrote so bitterly against Adrian himself when he venerated him in such a way as well as praised him after his death?

Next, it is certain that Charlemagne was a man learned in Latin and Greek, prudent and ingenious, but these books are of a barbarous and unlearned man, light and seem plainly stupid.

For to say that Constantinople, a very famous city, was in Bithynia when everyone knows that it is in Thrace, unless perhaps there were frequent earthquakes there that only changed it. Then, it asserts that a Council favoring the cult of images was celebrated at Constantinople, although every man knows that was celebrated at Nicaea unless he reads nothing at all. And how serious is it to attribute these many things to the fathers of Nicaea II by calumny and a lie, which they never said, and meanwhile which their adversaries had said, such is that the Eucharist is an image of the body of Christ, which not only the Fathers of Nicaea II did not defend, as this author dreams up, but they even avowedly reject. Wherefore Calvin takes up the occasion of another lie. Since the Iconoclasts said only one image must be adored, *i.e.* the Eucharist, and this pseudo-Charles attributed it to Nicaea, Calvin was pleased to so change the matter, as to say: "Moreover, lest the fable would lack solemn applause a little clause was added (namely by the Council of Nicaea), 'let them rejoice and exult who, having images of Christ, offer sacrifice to them'." This is a most impudent lie. God forbid that Nicaea II meant for sacrifice to be offered to images, as we see in act. 7 where they declared precisely that true latria is not to be offered to images, but only honorary adoration.

Finally, it happens that this book, like another Melchisedech, is without a father, mother or genealogy; for it appeared suddenly into the light, nor is it known when or where or how, or by whom it was found, nor does it have the name of the author nor of the printer, nor of the place where it was printed. Such are all the arguments and the marks of deceit. Be that as it may, what if it were a book of Charlemagne? What, then, would our adversaries gain? Absolutely nothing. For the author of this book clearly opposes nearly all the dogmas of Calvin when he clearly teaches that the final judgment on controversies of faith pertains to the Roman Pontiff, and he holds the primacy not from Councils but from God himself. The same would have it that exorcism is applied in Baptism, Churches are dedicated with certain rites, prayers must be offered for the dead, Saints invoked, relics venerated, chrism, water and salt are to be blessed and retained for use in the Church, that the body of Christ is truly present in the Eucharist and must be worshiped and offered as a true and proper sacrifice, all of which our adversaries cite as explored heresies.

So, if they want us to believe this author when he teaches that the Council of Nicaea erred, let them believe the same when he asserts as many things as we have already enumerated. What if it were certain that Charlemagne himself wrote this book and it agreed in all things with the Calvinists, what else would they have but the testimony of one lay soldier? To oppose this to a general Council of Bishops is manifest foolishness. For as St. John Damascene rightly says about images (*orat. secunda*), Christ did not consign the Church to kings and emperors, but to Bishops and pastors.

In the *fifteenth* place, they advance two Councils opposed between themselves, in which Roman Pontiffs presided. For the Roman Council under Stephen VII, it invalidated all the acts of his predecessor, Pope Formosus. Thereafter, the Council of Ravenna under John IX invalidated the acts of the Council under Stephen and approved the acts of Formosus. See Sigebert in his *Chronicum* for the year 903; Matt. Palmerius in *Chronicum* for the year 899 and Platina in the lives of these Popes.

I respond: This was a question of fact, *i.e.* whether Formosus was a true and legitimate Pope and because Stephen was badly informed, he thought that Formosus was not a Pope and invalidated his acts. Later, because John truly investigated the matter better, he discovered the contrary and corrected the error of the earlier Council, according to the rule of St. Augustine which says: earlier Councils are emended by later ones, without a doubt in particular cases of this sort.

In the *sixteenth* place, they advance the Roman Council under Nicholas II, in which it was defined that not only the sacrament of the body of Christ, but even the true body of Christ itself is taken up and broken in the hands of the priests and ground by the teeth of the faithful, as is clear from can. *Ego Berengarius, de consec.* dist. 2. But this is a manifest error against the glorious resurrection of Christ, about which the Apostle speaks: "Christ, rising from the dead, does not die again." (Romans 6:9) For if the true body of Christ is broken and ground, certainly it is corrupted and will die.

I respond: It was never a question of whether the body of Christ truly, as it is in itself, would be broken in the hands and ground up in the teeth; for it was always certain that the body of Christ, as it now exists, is incorruptible and cannot be broken and ground except in a sign of the Sacrament, so that it might be said to be broken and ground since its sign, *i.e.* the species of bread, is broken and ground. Yet, the question was whether the sign, which is broken and ground, were an empty sign or whether it truly and really contained the body of Christ, because Berengarius had taught it was an empty sign. Thus, the Council, while constituting the form of abjuration of this error, wanted him to say that it is not only a Sacrament, but also the true body of Christ that is broken and ground. Here, the sense of the words is not that it is ground and broken as an empty sign, but also as the true body of Christ, that is rather more a sign really having the body of Christ joined, or rather, even the true body of Christ existing there present, is broken and ground but not in itself, rather in the sign. This is how we also understand it with what Chrysostom says: "O how many times they say would that I might see his form and his shoe! You truly do see it, you touch it, you eat it." (Homily 83 in Matthew).

In the seventeenth place, Hermann advances the Lateran Council under Innocent III, in which it was defined that it must be held as an article of faith that the bread and wine are transubstantiated in the Sacrament into the body and blood of Christ. But at the Council of Ephesus anathema is said to all those advancing another creed.

I respond: a) the Lateran Council did not compose any Creed, but merely defined one question on faith, just as many Councils did after Ephesus.

I say: b) The Council of Ephesus declared anathema to anyone advancing another creed, *i.e.* against the Council of Nicaea, but not another, that is, one that is new and more explicit. I say: c) The Council of Ephesus forbade Bishops to compose a new Creed as well as particular Councils, but not the Supreme Pontiff or a general Council, for no one has the authority to command an equal or a greater.

In the eighteenth place, they advance the Council of Constance and Basel, for in sess. 13 they excommunicated anyone that communicated under both species, but conceded both species to the Bohemians.

I respond: Whatever might be the case on the authority of Councils, I say these are not opposed in themselves since Constance excommunicated those who communicated under both species without a license from the Church. So the precepts of the Fathers are understood, but one that commands does not thereby deprive himself of the authority to dispense. Moreover, the Council of Basel dispensed with the Bohemians and gave a license to them to communicate under both species.

Lastly, they advance from the same Councils of Constance and Basel that they ratified the position that a Council is above a Pope, whose contrary is held in the fifth Lateran Council, sess. 11, but we will speak on this matter below at the end of this book.

CHAPTER IX
The objection adduced from reason is answered

LASTLY, they object the following from reason. It often happens in every body of a multitude, that a greater part conquers the better part, therefore, in Councils of the Church, where all things are defined by a greater vote, it can easily happen that they fall into error. Thus: while legitimate Councils cannot err, still who knows whether there was ever a legitimate Council? For a Council is not legitimate unless it is made up of faithful Bishops; yet who can know whether those who gather together have true faith and true ordination? Then, in the ancient Councils, Bishops gathered together from many provinces, diligently examined a proposed question, then subscribed of their own will, not being coerced by some external force and did other things of this sort which legitimate Councils require; from what source do we know except faith in historians? But historians (except for divine oncs) often lie, and certainly they do not make firm and infallible faith. Therefore, it remains that all the decrees of Councils are doubtful.

We respond: In human assemblies it sometimes happens that a greater part conquers the better; but in a Council of the Church, where the Holy Spirit presides and where Christ is in the midst of them, in whose name they are gathered and where he is present, to whom it was said by Truth itself: "I have prayed for thee that thy faith would not fail, and when thou has been converted, confirm thy brethren," it is not such a thing that ought to be feared. Even if the greater part resisted the better, as happened in the Council of Armenia and the second Council of Ephesus, still it never conquered because acts of Councils of this sort were soon invalidated by the one for whom it is fitting to confirm the brethren by his office, in the same way as we see happened in the Councils of Armenia and Ephesus II.

Now, to respond to the second objection, it is not necessary that we know the Bishops that gather together at Councils have true faith and true ordination, rather, it is enough if the contrary were not certain. For even if the Supreme Pontiff (which we cannot believe would happen), and all the Bishops who are called to some general Council by the supreme Pontiff, were really heretics at heart and were only Catholics by external confession, nor truly received the invisible character of Sacred Order but an empty imposition of hands, nevertheless, we are certain that God would never permit that a Council of this sort would err in forming its decrees; for the Holy Spirit assists in a Council not because of the Council itself, but because of the universal Church which is held by divine precept to not argue with the teaching of the Bishops, rather, to venerate it. Therefore, divine providence saw to it that the universal Church would not err, so that even a Council of fake Bishops, whether they want to or not, would propose the truest faith for the Church to follow. Hence, for some gathering of Bishops to be legitimate it is also said that it is only required that these Bishops come together, who ordinarily preside in the Church and are true Bishops, and also are held publicly as Catholics by all, whatever might be the case on the things that they hide in their hearts.

Still, because we not only know that God has care of the salvation of his Church, but we also learn from the Scriptures that the providence of God sweetly disposes all things, consequently we believe for certain that God will never permit that in a Council, which is believed as legitimate by the Church, that either all, or the greater part of the Bishops gathered there would not be legitimate or even Catholics, for it would be terribly hard and violent (although it is not impossible for God, who also rebuked an insipid prophet with a beast of burden) that a whole Council of heretics, while opposing his will and teaching, would fashion a Catholic decree.

Certain men respond to the last objection, such as Vega (in Concil. Trid. lib. 3, cap. 39) that a Council is legitimate and held with Catholic faith by the faithful not because of the witness of historians but because the Council itself defined this; for Councils usually in the beginning of their acts define their gathering to be legitimate and gathered in the Holy Spirit.

But this certainly does not seem to be a solid response. *Firstly*, because the old Councils usually did not witness in the beginning that the assembly was legitimately gathered in the Holy Spirit; rather certain later Councils, such as Constance, Basel, Lateran V, Trent and others, give that witness but not as some decree formed *de fide*. Among the canons, properly so called, no canon of any Council has ever been found wherein it is defined that the Council itself is legitimate whereby those canons are fashioned. *Secondly*, either it is certain to us from another source that some Council was legitimate, when they meant to define that it was legitimate, or it is not certain. If it is certain, in vain is such a decree fashioned; if it is not certain, now we will begin to doubt the decree itself; if it were ambiguous whether a Council were legitimate before it defined that it was legitimate, it will also be ambiguous as to whether it would have erred in the very decree in which it pronounced itself legitimate.

So others respond that any Council you like is legitimate from the circumstances present at that time, and they can be evident without other proof. For they see that the Bishops come together as one who are held to be true Bishops by all, and come together from different provinces and are called by one who has the authority and if something else were required for a legitimate Council, they can also see since, as we said above, nothing invisible is required. Moreover, for posterity or those that were absent the very thing is known from human faith, but is most certain and such evidence can be compared by a natural mode. For the sake of example, not merely one or two historians witness that the Council of Nicaea was legitimate, but many different writers of that time as well as of the subsequent times and the Church which now is asserts this very thing; there is not, nor was there, anyone who would think or did think to the contrary.

This is why, in the same way that Cicero was a consul, Julius Caesar a dictator, Octavian fought with Mark Antony in a naval battle, and other things of this kind, even if they depend upon human faith, still they are so certain that they seem to have a certain evidence. So also Councils of the Church, which we say were legitimate, have so many testimonies of all ages that it leaves absolutely no doubt in our minds whereby we would believe them to be less than what they are said.

This is why we must hold with Catholic faith that legitimate Councils confirmed by the Supreme Pontiff cannot err, even from natural evidence, or that we would know from a most certain human faith that the Council of Nicaea, Constantinople, the first of Ephesus and others of this sort were legitimate and approved by the Supreme Pontiff, it certainly follows that we should believe decrees of this with certain faith. Please, see Melchior Cano in book 6 *de Locis,* last chapter, in the solution to the tenth argument, for more on this matter.

CHAPTER X

Particular Councils that were not approved by the Supreme Pontiff do not in any way make certain faith

NOW, another question follows namely whether Councils that have not been confirmed by the Supreme Pontiff would make certain faith. This is not a controversy among Catholics and heretics and scarcely ever among Catholics, therefore we will briefly explain the whole matter and first about particular Councils, then we will argue about general ones.

We assert two opinions from the common teaching of Catholics, 1) Councils of this sort *absolutely* can err; nevertheless *they are of great authority*, so that it would be rash to not acquiesce to them. We have, as a witness to the fact that Councils of this sort could err, the Council of Carthage under Cyprian, which was national, famous, legitimate and of 85 Bishops, of which many were martyrs or confessors, as is clear from the letter of Cyprian to Jubaianus, and still it erred. For a *second* witness, the fifth Roman Council under Symmachus, where we read that provincial Councils, because they do not have the presence of the Pope, lost their strength.

For a third, we have Prosper of Aquitaine in his *Chronicle* for the year 420, in which he says the Pelagian heresy was condemned by an African Council of 217 Bishops, no sooner was that heresy condemned by the Church of the whole world than Pope Zozimus approved the decrees of that Council. This is why St. Augustine (lib. 2 *Retract.* cap. 50) does not say that the Pelagian heresy was condemned by African Councils, which were particular, but by Popes Innocent and Zozimus in cooperation with the African Councils. As a *fourth* witness, the reason why general Councils cannot err is from a special twofold cause: 1) Because a general Council represents the whole Church and therefore, if it were to err, the whole Church would err; 2) because a Council does not become general without the Supreme Pontiff, for whom Christ prayed that his faith would not fail; but none of these causes have place in a particular Council.

But someone will object that, in cap. *Ad abolendam, extra de haereticis*, all those who are judged heretics by the Roman Church or by a provincial or diocesan Council are excommunicated; therefore, provincial and diocesan Councils make dogmas on faith, otherwise he would not be a heretic who would deny them.

I respond: One can be judged for heresy in two ways: 1) *secundum se*, in the abstract as it were, as when it is asked whether it is heretical to say this or that; 2) *in ordine ad hominem haereticum*, as when it is asked whether this man fell into a heresy that was condemned by the Church. Therefore, although provincial or diocesan Councils cannot constitute dogmas of faith, still they can judge whether someone falls into manifest heresy, just as inquisitors also judge. The Council of Aquileia was gathered in the time of St. Ambrose, but nothing was defined there except that a certain Palladius was a true disciple of Arius and that chapter, *Ad abolendam* seems to argue this about heretics. For even if this judgment is not infallible, still it suffices to excommunicate.

Besides, I say *secondly* that particular Councils can discern about heresy *secundum se*, when it is easy and in which nearly all Doctors agree; in the way that the Council of Antioch once made a judgment concerning the heresy of Paul of Samosata (cited by Eusebius, lib. 7 *hist.* cap. 24). The Bishops agreed on every side, not on a doubtful matter, but to expel a manifest wolf from the sheepfold of Christ. For, even if this judgment is not altogether infallible, still, private men should acquiesce to the judgment of the same and if they otherwise need, they should be duly excommunicated provided that the Apostolic See or a universal Council would not judge otherwise.

Next, I say thirdly that particular Councils can also define dogmas that are truly in doubt, and its decrees are strong if they do this from a commission of the Apostolic See, as the fathers of the Council of Araviscanus II and Toledo I did in the time of Leo I and the Council of Alcala in the time of Sixtus IV (On this see the *Summa Conciliorum*). Or at least, if they send the decision to the Roman Pontiff and they receive confirmation from him, just in the way it is certain that it was done in the Councils of Milevitanus and Carthage (Augustine, *epist.* 90, 91, 92 & 93). Nay more, it is believable that no particular Council ever defined something *de fide* without approval of the Apostolic See. From all these things that chapter *Ad abolendam* can be understood.

Furthermore, the fact that a particular Council that was not expressly confirmed would make the argument so probable that it would be temerarious for one not to acquiesce is obvious: 1) Because in the seventh Council (act. 3 and in the eighth Council, last act, first canon), the local Councils are honored and received; but no mention is made there as to whether they were confirmed or not; 2) because a great many of these Councils, such as Toledo, Braga, Arles, Hispalensia, etc. seem approved by the use of the Church; 3) Because if a few holy fathers coming together in the same opinion in a certain case make a probable argument, how much more 50 or 60 Bishops coming together and invoked by the Holy Spirit, establishing something by common consent?

CHAPTER XI

General Councils, before they receive confirmation by the Pope, can err unless the Fathers were to follow the instruction of the Pope in defining.

THERE are indeed different opinions on universal Councils. For some of the Parisians think, as well as all those that teach a Council is above the Pope, and some others besides, that legitimate general Councils cannot err even before the confirmation of the Pope. Others teach the contrary, such as Cajetan (*in Apolog*. part. 2 cap. 21) and Torquemada (lib. 3 cap. 32, 33, 34 & 38).

Note two things. *First:* Legates are sometimes sent to a Council with the instruction of the Apostolic See, just as we read happened in the fourth, sixth and seventh Council; sometimes without instruction, as happened in the Council of Trent. The reason for this is, because in those first Councils only one question was treated and therefore the Pope could easily explain to the legates what his teaching was on that question. But in the Council of Trent there were so many questions and they needed to be treated so differently that he could not suitably have applied an instruction of this sort.

Secondly, there can be four ways it can happen that a definition of a general Council is made. 1) that the fathers would agree and define while the legates of the Apostolic See dissent; 2) that they would define with the consent of the legates, but acting against the instructions of the Pope; 3) With the consent of all, even the legates, but they did not have a certain instruction; 4) All consent with the legates that have and follow the instruction of the Pope.

In respect to 1 and 2 there is no difficulty. For it is certain that such Councils can err. *In the first place* the second Council of Ephesus erred *de facto* because it wanted to define something against the opposition of the legates of Pope Leo (as is clear from epistle 2 and 25 of Leo), etc. Likewise, the Council of Constantinople in the time of Nicholas I erred when the legates of Nicholas acted against the instruction of the Pope, as is clear from the epistle of Nicholas to the Patriarch and the other Bishops of the east, as well as from Zonaras in the life of the Emperor Michael. *Secondly*, Councils of this sort not only should be said to not have been confirmed, but should also be said to have been condemned, since it is the same thing whether a Pope expressly condemns a Council, or whether a Council acts against the judgment of the Pope. Moreover, it is certain that Councils condemned by the Pope have no authority, as Gelasius shows with many examples in his volume *de Anathema*, and in his epistle to the Bishops of Dardania. *Thirdly*, they cannot be called legitimate Councils which are opposed with their head; and similarly when they agree with legates acting against their information because in that case the legates do not act as legates as they would not be acting in the name of the Pope; for St. Leo, in epist. 45 to Pulcheria and Agatho in his epistle to the emperor (which was read in the sixth Council, act. 4) precisely affirm they do not give authority to legates except that they would act according to the rules handed over to them.

Now, in regard to the third mode the matter is under opinion. Still, I think such a Council could err, nor is its judgment infallible before the confirmation of the Pope. *Firstly*, because the teaching of that Council is not the last judge of the Church, and still if it could not err, it would be the final and intractable judgment. Moreover, that the judgment of these Councils is not the last is plain. For Councils of this sort are sent to the Pope and the Pope can approve the Council or condemn it, as is clear from Gelasius in epist. to the Bishops of Dardania, and from Nicholas in his epistle to the Emperor Michael, as well as from the practice of Councils to seek confirmation; and namely from the bull of Pius IV in which he confirms the Council of Trent. (On that matter, see Torquemada, lib. 3 cap. 34).

Besides, *secondly*, the strength of the Council is born from the consensus and union of the body with the head, but the head has not yet made its judgment clear. Even if the legates preside in the name of the Pope, still they are not really Popes, nor know what the mind of the Pope is, nor do they have the privilege to not err that the Pope has.

Thirdly, the Council of Basel (sess. 2) together with a legate of the Pope established by common consent that a Council was above a Pope, which certainly is now judged to be erroneous.

Fourthly, a Council can err when it defines something against the instruction of the Pope, as in fact the Council of Constantinople erred with the consent of the legates of Pope Nicholas to the error; so it can also err when it has no instruction; for the Bishops in a Council are not held to follow that instruction, otherwise they would not be judges, nor would their votes be free.

But some object that a Council of this sort is general, legitimate and represents the universal Church, therefore it cannot err. Melchior Cano responds, that a Council cannot err in that mode in which the Church cannot err, *i.e.* just as the Church cannot err in those things on which everyone in the Church agrees, so also the Council cannot err in those things on which everyone agrees at the Council. But on the other hand, since the Church cannot err in regard to personal faith, therefore it cannot err only in that on which all agree. But a Council cannot err in a judgment of faith, *i.e.* in forming a decree; moreover, it is a true decree of a Council which is made by the greater part, otherwise there would be no legitimate decree of a Council since some will always dissent. Thus, a Council is said to err absolutely when the greater part errs, which forms the decree. This is why I think the objection must be answered with another reason.

So I say that Council cannot err which is absolutely general and perfectly represents the universal Church, moreover a Council of this sort does not exist before the judgment of the Pope would come. For the rest of the Bishops indeed represent the body of the Church, and what they do the body of the Church is thought to do; but the Papal legates do not so represent the head of the Church, *i.e.* the Pope himself, so that what they do the Pope is absolutely thought to have done, otherwise no confirmation would be required; rather they only represent the Pope as his vicars and intermediaries ought to refer to him when doubts arise and wait for his judgment and follow it. And so accordingly, such a Council, since it does not absolutely represent the authority of the head, only imperfectly represents the whole Church.

What if someone would altogether have it that a Council of this sort absolutely represents the whole Church, he could respond that the general Council is not thought to be entirely absolute until after the confirmation of the Pope; but when it is said that a general Council cannot err and its decrees do not make certain faith, it must be understood when it was altogether absolute and signed by all.

Secondly, they object that Councils impose anathemas upon those thinking the contrary before they are confirmed. I respond: They indeed impose anathemas, but it understands the force it is going to have if it is confirmed by the Pope, just as when a Judge, from whom one can appeal, imposes the death penalty against someone, it is understood he ought to die unless the prince retracts the sentence.

Now, on the *fourth mode* there can be hardly any doubt, for it seems to be certain that such a Council cannot err; for first, in such a Council express consent of the head and members is found, and hence of the whole Church, which without a doubt cannot err nor is it opposed that the instruction given by the Pope does not seem to be a definitive teaching of the Apostolic See. For when a Council agrees with the judgment of the Pope and a decree is formed by the legates in the name of the Pope, then it begins to be a definitive judgment and a final one, not only of the Council but also of the Pope, and the Pope cannot retract it, since he certainly understands his judgment was from God when it is approved by the Council, as St. Leo says in epist. 63 to Theodoret: "That which the Lord first defined by our ministry he has made firm by the assent of all fraternity that he would truly show that he produced what was first formed by the first see of all, has received the judgment of the whole Christian world so that in this also, the members are in harmony with the head, etc."

Now, so that it would be better understood, it must be known that the Pope usually sends Legates instructed about the judgment of the Apostolic See with that condition, that if the Council would consent to the judgment of the Apostolic See, the decree will be formed, but if not, the formation of the decree should be delayed until the Roman Pontiff, after he has been consulted, shall respond. This fact is clear from the Council of Chalcedon, since in act. 3 when the Council consented to the judgment of the Pope in regard to the deposition of Dioscorus, the next the legates formed the decree with these words: "The most holy and blessed Pope, head of the universal Church, Leo, through us his legates with the consent of this holy Council, provided with the dignity of the Apostle Peter which is the foundation of the Church and the rock of faith, named the porter of the heavenly kingdom, has stripped Dioscorus of his episcopal dignity and made him an exile from every priestly work."

Next, in act. 16, when the Council meant to establish something against the instruction of the Pope, the legates said it ought to first be shown to the Apostolic See. So when the Council defined something, following the express judgment of the Pope it is the same as if it were confirmed.

Add to these that the Council of Chalcedon (in an epistle to Leo which is contained in act. 3), when it sought confirmation of the decrees it clearly says it wrote to the Pope and sought confirmation because apart from the decree on faith against Dioscorus, they established certain other things without the express judgment of the Pope; therefore, they only sought confirmation of those things which they had defined apart from the judgment of the Pope. Even Leo himself, in epistle 61 to the Council of Chalcedon, in which he confirms it, shows that it did not need his confirmation except because some were uncertain whether the decree of the Council was really made with his consent, and this is the method whereby the Pope also confirmed many similar Councils, not because they could err, rather, so it would be ratified more certainly for all that what the legates had done was truly done at the express command of the Pope.

Lastly, in Councils of this sort another confirmation of the Pope was not awaited, next the execution is made, *i.e.* those who think the contrary are condemned as manifest heretics and deposed from the episcopate or priesthood. So in the Council of Nicaea, six Bishops were condemned and sent into exile together with Arius, as Ruffinus writes (lib. 10 *hist.* cap. 5); in the Council of Ephesus Nestorius was deposed and condemned, as Evagrius witnesses (lib. 1 cap. 4); in the Council of Chalcedon, act. 3, Dioscorus was deposed, and in act. 4 ten Bishops of Egypt were judged to be heretics because they refused to acquiesce to the decree that had been advanced in act. 3; at the sixth Council, in the 6th and 8th actions, Macharius, the Patriarch of Antioch, was condemned and deposed and sent into exile with some of his disciples, and in the 15th action Polychronius, a priest, was condemned and deposed. But if these Councils could err before the confirmation of the Pope, they were not manifest heretics who resisted before the confirmation.

CHAPTER XII
Whether the authority of a Council is greater than Scripture

WE spoke on the authority of Councils considered absolutely, now we must speak on the same by a comparison to other principles of faith, *i.e.* the written word of God (and for traditions the reasoning is the same), and the Pope. The heretics of this time everywhere cry out that we subject Scripture to Councils. Calvin, in the *Institutes*, book 4, cap. 9 §14, says: "To subject the oracle of God in this manner to the censure of men that it would be ratified because it pleases men is an unworthy blasphemy which is commemorated." Similar things are discovered everywhere in the writings of the others. Moreover, this is not our blasphemy, but is their strawman. For Catholics do not subject the Sacred Scripture to Councils, but places it before them; nor is there any controversy on this point. But if some Catholics sometimes say scripture depends upon the Church, or a Council, they do not understand this in regard to its authority, or according to what it is, but in regard to the explanation and in regard to us.

Therefore, it must be observed that there is a manifold distinction between Sacred Scripture and the decrees of Councils, from which it is understood that Scripture is put before Councils. 1) Scripture is the true word of God, immediately revealed, and in a certain measure at God's dictation according to what we read in 2 Peter 1:21 "Inspired by the Holy Spirit the holy men of God spoke," and in 2 Timothy 3:16 "All Scripture is divinely inspired." Nevertheless, it is not so understood to mean that all the sacred writers had new revelations and wrote things of which they were ignorant beforehand. It is certain that the Evangelists, Matthew and John, wrote those things which they saw while Mark and Luke wrote those things which they heard, as Luke himself declares at the beginning of his gospel: "Just as they handed it down to us who saw from the beginning." (Luke 1:2).

Therefore, the Sacred Writers are said to have had immediate revelation, and wrote the words of God himself, because either some new and previously unknown things were revealed by God, according to that in Psalm 50 (51):8, "You have made known to me the uncertain and hidden matters of your wisdom"; God immediately inspired and moved the writers to write the things which they saw or heard and directed them so that they would not err in some matter. Just like an epistle may truly said to be of a prince and dictated by the prince, even if he that transcribed the dictation already knew what he was going to write, so it is said to be and really is the immediate word of God which was written by the Evangelists at God's inspiration and direction, even if they wrote the things which they saw or heard. But Councils do not have, nor write immediate revelations, or the words of God, rather they only declare what indeed the word of God is, written or handed down, and how it ought to be understood; besides, they deduce conclusions from it by reasoning. Consequently, when Councils define what are the canonical and divine books, thcy do not cause them to be of infallible truth, but only declare that they are such.

So even the Council of Trent, in session 13, c. 1, when it defines that those words: "This is my body" must be understood properly, not figuratively, it did not publish but declared the word of God. And when the Council of Nicaea defined that Christ is *homoousion* (consubstantial) with the Father, it drew the conclusion from the Scriptures in which it is precisely contained that there is one God, and the Father is God, as well as the Son, from which it necessarily follows that the Father and the Son are of the same substance and divinity. Likewise, in the sixth Council, when it defines that Christ had two wills, divine and human, it drew the conclusion from Scripture in which it is contained that Christ is perfect God and perfect man.

The second distinction arises from this first, and is that the sacred writers ought not labor much in in producing these books; for it was enough if they would labor by writing or dictating if they were giving prophecies; or to the chief point by recalling to memory what they had seen or heard, and thought the words which they should write, if they were writing histories or epistles or something similar. But the Fathers in Councils ought to seek the matter itself, *i.e.* to investigate conclusions by disputation, reading and reflection. For that reason, we read in Acts 15 in the first Council that there was a great deal of questioning. Ruffinus witnesses about the Council of Nicaea in book 10, cap. 5, *hist. Ecclesiasticae*, in regards to Acts 15 the fathers of the Council say: "It has been seen by the Holy Spirit and us," *i.e.* the Holy Spirit assists our industry and diligence. But the sacred writers only attribute the things which they write to God and this is why the prophets so often repeat: "Thus speaks the Lord."

The third is that in the Scripture there is no error whether it is treated on faith or on morals, and whether some general thing is affirmed, even common to the whole Church, or some particular thing pertaining to one man. But it is both certain and of the faith that without the grace of the Holy Spirit no man is saved, and Peter, Paul, Stephan and certain others truly had the Holy Spirit and were saved, seeing that the same Scripture witnesses that both are most true, but Councils can err in particular judgments.

The fourth is that in Scripture not only teachings, but even each and every word pertains to faith. We believe no word in Scripture is in vain or not correctly placed, but in Councils the greater part of the acts does not pertain to faith. For disputations that are prefaced, or reasons which are added, or the things that are advanced to explain and illustrate matters are not *de fide*, rather only the bare decrees and not even all of these, but only those which are proposed as *de fide*. Sometimes Councils define something not as a decree but as probable, such as when the Council of Vienne decreed that it must be held as more probable that grace and the virtues are infused into infants at Baptism, as it is contained in *Clem. uni. de Summa Trinitate et fide Catholica.* But when a decree is proposed as *de fide*, it is easily discerned from the words of the Council because they usually say they explain the Catholic faith or they must be held as heretics who think the contrary; or what is most common, they say anathema and exclude anyone from the Church that thinks the contrary. But when they say none of these, the matter is not certain *de fide.*

Next, in the very decrees on faith, not the words but only the sense pertains to faith. It is not heretical to say that in canons of Councils some word is superfluous or not correctly placed, except perhaps the decree were formed from the word itself, such as when in the Council of Nicaea they decreed the word ὁμοούσιον must be received, and in Ephesus the word Θεοτόκον.

The fifth is, that Scripture does not need the approval of the Pope to be authentic, but only that its authority would be known; but Councils, even legitimate and general ones, are not ratified until they are confirmed by the Pope, as we showed in a previous question.

But certain men object. Gratian, in d. 19, can. *In canonicis*, affirms the decretal epistles of Popes ought to be numbered among the canonical Scriptures, and in d. 20, can. *Decretales*, says the canons of Councils are of the same authority with the decretal epistles, therefore even the canons of Councils are numbered among the canonical Scriptures; consequently the Scriptures are not placed before Councils. Besides, St. Gregory says that he venerates the first four Councils as the four books of the Gospels (lib. 1 epist. 24).

I respond twofold to Gratian.

Firstly, he was deceived from a corrupted codex which he held to be of St. Augustine, for he attributed that canon to Augustine (lib. 2 *doct. Christiana*, cap. 8); but the true and corrected codices of St. Augustine do not have what Gratian relates but differ by far. Augustine does not say that the epistles that the Apostolic See usually gives or receives are canonical Scripture, as Gratian read, but a judgment on holy writings that pertain to the Churches and chiefly to those which are Apostolic Sees or merit to receive epistles, such as are Rome, in which Peter sat and to which Paul wrote; Ephesus, in which John sat and to which the same Paul wrote, and certain others.

I say *secondly*, with this error posited, Gratian did not mean to say that decrees of the Popes are properly sacred and canonical Scriptures like the Gospels or the Psalms, but that they are holy writings so as to distinguish them from profane writings, and canonical so as to distinguish them from the sacred writings of the Fathers, which are not rules nor have the authority to oblige. Although the canons of Popes and Councils are distinguished and placed after the divine Scripture, nevertheless they may and must be called sacred writings as well as canonical, just as the seventh Council, in act. 3, calls decrees of Councils divinely inspired constitutions. Nay more, Innocent, cap *Cum Marthae extra de celebratione Missarum*, calls the teaching of St. Augustine a sacred writing: "He does a martyr an injury that prays for him," serm. 17, from the words of the Apostle. Moreover, that Gratian felt the decrees of Councils must not be equated with the divine scriptures properly so called, is clear from 36 *caussa, quaest. 2 can. Placuit*, where he placed the opinion of Jerome, because it was fortified with the testimony of divine Scripture, ahead of a decree of a Council.

I respond to that of Gregory: it sounds like a similitude, not equating, as that of Matthew 5:48, "Be perfect just as your heavenly father is perfect." Or if it would sound like equating, it will need to be said that Gregory does not compare the Councils with the Gospels in all things, but only in the same certitude whereby it is spoken of in the Scriptures as well as in the decrees of Councils. Since both are of infallible truth, they can be said to be equally certain; but just as Councils are not of a greater authority than the Scripture, it remains that we explain at least whether the authority of an ecumenical Council were greater than that of the Supreme Pontiff.

CHAPTER XIII
Whether a Council is above a Pope

THIS question arose at the time of the Council of Pisa. when there were two Popes who sat at the same time in schism, Gregory XII and Benedict XIII. They did not seem to think in earnest of abolishing the schism by a willful abdication, just as before the Pontificate the Cardinals of each party vowed and swore they would leave Pisa and begin to treat whether it were lawful to call a general Council against the will of those Popes to depose them. Antoninus calls this disputation to mind which took place in Florence, in 3 part. *Sum. hist.* tit. 22 c. 5 §2.

Next, when a little later the Council of Constance was called, and John XXIII, who alone had come to the Council left it in secret, then the Council remained without a head and the Fathers began to treat on whether a Council could judge a Pope and depose him against his will. Yet, the controversy particularly arose in the time of the Council of Basel, because Pope Eugene IV wanted to dissolve and impede the Council from beginning, lest it would progress any further, so the Fathers began to ask whether they were held to obey the Pope, or rather more whether the Pope was held to obey them, *i.e.* the Council; and because a little earlier they saw two Popes, John XXIII and Benedict XIII were deposed by the Council of Constance, and imposed an end upon the greatest schism, they began to fear that if the Pope was not held to obey the Council the schism would again be renewed and the Church would remain without any remedy. Consequently, on this occasion, then many entered into the opinion that a Council was above a Pope. But while they wanted to close the path to schisms, they made a new one, and created the anti-Pope Felix V who later, after he recognized his error, abdicated the pontificate. Although later at the Council of Florence and the last Lateran Council the question seemed to have been defined, still, because the Council of Florence did not so expressly define it, and from the Lateran Council which most expressly defined the matters, some were uncertain whether it was truly a general Council; therefore, even to this day the question remains, even among Catholics.

Furthermore, it must be observed that a Pope can be compared with a Council in two ways: 1) that only a true and undoubted Pope were taken on the one hand, on the other a general Council over which the Pope presides in himself or through legates, so that nothing would be defined without his consent.

2) In the second mode, that the Pope alone were taken on the one hand, and on the other a general Council over which he presides neither in his person or in his legates. I do not, however, understand him to preside through his legates even when he sends a legate to preside over a Council, if the latter acts against the will of the Pope since then he is not truly a legate, although he holds himself out as such.

The present question, although it seems to several authors to turn especially on the first comparison, nay more, those who think a Council without a Pope is not a true Council, and hence, without a doubt, the Pope is greater than such a Council; still, really the particular question is on the second comparison. That is clear *firstly*, because this question was introduced on account of the deposition of Popes, *i.e.* it must be inquired whether the Pope could also be judged, condemned and deposed by a Council against his will. Moreover, for this purpose the question is superfluous, whether a Council with a Pope were greater than the Pope alone, for whether it is greater or lesser it will never judge nor condemn nor depose the Pope against his will. For how would this Council do it when it does nothing without the consent of the Pope? Would the Pope will himself to be judged and condemned against his will?

Secondly, the same is clear from the Council of Basel, for the Fathers at Basel, who defined that a Council was above a Pope, asserted that their Council was above Pope Eugene, at a time in which neither the Pope nor his legate were present at the Council. In fact, they even undertook to depose the Pope opposing them by all means.

Therefore, this is the particular question, and it must be treated alone. It will be clear from its explanation what must be said about the first. For those who teach a Pope is above a Council celebrated without him also teach the authority in the Pope alone and in a Council with the Pope intensively, although extensively it would be greater in a Council; and hence the Pope cannot be judged or condemned in such a Council, nor can he be obliged coercively by the decrees of such a Council, but only as a guidance, and he can dispense against them with the exception of decrees on faith which are immutable. The reason is because an equal does not have power in an equal matter. But those who teach a Council without the Pope is above the Pope, consequently also teach that a Council with the Pope is above the Pope and affirm it obliges the Pope just as a minister of the Church dispenses against general Councils, but if he badly dispenses, he can be corrected and punished later by a general Council. Thus, omitting the first comparison, only the second must be treated.

CHAPTER XIV
Different opinions are explained

HENCE, on the proposed question I find three opinions of the doctors. 1) The position that a Council is above the Pope, which all the heretics of this time especially assert, namely Herman Hamelmann, who tries to prove it with many arguments in book 3, cap. 13 *Prolegomenorum.* Cardinal Cameracensis, John Gerson, Jacobus Almainus and several others asserted this in their treatises on the power of the Church. Likewise, Nicholas of Cusa, in his treatise *de concordantia canonica*, lib. 2, last chapter. Panormitanus, in *cap. Significasti, extra de electione*, and in the same place his teacher, Cardinal Florentius, and Abulensis in cap. 18 of Matthew, quest. 108, and in defense of three conclusions, as well as certain others.

So, that this opinion would be understood, it must be known that there are two foundations for it. The first is that the Pope is not properly head of the universal Church gathered together, but not in the same way as the heretics and other authors understand it. For the heretics would have it that the Pope is in no way head of the whole Church, but only a Bishop of his particular Church, and at the most, patriarch of the West.

But the other cited authors teach that the Pope is the head and shepherd of individual Christians as well as individual Churches, if they are taken separately, but not of the whole Church gathered together in a general Council. For then the Church receives, as a form of the body, and the whole power which is separated into different members is united there so that to compare the Pope with other Christians taken apart is to compare the most noble member with a less noble one, but to compare the Pope with a Council is to compare a part with its whole, and hence the lesser with the greater.

And lest we were to say that a Council without a Pope is not wholly perfected but a body without the head, they add a second foundation, which is that supreme Ecclesiastical power is both in a Council and in a Pope, but more principally, immediately and immovably in a Council. They say that Christ immediately gave all power to bind and loose to the Church, and since the Church will always endure, this power always remains immovably in it; since the Church cannot always remain gathered and exercise this power by itself, Christ established the Supreme Pontiff as a general instrument for all the actions of the Church, and placed in him this supreme power that he would exercise it in the name of the Church.

These authors differ among themselves because some place this power formally and subjectively in the Pope alone, but place it in the Church as in the end, because it is on account of the Church as in regulating since it is for the Church to regulate and direct the Pope, since she cannot err, but the Pope could and thereupon that in supplying, because the Pope lacks it on account of natural death, or civil, the Church supplies his office.

But others would have it that it is formally and subjectively principally in the Church, but instrumentally in the Pope, still all agree on this: they teach this power is immediately in the Church and hence, when the Pope dies or is deposed, or when he refuses to be present at a Council, a Council is not on that account an imperfect body, but a perfect one and has the Papal power to define on faith, ratify laws, grant indulgences, etc., from which they deduce that a Council is above a Pope and can judge and punish him; it is the same thing to ask whether a Pope is greater than a Council as if one were to ask whether a part were greater than the whole.

Next, they would have it that the Pope is in the Church in the way that the Venetian Doge is in the Republic of Venice, or a superior general in some religious order. For it is certain the Venetian Doge is above individual magistrates, and above individual senators and citizens of Venice, still, he is not above the whole senate gathered together; when the Doge dies, it is certain that his whole authority is in the senate. In the same way a superior general is over individual religious and even priors, provincials, etc., still, he is not above the general congregation, since he ought to obey it and not command it.

Now, the *second opinion* is of some canonists, who would have it that the Pope is above a Council and can be judged by no man against his will, yet he can subject himself to a Council and grant it power over him; if he did this he ought to acquiesce to the judgment of the Council, even if it were a question of his deposition. So the Gloss teaches in can. *Nos si incompetenter,* 2. q. 7, and in can. *In Synodo,* d. 63.

The last opinion is nearly common, namely that the Pope is so above a Council that he could not even subject himself to its judgment if it were a question of a properly coercive judgment. This opinion seems to be of all the old Scholastics, such as Albert the Great, St. Thomas, St. Bonaventure, Richardus, Paludanus and others commenting on the Sentences (4 dist. 19) where it is argued on the keys, even if they did not avowedly dispute this point. Moreover, St. Antoninus[10] expressly teaches it in *Summa Historialis,* 3 part. tit. 22 cap. 10 § 4; and *Summae Theologicae,* 2 par. tit. 3 cap. 11; Juan Torquemada in lib. 2, cap. 93 and 104 of *Summa de Ecclesia,* as well as in response to the orators of Basel on the Supreme Pontiff and a general Council. Alvarus Pelagius, *de planctu Ecclesiae,* lib. 1, art. 6; Dominic Jacobatius in book 10 *de Conciliis,* art. 7, in which he most profusely disputes the question and answers sixty-three arguments of opponents. Cardinal Cajetan, in his treatise *de Comparatione Papae et*

---

[10] Translator's note: Although Bellarmine cites St. Antoninus in favor of this opinion, St. Antoninus does not quite say this. Rather, after he asserted that the Pope is above a Council, he adds three exceptions from the Gloss, of which one is: "When he submits himself to the judgment of the Church, a Council or another of his own will." (*Summ.*, part. 2, tit. 3, cap. 11, §10).

Conciliorum, and in *Apologia* of the aforesaid treatise. Albert Pighius, lib. 6 *de hierarchia Ecclesiae*. Francis of Ferrara, in lib. 4 contra Gentes, cap. 76. Augustino de Ancona in his treatise *de potestate Ecclesiae*, and Peter de Monte in his book *de potestate Papae et Concilii*. Francis Turrianus in three books in which he wrote on the question, and nearly all Canonists commenting on cap. *Significasti, de electione* and can. *Si Papa,* dist. 40. John Anto. Dephinus, lib. 2 *de Ecclesia*, cap. ult.; Thomas Campeggio in his treatise *de potestate Romani Pontificis*, cap. 22 *et seq.* Nicholas Sanders, lib. 7 *de visible monarchia*, where he argues about the Council of Constance, pg. 540.

CHAPTER XV
The Supreme Pontiff is head of the whole Church

INDEED, so as to declare the truth of the matter, we will convey and demonstrate several propositions, of which this is the *first. The Roman Pontiff is pastor and head not only of all particular Churches, but even of the whole universal Church gathered together, being constituted immediately by Christ.* This is against the first foundation of our adversaries, which, even if it was profusely proven in the books *On the Roman Pontiff*, still it also must be briefly proven in this place.

Therefore, it is proved: 1) from Scripture. Peter is the foundation of the Church, a foundation which was laid by Christ according to that of Matthew 16:18, "You are Peter, and upon this rock I will build my Church," hence head and pastor, for what the foundation is in the house the head is to the body and the shepherd to the flock. Just as the foundation does not depend upon the house, but the house on the foundation, so also the head does not depend upon the body, but the body upon the head, and a shepherd does not depend upon the flock, rather the flock upon the shepherd. Moreover, in this place the universal Church is understood by the word Church, even gathered together, as it is in a general Council, which is proven from Matthew 18:17, where Christ says on the same Church: "If he will not hear them, let him go to the Church." In such a passage, our adversaries understand a general Council by "church".

Besides, once the Church has been gathered, a Council is more properly the Church of Christ, as even our adversaries concede, for the Church is a congregation of the faithful, therefore, the more the faithful are gathered and united the more properly they are the Church. Yet, it is stupid when something is pronounced absolutely on another thing, to remove that which is most properly meant by it; consequently when Christ says, "Upon this Rock I will build my Church," the universal Church gathered together is stupidly removed since it is most properly the Church.

Next, the Church of Christ is always formally gathered together, because it is one kingdom, one household, one flock, even if it seems to be so much dispersed to a place. Thus, if the Pope is the shepherd and head of the Church, certainly it is not a dispersed Church, which is null, rather he is pastor and head of the Church gathered together. The same is held from the last chapter of John: "Feed my sheep." For even if our adversaries say that the Lord had said "feed my sheep" not my Church, still the Church so explains this in the prayer for the Pope: "O God, pastor and ruler of all the faithful, who willed your servant N. to preside over your Church." And besides, either the Church gathered together (or a general Council), pertains to the sheep of Christ, or it does not. If it pertains, consequently Peter is the pastor of the Church gathered and of a general Council; if it does not pertain, therefore Christians, through being gathered cease to be the sheep of Christ, which is most absurd.

2) It is proven from Councils, for in the Council of Chalcedon, in its epistle to Pope Leo, it declares with precise words that St. Leo was head of that Council, which was the greatest of all, in which the whole Church was seen gathered together. It says: "Who you preside over as the true head." Likewise, the Council of Lyons, as it is held in the chapter *Ubi periculum, de elect.* in 6, calls the Pope ruler of the universal Church, not merely the ruler of particular Churches. Similarly, at the Council of Florence it was defined that the Pope is head of the whole world and received the fullest power from the Lord to rule the universal Church. The Council of Constance, sess. 15, condemned the heresy of John Hus, saying that the Pope is not head of the Church.

3) It is proven by reasons. *Firstly*, the Pope is one head, therefore he is the head of one body, but particular Churches

taken separately are not one body, therefore the Pope is head of the universal Church. *Secondly*, the universal Church is one visible body, consequently, it ought to have one visible head, otherwise it would appear to be a monster. But it produces no other head than the Pope. Therefore, the Pope is head of the whole Church at the same time. *Thirdly*, the Pope is immediately Vicar of Christ, as is held in the cited Councils of Lyons and Florence, and also in the Council of Constance, sess. 8, where the heresy of Wycliffe is condemned, saying the Pope is not immediate vicar of Christ; nor do our adversaries deny it, as a result he presides over all of them in place of Christ, over whom Christ himself invisibly presides; but Christ presides and would do so visibly if he were visibly present, not only over particular Churches, but even over the whole universal Church and general Councils; therefore even the Pope presides over the universal Church.

CHAPTER XVI
Supreme Power is not in a Council

NOW for the second proposition: *Supreme Ecclesiastical Power is not in the Church or a Council without the Pope either formally or supplied.* This is against the second foundation of our adversaries and that supreme power is not formally in the Church or in a Council in the way it is in the Pope is clearly gathered from the Scriptures. According to the Scriptures, the Church is not a democracy, or an aristocracy, but a monarchy, or the kingdom of Christ, according to that of Psalm 2:6, "I have been set up as King by him over mount Sion, his holy mountain." And in Luke 1:33, "Of his kingdom there will be no end." and John 18:37, when Christ is asked "Are you a king?", he does not say "I am not", or my kingdom is not in this world, rather he says: "My kingdom is not of this world," *i.e.* it is indeed in this world, but it is not such a kingdom as you think of, such as that of Herod and similar kings. Thereupon, Scripture everywhere calls Christ a King and the Church his kingdom, from which it follows that the Church herself ought to be ruled by one, not by many just as all kingdoms are governed.

But that this authority in the Church is not supplied is shown by this reason. The Church does not hold this authority of itself, nor from another, therefore, in no manner does it hold it. A distinction between the kingdom of Christ and other kingdoms manifestly shows that the Church does not hold this authority of itself. For, the Church is not such a kingdom as the kingdoms of this world in which supreme power is in the king, rather, the same power, proceeding and derived and hence radically supplied by the people is in the kingdom, because the people make the King who would otherwise be a private citizen, just as the rest, for all men are naturally free and equal, nor can one command the rest unless they would subject themselves to him and concede power to him.

But Christ is God and man, and to the extent that God is naturally the lord and king of all creatures, insofar as he is man he has all power from God, nor was he made king by the Church, rather he made himself its king. Apocalypse 5: "You have made us a kingdom for our God," hence it is that in Scripture, the kingdom of Christ is the Church. Now, lest someone would think it were like other kingdoms, it is also compared to a household: "Who is a faithful and prudent servant whom the Lord constituted over his household?" (Matthew 24:45); and in Hebrews 3:2, St. Paul says that Moses was faithful in the whole house of God as a servant, but Christ was faithful in the whole house as the Lord. For it is certain that the householder does not have any authority from the household, but of himself; because a father is not constituted by the family, rather he makes the family for himself by begetting sons and correcting servants. For that reason, a householder, even if he were the worst, can never be judged by the household or expelled, just as a king can when he degenerates into tyranny. The Church is also compared to a sheepfold in John 10:1, likewise to a body and a spouse in Ephesians 4 and 5, that we would understand that a pastor does not receive authority from the sheep, nor the head from the body, nor a man from his wife, so neither does Christ from the Church.

From these, we hold that the Church of itself has no authority, rather all is in Christ and those to whom Christ communicated it. Moreover, that it does not have it from another, namely from Christ, is proven. For Christ is read to have given the keys of the kingdom of heaven to Peter in Matthew 16:18, and to have put the same in charge of his sheepfold in the last chapter of John, he also gave power to the other Apostles to preach, Baptize, forgive sins and do certain other things which look to the Episcopal office, but this power

Christ gave to individuals so that everyone would be able to exercise all these without the gathering of all, as is known; but that he gave some power to the Church itself, *i.e.* to the corporate body of the faithful in itself, that is, by reason of its totality is read nowhere; nay more we read the contrary, the people are commanded to be obedient and subject to their pastors (Hebrews 13:17). But if no authority were given to the corporate body of the Church therefore, neither was it to a general Council, to the extent in which it represents the whole Church. Therefore, supreme authority is not in a Council, nor Papal, but only Episcopal or Archiepiscopal, exactly as the persons are who come together there. At least supreme or Papal authority is not placed in a Council by our adversaries, except insofar as the Council it manages the universal Church in his place. If, therefore, the universal Church, without the Pope, does not have papal authority, as a result so much the less does a Council have it.

Secondly it is proved: If a general Council without the person of the Pope would have Papal authority formally, or supplied, it would not need the confirmation of the Pope. But that is false, as it is certain that all general Catholic Councils sought confirmation.

Thirdly, a Council without the Pope can err even in decrees of faith, as is clear in the Council of Sirmium, to which Hosius subscribed. Likewise, Milan, Armenia, Ephesus II, Constantinople under Justinian II, Constantinople under Leo the Isaurian, and another under Constantine Copronymus. But a Council with the Pope cannot err; therefore, it cannot do all things without the Pope which it can with the Pope. Nor can one respond that these Councils erred because they were not legitimate, for many of them lacked nothing other than the assent of the Pope; nay more, Ephesus II was altogether similar to Basel; for both were summoned by a Pope and in both a legate of the Pope was there in the beginning; shortly after the Papal legate departed at both Councils, the Pope was excommunicated at both, and all of these things were certain at Basel from its deeds described by Aeneas Sylvius. Moreover, in regard to the Council of Ephesus, it is certain from the epistles of Pope Leo, 12, 13, 15, 21, and 22 as well as from the Council of Chalcedon, act. 3; but just the same our adversaries cannot deny the second Council of Ephesus erred.

Fourthly, if supreme power were principally in the Church, but instrumentally in the Pope, as in a minister of the Church, as they themselves say, it would follow that the Pope is not the *immediate* vicar of Christ, rather he would be a mediate one; for the Church would *immediately* be the vicar of Christ, but the Pope would be the mediate vicar of the Church, which is expressly against the Council of Constance, sess. 8, where the heresy of Wycliffe was condemned, that said the Pope is not the immediate vicar of Christ.

CHAPTER XVII
The Supreme Pontiff is absolutely above a Council

THE third proposition. *The Supreme Pontiff is simply and absolutely above the universal Church as well as above a general Council, so that he would recognize nothing on earth above his judgment.* This is also truly *de fide*, and proven. 1) From the two preceding propositions; for if the Pope is head of the universal Church, even when it is gathered together, and the universal Church gathered together does not also have any power by reason of its totality, then it follows the Pope is above a Council and above the Church, not vice versa.

2) It is proven from reason, and founded in the scriptures; for all the names which are given to Christ in the Scriptures whereby it is certain that he is above the Church, all the same are attributed to the Pope. *First*, Christ is the householder in his house, which is the Church, the Pope in the same house is the supreme steward, *i.e.* in the place of Christ the householder: "Who is a faithful steward, and prudent, whom the Lord constituted above his household, etc." (Luke 12:42) Here, by steward, or *oeconomon*, as it is in the Greek text, the Fathers understand a Bishop. Ambrose, as well as Hilary and Jerome (in cap. 24 Matth., where a similar sentence is contained) understand this passage in the same way. And although the Fathers do not speak expressly about the Roman Bishop, nevertheless, without a doubt the teaching of that Scripture is: as particular Bishops are supreme stewards over their Churches, so the Roman Bishop is in the universal Church. Wherefore, Ambrose, on 1 Timothy 3. That you would know how you ought to be preserved in the house of God, etc., he says: "The Church is called the house of God, whose ruler today is Damasus." And Chrysostom, in lib. 2 *de sacerdotio*, near the beginning, cites this passage: "Who is a faithful servant," etc., explaining that it is about Peter.

However, the supreme steward is over the household, and he cannot be judged and punished by it, as is clear from the same passage, for the Lord says: "whom the Lord constituted over his household ... But if the servant would say in his heart: 'the master delays his coming', and would begin to strike the servants and the maidservants, to eat and drink and be drunk, the Master will come on a day in which he hopes not, and divine him and place his lot with the infidels." There you see the Lord saves that servant for his judgment and does not consign him to the judgment of the household. The use of all household teaches the same thing; for there is no household in which it would be lawful for inferior servants to punish even when gathered together, or expel the steward, even if he were the worst, for it pertains to the Lord of the household alone.

The *second* name of Christ is shepherd, "I am the good shepherd, etc." He shares the same with Peter in the last chapter of John: "Feed my sheep." It is certain, however, that a shepherd is so in charge of the sheep that he cannot be judged by them.

Thc *third* is "head of the Body of the Church," (Eph. 4:15-16), and he shares the same with Peter, as we have it in the Council of Chalcedon, act. 3, where the legates pronounce sentence against Dioscorus, and in the epistle of the Council to Leo. Moreover, that the head would be ruled by the members and not rather rule them is against nature, just as also it is against nature for the members to cut off their head when it is gravely sick.

The *fourth* is husband, or bridegroom (Ephesians 5:25), "Men, love your wives just as Christ loved the Church and gave himself up for it, etc." The same agrees with Peter, for in the general Council of Lyons, as it is found in c. *Ubi periculum, de electione, in Sexto*, the Council speaks on the election of a Roman Pontiff: "Let a useful provision make haste for the necessary things of the whole world, for a suitable bridegroom to speedily be given to the Church." But it is against the

Apostle in Ephesians 5:25 as well as against the order of nature that the bride would be in charge of the bridegroom, and not rather subject.

In the second place, it is proven from the express words of Councils and Popes; for although the controversy is on the power of Councils and of Popes, if Councils and Popes agree between themselves, why is it necessary for us to argue? *First*, the Council of Sinvessano under Marcellinus is extant, in the end of which we read: "The first see is judged by no one." A little after, the Roman Council under Sylvester stands out, in the last canon of which we read likewise: No one will judge the first see."

Besides, it is gathered from the Council of Chalcedon that a Pope is greater than a Council, for in act. 3 many written epistles are cited from different places to the Council, which all so begin: "To the most holy, blessed and universal Patriarch of great Rome, Leo, and to the holy universal Council gathered in the city of Chalcedon, etc." But there was no man in the whole Council that cried out and said that the Pope ought not be placed before the whole Council. Nay more, in the end of that action there is extant an epistle of the Council to the same Leo, in which they acknowledge him as their head and father. Besides, in the same action Dioscorus was condemned along with the whole second Council of Ephesus, not only for different reasons, but especially because it had dared to judge and condemn the Roman Pontiff, Leo. For, as Nicholas I says in his epistle to Michael, Dioscorus was not condemned so much for heresy as for the horrendous presumption in which he dared to impose sentence against the Supreme Pontiff. There it must be noted that if Dioscorus, who was the Patriarch of Alexandria, that is, the first after the Roman patriarchate, could not lawfully judge the Roman Pontiff with a general Council, clearly it follows that a Council is not above a Pope. For why could it not judge the Pope if it was above him, nay more his judge as our adversaries would have it?

Likewise, the fifth Roman Council under Symmachus received and approved as if they were its own decrees, a book of Ennodius the deacon, in which we so read: "God willed the cases of other men to be concluded by men. The prelate of this See without question he reserved to his own judgment, for he willed that the successors of Peter the apostle ought to have their innocence judged by heaven." In the eighth general Council, act. 7, we read the Roman Pontiff judges in regard to the prelates of every Church, while on the other hand no man ever judged him. Here it must be understood *legitimately*, so that a judgment of this kind was received by the Church. Platina, in *vita Leonis III*, and Paulus Aemilius in lib. 3 *historia Francorum* write that when Charlemagne came to Rome to discern the case of Pope Leo III, against whom many crimes had been objected, and at the same time he convened a great Council of Bishops, all the Bishops cried out in one voice that no man is allowed to judge the Supreme Pontiff; then Charlemagne desisted from that office of judgment, and Leo purged himself with an oath.

Besides, the Lateran Council under Alexander III, as it is held in c. *Licet, extravagantes, de elect.* says: "In the Roman Church, something is specially constituted because recourse may not be had to a superior." There, the Council teaches that the Roman Pontiff should be chosen with greater caution than other Bishops, because if a bad Bishop were chosen, he can be corrected and deposed by the Roman Pontiff; but if a bad Pope were chosen, there is no remedy, for he has no superior whereby he could be deposed. Likewise, at the Council of Constance, a Bull of Martin V was published with the approbation of the Council, in which anyone suspect of heresy is commanded to be interrogated as to whether or not they believe the Roman Pontiff has supreme power in the Church of God. But certainly it is supreme, in which there is no greater and for whom there is no equal.

Next, the fifth Lateran Council under Leo X, in its eleventh session, precisely and avowedly taught that the Pope is above all Councils and rebuked the contrary decree published at the Council of Basel: "It is evident that the Roman Pontiff alone, as one having authority over every Council, and the right and power to summon Councils, transfer them, and dissolve them, not only by the testimony of Sacred Scripture, the aforesaid Holy Fathers and other Roman Pontiffs, but so much more even by the very confession of the same Councils."

There is no response to this passage, except that it was not a general Council or was not received by the Church, or that it did not define this *de fide*. Yet, it can scarcely be said that it was not a general Council, for even if there were few Bishops (as it did not attain to 100), still it was clearly a Council to all, and all were called to it, and in it the true and unquestioned Supreme Pontiff presided. But that it was not received it is hardly related, since the decrees of Councils do not need the approval of the people, since they do not receive their authority from them. It is true that decrees on customs, if they were not received and the Pope would turn a blind eye to them, at length are abrogated by custom; but this does not happen because those things needed the approval of the people, rather because the decrees were mutable and when the Pope sees that after a long time they are not preserved, and is silent, he is considered to abrogate them. But decrees on faith are immutable, nor can they be abrogated in any manner, once they have been established. But such is this, on which we are arguing. But the Council did not so define the matter, properly, as a decree that must be held with Catholic faith, so there is a doubt and therefore they are not properly heretics who think the contrary, but they cannot be excused from great temerity.[11]

[11] Translator's note: While this claim that a Council is above the Pope was hardly tenable after Bellarmine's time, after the decree of Vatican I it is properly heretical.

Now we add *thirdly*, Popes. Leo the Great, in epist. 48 to Anastasius, says: "By the great disposition of God it has been provided lest everyone would have to defend all things themselves, rather there would be in each province individuals of whom among the brethren would have the first judgment, and again certain men were constituted in the greater cities that received a greater solicitude, through which to the one See of Peter the care of the universal Church would be brought, that no one would ever be at variance from its head." Now, if care of the universal Church pertains to Peter, certainly also of a Council, which in turn acts for the universal Church.

Pope Gelasius, in his epist. to the Bishops of Dardania, says: "The Church through all the world knows that the most holy Roman See has the right to judge all things, nor is it lawful for anyone to judge its judgment."

Nicholas I, in his epistle to the Emperor Michael, repeats the same thing: "It is clear that there is certainly no authority greater than that of the Apostolic See, whose judgment is retracted by no man."

St. Gregory in his epistle to Theotista (lib. 9 epist. 39) says: "If Blessed Peter, when he is reproached by the faithful, were to attend to the authority which he received in the Holy Church, he could respond that the sheep ought not dare to rebuke their shepherd, but if in the quarrel of the faithful he were to say something of his power, he would not be a mild doctor; therefore he placated them with humble reason."

Pope Paschal, as it is held in c. *Significasti, extra. de electione*, says: "They say in Councils it is not found stated as if the law of the Roman Church was set in front of any Councils, since all Councils are made and are fortified by the authority of the Roman Church, and in their statutes, the authority of the Roman Pontiff is clearly received."

Innocent III, in serm. 2 *de consecr. Pontificis*, says: "In so great a matter, it is necessary that I have faith, since I have

God as a judge on the rest of my sins, only on account of sin which is committed against faith, could I be judged by the Church."

Boniface VIII, *in extravag., Viam Sanctam, tit. de major. et obed.*, says: "If earthly power would stray, it will be judged by the spiritual power. If the spiritual would stray, the lesser by the greater. But if the supreme power would stray, it can be judged by God alone, not by man." He adds the testimony of St. Boniface, the Bishop of Fulda, who, even if he was not a Pope, still was of great authority. Therefore, it is held in dist. 40, can. *Si Papa*, where he says: "He that will judge all must be judged by nobody unless he is found to have deviated from the faith."

It is proven *fourthly*, from the appeals from a Council to the Pope. A lesser can always appeal to a greater without any controversy; that one can appeal from a Council to a Pope, not the other way around, is clear from the epistle of Gelasius to the Bishops of Dardania: "To the Apostolic See one may appeal from every part of the world, but nobody is permitted to appeal from it."

And lest we might think he speaks on appeals from some Bishop, not from a Council, he adds that often the Roman Pontiffs absolved those whom Councils had unjustly prosecuted. Famous examples of this fact are extant. For, Athanasius, the Bishop of Alexandria, and Paul, the Bishop of Constantinople, were deposed by a Council; they appealed to Pope Julius I, and they were restored to their Sees by him, as the author Sozomen notes (lib. 3, *hist.* cap. 7), and similarly Flavian, the Bishop of Constantinople, appealed from the second general Council of Ephesus to Pope Leo, as Leo witnesses in epist. 25 to the Emperor Theodosius. Likewise, Theodoret, the Bishop of Cyprus, appealed from the same Council to the same Pope Leo, as is clear from Liberatus in his *Breviarium*, cap. 12, and from that epistle of Theodoret which is extent at the end of the works of Leo. Lastly, John

Chrysostom was deposed by a Council and he appealed to Pope Innocent, as Gelasius witnesses (*loc. cit.*) and the same is gathered from the epistles of Chrysostom to Innocent.

It is proved *fifthly* from the approval and condemnation of Councils; for all are recalled, at length, to the examination of the Roman Pontiff, and those which he approves are received, but those which he condemns are rejected, as Gelasius witnesses in the same epistle to the Bishops of Dardania, and even that the Pope approved many Councils at their request is clear from the deeds of these very Councils, especially the first, second, third, fourth and sixth Councils.

Moreover, that the Popes at some time condemned the decrees of Councils, which is a clear sign of superiority, is certain from St. Basil, who writes in an epistle to St. Athanasius (which is number 52), that it seemed good to him that the Pope might be asked to send some men into Greece to invalidate the Council of Armenia in his name. Pope Damasus himself, in his epistle to the Bishops of Illyria condemned that Council. Likewise, Leo, in epist. 55 to Pulcheria, says: "We make void the agreement of the Bishops opposed to the rules of the holy canons enacted at Nicaea, by the piety of your faith united with ours, and through the authority of Blessed Peter the Apostle we altogether invalidate it by a general definition." St. Gregory the great says: "All the acts of that Council opposing the Apostolic See have been scattered."

CHAPTER XVIII
The Pope cannot subject himself to the coercive judgment of Councils

THE fourth proposition. *The Supreme Pontiff cannot consign himself either to the coercive judgment of a Council or any man, rather, only to discretionary judgment.* Now, in a perfect judgment two things are required. *Firstly*, the power to discus the case and to discern or judge what must be done. *Secondly*, the power to compel him who falls in the case to obey the judgment imposed against him. Both are found in a judge properly so called, such as a prince is, or a judge constituted by the prince. But the first is only found in arbiters, whose judgments, even if men are held to stand from the law of nature, because they are held to keep their promises, still not from the force of the sentence, because arbiters cannot compel.

Now, the Supreme Pontiff cannot constitute a judge, properly so called, over himself, but only in the manner of arbiters, whose judgment if he is not held to obey, he might do what he ought not, but not what he cannot.

The first part is proven. *Firstly*, because the power of the Pope is above all, and of divine law as is clear. But the Pope cannot dispense against divine law. *Secondly*, because an inferior cannot consign judgment to someone that is reserved to a superior. A Bishop cannot consign to his penitentiary that he would absolve in cases reserved to the Pope; but judgment in the case of a Pope is reserved to God, as we taught above. *Thirdly*, because it would follow that the Pope is a superior and not a superior in respect to the same thing, which is a tautology. It is shown to follow from this reason. The Supreme Pontiff, when he consigns himself and his case to the judgment of another, does not cease to be Pope, consequently, he does not cease to be the superior of every Christian; but just the same, if he can be compelled then he is not a superior, rather an inferior. Therefore, he would be a superior and not a superior at the same time.

The second part is clear from Sixtus III, Leo III, Symmachus, Leo IV and others, who when they were accused, wanted their cases to be discussed in a Council of Bishops, just as is clear from can. *Mandastis,* and can. *Auditum*, 2. q. 5, as well as from the fourth Council under Symmachus; still the Bishops did not dare to judge such things. For this reason, in the fourth Council under Symmachus, all the Bishops subscribed, and affirmed that they relinquished the whole judgment to God.

CHAPTER XIX
The responses of our adversaries are refuted

IT remains to answer arguments. In the first place are those of Hermann, who objects in book 3, c. 12 *Prolegomenorum* with some old examples. Secondly, certain arguments from Gerson; thirdly, something else from the Council of Basel.

1) The example of Marcellinus, who in the Council of Sinvessano was condemned by the Bishops and deposed. I respond: a) Marcellinus was accused of an act of infidelity, in which case a Council can discuss the case of the Pope and if they were to discover that he really was an infidel, the Council can declare him outside the Church and thus condemn him. b) I say the Bishops did condemn Marcellinus, but only after the very man had condemned himself, *i.e.* he abdicated the Papacy, for before they had often declared: "The first see will be judged by no one, you are guilty, you are the judge, do not be judged by us, etc." See Nicholas I in his epistle to Michael.

2) The next is the example of Pope Miltiades. After he had imposed judgment the Bishop of Arles judged the very same case, as Augustine witnesses in epist. 162 to Glorius and Eleusius, where he also adds: "Behold, we think the Bishops that judged at Rome were not good judges. Still a plenary Council of the universal Church remained, where even with these judges the case could be argued. So that if they are found to have judged badly their sentence will be lifted."

I respond: To that of the Bishop of Arles from the same Augustine and in the same place, not because it needed to be done, but because the Emperor wished to acquiesce to the Donatists who were begging for another judgment, so that maybe the guilty party would be cleansed in two judgments. To that about a general Council, I say Augustine did not discuss a Pope without a Council so as to support a Council without a Pope, as we recently discussed, rather he discusses a particular Council over which the Pope would preside, then a general Council, over which also the Pope would preside. Moreover, there can be no doubt that a case judged by the Pope in a particular Council can again be judged by the same in a general Council, especially in a question of fact, which depends upon information and in which the Church can err, such as the question was that was being argued then. Nay more, even ordinarily, after a general Council has been summoned, if formerly there were particular Councils held earlier in individual provinces—even at Rome, and later the matter which was treated in those particular Councils was defined in a general Council, then the final judgment and definitive sentence of the Roman Pontiff with the assent of a Council is imposed.

3) The example of Liberius, whom the Emperor deposed and later restored in his see, bidding him to rule the Church of Rome with Felix, and the Council of Sirmium commanded the same thing, after letters were given to Felix, as Sozomen relates (lib. 4, cap. 14).

I respond: An Arian emperor did this unjustly and tyrannically, in the way that Nero also killed Peter and Paul. But the Council of Sirmium did not command, rather it only sent exhortatory letters to Felix asking him to suffer Liberius to sit at the same time as himself. Add the fact that the Council was especially made up of Arians, and is of no importance.

4) The example of St. Leo, whose epistle in the Council of Chalcedon was examined by many Bishops, as Evagrius relates in lib. 2 cap 18, and Leo also boasted, in epist. 63 that his epistle was approved by the Council.

I respond: From here it does not follow that a Council is above a Pope. Leo had sent his epistle to the Council not as something containing a final and definitive sentence, but merely as an instruction, whereby bishops are assisted to judge better. Moreover, after they all consented to the epistle of Leo, then at length a final definition was published in the name of the Pope and the Council. That is enough for examples.

In the second place, he proposes arguments of John Gerson: 1) The first is that of Matthew 18, where it is said: "If your brother sins against you, etc., tell it to the Church." But the Pope is also our brother, since he is a Christian, and ought to say the *Our Father*, therefore, the Pope can be called to judgment, moreover he can be judged by the Church and punished; but the Church does not do anything except by its prelates, therefore the Pope can be judged by a Council of prelates.

I respond: By the word *Church*, either a Bishop is understood, as Chrysosotom explains on this passage, as well as Innocent III in c. *Novit, extra, de judiciis*, and the praxis of the Church demonstrates this. Daily they are denounced to a Bishop, on whom the Lord said: "Tell it to the Church"; or it would mean the body of the faithful with their head. As Cyprian says in his letter to Florentius, which is the ninth in book 4: "The Church is the people united to the priest and a flock adhering to its shepherd." This is why in each episcopate sinners are brought to the Church and the Bishop of that place, but if the Bishop were to sin, he cannot be brought to that Church unless he were to be brought to himself, since he would be the head of the same Church; rather he must be brought to some higher Church, over which an Archbishop or a Patriarch presides; but if the Patriarch were to sin, he cannot be brought to his own Church but to a greater one, that is to the Roman Church, or a general Council, over which the Supreme Pontiff would preside. Still, if the Supreme Pontiff himself were to sin, he must be reserved for the judgment of God, for there is no other Church to which he could be brought, since without him no Church would be discovered with a head.

But again, they insist. These words: "Speak to the Church", were said to Peter, therefore even Peter and his successors ought to bring sinners to the Church, therefore he ought to acknowledge a certain tribunal of the Church greater than his own.

I respond: When these things were said to Peter, he was not yet the Pope, but a private man, hence what was said to him is fitting to those who acknowledge some superior. I add besides, in his own way the Pope can fulfill this precept: first he ought to privately correct one who is a sinner, then apply witnesses, lastly speak to the Church, that is himself, as the president, and to the Church over which he presides, *i.e.* to publicly excommunicate him. This is how St. Gregory understood this passage, in lib. 4, epist. 38 to John, the Bishop of Constantinople.

2) The Pope is a member of the Church, therefore he is lesser than the whole, which is the Church, and may and must be cut off if he would corrupt the Church because it is from natural law that members corrupting the whole body must be cut off.

I respond: in regard to the first consequent, when the Church is gathered, it is either received with the Pope or without the Pope, thus, the Pope, as a member, is lesser than the Church which is a whole. If the Church were received without the Pope, it is false that it is whole, for it is not whole, but a part, and indeed a greater part than the head, like a boulder in magnitude, but lesser in the magnitude of strength, or authority, as is clear in every body. Yet, what our adversaries say, that the authority of the head remains in the Church as an assistance, was already refuted earlier. But if the Church were received with the Pope, then, as we otherwise said, the authority of the Church is extensively greater than that of the Pope alone, intensively, however, it is equal. Just as being, as it embraces God and creatures is not greater than if it were only God intensively even if extensively it is greater since there are many goods, so also Christ, as man, is the head of a homogenous Church, and hence part of it, and still the whole Church is not greater than Christ alone.

But they insist against this: "All power to act is more principally in the whole than in the parts, which are instruments of the whole; for a man is said to see more principally than the eye, this is why when the Pope is also included in the Church, it makes a certain whole, and the Pope is a certain part and instrument of this whole, so it follows supreme ecclesiastical Power more principally fits the Church itself than the Pope."

I respond: a judgment on the body of the Church is one thing, and on natural bodies another; for in natural bodies the power proceeds from the essence to the powers, therefore, it is said more principally the whole acts rather than any part or power; but in the body of the Church the power does not proceed from essence to the powers, or parts, but from an outward power. For the Pope, who is head of the Church, does not hold authority from the Church, but from God, and so the principal agent is not the Church, but God. *In the second place*, it may be said that the principal agent in whatever body you like is always supposed to be the very thing which sustains and moves all the members. Hence, for the body of the Church Christ is supposed, as when we say this is the body of Peter, or Paul, it declares it is supposed of Peter or Paul, so when we say the Church is the body of Christ, it declares that of Christ is supposed. Nor is it opposed that Christ is also the head of the Church, for Christ, as flowing into all the members, is called the head that he would sustain and move all things, it can be supposed, and in this way we concede the Pope is the instrument of the body of the Church, and in a certain measure less than the whole itself, just as without a doubt we include Christ himself in the whole, as supposed.

To the second consequent it can be said: *firstly,* on the law of nature, that putrid members should be cut off with the exception of the head. For it is better to have a putrid head than none. But this answer avails little, for in natural bodies the head ought to be cut off because by that amputation the whole body dies. But the body of the Church does not die when the Pope does, and for that reason we also see in temporal states that if the King degenerates into a tyrant, it will be permitted for the head of the kingdom to be deposed and another chosen. So I say *secondly*, in a natural body and in temporal states corrupting members are cut off because they depend upon the body and have their force from it; but the body of the Church does not have the same arrangement, whose head does not receive authority from the body, but from God, just as even it is not lawful for a household to depose the supreme steward, even if he is the worst, because he was not set up by the household, but by the master.

But they will say, therefore, only the Church is without remedy if it has a bad Pope, and the Pope can disturb all things unpunished, and destroy and no one will be able to resist.

I respond: No wonder, if the Church remains without an efficacious human remedy, seeing that its safety does not rest principally upon human industry, but divine protection, since God is its king. Therefore, even if the Church could not depose a Pope, still, it may and must beg the Lord that he would apply the remedy, and it is certain that God has care of its safety, that he would either convert the Pope or abolish him from the midst before he destroys the Church. Nevertheless, it does not follow from here that it is not lawful to resist a Pope destroying the Church; for it is lawful to admonish him while preserving all reverence, and to modestly correct him, even to oppose him with force and arms if he means to destroy the Church. For to resist and repel by force of arms, no authority is required. See more on this with Juan Torquemada, lib. 2 cap. 106.

The third argument of Gerson, related by Herman, is taken from the Council of Constance. Constance defined, in session 4, that a general Council has authority immediately from

Christ, which all are held to obey even if it is provided with papal dignity. Either this Council is approved or not; if it is approved, therefore it is true and must be received, because it defined it; if not, it wrongly deposed John XXIII, Gregory XII and Benedict XIII and chose Martin V, whom all other Popes succeeded thereafter. Add, Pope Martin V, in the last session, confirmed all the decrees of this Council that were on faith, moreover, this decree seems to pertain to faith.

I respond: 1) The Council of Constance was legitimate and approved, but that is not opposed to those things which we said. For it did not define absolutely that general Councils have power from Christ over Popes, but only in a case, that is, in a time of schism when it is now known who is the true Pope; for a doubtful Pope is held for no Pope, and so to have power in that case is not to have power against the Pope. So think Torquemada, Campeggio, and Sanders (*ll.cc.*)

2) The response can be made that the Council of Constance was not, when it asserted something of this kind, that it could define questions of faith; for in the first place it was not yet a general Council then, since only a third of the Church was present, *i.e.* only those prelates who obeyed the anti-Pope John XXIII, for those who obeyed Gregory and Benedict opposed the things which were being done by the Council. Next, a certain Pope was not present in the Church, without which doubts on faith could not be defined; thus there was no Pope in the Council. For John XXIII, who began the Council, already departed when the fourth session was being held.

Nor is it true that Martin V confirmed this decree. For he precisely said that he confirmed only those decrees on faith which were done *Conciliariter*, that is, by the custom of other Councils, after the matter was diligently examined. Furthermore, it is certain this decree was made by the Council without any examination. Consequently, Martin, when he confirmed decrees on faith that were concluded in a conciliar fashion, understood only the condemnation of the heresies of Wycliffe and Hus.

And it does not follow that if the Council erred in this, it also erred in deposing Gregory XII, John XXIII and Benedict XIII. For, even if the Council without a Pope cannot define new doctrines of faith, still it can judge in a time of schism who is the true Pope and prove to be a true shepherd for the Church when there is not one, or there is a doubtful one, and this is what the Council of Constance rightly did. Besides, John and Gregory were not deposed against their will, for even they renounced the Papacy freely, as is clear from the acts of the Council in session 12 and 14. Moreover, Benedict did not yield, but after his death Clement VIII, his successor yielded to Martin V, who all the Church venerated as a true Pope.

Lastly, Herman advances the Council of Basel, which in sess. 33 defined that it must be held with Catholic faith that a Council is above a Pope. Moreover, this Council was summoned by Martin V, as we see in sess. 1, and then declared legitimately continued from its beginning in sess. 16 by Eugene IV. Lastly, it was confirmed by Nicholas V with its acts.

I respond: The Council of Basel was legitimately begun, but illegitimately completed. Moreover, it is a clear lie of Hermann that it was confirmed by Nicholas V with its acts. For Nicholas, as is obvious from his Bull connected to the same Council, only confirmed those things which the Council did in regard to benefices and ecclesiastical censures. Such things, however, as the Council of Basel had defined on its authority over the Pope, no Pope approved, rather condemned avowedly, especially Pope Eugene IV, as is clear from the Council of Basel in sess. 38, then Leo X in the last Lateran Council, sess. 12, and again by the whole Church, which, when the Council deposed Eugene, always held him as a true Pope. Lastly, those at the Council of Basel and Pope Felix, whom they created, as Pope Felix at length yielded to Nicholas, Eugene's successor, and those at Basel, who transferred the Council to Lausanne and at length subjected themselves to Pope Nicholas, as Nicholas witnesses in the same Bull. Many other arguments could be proposed and answered, but these are answered in our treatise *On the Roman Pontiff.* See also what we will say about the Council of Basel, in the following book, chapter 16.

END BOOK II

Book III
On the Church Militant Diffused Throughout the World

FOREWORD

MICHAEL G. SIRILLA, Ph.D.
Franciscan University of Steubenville

ST. ROBERT BELLARMINE (1542–1621), a preeminent and officially-recognized Doctor of the Church, is the most important figure in the Catholic Counter-Reformation. His prodigious works have been received for centuries as standard and decisive for the promotion and defense of the truth of Christ's revelations on justification, the sacraments, the four last things (eschatology), and Christian spirituality. Even more importantly, his theological writings on the Church of Christ constitute an invaluable treasure not only for Catholics, but for the commonweal and eternal salvation of humanity itself. This is no slight exaggeration. His is the very first independent theological and dogmatic treatise on the Church. Patristic and medieval Catholic authors treated on the mystery of the Church, to be sure; but they provided no free-standing treatment *de ecclesia*. Bellarmine's is the first and the best of its kind. And yet, his writings–mostly composed in Latin–have remained largely unavailable to the English-speaking world until several years ago, when Mr. Ryan Grant began publishing superbly readable translations of the works of this great doctor. But why were Bellarmine's works available only in Latin for so many years?

There are two principal reasons for this. The first is that the theologians who needed to access them were scholars who had a command of the Latin language—something standard for Catholic theologians at least until the mid-1960s. For example, up to this time the final examinations for the licentiate and doctoral degrees in both philosophy and theology in the Church were administered orally and in Latin. And, of course, it is much better to read the writings of your primary sources in their original language instead of depending on the work of a translator. The second reason is more political and ideological in nature. St. Bellarmine, being the most prominent Catholic intellectual behind the counter-reformation, was viewed just before, during, and most certainly after Vatican II, as the prime example of the rigid, self-enclosed, anti-ecumenical, and anti-modern thinker that those inebriated with the ersatz spirit of Vatican II wanted to eschew. Those possessed of this mentality relegated Bellarmine and all early modern Catholic thinkers (and this includes the countless other venerable doctors such as Ligouri, De Sales, Suarez, Melchior Cano, among others) to the dust heap of Catholic history as "ghettoizing" throwbacks who foolishly clung to an untenable form of Catholic life and thought made irrelevant by the modern political and religious revolutions.

And yet these claims cannot stand. In fact, the Second Vatican Council itself vindicates St. Bellarmine's definition of the Church militant (the Church on earth) in article 14 of the "Dogmatic Constitution on the Church" where we read, "The bonds which bind men to the Church in a visible way are the profession of faith, the sacraments, and ecclesiastical government and communion." This is essentially how St. Bellarmine defines the Church on earth with in "De Ecclesia Militante," book 3, chapter 2, as translated by Mr. Grant: The Church is "that one and true ... body of men of the same Christian profession and of the same Sacraments gathered in communion, under the rule of legitimate pastors and especially of the one Vicar of Christ on Earth, the Roman Pontiff." Thus, the current English translation of Bellarmine's *De Ecclesia* is of inestimable value for those English-speaking students of Catholic theology who wish not only to understand properly the essence of the ecclesiology of Vatican II, but the official magisterial teaching of the Church on Her essence and mission as the sole institution established by our Lord for the salvation of souls and the glory of God.

On a personal note, for over a decade I have had to provide my ecclesiology students with my own translations of select portions of

St. Robert Bellarmine's treatise on the Church. With this and his other translations of St. Bellarmine's works on the Church, Mr. Grant has provided an unmatched service to the English-speaking world of Catholic theologians and students of theology. I strongly recommend this volume, along with his others in this series, as a principal text for teachers and students of Catholic ecclesiology. Mr. Grant's translation is precise and consummately readable. Let us look forward with hope to his further translation projects.

Steubenville, Ohio
June 6, 2016
Feast of St. Norbert

CHAPTER I
On the term "Church"

THE CONTROVERSY on the Church Militant has many parts. In the first place, what the Church itself is must be argued, and then on the members, that is, clergy, monks and laity. Again, the Church Militant must be considered according to what it is, and this is what we now hasten to dispute. There are three particular controversies: 1) On the term "Church" and its definition; 2) On the quality or the visibility of the Church; 3) On the marks whereby it can be known for certain.

We now commence with the first, but before we get too far into it we ought to note those who have written about the Church, or rather, whose books we have read since we have not read everything. So, the following authors have written on this point about the Church: St. Augustine;[12] St. Cyprian;[13] Optatus;[14] and from more recent authors who have written on this matter we have Thomas Waldens;[15] Juan Torquemada;[16] John Driedo;[17] Albert Pighius;[18] Cardinal Hosius in his confession, as well as in his explication of the Creed, and his *Contra prolegomena Brentii*, lib. 5;

---

[12] *De Unitate Ecclesiae.*

[13] *De Unitate Ecclesiae.*

[14] *Contra Parmenianum*, in six books.

[15] Lib. 2. *doctrin. fid.* cap. 8.9.10, etc.

[16] *Summam de Ecclesia.*

[17] in lib. 4 de dogm. Ecclesiast., cap. 2.

[18] *Controversia*, 3.

Pedro de Soto;[19] John of Daventria;[20] John Cochlaeus,[21] Johan Eck;[22] Alonso de Castro;[23] John of Louvain;[24] Francis Turrianus[25] and Melchior Cano.[26] After these, in the beginning of the year 1577, we disputed this very treatise (which we are now publishing) in the schools, and in that time Gregory of Valentia also wrote on the same issue[27] and others also wrote, but he was not free from other occupations to explain their books.

I come now to the proposed disputation, which is on the first point, the term "Church". The name is Greek and is deduced from the word εκκαλέώ, (*ekkaleō*), which means *I call out.* Therefore, Church is an evocation, or a body of those called out. Moreover, the people of God is a body of those called out, because no man joins himself to this people by himself and by his own instinct, but any whosoever that come have been preceded by the calling of God. For the calling is the first benefit, which the saints receive from God, as the Apostle says in Romans, "He called them and justified them, and glorified those whom he had justified."[28] The Apostle says often enough that Christians are called, in fact in nearly every epistle.

Moreover, three things must be noted on this term. 1) The name of Church can be joined with another thing, and can be received on the side of the good and the bad. For the Psalms speak of the

[19] 1 parte defensionis suae contra Brentium.

[20] in confut. 7 artic. Confessionis Augustanae.

[21] Philippica 4, et in lib. de Scripturae et Ecclesiae Auctoritrate.

[22] *Enchiridium.*

[23] lib. 6 contra haeres.

[24] In explicat. Symboli and all others who have written on the Creed.

[25] In two books de Ecclesia et ordinat. Ministr.

[26] *de Locis*, lib. 4.

[27] In his *Analysis fidei Catholicae*, parte 6.

[28] Romans 8:30.

"Church of the malignant,"[29] and "the Church of the Saints".[30] Moreover, this term is placed absolutely, it is not understood unless it is about the Church of Christ, with the exception of one passage, that is Acts 19 where it says about the people of the heathen "For the Church was confused."

2) Mark with St. Augustine, "God stood in the synagogue of the gods,"[31] although the Church of the Old Testament and the New are the same, nevertheless the state of the new Testament Church is by far more excellent, thus, the names are also distinct, for the people of the Old Testament are properly called the Synagogue, that is the congregation; but the people of the New Testament is never called the Synagogue, but always the Church, that is the evocation. To be gathered is common among both men and beasts, but to be called out is proper to men. It is not related that the people of the Jews in the Old Testament are also everywhere called the Church; for both the Synagogue and the Church are called in Hebrew by the word "congregation" חדע, [e-dah] which we translate into Synagogue, and is said to be from דעי [ya-ad] "to assign or gather". Likewise, לחק [qa-hal] that is "the Church," is said to come from from לחק, "to gather". Therefore there are two names, but they mean altogether the same thing.

3) It also must be noted that in the same way as the city on the one hand means a body of men, on the other the place in which that body lives, so also the Church in the Scriptures means the body of the faithful, as it says in Romans 16: "All the Churches of Asia greet you." Now, all the faithful are gathered in that very citation, just as in Judith 6: "every people prayed through the whole night within the Church," although we now only mean the body of the faithful when we dispute on the Church.

---

[29]Psal. 25(26).

[30]Psalm. 88 (89).

[31]*In Psal. 81 (82).*

CHAPTER II
On the Definition of the Church

THERE are five heretical opinions on the definition of the Church. The first is that the Church is the congregation of the predestined, so that only all those who have been predestined would constitute the Church. This is the opinion of John Wycliffe[1] and Jan Hus whose position is contained in a condemnation by the Council of Constance: "A man foreknown, although he might be in grace for a time according to the present justice, is still never part of the Holy Church whereas a man predestined will always remain a member of the Church, although at some time he may fall from the grace he has attained thus far, still not from the grace of predestination.[2]

The second is that the Church would be a multitude of perfect men having no sin. Certain Pelgians taught this, as St. Augustine relates where he says: "To it also come the Pelagians, in order to say that the life of the just in this world is entirely free from sin, and that the Church of Christ is formed of men of this kind in this mortal life."[3] Calvin attributes the same teaching to the Anabaptists of this time.[4]

The third is that the Church might be a congregation of the just, or better still those who have never failed to make the confession of faith. This is distinguished from the second opinion in that it excluded each and every sinner, but this does not exclude anyone except notable sinners. Formerly, St. Cyprian thought Novation was

[1]Quoted in Waldens, tom. 1, lib. 2, cap. 8.

[2]Artic. 1,2, 3, 5, 6 as is contained in the Council of Constance, sess. 15.

[3]*De haeresibus*, ca. 88.

[4]*Instit.*, lib. 4, cap. 1, §13.

the author of this opinion,[5] and Augustine the Donatists,[6] for I believe Calvin and others were deceived who thought that the followers of Novation and the Donatists excluded every kind of sinner. For, Cyprian and Epiphanius clearly say that they retained swindlers, adulterers and the like in the Church but only excluded those who had lapsed under persecution.[7] Moreover, what Ambrose[8] and Theodoret[9] say does not appear opposed to this, that the Novationists abolished the power of forgiving all sins, save for the lightest. For even if they did not absolve grave sinners they still retained them in their body unless they lapsed in the confession of faith. Augustine also teaches[10] that the Donatists did not abhor all sins, but only certain greater crimes; one that they objected to is that they thought Catholics were traitors to the divine books.

The fourth is of the Confessionists, who, although they condemn the Pelagians, Novationists and Donatists by name, still their opinion is a composite of those heresies. For: 1) Not only the Confessionists, but all Lutherans and Calvinists teach that there is no sin that is venial by nature, rather, all are in and of themselves mortal, but venial by the mercy of God, who does not impute these to believers. Luther teaches this[11] as well as Melanchthon[12] and Calvin.[13]

2) The Augsburg Confession, in article 7, teaches that the Church is the congregation of the Saints who truly believe and obey God. And Melanchthon, in his defense of it, tries to show that sinners do

---

[5]Lib. 1, epist. 2

[6]lib. *De Haeres.* cap. 69.

[7]Cyprian lib. 4, epist. 2; Epiphanius *in haeres. Catharorum.*

[8]lib. 1 *de poenitentia*, cap. 1-2.

[9]lib. 3 *de fabulis haereticorum.*

[10]*Contra Parmenianum*, lib. 3, cap. 2.

[11]*in assert.* art. 32.

[12]*In locis* cap. de discrimine peccati mortalis et venialis.

[13]*Instit.* lib. 2, cap. 8, §58 et 59.

not pertain to the Church except in name. John Brenz teaches similar things in the Prolegomena against Pedro de Soto. Nor is it opposed that Melanchthon and Brenz both say that the wicked are mixed with the good, for they in effect create two Churches. One that is true, and to which the privileges related in the Scriptures pertain; this is the congregation of the Saints who truly believe and obey God, and this one is not visible but can only be seen with the eyes of faith. The other is external, which is a Church in name only, and this is the congregation of men coming together in the doctrine of faith, and the use of the sacraments; in this the good and bad are discovered. Consequently, they never mean that the wicked are parts of the true Church and so Melanchthon cautiously does not say the Church consists from the wicked as well as the good, but says the wicked are mixed into the Church. Moreover, Brenz says that the wicked are in the Church in some manner, but they are not of the Church.

Luther in his work *de Conciliis et Ecclesia*, in the third part, says that the Church is the holy Christian people. That he might show himself to speak on the sanctity of each of the members, he tries to show the Pope and Cardinals are not of the Church because they are not holy. Therefore, if only the just are part of the true Church, and all sins, in so far as they are light, are mortal sins and make a man unjust; it follows that only the perfect and those lacking all sin are in the Church, which was the opinion of the Pelagians.

3) The Confessionists say, and in this they agree with all Lutherans, that all the works of man, even of the justified, are mortal sins. The *Augsburg Confession*[14] indicates this, but Luther more clearly asserts it in his *Assertions*,[15] whereby it seems to follow that no man is in the Church. For, if only the just are in the Church, and there are altogether no just in the world, and naturally when the works of every man are sins, who, I ask, will constitute the Church? But they easily explain the whole matter when they say the works of

[14] Articl. 6 & 20.

[15] artc. 32.

the just are all mortal sins, but still they are not imputed to them if they have the faith, and hence he who has faith, at the same time is the most just and also sins by every work. In some manner the Confessionists agree with the Donatists and the Novationists. For, as they did not exclude all sinners from the Church, but only those who committed idolatry, so the former do not exclude all sinners, but only those who do not truly believe. For they think, as we said, that no crime is imputed to believers.

The fifth opinion seems to have been raked together from all these. For it teaches that the Church is constituted from the predestined. Thus Calvin taught three things in this regard. 1) Once someone has faith, he can never be damned, and furthermore all who have the faith are necessarily predestined. He holds this in the *Institutes*,[16] but the ancient heretic Jovinian expressly taught this same thing in the ancient Church, as we see from St. Jerome.[17] 2) He also teaches that the true Church can be recognized by God alone since its foundation is divine election, because it is constituted from the faithful, who are necessary from the number of the elect.[18] 3) he teaches besides a certain external Church, wherein the good and the bad dwell, as the Confessionsts said above, he holds in the same book and chapter, in the subsequent sections. Martin Bucer seems to think the same thing and he defines the kingdom of Christ as the charge of salvation of the elect of God, whom God has gathered on earth.[19] Tilman Hesch teaches the same thing.[20]

The Catholic teaching is that the Church is only one, not two, and that the body of men of the same Christian profession and of the same Sacraments gathered in communion is one and true, under the rule of legitimate pastors and especially of the one Vicar of Christ on Earth, the Roman Pontiff. From such a definition it can be clearly

---

[16]lib. 3, ca. 2, §8-11.

[17]*Contra Iovinianum*, lib. 2.

[18]*Instit.*, lib. 3, cap. 1, §2 and to a lesser degree in cap. 8, §4 et sequentibus.

[19]*De regno Christi*, lib. 1, cap. 5.

[20]*De erroribus Pontificorum*, locus 12; *de Ecclesia*, lib. 1, cap. 3.

understood which men pertain to the Church and which do not. For there are three parts of this definition; the profession of the true faith, the communion of the Sacraments, and subjection to the legitimate pastor, the Roman Pontiff. By the reasoning of the first all infidels and those who have never entered the Church are excluded, such as Jews, Turks, and Pagans; then those who were in the Church but left, such as heretics and apostates. By the reasoning of the second part, all Catechumens and excommunicates are excluded, because they have not been admitted to the communion of the Sacraments, these are sent out; by reasoning of the third, all schismatics are excluded, that is those who have the faith and the Sacraments, but are not under the legitimate pastor, and therefore profess the faith and receive the Sacraments outside of the Church. Yet, all others, even the base, wicked and impious are included.

This is the difference between our teaching and all others, that all others require external virtues to constitute someone in the Church, and for that reason they make the Church invisible; but even though we believe all virtues (e.g. faith, hope and charity and the rest), are discovered in the Church, still that someone could absolutely be called part of the true Church, on which the Scriptures speak, we do not think any internal virtue is required, but only the external profession of faith, as well as the communion of the Sacraments which is taken up in that sense. For the Church is a body of men that is just as visible and palpable as the body of the Roman people, or the Kingdom of France, or the Republic of Venice.

Furthermore, it must be noted with Augustine,[21] that the Church is a living body in which there is a soul and body, and in the soul there are internal gifts of the Holy Spirit, namely Faith, Hope and Charity, etc. The body is the external profession of faith as well as the communication of the Sacraments. From there it happens that some men are in the soul and body of the Church and furthermore are united to Christ the head inwardly and outwardly, and such are perfectly in the Church, since they are as living members in the

[21] *Breviculus collation.*, collat. 3.

body, although among them are also some who participate more or less in the life of the Church, and some even who might hold only the beginning of life like a sense but not a motion, just as those who only have faith without charity. Again, some might be in the soul of the Church and not in the body, such as Catechumens or the excommunicated if they might have faith and charity, which can happen. Then, some may be in the body, but not the soul, such as those who have no internal virtue, and still by hope, or by some temporal fear profess the faith and communicate in the Sacraments under the rule of their pastors, and such are like hairs or nails, or bad humors in the human body.

Therefore, our definition holds true in this last manner of being in the Church, because this at least is required, that one can be said to be apart of the visible Church. Therefore, it must in the proper order be proved that the following do not pertain to the Church: the unbaptized, heretics, apostates, excommunicates and schismatics. Next, that those who are not predestined do in fact pertain to the Church, along with the imperfect and also manifest sinners; then lastly, secret heretics, if they would have the Sacraments as well as the profession of faith and subjection to the Church, etc.

CHAPTER III
On the Unbaptized

PAUL certainly speaks about the unbaptized infidels when he says,[1] "Why do you ask me to judge concerning those who are outside?" He says generally in that passage that they are outside who did not give their names for Christ through Baptism, but followed some other religions.

On Catechumens, there is a somewhat greater difficulty because they are faithful, and can be saved if they die in that state but still no man can be saved outside the Church, just as no one could outside of the ark of Noah, according to that which is held in the first chapter of the Lateran Council (III): "The universal Church of the faithful is one, outside of which altogether no one is saved." But just the same, it is certain that Catechumens are not in the Church properly and by act, but only in potency, just as in the way a man being conceived but not yet formed and born is not called a man, except in potency. For we read in Acts II: "Therefore those who received the word were baptized and on that day around three thousand were added." Likewise, the Council of Florence in the instruction of the Armenians teaches that men become members of Christ and concern the body of the Church when they are baptized, and the Fathers teach likewise.

St. Gregory Nazianzen, in his oration on holy Baptism, says that Catechumens are in the vestibule of piety, but still they cannot be called faithful unless they enter in through Baptism. John Chrysostom says that Catechumens are foreign to the faithful and have nothing in common with them, not citizenship, nor table, etc.[2] Tertullian in the *Praescriptiones*, condemns among the heretics those that refused to distinguish the Catechumens from the faithful. Cyril

[1] 1 Cor. 5:12.

[2] hom. 24 in Ioannem.

teaches that Catechumens are with Christians just as the uncircumcised were among the Jews, who on that account could not feed on the Paschal lamb.[3] Augustine distinguished Catechumens from the faithful, which other Fathers also do.[4] Moreover, it is certain that the Church is the body of the faithful.

Therefore, Catechumens do not have the right to any sacraments, nor to other things which are common to the universal Church. Therefore Catechumens do not pertain to the Church properly or in act. Therefore, how, you will ask, are they saved, if they are outside the Church? The author of the book on Ecclesiastical dogmas (cap. 74) clearly responds, that Catechumens are not saved. But this seems too harsh. Certainly St. Ambrose in his oration on the death of Valentinian affirms with clear words that Catechumens (in which Valentinian was numbered) can be saved when they have departed from this life.

Therefore, there is another solution. Melchior Cano says that Catechumens can be saved because even if they are not of the Church, which properly is called Christian, still they are part of the Church which embraces all the faithful from Abel even to the consummation of the world. But this does not seem to satisfy. For after the coming of Christ there is no true Church but that which is properly called Christian; consequently, if Catechumens are not in it, they are in nothing.

Consequently, I respond that it is said outside the Church no man is saved, and this ought to be understood on those who are neither in fact nor in desire within the Church, just as all the Theologians commonly teach on Baptism. Moreover, if the Catechumens are not in the Church *de facto*, at least they are in the Church in desire, therefore they can be saved. This is not opposed to the similitude of the Ark of Noah (outside of which no man was saved), even if he were in it by desire since similitudes do not agree in all things. For

---

[3]Lib. 12 in Ioan., cap. 50.

[4]Tract 4 in Ioannem and elsewhere,

that reason, 1 Peter 3 compares Baptism to the ark of Noah and still it is certain that some are saved without Baptism in fact.

But, one might say, Augustine says that Catechumens are in the Church;[5] it is true, but in the same place he separates them from the faithful. Therefore, he meant that they are in the Church not by act, but by potency, which he explains in the beginning of the 2nd book on the Creed, where he compares Catechumens to men who are conceived but not yet born.

---

[5]Tract. 4 in Ioannem.

CHAPTER IV
On Heretics and Apostates

ALONSO DE CASTRO teaches that heretics and baptized apostates are members and parts of the Church, even if they openly profess a false doctrine.[1] Such an opinion is clearly false, and it can easily be refuted. 1) Scripture shows this, since in 1 Timothy 1:19 it says that certain men are shipwrecked in regard to the faith. In that passage, it understands heretics by means of a metaphor of a shipwreck, after being broken from one part of the boat of the Church, after which they sink into the sea, which also is meant by the Lord's parable of the net which is torn before the multitude.[2] Besides, to Titus he says, "after a heretic has been given one or two corrections, knowing that he is subversive, who is of this sort, he has been condemned by his own judgment." There the Apostle commands the Bishop that he should avoid heretics, because certainly he would not command it if they were within the Church. For a shepherd ought not avoid those whom he has care of when they pertain to his own flock. And he adds the reason that such a pertinacious heretic is condemned by his own judgment, that is (as Jerome explains it), he has not been thrown out of the Church by excommunication, as many other sinners, but he cast himself out of the Church. Likewise, 1 John II says, "They went out from us, but they were not from among us," in other words, they went out from us because they were with us in the same Church but they were not from us according to divine election, as St. Augustine explains.[3]

2) This is proved from the 18th and 19th chapter of the Council of Nicaea, where heretics are said to be able to be received in the Church if they wish to return to it, although under certain

---

[1] *De Justa haereticorum punitione*, lib. 2, cap. 2.

[2] Luke 5.

[3] *de bono persever.*, cap. 8.

conditions. In like manner, from the chapter *Firmiter* of the Lateran Council, on the Supreme Trinity and the Catholic Faith, where the Church is called the congregation of the faithful. It is certain that heretics are not in any manner among the faithful.

3) From the Fathers, Irenaeus says that Polycarp converted many heretics to the Church,[4] whence it follows that beforehand they had gone out from the Church. Tertullian says that when Marcion wanted to rejoin the Church, he received the same condition as the others that he had perverted, that he should be restored to the Church.[5] Cyprian says, in an epistle to Jubaianum, that heretics, although they are outside the Church, still claim the power of the Church for themselves after the fashion of apes who, although they are not men, nevertheless wish to appear as men.

Jerome says, in his Dialogue against the Luciferians, "If you will have heard anywhere some who are called "Christs", not by the Lord Jesus Christ, but by some other name, as the Marcionists, Valentinians, Montanists, or Campenses, know that this is not the Church of Christ, but it is the Synagogue of Antichrist."

St. Augustine says sometimes it may happen that a heretic who is outside the Church might not act against it, while a Catholic inside the Church might act against it.[6] And in his book on the Unity of the Church, chapter IV: "Those who do not believe that Christ came in the flesh from the Virgin Mary, from the seed of David or that he rose in his own body in which he was crucified and buried, indeed they are not in the Church."

Lastly, it happens that when the Church was a united multitude (for a certain people are either a kingdom, or one body) and this particular union consists in the profession of the one faith, the observance of the same laws and rights; no reason permits that we might say they are of the body of the Church who have altogether no union with it.

---

[4] Lib. 3, cap. 3.

[5] *De Praescriptionibus.*

[6] *Contra Donatistas*, lib. 4, cap. 10.

On the other hand, some object firstly with what is said in Matthew on the parable of the cockle the three that are discovered in the same field, wheat, the husks and the chaff, which mean good Catholics, bad Catholics and heretics, as Augustine[7] and Jerome explain on this passage, as well as Chrysostom. Moreover, the Church would be sick, as Cyprian[8] and Augustine[9] teach.

I respond: Some understand through cockle not heretics but wicked men who are in the Church. Thus Cyprian (loc. cit.) and often Augustine,[10] speaking not so much from his own opinion as much as by the mind of Cyprian. Moreover, the fact is Cyprian does not understand heretics by cockle, thereupon it can be understood that in those citations, where he says the cockle is in the Church, he says that heretics are not in the Church. Besides, the fact is made plain from the intention of Cyprian who writes in those places against the Novatianists, who refused to admit the lapsed penitents into the Church, fearing lest they might communicate their sins with others. Cyprian showed them that by the Lord's parable there are not only strong men in the Church but also weak who fall at some point, just as the cockle is in the field at the same time as the grain.

But although such an exposition might not be condemned and is not contrary to our position, nevertheless it seems better to respond with what Augustine says, that the field does not mean the Church, but the whole world.[11] For the Lord, explaining the parable, says the field is the world. Hence, by the name of "cockle," although heretics are rightly understood, still perhaps we might understand it more literally as all the wicked in general, whether they be heretics or not. The scope of the parable, therefore, is to show that there were always going to be some wicked men in the world, nor can any human diligence cleanse the world before the day of judgment. For

---

[7]Quaest. 11 super Matthaeum.

[8]Lib. 3, epist. 3.

[9]Lib. 2, *Contra Cresconium*, cap. 34.

[10]Lib. 4, ep. 2.

[11]Quest. 11 super Matthaeum.

that reason, the Lord says that the cockle are the wicked sons, and all those who at length will be cast into eternal fire.

Secondly, they object with the verse in 2 Timothy 2:20, "In a great house there are vessels, some golden, some silver, some wooden, and some clay." There by the name *house* it seems that Paul understands the Church and by the name of the wooden and clay vessels, heretics. Thus he said a little earlier: "Their word creeps like a crab, from which are Hymnaeus and Philetus who are cut off from the truth."[12] Moreover, the house is understood as the Church which Cyprian,[13] Ambrose (in his commentary on this passage), and Augustine[14] teach.

I respond: This varies in the expositions of the Fathers. One is of the Greek Fathers, Chrysostom and Theophylactus who understand by the word house not the Church, but the world just as we said about the field in which there is cockle. The other is of the Latins, Cyprian, Ambrose and Augustine, who understand the house to be the Church. Although Augustine and Ambrose would have it that the wood and clay vessels represent heretics, nevertheless Augustine explains that same passage must be understood in the sense that they are in the Church, when he says they are in it before they are separated from it by obstinacy and pertinacity, and this is the time the Apostle considers, so that they are not heretics as much as they are said to be erring in the Church.[15] He also adds that it can be said they are in the Church after they have left it, on account of the administration of the Sacraments, because even they truly administer some sacraments. In other words, they are in the Church according to something, not on their own account. Ambrose receives it as the Church in a broad sense that is more common than proper, according to how it embraces all who are named Christians in any

[12] 2 Tim. 2:17.

[13] Lib. 3, epist 3; lib. 4 epist. 2.

[14] Lib. 4 de Baptismo, cap. 12.

[15] *De Baptismo*, lib. 3, cap. 19.

manner, in the same way that the Pagans usually said that in the body of Christians there are many opposed opinions and sects.

But according to Cyprian (whose explanation I reckon is more true), through wooden and clay vessels heretics are not understood, but the weak and frail who are easily seduced. When the Apostle says that in a great house there are vessels of gold, silver, etc., he is not referring to "whose word lurks like a crab", whereby Hymnaeus and Philetus are cut off from the truth, but to the part where he says: "And they overturn the faith of some men." The Apostle means that if they overturn some, they are not a danger for this reason, lest all would be overturned. For in the Church there are the strong and the weak, etc.

But one might say that Augustine, who understands heretics by the wooden and clay vessels, says he is moved to think this by Cyprian's words in his epistle to Antioninus, which is the second of book 4.

I respond: Augustine thought these words of the Apostle were related by Cyprian: "In a great house there are golden vessels, etc.," referred to the verse "whose word creeps like a crab," just as he says. Moreover, the words of Cyprian do not sound that way, and Cyprian correctly did not mean that heretics are in the Church, as is clear from the same epistle, where he clearly says that Novation is outside of the Church because he is a heretic.

Thirdly, the argument is made that the Church can judge and punish heretics, therefore they are within it, "For what is it to me to judge those who are on the outside?"[16] Besides, heretics retain the character of Baptism and priesthood, therefore they are Christians and priests.

I respond: Although heretics are not in the Church, nevertheless they ought to be; hence they pertain to her like sheep to the sheepfold when they roam outside the sheepfold. The Church can judge concerning those who are inside by that very fact, or who ought to be, just as a pastor really can judge and compel the sheep

[16] 1 Cor. 5:12.

who wander outside of the sheepfold through the mountains to return to it. In the same way, a general can compel by force a deserter from the army who has fled across to the camp of the enemy to return or even to hang him. The Apostle, on the other hand, speaks on those who were never truly in the Church.

Now I speak to that which relates to the character. Heretics retain those indelible characters outside of the Church, just as lost sheep retain the branding in their back and deserters of the army military signs: but they are not in the Church for that reason because those characters do not suffice to constitute someone in the Church; otherwise the Church would also be in hell. St. Thomas Aquinas says that the damned are not members of Christ in either act or potency.[17] Besides, the character does not properly unite a man with the head, rather it is a sign of the power of a certain union, and consequently, in hell they are recognized by that sign as men who were members of Christ. Nevertheless, that it does not unite them is clear since something that is invisible cannot unite outwardly, nor interiorly when it is not in act or when it is not an operative habit. For that reason St. Thomas places the first internal union in faith.

---

[17]III, Q. 8, art. 3.

CHAPTER V
On Schismatics

SEVERAL Catholics deliberate whether schismatics are in the Church, on the other hand there are those who affirm that they are in the Church, such as Alonso de Castro in the place we cited. Yet it is easy to teach the contrary from the Scripture and from the tradition of the Fathers. In the first place, when it is said in Luke that the nets were torn,[1] schisms in the Church are understood through the tearing of the nets and the exit of the fish from it, and the exit of heretics and schismatics, as St. Augustine explains.[2]

Besides, Scripture calls the Church, "One sheepfold,"[3] "One body,"[4] "One spouse, friend and dove."[5] Moreover, schism tears that which was one into parts, as is clear from its very name, as σχιζειν [schizein] is to tear, and σχισμή [schismē] means a tear. Consequently, schismatics are not in the Church nor are they of the Church. For the part that is torn from the body is no longer a part of that body. For that reason Cyprian beautifully says that the Church is signified through the seamless garment of Christ which was not torn, that we might understand the Church can be torn, but not in that manner in which a garment is torn, so that some parts remain equally part of the garment, but how a branch is torn from a tree, which dies right away while the tree still lives.[6] In like manner, he adds it is similar to a river from its source which soon dries up while the source flows, and the ray from the sun, which fails right away while the sun remains as it was. Or, if one were to contend that the

---

[1]Luke 5:6.

[2]Tract. 122 *in Ioannem.*

[3]John 10:16.

[4]Rom. 12:5.

[5]Cant. 6:8.

[6]*De Unitate Ecclesiae.*

part torn from the Church is also a certain Church, then he would make many Churches; but that is against the Scriptures recently cited.

Secondly it is proved from the decrees of Pope Pelagius, who clearly proves that schismatics are not part of the Church.[7] Moreover, the testimony of the whole Church witnesses the fact, since on Good Friday it prays for heretics and schismatics that God would deign to recall them to the Catholic Church, which would not be the case if it believed they were in the Church. The testimony of the Roman Catechism also pertains to this, which is of no scanty authority in the Church of God. Thus the Catechism separates schismatics from the Church in its explanation of the Creed.[8]

Thirdly, it is proved from the Fathers. Irenaeus, after he had said earlier in his work that a spiritual man judges all heretics and schismatics and had enumerated them into many particular heresies, he also had added them under those properly called schismatic, and he concludes in the end: "He will judge all those who are outside the truth, that is outside the Church."[9] St. Cyprian says, "The people has been joined to the priest even as the flock adheres to its shepherd, for that reason you ought to know that the Bishop is in the Church and the Church in the Bishop, and if there would be someone who is not with the bishop, he is not in the Church."[10] But certainly schismatics are not with the Bishop; therefore they are not in the Church.

Chrysostom said, "The meaning of schism convicts them enough, or rather more its name is enough to strike them, since they had not become many parts, rather the one had perished. For they constituted these many into whole Churches."[11] And in another homily he teaches that schismatics are like a hand that is cut from

---

[7]24.q.1, can. *Pudenda*, et can. *Schisma*.

[8]*Catechism of the Council of Trent*, Part I: The Creed, Article IX.

[9]Lib. 4, cap. 62.

[10]Lib. 4, epist. 9 ad Florentium Papianum.

[11]Hom. 3 in 1 Cor.

the body which soon ceases to be a member and he says in the same place that schismatics are in another Church even if they agree with the true Church of Christ in faith and doctrines.[12]

Jerome says, "Schismatics really separate a deceived multitude from the Church of God; still they do not do this from belief, as heretics do."[13] And again, "We hold this is between heresy and schism, because a heresy holds a perverse doctrine, but schism equally separates from the Church by reason of Episcopal dissension."[14] There note the word *equally.*

Augustine says: "We believe in the Holy *Catholic* Church, since even the heretics and schismatics call their congregations "Churches", but the heretics violate faith in God by believing false things, while the schismatics leap from fraternal charity by wicked dissensions, even if they believe what we believe. For that very reason neither the heretic pertains to the Catholic Church because he loves God nor the schismatic because he loves his neighbor."[15]

Optatus of Miletus, speaking of schismatics, says: "After deserting their Catholic mother, the wicked sons run about outside of her and separate themselves, as you have done, being cut off from the root of the hated mother Church by sickles, like rebels who recede by wandering away."[16] In book 2 of that work he compares schismatics with branches, rivers and rays cut off from the tree, font and sun. Fulgentius says: "Hold most firmly and do not by any means doubt that not only Pagans but also Jews, heretics and schismatics who end the present life outside the Catholic Church are

---

[12]Hom. 11 in epistolam ad Ephesios.

[13]In Caput Primum Amos.

[14]in cap. 3 ad Titum.

[15]*De Fide et Symbolo*, cap. 10.

[16]*Contra Parmenianum*, lib. 1.

going into the eternal fire."[17] Next Thomas Waldens holds the same thing,[18] as well as John Driedo,[19] and other more recent writers.

Lastly, it is proven from reason. From the very notion of what the Church is, that it is one in regard to the union of members within her, and with her head, but schism abolishes this union since it separates itself from communion with the head and other members. Moreover the essential unity of the Church consists in that union of that joining of the members among and with the head is proven, since there is a manifold unity discovered in the Church. 1) The unity of the same beginning; that is the calling of God. "No one comes to me, etc."[20] 2) The unity by reason of the same final end, which is signified in Matthew 20 in that one denarius promised to all the workers. 3) By reason of the same means, that is the Faith, Sacraments, and laws according to what is said in Ephesians 4, "One faith, one baptism." 4) By unity of the same Holy Spirit, by whom the Universal Church is steered as if by an external and separate Captain, "There are divisions of grace, but the same Spirit."[21] 5) By reason of the same head, just as an internal and continuous Captain; for every Church obeys the same Christ and his vicar just like a head, "He gave the him as the head over the whole Church,"[22] and, "Simon Peter, feed my sheep."[23] 6) By reason of the connection of the members among themselves and especially with the head as the principal member, "We are one body, each one members of another."[24]

---

[17] *De fide ad Petrum*, cap. 38 et 39.

[18] 1 lib. 2, cap. 9 doctrinalis fidei antiquae.

[19] Lib. 4 de Scripturis et dogmatibus Ecclesiasticis, cap. 2, part. 2.

[20] John 6.

[21] 1 Cor. 12:4.

[22] Ephesians 1:22.

[23] John 21.

[24] Romans 12:5.

Moreover, among these unities we have enumerated that properly make one Church there are two ends. By the first, the Church is not one as much as it is from one. By the second, it is not as much one as to one. By the third it is not as much one as through one. By the fourth it is not as much one as under one. By the fifth and sixth, it is properly one, that is one body, one people and one society. Schism, however, is opposed to these last unities; consequently there is schism when one member refuses to be any longer a member of that body, nor under the head, this is the reason why it abolishes the essential unity and also the Church herself; therefore a schismatic is not of the Church.

Now they object: 1) The Church is a congregation of Catholics, as Pope Nicholas defined (*De Consecrat.*, distinctione prima, can. Ecclesia), But schismatics are Catholics, therefore they are of the Church.

I respond: Firstly, even if schismatics have the Catholic faith, nevertheless, they cannot properly be called Catholics even if they profess the faith in the Catholic Church, as is clear from the citations we provided from St. Augustine and Optatus. I say secondly, this is not the full definition of Pope Nicholas, nor did he mean to define the Church but only exclude heretics from the Church. Just as Innocent did when he said that the Church is the congregation of the faithful.[25]

They object 2) Even if schismatics refuse to submit to the Pope, nevertheless they mean to submit to Christ the Supreme Head, and although they refuse to communicate with this Church on earth, nevertheless, they mean to communicate with the Church that is in heaven, namely the better part of the Church, therefore they do not abolish the unity of the Church nor are they absolutely outside it. This argument is confirmed from like things. For if anyone would refuse to be under his particular Bishop nor communicate with that particular Church under that Bishop, and nevertheless he means to

---

[25] cap. *Firmiter, de Summa Trinitate et fide Catholica.*

be under the Roman Pontiff and communicates with the universal Church, he cannot be said to be outside the Church.

I respond: No man can be under Christ and communicate with the Church who is not subject to the Pope and is not in communion with the Church militant—even if he wishes to be. For Christ said, "He who hears you, hears me," (Luke 10:16) and besides, just as Christ is the supreme head in regard to the interior life (since he breaths sense and motion into his members, that is faith and charity), so the Pope is the supreme head over the Church militant, in regard to the exterior life of the doctrine and the sacraments. Furthermore, the Church triumphant is united, nay more, it is one with the Church militant, and hence no man can be separated from one without being separated from the other.

In a similar fashion I respond with a confirmation. One who separates himself from a particular Church and Bishop is necessarily separated from the Church and the universal Bishop (unless perhaps someone had done it because that particular Church and its bishop were heretics or schismatics). For Cyprian rightly says, "They deceive themselves in vain, who, not having peace with the priests of God, creep and believe that they secretly communicate with the Church, which is Catholic and one and that it would not be torn nor divided but really is the connection of those adhering to each other and joined with the glue of the priests.[26]

---

[26]Lib. 4, ep. 9.

CHAPTER VI
On the Excommunicated

CONCERNING the Excommunicated, the Roman Catechism teaches they are not in the Church.[1] Furthermore, Thomas Waldens,[2] Juan Torquemada,[3] John Driedo[4] and several others teach the same thing. It is proven first from what we read in Matthew 18:17, "If they will not listen to the Church, let him be to you as a heathen and a tax-collector." There the Lord speaks about the excommunicated according to the exposition of all. Heathens are not in the Church. Likewise we see in 1 Corinthinas, "Have you not rather not mourned that he is taken away from your midst, that did such a thing? ... Do you not know that a little leaven corrupts the whole mass? ... Put away the evil one from yourselves."[5] With these words, the Apostle describes what it means to be excommunicated. For he bids anyone to be excommunicated who would have the wife of his father.

Secondly it is proved from Canon law, "It is canonically established, following the examples of the holy Fathers, that we eliminate violators of the Church of God from the lap of holy mother the Church and the consort with the whole Christian world by the authority of God and the judgment of the Holy Spirit."[6]

Thirdly from the Fathers. Eusebius, relating the extent to which Pope Victor had excommunicated all the Galatians says, "He sent a letter in which he separated everyone at the same time without

[1] Part I, *In explication of the Creed*, Article IX.

[2] *Doctr. fid. antiquae*, tom. 1, lib. 2, cap. 9.

[3] *Summae de Ecclesia*, lib. 1, cap. 3.

[4] *De Script. et dogmatibus Ecclesiasticis*, lib. 4, cap. 2, part. 2

[5] 1 Cor. 5:2, 6, 13.

[6] 11, q. 3, can. *Canonica.*

distinction from Ecclesiastical union.... Irenaeus argued with Victor because it was not right to cut so many and such Churches from the unity of the body."[7] Epiphanius, speaking about Marcion (who had professed virginity prior to becoming a heretic and nevertheless violated a woman who also had professed virginity and consequently was excommunicated by his father), said, "He was ejected from the Church by his own father, for his father was famous due to the excellence of his piety and persevered living honestly in the ministry of the episcopate."[8]

Hilary, commenting on that verse, "Let him be to you as a heathen and a tax-collector," says that God did that very thing with the people of Israel as Christ advises must be done. Firstly, he corrected the people between him and it alone, when he appeared to them with majesty on mount Sinai. Secondly, he applied two witnesses to himself, that is the Law and the Prophets. Third, he spoke to the Church, that is, he sent Christ as the Supreme Prelate of the Church who reproached the Jews. Lastly, when they did not listen to the prelate of the Church, he neglected them and left them behind, just as the heathen and the tax-collectors. With such words he showed that through excommunication a man becomes just as a heathen and a tax-collector, cast out from the people of God, and no longer governed by that peculiar providence whereby the Church is governed.

Chrysostom and Theophylactus explain on this citation that one is said to be cast out from the Church because he becomes as a heathen and a tax-collector. Jerome says that some sinners are pushed outside the Church through the excommunications of bishops and become heretics and schismatics by their very own will. Augustine says that those who are excommunicated are visibly cut from the body of the Church.[9] Likewise he says that through excommunication diseased sheep are separated from the healthy lest

---

[7] *Historiae*, lib. 5, cap. 24.

[8] Haeres. 42, which is of Marcion.

[9] Lib. *de unitate Ecclesiae*, last chapter.

dangerous plagues creep through a great many of them.[10] This opinion is cited by Augustine: "Every Christian who is excommunicated by priests is handed over to Satan. How? Because obviously the devil is outside the Church, just as Christ is in the Church."[11] Anselm subscribes to this when says that a man is handed over to Satan that is pushed out of the Church through excommunication.[12]

Lastly it is proven by reason. Firstly, by excommunication men are deprived from all the spiritual privileges that men in the Church have, as Tertullian teaches;[13] consequently they are no longer in the body of the Church. What is it for some citizen to be deprived of his city except to be deprived of all privileges that are due to men of that city? Secondly, excommunication has that place in the Church that the death penalty had in the Old Testament as well as in the temporal commonwealth. Yet, through death men are clearly separated from the whole commonwealth. Augustine says, "Excommunication now does in the Church what death did formerly."[14] There he compares what is said in Deuteronomy 24:7, "You will abolish the evil one from your midst," with what Paul says, "Remove the wicked man from your presence."[15] Thirdly, there is no penalty that the Church can inflict that is more severe than excommunication, as St. Augustine teaches,[16] therefore by excommunication a man is cast out from the Church. It is more serious to be cast from the Church than any penalty you like that remains for the Church to take up.

Fourthly, excommunication can not be imposed except upon those who are contumacious and incorrigible, as St. Augustine

---

[10] *De Corrept. et Gratia*, cap. 15.

[11] 11, quaest. 11, 3 can. Omnis.

[12] In 1 Cor. V.

[13] *Apologeticus*, cap. 39.

[14] Quaest. 39 in Deuteron.

[15] 1 Cor. V:13.

[16] *De Correptione et Gratia*, cap. 15.

teaches.[17] And indeed, even all Theologians deduce this from that passage of Matthew 18:17 which we have been citing. Consequently, excommunication is the ejection from the Church; for if excommunication were to be imposed for some penalty short of ejection, it would also be imposed in every degree whatsoever upon murderers, adulterers and other malefactors even if they are not contumacious. Add to this that when the excommunicates are absolved, it is said: "Now you have been restored to the unity of the Church and the participation of the members." That is a clear sign that the excommunicates were separated from the unity of the Church.

But some object to the contrary. First, an excommunicated man remains baptized, retains the profession of faith and the subjection of the legitimate prelate, and to the extent that he is a friend of God, if he will be unjustly excommunicated then the excommunicate can also justly do penance and have those three before he is absolved, therefore he will be in the Church, even while remaining excommunicated.

I respond: Such a person is in the Church by his mind, or by desire, which suffices to salvation, but still not in the body or the external communion which properly causes a man to be in this visible Church which is on Earth. Augustine says, "Often divine providence may permit that even good men may be expelled from the Christian congregation. If men will bear such contumely or injury very patiently for the peace of the Church, nor will have created any novelties, schisms or heresies then they will teach men how truly God must be served by good will and by such genuine charity. The Father who sees in secret will crown men of this sort in secret."[18]

---

[17] *De Vera Religione*, cap. 6.

[18] *De Vera Religione*, cap. 6.

Secondly, our adversaries raise objections because Augustine says, "And we do not separate from the people of God those whom we reduce to a lower place by degradation or excommunication."[19]

I respond: I suspect this passage has been corrupted and thus the phrase "And we do not separate from the people of God," must be picked out, since what follows after that is, "And we are not allowed to do this for the sake of peace and tranquility of the Church, still we do not so neglect the Church, but we tolerate that which we refuse to arrive where we wish, using the precaution of the Lord's precept, lest we might wish to gather the cockle before its time and eradicate the wheat with it." But if this passage has not been corrupted then the response can be made that through the words, "the people of God," not only the Church militant is understood but the absolute number of those going to be saved, whether they might be in the Church or whether they can be; since by excommunication pastors do not intend to separate men from the number of those who can be saved, but rather more to help them to salvation by that correction.

Our adversaries object thirdly that excommunication is a type of spiritual medicine established for the assistance of those who are excommunicated. For this reason the Apostle says, "But if any man does not obey our word by epistle, mark such a man lest you keep company with him so that he shall be ashamed."[20]

I respond: Excommunication, even if it tears a man from the Church, nevertheless does not take away potency so that he cannot again be inserted into the Church when he is cut off from it if he should do penance. Therefore, the Church, through excommunication, separates certain men from its body, but for their sake because she desires them to be humbled by that shame, and once humbled then received again into the body of the Church.

---

[19] *Contra Donatistas*, cap. 20.

[20] 2 Thess. 3:14.

CHAPTER VII
On the Predestined

MOREOVER, the fact that not only the predestined but even the reprobate can pertain to the Church (contrary to Wycliffe and Calvin) must be proved. 1) From the very clear parables of the Lord. In Matthew the Church is compared with a threshing floor, "He will clear his threshing floor and will gather the wheat into his barn, but he will burn the chaff in the inextinguishable fire."[1] Certainly the term "threshing floor" cannot be understood except about the Church, in which the threshing floor is discovered, but the part about the inextinguishable fire cannot be understood about the elect. Later in Matthew he compares the net let down in the sea that gathers every kind of fish but at length some of them are sent into the furnace of fire,[2] but that certainly is not said about the predestined.

Later in Matthew's Gospel the nuptial dinner is compared to that in which the good and the wicked enter and afterward the wicked do not have the nuptial garment and are cast into exterior darkness. Then the Lord concludes it saying, "Many are called but few are chosen,"[3] *i.e.*, many are in the Church, which is a certain evocation, or the body of those called who still are of the elect. Likewise he compares it to ten virgins, of whom the five prudent will enter the nuptials with the spouse on the day of judgment, but the five foolish will be excluded.[4] In the same place it is compared to a sheepfold in which there are sheep and goats and the former, as the Lord himself explains, are the elect while the latter are the reprobate.[5] Paul bids

[1]Matthew 3:12.

[2]Matthew 13:47-50.

[3]Matthew 22:14.

[4]Matthew 25:1-12.

[5]Matthew 25:33.

the incestuous to be expelled from the Church,[6] and still he could not cause him to be cast out from the predestined, nor did he will it, since he cast him out that, having been humbled, he would return and be saved on the day of the Lord, as he says in the same place.[7] Likewise in 2 Timothy 2:20 he says, "In a great house there are vessels, some gold and silver, some wooden and made of clay, some in glory and some in contumely." There does not seem to be a doubt that the vessels in glory are the elect while the vessels in contumely are the reprobate even though they are in the same house.

St. Cyprian confirms the same thing[8] and he clearly teaches that in the Church there are wheat and cockle, as well as golden and wooden vessels, since it is certain that the cockle is burned and the wooden vessels are in contumely. Moreover St. Augustine says, "According to foreknowledge and predestination how many sheep are outside and how many wolves inside?"[9] There he says that many predestined are outside the Church and many reprobates are within it.

Besides, the examples of Paul and Judas agree with it. Jan Hus said that Paul was always in the Church but Judas was never in it. On the other hand, Paul himself says that he had persecuted the Church of God, just as Luke affirms.[10] Therefore I ask, was the Church which Paul persecuted the true Church, or it was not? If the true Church, then Paul was not a member of the true Church at some point. For how was he of the Church which he opposed with all his strength? If that was not the true Church, then Paul and Luke lie when they unreservedly call it the Church of God.

---

[6]1 Cor. 5:1-3.

[7]1 Cor. 5:5.

[8]Lib. 3, epist. 3; lib. 4, epist. 2.

[9]Tract. 45 in Ioannem. He repeats the same thing in *Contra Cresconium*, lib. 2, cap. 34.

[10]1 Timothy 1:13; Galat. 1:13; Cor. 15:9; Acts 9:1.

Hence, St. Augustine teaches that Paul, although he was predestined, was a wolf before the fact and a sheep afterward.[11] Chrysostom says that Paul was a clay vessel but turned into gold while Judas was gold but turned into clay.[12] Hence Judas became reprobate, as is clear from the Acts of the Apostles,[13] and nevertheless, was at some point in the true Church. It is said in the same passage of Acts that he was an Apostle from the twelve and was called a Bishop by David,[14] This could not be true unless he were in the Church at some point. For this reason Augustine says that Judas was a son of Christ and still persecuted his father just as Absalom did David.[15] He also says that Judas was in the Church in which the rest of the Apostles were.[16]

Reason also agrees for if predestination alone makes a man in the Church, it would follow that if the Turks, Jews, heretics or any impious men were predestined, then they are now in the Church and the living members of Christ; but on the other hand certain holy and pious baptized men, if they might not be predestined, are not in the Church or the body of Christ. But each is false and against what is expressed in the Scripture. For above we showed the fact that the unbaptized and heretics are not in the Church, and the impious are not living members as it says in Romans, "If anyone does not have the spirit of Christ, he is not of him,"[17] *i.e.* a living member. That the impious do not have the spirit of Christ, but the spirit of the devil is clear from their works. For they are not patient, chaste, etc., which are works of the spirit, rather they are adulterers, murderers,

[11]Serm 1, de conversione Sancti Pauli.

[12]Hom. 6 in II Tim.

[13]Acts 1.

[14]Psalm 108 (109).

[15]in Psalm 3.

[16]*De Unitate Ecclesiae*, cap. 13.

[17]Romans 8:9.

blasphemers, etc., which are works of the flesh.[18] On the contrary, we find that all pious baptized men are members of the Church in Paul, "We are all baptized in one spirit into one body,"[19] and again, "You are all sons of God through faith in Christ Jesus, whoever you are that have been baptized in Christ, have put on Christ."[20] And still it is not believable that all the Corinthians and Galatians were predestined.

Next, Augustine says, "In the bond of Christ, just as in a living building of the temple of God, which is the Church, men are born not from the works of justice that they do rather they are transferred by works of grace just as from the mass of a ruin to the solidity of a building."[21] Again, showing that the impious do not pertain to the living members of Christ, he says, "God forbid that they could enter the confines of the enclosed garden that has such a guard as cannot be deceived, who nevertheless if they confess and are corrected, then enter, then are cleansed, then are enclosed among the trees of the garden, then are numbered in the members of the singular dove."[22]

Lastly it is proven from what is disagreeable; for if only the predestined were in the Church, then everything would be uncertain. Then no man could recognize his brothers, nor would shepherds know their sheep or be recognized by them, since nobody would know who is predestined. Besides nobody would know which would be the true Scripture, which would be the true Sacraments, or the true faith, etc., since all these depend upon the testimony of the true Church.

Yet they object to this with several arguments. 1) That verse in the Canticles, "An enclosed garden, a sealed font, a well of living

[18]Gal. 6:8.

[19]1 Cor. 12:13.

[20]Gal. 3:27.

[21]Epist. ad Dardanum.

[22]*Contra Cresconium*, lib. 2, cap. 21.

water, etc.," without a doubt means the Church, and still St. Augustine explains all of these about the elect alone.[23]

I respond: Firstly, Scripture often attributes one thing by a figure of speech to the whole which only agrees with a part. In Matthew it says that the thieves that were crucified with the Lord blasphemed against him,[24] when it is certain from Luke that only one of them blasphemed.[25] In Philippians it says "All seek what is their own,"[26] and yet there were not very many saints like this who lived then and especially the Philippians. Secondly I say that what is said about the spouse in the Canticles must not necessarily be understood on the Church. Some men understand this to be about the Church, and others about the Blessed Virgin, and others every perfect soul (which seems more probable), for it is said, "There are sixty queens and eighty concubines and the young women are beyond number. One is my dove, my perfect, my mother is one chosen by her mother."[27] In that passage, if you understand the Church through that one spouse, what will you understand by the queens, concubines and young women? Therefore the Church is understood by the mother while the souls of the more imperfect by the queens, concubines and young women and at length the faithful and good souls. For it is said, "For that reason the young women have loved you."[28] But through the one perfect spouse and dove is understood a perfect soul. Thus it is also said in that very place, "Just as a lily among thorns, so my beloved among the daughters."[29] If you understand the Church through the beloved, what will you understand for the other daughters? Would it be the congregation of the unfaithful? God forbid. Thus, it speaks on the perfect soul, which is called to mind

[23] *De Baptismo*, lib. 5, cap. 27.

[24] Matt. 27:39.

[25] Luke 23:40.

[26] Philippians 2:21.

[27] Canticle of Canticles 6:8.

[28] cap.1.

[29] cap.2.

amidst the multitude of sinners in the same garden of the Church. St. Augustine says, "The thorns are described on account of the malignity of morals, the daughters are described on account of the communion of the Sacraments."[30]

2) They make the second objection that the ark of Noah was a figure of the Church, as Augustine teaches,[31] but there was nobody in the ark but those who were going to be saved from the waters, therefore only the predestined are in the Church.

I respond: Similitudes do not agree in all things, otherwise every baptized person would be predestined, since Peter compares Baptism to the ark of Noah,[32] thus not only the good but even the wicked would be saved because in the ark both the clean and unclean animals were saved. For that very reason the ark agrees with the Church; for just as outside the ark no man could be saved, so not outside the Church, as Augustine remarks on that citation, as well as Cyprian and Jerome,[33] nor must any other similitude be sought out.

3) They make their third objection that Christ is not the head except of his Church which he will save, and which he will show to himself on the glorious day of judgment, not having spot or stain, as Paul says.[34] But only the predestined will be saved and glorious, consequently, only the predestined pertain to the Church of Christ.

I respond: When it is said that Christ is not the head except of his Church which he will save, that, "of his Church," can mean of his part of the Church which he will save, and then the proposition is false. For he is the head of his whole body although certain members are going to cease to be members and will perish in eternity. It can also mean, "of his Church," as in the whole Church, as is distinguished from other congregations of infidels and then the

---

[30]Epist. 48.

[31]*de Baptismo,* lib. 5, cap. ult.

[32]1 Peter 3:20.

[33]Cyprian, *De unitate Ecclesiae.*; Jerome, epist. ad Damasum, de tribus Hypostatibus.

[34]Ephes. 5:27.

proposition is true but the consequent is bad. Although some members of this Church will not be saved, it does not follow on that account that Christ did not save his Church, of which he is the head.

4) They argue fourthly that the mystical body is like a true body, but the whole true body of Christ is safe and glorious with all its parts, therefore the mystical body in all of its members and parts ought to be saved.

I respond: Firstly, similitudes do not agree in all things. Secondly, just as the body of Christ is true, saved and glorious in regard to all its formal parts, still not in regard to all its material parts, for the material parts flowed out from and were changed in Christ as we see happens among us, so also the mystical body is going to be saved in regard to all the formal parts, which are Apostles, Prophets, Pastors, Teachers, etc.; some will be saved from every race of men, but not in regard to all material parts, which are all men individually.

5) The Church is one sheepfold,[35] but there are no sheep except the predestined,[36] therefore, only the predestined are in the Church.

I respond: In some places of Scripture the word "sheep" means only the predestined as in Matthew 25:33 where the sheep are separated from the goats, and in John 10:3, "My sheep hear my voice." In other places it means everyone in general, both the good and the bad who are in the Church, as in the last chapter of John, "Feed my sheep," and in the Psalms, "Your furor has been aroused over thy pasture,"[37] and in Ezechiel 34:4, the sheep of God are described as some fat, some lean, some healthy and some sick, but according to this second meaning the argument does not have any force.

Still, we respond following the earlier meaning that in the sheepfold there are not only sheep but also goats, as is clear from Matthew 25:33, where they are separated since beforehand they were present together in the same sheepfold. Moreover, the

---

[35]John 10:16.

[36]Augustine, Tractatu in *Ioannem* 45.

[37]Psal. 73 [74]:1.

sheepfold may still be so called even if it does not, for the most part contain only sheep. Just the same, Rome is called a city although she embraces many who are not her citizens.

6) They argue from John, "I have other sheep who are not from this sheepfold,"[38] and also, "Jesus was going to die for the nation, but not only for the nation but even that the sons of God who were dispersed would be gathered into one."[39] In such passages the predestined are called sheep and sons of God, even when they lived amidst the errors of the Gentiles, for this reason the predestined are always in the Church. Likewise we see in 2 Timothy, "The strong foundation of God stands having this seal, the Lord knew who were his own,"[40] and in 1 John, "They went out from us but they were not from us, for if they were from us they would certainly have remained with us."[41] Therefore, even before they went out they were not from us but seemed to be. And it is confirmed by Augustine, "Some are sons of God because they received grace temporally, as when it says 'from us,' nevertheless they are not of God.... They went out from us, but they were not of us, *i.e.* even when they seemed to be among us they were not. Likewise, they were not sons even when they seemed to be in profession and in the name of sons. ... because they did not have perseverance, just as they were not truly disciples of Christ so they were not truly sons of God, even when they seemed to be and were so called."[42] Besides, in *Doctrina Christiana*, arguing with Ticonius who called the mystical body of the Lord, *i.e.* the Church, divided, he also says, "It ought not be so called, for that part which will not be with him forever is not really the Lord's body."[43]

---

[38]John 10:16.

[39]John 11:52.

[40]2 Timothy 2:19.

[41]1 John 2:19.

[42]*De Corrept. et Gratia*, cap. 9.

[43]*loc. cit.*, lib. 3, ca. 32.

I respond: Two distinct things must be noted for the explanation of these passages. The first is that a man can be called a sheep, a son, and a member of Christ in two ways: a) according to predestination; b) according to present justice. This distinction is contained with Paul, for when he says, "Whoever does not have the spirit of Christ is not of him,"[44] and nevertheless in 2 Timothy he says about the predestined, "The Lord knows who are his own."[45] Therefore, a member and a non-member of Christ can be one and the same. For he will be his if he has been predestined, and he will not be his if meanwhile he does not have his spirit. Likewise Augustine teaches, "According to foreknowledge, many who are certainly outside, and even those who are called heretics, are better than many and good Catholics." And again, "According to foreknowledge and predestination how many sheep are outside? But how many wolves are inside?"[46]

The difference between these is that those who are the sheep, sons, or members, are only so according to predestination, such as are by potency but not by act. For predestination places nothing in man, rather it is an act remaining in God himself. But those who are such according to present justice are simply such by act, because they really have this act in themselves, whence they are called such. Augustine clearly teaches this when he says, "Why is it that I said how many sheep are outside? How many that revel are going to be chaste? How many that blaspheme Christ are going to believe in Christ? And these are sheep. Even so, they only hear a foreign voice, they follow strangers. Likewise how many praise God on the inside but are going to blaspheme? How many are chaste but will fornicate and who now stand but are going to fall? And we say they are not sheep from the predestined."[47] There you can see how he speaks

[44]Romans 8:9.

[45]2 Timoth. 2:19.

[46]Tract. 45 in Ioan.; he says similar things in *de bono persever.*, cap. 8; *de corrept. et gratia*, cap. 9.

[47]Tract. 45 in Ioan.

about the future, "they who revel are going to be chaste, etc." For in the same way it can be said that those who are outside are going to be inside, and from this distinction it should be clear enough from the Scriptures we have brought forth. For there the sheep are spoken of, as well as the sons of God who still were not in the Church because they were such according to predestination and in potency, not however in act and simply.

For equal reasoning, it is said in 2 Timothy 2:19, "The Lord knows who are his," this phrase is about those who are his through predestination but not on the whole Church, since he adds in verse 20, "In a great house there are many vessels, some of gold, some silver, some wooden and others of clay." And the reprobate are similarly called those who went out from the Church and were not from us, because they were not from us according to predestination, although they were according to the communion of the Sacraments. In this way it ought also be understood what the author of the incomplete work says in homily 20 on Matthew, namely, that one who falls from the Church was never Christian; there he understands it according to predestination.

The second distinction is that one can truly be said to be a son of God or a member of the body of Christ in two ways, in one way by the truth of essence, or the form, and in the other way by the truth of the end, or as others say, from the truth of permanence. By the truth of essence it is the son of God who has charity. "Everyone who loves is born of God."[48] And likewise by the truth of essence is the member of Christ who lives in the same spirit. "In one spirit you all were baptized into one body."[49] But by the truth of the end one is called a son of God, who attains inheritance; and who will not attain it seemed to be a son but was not. For the purpose of descent is inheritance, "Such if a son and heir through God."[50] thus even by the truth of the end one is a member who will be saved, for Christ

[48] 1 John 4:7.

[49] 1 Cor. 12:13.

[50] Galat. 4:7.

united the Church to himself for this purpose, just as the body to the head that he would save her, as it is said in Ephesians 4:16. Therefore, who is in grace and still has not been predestined, is truly a son and member by the truth of essence and is not truly a son or a member by the truth of the end. On the other hand, one who is not in grace, and still has been predestined, is not truly a son or a member by the truth of essence, and nevertheless is truly both by the truth of the end. The verse, "Who keeps his word, truly the charity of God has been perfected in him,"[51] is understood on the first truth; while the verse, "If you will have remained in my word, you will truly be my disciple,"[52] is on the second.

Since we have noted these things, the passages of Augustine will be easily understood, where he says that the just who are not predestined are neither truly sons nor members. For he speaks on the truth of the end, not on the truth of the essence, as he explains himself in the same passage. Likewise in his book on *Rebuke and Grace*, after he had said the predestined—not the good—were truly sons,[53] he added, "Not because they feigned justice but because they did not remain in it." and in *Doctrina Christiana*,[54] rendering an account as to why he had said that those who will not be with Christ in eternity do not truly pertain to his body he said, "Now they are in one, still they will not always be in one. He is indeed that servant called to mind in the Gospel, of whom when the Lord will have come he will divide him and place him in the lot of the hypocrites."

---

[51]1 John 2:5.

[52]John 8:31.

[53]*De Corrept. et Gratia*, cap. 9.

[54]lib. 3 cap. 32.

CHAPTER VIII
On Those who are not Perfect

IT can easily be proven that there are imperfect men in the Church, against the opinion of the Pelagians and the Anabaptists. If those who had any imperfection were not in the Church, then there never would have been nor would be any Church on earth. For with the exception of Christ and the Blessed Virgin (who by themselves do not make the Church), there is no one, even if he were very holy in this life, who does not have some venial sins, even though they do not abolish justice nor make man an enemy of God, as the Pelagians thought. That is particularly taught in Scripture. "You forgave the impiety of my sin, for this every holy man will pray to you in due season."[1] What is the "for this," except for this remission of sin? Furthermore, the holy man is a man, and he still has something that he begs to be remitted him. In the Old Testament it says, "For there is no man who shall not sin,"[2] and again, "The just man falls seven times a day and rises again,"[3] and, "No man is so just on earth that he does good and does not sin."[4] In Matthew all are bid to say, "Forgive us our sins." James says, "We have all offended in many things."[5] and "If we will have said that we do not have sin, we deceive ourselves and we do not have the truth."[6] Such testimonies are certainly so clear that they hardly need any explanation.

---

[1]Ps. 31(32).

[2]3 Kings (1 Kings) 8:46.

[3]Proverbs 24:16.

[4]Eccles. 7:21.

[5]James 3:2.

[6]1 John 1:6.

Likewise the Council of Miletus defines in canons 7 and 8 that the just say "forgive our sins," not just out of humility but also in truth—not just for others but even for themselves.

The Fathers witness the same thing. St. Cyprian said, "Whoever says he is without fault is either proud or stupid."[7] St. Gregory Nazianzen said, "To be free from every sin altogether is something God constituted above the mode of human nature."[8] St. Ambrose said, "The just man cannot deny this because no man is without sin."[9] St. John Chrysostom says, "The Church is not constituted from the perfect but contains those given over both to industry and sluggishness."[10] St. Jerome said, "I concede there are just men, but I do not agree they are without any sin."[11] In book 3 of the same work, Jerome proves this same thing from the whole matter, when he at length admits that a man can go a very brief time without sin, but not long.

St. Augustine teaches that a man can live without any sin by a singular privilege from God, but really there is no one who lives or has lived thus but Christ.[12] He says the same thing in *de natura et gratia*, cap. 34, where he also exempts the Blessed Virgin, and in epist. 89, 95 and in the whole book on perfect justice, and finally in book 1 against the two Pelagian epistles, cap. 14. "There is no one in the Church that could rightly be ordained a minister, if the Apostle would have said if anyone is free from sin, where he said free from crime; or if he had said those having no sin when he said those having no crime. To be sure, there are many baptized faithful that are not guilty of a crime, but in this life I say there is no one without

[7] *de Eleemosyna.*

[8] Orat. 2, in Iulian.

[9] Serm. 16 in Psal. 16.

[10] in Psal. 39.

[11] *Contra Pelagionaos*, lib. 2.

[12] *De Spiritu et litera*, cap. ult.

sin." St. Gregory the Great said that in this life there are many not guilty of a crime, but no one that lives without sin.[13]

There are many arguments to the contrary, but they do not all need to be answered here. Those which are advanced to prove that any sin destroys justice, or that a man can live without any sin, do not lack an answer since a little later we will show that the best and the most wicked men are in the Church. There are only two arguments proper to this place. One is from the Canticles, "You are all beautiful, my beloved, and there is no stain in you,"[14] and the other, "That he might show the glorious Church to himself, having no stain or blemish, or anything of this kind."[15] That passage must be understood about the Church, as the sixth Council of Toledo teaches in its first chapter, explaining the confession of faith.

I respond: To the first, it is either understood on the Church by reason of only one part (*i.e.* by reason of just souls), or on the perfect soul, which I would prefer to argue. For the just soul is called all beautiful, either through hyperbole (which is familiar to lovers), or because the just and perfect soul lacks mortal sins, which properly leave behind a stain and avoids venial sins as much as it is permitted for human frailty to do so, and if it were to commit such it will soon labor to blot them out. Even if it is not immaculate simply, still it is immaculate for the state of this life, as Augustine explains in his book on the perfection of justice. In this way no one is perfect in this life absolutely, and nevertheless many in the Scriptures are said to be perfect because they were such for the state of this life. In Genesis it says, "Noah was a just man and also perfect,"[16] and, "Let all of us who are perfect be of this mind."[17] Nay more they are also called Immaculate who lack venial sins, "And I will be Immaculate with

---

[13]Moral., lib. 21, cap. 9.

[14]Cantic. 4:7.

[15]Ephes. 5:27.

[16]Gen. 5:9.

[17]Philipp. 3:15.

him."[18] "Blessed are the immaculate on the way."[19] "He chose us in himself, that we might be holy and immaculate in truth."[20]

I say to the second argument that a) it can be understood about the Church, not as it now is but as it will be after the resurrection, as St. Jerome explains it,[21] as well as St. Augustine,[22] and St. Bernard.[23] The Council of Toledo is not opposed to this either, because even if the Council understood those words on the Church in this time, nevertheless it did not define it. Still, I say b) it is more probable that the Apostle spoke about the Church of this time but attributed it through a figure of speech to the whole Church, which agrees with one part of it. For those who are now the just in the Church, that are glorious through the beauty of grace which is an innate glory, who are the ones without stain, as it was expressed a little earlier, without blemish, because they have been renewed through baptism; they have laid aside the old man and put on the new, the blemishes are signs of the old man. So all understand this passage apart from the Council of Toledo that has already been cited, such as Chrysostom, Jerome and Theophylactus in their commentaries on those passages.

---

[18]Psal. 17[18]:24.

[19]Psal. 118 [119]:1.

[20]Ephesians I:4.

[21]*in Hieremiae*, cap. 31.

[22]de Perfect. Iustit., et other places.

[23]Serm. 3, *de festo omnium Sanctorum.*

CHAPTER IX
On Great Sinners

MOREOVER, in the one true and Catholic Church of Christ there are not only imperfect men but even great sinners, and not only secret ones but even manifest ones. This is proved against the error of the Novationists, Donatists and Confessionists. First, it is proved from the parables of the Gospels on the chaff, on the net, on the nuptial dinner, the ten virgins and on the sheepfold that we cited above, with which Catholics once so refuted the Donatists that the latter found no way to escape them, as Augustine relates in his short work on the conference with the Donatists, explaining the conference of the third day.

Besides, there are other very clear passages. In Matthew it says, "If your brother might have sinned against you, go correct him, etc. If he will not hear you, speak to the Church, if he will not hear the Church, let him be to you just as a pagan and a publican."[1] Here it cannot be denied that the discourse is on the true Church, for Christ speaks about his Church and in this Church it is certain that sinners are discovered, even such sinners who often are not mended by fraternal correction, nor by the application of two witnesses, and still they remain in the Church until they are thrown out of the Church by the judgment of a prelate. We also see in Matthew that the Lord commands in regard to wicked overseers that we should do what they say but not what they do.[2] Next the Lord describes a wicked overseer who strikes the converted, eats and drinks with the drunkards, and he says, "The Lord will come on a day which he hopes not and he will divide him and place his share with that of the

[1] Matthew 18:17.

[2] Matthew 23.

hypocrites."[3] Hilary, Jerome, Chrysostom and others teach on that passage that it is in regard to those in charge of the Church. Likewise Paul says that he writes to the Church of God, which is in Corinth, and soon he adds, "It has been shown to me that there are contentions among you."[4] And in chapter 5, "fornication is heard of among you and such fornication that is not known among the nations, so that a man has the wife of his father."[5] What will they say here? That it is not the true Church? But the Apostle calls it the Church of God; that it was not a very great and manifest sinner? Yet the Apostle says it. That he was not in that Church? But the Apostle commands that they expel him through excommunication. "Let him be taken away from your midst, etc."

Additionally, St. John writes in the book of the Apocalypse to the seven Churches of Asia,[6] and condemns individuals for no light matters. As Augustine remarks, John not only condemns the Churches, but even the Bishops, signified by the Angel of the Church of Sardis, "You have the name which you could live, but you are dead, be watchful, etc."[7] Add that in the time of the Old Testament the people of God never lacked very serious sins, and still we never read that Moses or Samuel or other Prophets who lived in different times, or Mary, Anna, Elizabeth, Simeon, Zachariah, John the Baptist and the other just, whom the Lord discovered in the people of the Jews, separated themselves from the other very evil men in regard to the temple, altar, sacrifices and other things which are of religion, hence, the good and the bad remained in the same congregation. St. Augustine duly urges this very argument.[8]

Secondly it is proven from the testimony of the Catholic Church in St. Augustine's time. For Augustine relates a famous conference

---

[3]Matthew 24:50.

[4]1 Cor. 1:11.

[5]1 Cor. 5:1.

[6]Apocalypse 2 et 3.

[7]lib. 2, *contra Parmenianum*, cap. 10.

[8] *Breviculo, loc. cit.*

held in Carthage among 306 Catholic Bishops (of which he himself was one), with 296 Donatist Bishops. Augustine indicates that there were that many on the first day, then in the conference on the third day the Donatists were compelled to admit that the good and the bad are in the Church, and the Catholics advanced the parables on the net gathering the good and bad fish, but the Donatists still said those who are secretly wicked are in the Church, just as in the net while it is in the sea the good fish are not known from the bad, but on the shore they will soon be separated. The Catholic Bishops responded to this that on that account the Church is compared to a seine, in which the chaff is discerned from the grain, nay more the chaff appears more than the grain. Further they argued that in the ark of Noah, after the exit of the raven (which signifies heretics), the clean and unclean animals still clearly remained in the ark.

Augustine also adds that when the Donatists misrepresented Catholics as making two Churches, one on earth which would have the good and evil but the other in heaven which had none but the good, then the Catholics responded that they do not make two Churches but distinguish two periods of the Church, "They said that there is now one and the same holy Church, but later it will be otherwise, now it is mixed with the wicked, then it is not going to have them just as there are not two Christs because Christ was at one point mortal and then immortal." Such things must also be noted against the Confessionists and the Calvinists who create two Churches.

Thirdly, it is proven from the testimonies of the Fathers. Cyprian said, "Neither faith nor our charity ought to be impeded; just because we discern that cockle is in the Church, is no reason to depart from the Church."[9] St. Gregory Nazianzen compares the Church to a vast sea monster composed of many such creatures, that is from the great, the small, wild, meek, etc. to show that the greatest labor is that of Bishops who ought to rule so many kinds of men, the

[9]lib. 3, *epist. 3 ad Maximum.*

perfect and the imperfect, the good and the bad.[10] St. John Chrysostom says many similar things on the sins of those who are ruled by Bishops.[11] Commenting on Psalm 39 (40), on that verse, *They are multiplied over the hairs of my head,* he said: "The whole Church is certainly not constituted from the perfect, but it also has those who from laziness give themselves over to inaction, and embrace a soft and dissolute life, and gladly serve their desires, at length both the former and the latter announce that it is one body from one person."

Jerome says, "The ark of Noah was a type of the Church, just as in it were all kinds of animals so also in the Church there are men of all kinds of nations and morals, just in the ark there were leopards, goats and wolves as well as sheep, so also in the Church there are the just and sinners, *i.e.*, vessels of gold and silver along with those of wood and clay."[12] Augustine says, "We affirm that both the good and the wicked are in the Catholic Church, but just as the grain and the chaff."[13] Fulgentius says, "Firmly hold and in nowise doubt the threshing floor of God is the Catholic Church, and within it even to the end of the world it contains the chaff mixed with grain, that is, the wicked are mixed with the good in the communion of the Sacraments."[14] St. Gregory also teaches the wicked are in the Church and proves it with many arguments.[15]

Lastly, it is proved from reason. For if only the good were in the Church then the Sacrament of Penance would be in vain since it is administered only to those who are in the Church. Besides no man would know for certain who was or was not in the Church, since it

---

[10]Orat. 1, *Apologetica.*

[11]lib. 3 *de sacerdotio.*

[12]*Dialogus contra Luciferianos.*

[13]*Tract. 6 in Ioannem. cf. Retract.*, lib. 2, cap. 18; liber *post collationem*, cap. 7 et 20; *de Unitate Ecclesiae*, cap. 13; *De Civitate Dei*, lib. 18, cap. 4, 9, and other places.

[14]*de fide ad Petrum*, cap. 43.

[15]Hom. 11 et 38 in Evangelia.

would be uncertain who was really good or not. Likewise, if some prelate were to sooner or later fall into sin then he would no longer be in the Church and hence no longer a prelate and therefore it would not be necessary to obey him any longer; just the same if his subjects sooner or later would sin, they would no longer be in the flock and therefore it would be lawful for the pastors to omit their care; but from such confusion great disturbance would arise.

Still they object; 1) from the Scripture: "He will not add beyond that he should pass over to the uncircumcised and the unclean.... Withdraw, withdraw, go out from there, do not touch anyone polluted, go out from their midst."[16] The Apostle explains this passage thus, "I will receive you, says the Lord."[17] Therefore, God does not receive anyone in his Church except those who separate themselves from the unclean and sinners. Paul gives the reason (*loc. cit.*) saying, "What participation does justice have with iniquity? What compact does Christ have with Belial?" In 1 Corinthinas he says, "One bread and one body we are many."[18] But bread is only effected from grain, not chaff and grain. In Romans he says, "Whoever does not have the spirit of Christ is not of him,"[19] and, "In the one spirit we are all baptized into one body."[20] Therefore, whoever does not have the spirit is a sinner, and not a member of Christ. If one were to say he is not a living member but still he is a member, on the other hand because he is a dead member he is not a member except by a figure of speech, therefore he is not a true member and thus not one at all.

St. Augustine responds to the first argument.[21] The Church triumphant is understood in that passage, "he will not add more that

---

[16]Isaiah 52:11.

[17]2 Cor. 6:18.

[18]1 Cor. 10:17.

[19]Romans 8:9.

[20]1 Cor. 12.

[21]lib. *contra Donatistas post collationem*, cap. 8 et 20, et in *Breviculo Collationis tertia diei.*

he should pass over to the uncircumcised and unclean." What is added, "Recede, go out, etc.," is understood on the separation which ought to happen in the soul and the dead but not in the corporal separation from the same temple and Sacraments, etc.

But Cyril of Jerusalem says it better when he comments on this passage of Isaiah (and it does not seem that Jerome disagrees). He teaches that it is according to the historic sense, and it is a question of the temporal persecution of the Jews that the sense might be when you return from captivity an addition should not be made, *i.e.* for a long time, some infidel persecutor shall pass through your lands, devastating them, but according to the mystical sense it is a question of the Church, and Isaiah foretold that the gates of hell would not prevail against it. For the uncircumcised and the unclean are principally the enemies of the Church, that is the demons. For equal reasoning it follows that, "recede, recede, etc." according to the historic sense is understood about the Jews whom Isaiah exhorts go out from Babylon since the time of captivity was limited; but according to the mystical sense it is understood about Christians who ought, after Baptism, to be separated from the bodies, temples and sacrifices of unbelievers, along with their spouses and all the rest which also pertain to religion. And St. Paul understands this passage in that manner when he says speaks not on the commerce with certain sinners, but only with the infidels, "Do not take up the yoke with infidels, what share do the faithful have with the unbelievers? What union is there with the temple of God and idols?"

To what was said on the one bread, which is from the wheat alone, I respond: the similitudes do not agree in everything. This similitude consists of the bread and of the Church, as Cyprian and Irenaeus explain,[22] just as one bread is made from many grains through water, so also from many men through the waters of Baptism, or through the Holy Spirit, who is also called water,[23] one people of God is made. No man is in the Church who has not been

[22]epist. 6, lib. 1 *ad Magnum*, Irenaeus, lib. 3 cap. 19.

[23]Ezechiel 36.

baptized and does not participate in either an internal or external gift of the Holy Spirit. Although it is also not true that bread consists of wheat alone. Meanwhile either from negligence or from their malice, were those who make bread to mix in even a grain of chaff, just as often in wine from the malice of the sellers it is mixed with water. Next, the same is shown from the very words of Paul in 1 Corinthians 10:17 when he says, "We are one bread and one body, we who participate in one bread." But the good and the bad participated in the one bread, otherwise Paul would not have argued that some communicate unworthily.[24]

To the last point I say that the wicked are not living members of the body of Christ and the Scriptures themselves signify this. To that which is added, that they are members by a figure of speech, etc., it is usually conceded by many men that the wicked are not true members of the body of the Church, nor simply, but only according to something and by a figure of speech, such as Juan Torquemada[25], and he tries to show it from Alexander of Hales, Hugh and St. Thomas. Pedro de Soto, Melchior Cano and others also teach the same thing, even if they say the wicked are not true members, just the same they say they are truly in the Church, or in the body of the Church and are faithful, that is Christians simply. For not only are members in the body, but also the humors, the teeth, the hair and other things. And faithful or Christians are not called such from charity, but from faith or by the profession of faith. But if that is so, it follows that a bad Pope is not the head of the Church, and bishops, if they will be bad, are not the heads of their Churches. For the head is not a humor, or a hair, but a member and certainly a special one; but this is against the Council of Constance wherein the error of Jan Hus was condemned which asserted that a bad shepherd is only a shepherd by a figure of speech. It also condemned his error which asserted that a bad prelate is not truly a prelate.[26]

---

[24]1 Cor. 11:27.

[25]Lib. 1, cap. 57.

[26]In quo sess. 15 damnatur error XXII; XXX error.

Consequently, I respond that members can be considered in two ways: a) as there are certain matters according to themselves or according to their essence and substance; b) as they are operative instruments, *e.g.*, a man's eye and a cow's eye, as they are certain substances they are different in regard to species, by reason of different souls. But as operative instruments, they are species of the same thing because they have the same object.

So, I say a bad Bishop, priest, teacher, etc., are dead members and so they are not true members of the body of Christ in so far as it attains to the purpose of the member, as it is a certain part of the living body, nevertheless they are truly members by reason of the instrument, *i.e.* the Pope and the Bishops are true heads, the Doctors true eyes, or a true tongue of this body, etc., and the reason is because they are constituted living members by charity, which the impious lack. But the operative instruments are constituted either by the power of order or of jurisdiction, which can also exist without grace. For even if in the natural body a dead member cannot be an instrument of operation, still it can, in the mystical body. In a natural body the work depends upon the goodness of the instrument, because the soul cannot operate well unless it does through good instruments, nor can it exercise works of life except through living instruments. The soul of this body, *i.e.*, the Holy Spirit works equally well through good and bad instruments, as well as living and dead, etc.

The second objection. The Church is called "Holy" in the Creed, therefore it is constituted by none but the holy. Those who make this objection will say that the response that the Church is called holy because one part of the Church is holy does not suffice. For then, the Church could also be called sinful because one part, nay more the greater part is sinful.

I respond: The Church is truly said to be holy because all the things that pertain to her constitution are holy. First baptism, which no man denies is holy. Secondly, Christian profession, that is the profession of faith, as well as of morals, doctrines and Christian precepts. It is certain that she is holy and that only she is holy by this profession since the profession of the Jews, Turks, Heathen and heretics is not holy; and only that of Christians is. Thirdly, the union of members among themselves and with the head, at least the external head, and in regard to those things which pertain to religion is also certainly holy. She is called holy on account of the saints that she has, but she ought not be called sinful on that account since a denomination is made from its better part. Besides, it is proper for the Church to have saints because she alone truly has holy people, but to have wicked men is not proper to the Church, for that agrees with other bodies as well. Next, she is called holy because she is wholly consecrated to God and because Christ her head is the holy of holies.

The third objection. He who does not have the Church as a mother does not have God as a Father, as St. Cyprian teaches; likewise one who does not have the Church as a mother does not have God as a father. But none of the wicked have God as a father, "For those who are urged by the Spirit of God, these are the sons of God,"[27] and it is said to the wicked, "You are from your father the devil."[28] and again, "In this you are manifested as sons of God and sons of the devil, everyone who is not just is not from God." Therefore, only the good have the Church as a mother, so only the good are in the Church.

I respond with St. Augustine,[29] that the name of "son" is received in three ways in the Scriptures. In one way sons are called according to production, whether that is properly by generation, or creation, or regeneration; thus Christ the Lord is properly called the Son of God because he was generated by God the Father, all men also are sons by reason of creation. "Is he not your father who made and created you?"[30] Still by reason of a new regeneration all sons are called just, and only just as in the places we have cited, Romans 8 and 1 John 3.

---

[27]Romans 8.

[28]John 8.

[29]contra Adimantum, cap. 5.

[30]Deut. 32.

Secondly, some are called sons by reason of imitation, just as the Apostle calls the sons of Abraham those who imitate the faith of Abraham,[31] and again, "Love your enemies and do good to those who hate you that you might be sons of your father, etc."[32] And in this way only the good are sons of God, for all the wicked are sons of the devil, as it says in John 8 and 1 John 3. Thirdly, they are called sons by reason of doctrine, this is why the Apostle calls the Corinthians sons,[33] because he taught them the Gospel, and again he says, "My children, whom I give birth to a second time until Christ will have been formed in you."[34] In this way all who are in the Church are sons of God and the Church, because they adhere to the true doctrine of God and the Church, but they can still be good and wicked. This is why Isaiah says, "I nurtured the children and raised them up, and they hoped in me,"[35] and the Canticles declare, "My beloved is among the daughters as a lily among thorns." There, Christian souls are called daughters, but wicked.

With these being noted we respond to the argument. If it is a question of the sons of doctrine, the assumption is false, for it is not true that only the just are sons of God if only the reason of doctrine is considered; but if it is a question of the sons of God by regeneration or imitation, the last consequent is bad, therefore only the good are in the Church; for not only the sons but the servants also, although these do not remain in the house for ever, the sons remain forever,[36] and this is the mind of St. Cyprian. He did not mean that in the Church there are none but the sons, but there are not any sons outside the Church, just as there are not any good men outside, although there might be evil ones within. He meant to

---

[31]Gal. 4; Rom. 4.

[32]Matthew 5.

[33]1 Cor. 4.

[34]Galatians 4.

[35]Isaiah 1.

[36]John VIII.

terrify heretics and schismatics, and to warn them to not think they can be either good, or sons outside the Church.

The fourth objection is also from St. Cyprian, when he says, "Only the peaceful and harmonious dwell in the Church, as God who makes those in unity dwell in his home, as it is in the Psalms through the Holy Spirit."[37] Thus, sinners who fight and make contentions with others are not in the Church."

I respond: Cyprian does not speak on every peace, but on that which is properly said to be opposed to schismatics. Besides, there can be other dissensions in the Church and in fact one often finds them, as Cyprian himself witnesses in his sermon *de Lapsis*, where among other sins, he also places among men in the Church who separated themselves from pertinacious hatred for each other.

The fifth argument is from St. John Chrysostom and Theophylactus commenting on 2 Timothy 2, where they say, "In a great house there are golden vessels, etc." They say that this cannot be understood about the Church but about the world, because in the Church there are no vases but gold and silver.

I respond: They do not deny that the wicked can be in the Church but they say it is not necessary that they be in the Church because when the Apostle says that in a great house there are golden, silver, clay and wooden vessels, it is known that all these are necessary lest someone might think the Church cannot exist without the wicked. So these Fathers say that by the term "house", not the Church but the world should be understood since the Church does not need the wicked, nay more when it will be in its best state, *i.e.* in heaven, it will have no wicked members. Yet the world is furnished with the wicked, not *per se* but *per accidens*, if there were no wicked men then the patience of the just would not be exercised in this world, nor the justice of God.

The sixth argument is taken from St. Jerome in his commentary on Ephesians 5. He says on the subjection of the Church to Christ, "The Church of Christ is glorious, having no stain, no blemish, nor

---

[37]lib. 1, epist. 6 ad Magnum.

anything of this sort. A sinner or anyone stained with filth cannot be said to be of the Church nor subject to Christ."

I respond: Jerome means that the wicked cannot be said to be in that part of the Church that contains only the perfect. He explains in his commentary on Galatians 1 on that verse, "Paul, an Apostle, ... to the Churches of Galatia," he means to explain how the words of the Apostle embrace in themselves those who now seem to praise all the Churches, then reproach and rebuke them; he says the Church is received in a two-fold sense, *i.e.* not that there are two Churches, but on the one diverse-mode the Scriptures speak; sometimes Scripture attributes that which is proper to the perfect to the whole Church, namely, that it lacks stain or blemish, and sometimes that which is proper to the imperfect, such as to sin and the need for correction. When the Church is praised it must be taken in respect to that part which contains the perfect, when it is rebuked then to that which contains the imperfect.

The seventh argument is from Pacianus, who says, "In the Church there is no stain or blemish because sinners are not in the Church until they will have done penance for their prior life, and after that are cleansed."[38]

I respond: He does not speak about all sinners, but only on sinners who fell into heresy, for before that he had said the Church lacks stain and blemish because she lacks heresy.

The eighth argument is taken from St. Augustine who says, "But by this, even without the knowledge of the Church, on account of the wicked and polluted conscience, those damned by Christ are not in the body of Christ, which is the Church, because Christ cannot have damned members."[39] He holds similar things in other places.[40]

---

[38]Epist. 3 ad Sympronianum.

[39]*Contra Cresconium*, lib.2, cap. 21.

[40]*Contra Petilianum*, lib. 2, cap. ult.; *de Baptismo*, lib. 4, cap. 3, lib. 6, cap. 3, lib. 7, cap. 49, 50, 51; *de Unitate Ecclesiae*, cap. ult.; *Doctrina Christiana*, lib. 3, cap. 32.

I respond, on account of these citations, not only Brenz and Calvin, but even some Catholics imagine that there are two Churches, but they really imagine it, for neither the Scriptures nor Augustine ever call to mind two Churches, but only one. Certainly in the short conference with the Donatists, where they falsely asserted that Catholics make two Churches (one for the good and another which contains the good with the wicked), the Catholic side responded that they never dreamed of two Churches, but only distinguish parts, or times of the Church. Parts, because on the one hand the good pertain to the Church, and on the other the wicked, since the good are the interior part, just like the soul of the Church, and the wicked are the exterior part, just like the body. Then they gave the example concerning the interior man and the exterior, which are not two men but one part of the same man.

With regard to times, they spoke distinguishing on the one hand the Church today, and on another the Church after the resurrection; today it has good and wicked men, after the resurrection it will not have any but the good. They also placed the example of Christ, who is always the same but nevertheless was mortal and passible before his resurrection, but afterwards immortal and impassible. St. Augustine often confirms the same doctrine in other places and explains it with various similitudes. Against the Donatists he says that the good are in the house of God, which is the Church, so that the house of God might be built upon living stones, while the wicked are in the same house, but these, nevertheless are not the house.[41] In the last chapter of his book *On the Unity of the Church*, he says that the wicked are cut off from the Church in spirit but not in body; in other words they pertain to the Church as to the exterior man, but not to the interior. In *Doctrina Christiana*, while explaining the verse in the Canticles, "I am black but beautiful, just as a cedar tent, just as the skin of Solomon," he notes that it was not said "I was black and I am beautiful," but "I *am* black and beautiful," because the Church now is one and the same, black just as a cedar tent, on account of the

[41] *Contra Donatistas*, lib. 7, cap. 51.

sinners which she has in her, and at the same time beautiful, just as the skin of Solomon, *i.e.*, just as the halls of a king, because of the good which she has in her.[42]

Augustine says the same thing on the epistle of John, where he teaches that the wicked are indeed in the body of the Church, not as members, but as corrupted humors which remain in the breast and really are in the body, and nevertheless are also truly separated from the members of the body. From the latter the response is made that when Augustine says the wicked are not in the Church, it ought to be understood to be in that way in which the good are, that is, they are not living members of the body.

But one might object that St. Augustine also teaches that only the saints are the Church, which is founded upon the rock, and to which the keys of the kingdom were given,[43] and about which it was said if he will not hear the Church, let him be to you just as a heathen and a publican.

I respond: Augustine meant nothing other than that all privileges which were conceded to the universal Church by God were conceded on account of the saints alone for the advantage and benefit of those who obtain eternal salvation. Otherwise, Augustine frequently repeats the same thing; wicked Christians advantageously administer the Sacraments and hence rule men, loose them, bind them, etc. Consequently,[44] he compares evil ministers to a stony channel, through which water passes to the garden, and although it acquires no advantage for itself, nevertheless it is the cause for grass and flowers to be born and grow in the garden.[45]

The ninth argument is of the Lutheran Centuriators of Magdeburg. They try to show that there are two Churches, one of the good and one of the wicked.[46] They distinguish the justice of the

---

[42]lib. 3, cap. 32.

[43]*de Baptismo*, lib. 3, cap. 18, lib. 1, cap. 21 et 22, lib. 6, cap. 3, lib. 7 cap. 51.

[44]Tract. 5 *in Ioannem.*

[45]*C.f. Contra Parmenianum*, lib. 2, cap. 10 et 11.

[46]*Centur.* 1, lib. 1, cap. 4, col. 171.

disciples in Matthew 5 from the justice of the Pharisees, in Matthew 6 of the pious from the hypocrites, in Matthew 7 the body of wayfarers traveling on the narrow path from the body of those going through the broad road, and in the same place they distinguish the house founded upon the rock from the one founded upon sand. Moreover, they say it is certain that the Church of the wicked is not one holy Catholic Church, therefore the true Church of Christ only embraces the good.

I respond: Two Churches are not distinguished in any of those passages, but only different qualities of those who are in one and the same Church. Just the same, Matthew 13 distinguishes good fish from bad fish, and still they are in the same net, which signifies the Church. Thus, they are also in the same Church who make the profession of the same faith and are in the communication of the same Sacraments, indeed they are those who walk on the broad road of vices, just as those who walk on the narrow path of virtue; just as those who are truly pious and those who are hypocrites; and those who follow the justice of the Pharisees as well as those who follow the justice of the Apostles. Lastly, there are some just as a house founded upon a rock, and those who are like a house founded upon sand. For in this passage it does not signify two Churches, as if we wanted to make as many Churches as there are men, for the Lord says, "Therefore, everyone who hears my words and does them, he will be compared to a wise man who built his house upon the rock, etc."

The tenth argument. If the body of Christ is the Church they cannot be parts and members of this body, among whom Christ works nothing. For he works nothing in the impious and the hypocrites; as a result, they are not of the same sort as those who can pertain to the Church of Christ. Likewise, it is altogether fitting to distinguish the kingdom of Christ from the kingdom of the devil, but all the impious pertain to the kingdom of the devil, therefore, only the pious pertain to the kingdom of Christ, which is the Church.

I respond: It is not necessary that Christ work something in all his members, for there are some dead members, some shriveled, which only adhere to the rest by an external connection. Moreover, if the kingdom of Christ is distinct from the kingdom of the devil, still the same men can pertain to each kingdom: those who are provided with bad morals yet persevere in the Catholic faith, and the union with the other faithful, they pertain to the kingdom of Christ insofar as the profession of faith. Yet, they pertain to the kingdom of the devil in respect to the perversity of morals. For this reason Augustine says the impious who are in the Church are sons and foreigners; sons on account of the form of piety, but foreigners on account of the loss of virtues.[47]

---

[47]In Psal. 47(48).

CHAPTER X
On Secret Infidels

LASTLY, it remains to speak of secret infidels, *i.e.* those who have neither internal faith nor any Christian virtue, but nevertheless profess the Catholic faith due to some temporal advantage and mix with the true faithful by the communion of the Sacraments. Both the Confessionists and Calvinists teach that such men in no way pertain to the true Church, and even some Catholics, one of whom is Juan Torquemada,[1] although this author perhaps meant nothing other than that they require faith for someone can be said to be united by an internal union to the body of Christ, which is the Church, which would be very true.

Nevertheless, we follow the manner of speaking of a great many authors who teach that they who are joined with the remaining faithful only by an external profession are true parts and even members of the Church but withered and dead.[2]

1) This opinion can be demonstrated from those words of John: "And now many have become Antichrists, they went out from us, but they were not from us; for if they were from us they would have remained with us."[3] John speaks in this place on heretics, whom he calls Antichrists, and he says that before they went out, they were not from us, *i.e.* they were not Catholics in spirit and will but heretics and Antichrists, and still they went out from us because if

---

[1]Lib. 4, *de Ecclesia*, par. 2, cap. 20.

[2]Thomas Waldens, tomus I, lib. 2 cap. 9, nu. 10, et cap. 11, num. 5; John Driedo, *de Ecclesiasticis Scripturis et dogmatibus*, lib. 4, cap. 2, par. 2; Pedro de Soto *Confessio Catholica*, (which was opposed to the Augsburg Confession), cap. de Ecclesia, et cap. de Conciliis, et in Apologia pro eadem Confessione par. 1, cap. 11; Cardinal Hosius, *contra Prolegomena Brentii*, lib. 3; Melchior Cano, lib. 4 de Locis Theologicis, cap. ult. ad argumentum XII.

[3]1 John 2:19.

they were not from us, in spirit and will, nevertheless they were by external profession; but after they betrayed themselves and broke out into open schism, they already ceased to be from us in every way.

And, although at some time St. Augustine explained those words, "They were not from us," about predestination, still in his commentary on this passage, he explains they are about secret heretics. He speaks thus: "All heretics, all schismatics, went out from us, that is, they went out from the Church, but they would not have gone out if they were from us, namely, they went out from the Church, but they would not have gone out if they were from us. Before they went out, therefore, they were not from us, if before they went out they were not from us. Many are inside that did not go out, and yet they are Antichrists.... And those who are inside are certainly in the body of our Lord Jesus Christ since he still takes care of his own body; but health will not be restored except in the resurrection of the dead; thus they are in the body of Christ in the same way as bad humors. For, when they are vomited then the body is relieved; thus even the wicked, when they go out, then the Church is relieved and when she vomits them out, and the body casts them out, she says these humors go out from me, but they were not from me. Why were they not from me? They were not cut from my flesh but pressed from my breast when they were present there."[4] He explains it in the same way in other places,[5] which we will present below.

2) Next the same thing is proven from the testimonies of those Fathers who teach in a common consensus that those who are outside the Church have no authority or jurisdiction in the Church.[6]

---

[4]Tract. 3, *in epistolam Ioannis.*

[5]De Baptismo lib. 3, cap. 18, Tract. 61 in Ioannem.

[6]Cyprian, lib. 1, epist. 6, lib. 2 epist. 1; Optatus, *contra Parmenianum*, lib. 1; Ambrose *de poenitentia*, lib. 1, cap. 2; Jerome *dioalogus contra Luciferianos*; Augustine, *in Enchiridio*, cap. 65; Pope Celestine *epistola ad Clerum Constantinopolitanum*, *epistola ad Ioannem Antiochenum*, *c.f.* 1 Tomo Concilii Ephesini, cap. 18 et 19, cited by Nicholas I in his epistle to the Emperor

Moreover, right reason manifestly teaches the same thing: By what arrangement can it be devised or imagined that one might have jurisdiction and hence be the head of the Church, who is not a member of the Church? Whoever heard of a head which was not a member? Moreover it is certain, whatever one or another might think, a secret heretic, if he might be a Bishop, or even the Supreme Pontiff, does not lose jurisdiction, nor dignity, or the name of the head in the Church, until either he separates himself publicly from the Church, or being convicted of heresy is separated against his will; for this reason, Celestine and Nicholas say (*loc. cit.*) that a heretical Bishop, to the extent that he began to preach heresy, could bind and loose no one although without a doubt if he had already conceived the error, were it before he began to preach publicly, he could still bind and loose. The fact is likewise confirmed from the canon *Audivimus*, 24, q. 1, where we read: "But if he will have devised a new heresy in his heart, to the extent that he begins to preach such things, he can condemn no man." Besides, if it were the case that secret heretics could have no jurisdiction, every act that depends upon jurisdiction would be rendered uncertain, which would disturb the universal Church in no small measure. Therefore, now if he who is not in the Church cannot have authority in the Church and a secret heretic can have it, and at some point really has authority in the Church, certainly a secret heretic can be in the Church.

3) The same thing is proven from Origen, Augustine and Gregory. Origen says, "Even here in Jerusalem (*i.e.* in the Church), there are some Jebusites who are perverse in their faith and deeds."[7] There is no doubt whether he spoke about secret heretics, for he adds: "Nor do we speak about those who are manifestly and evidently guilty enough to be expelled from the Church."

Augustine says, "The enemies of this fraternal charity are either clearly outside or seem to be inside, as pseudochristians and

Michael.

[7] *Homil. 21 in Iosue.*

Antichrists, for after they have discovered opportunities, then they go out. But even if they lack opportunities, although they seem to be inside, they have been separated by the invisible bond of charity."[8] When Augustine says these things about secret heretics, that they seem to be in the Church, he does not mean they are not really in the Church, but that they are not in the manner in which they seem. They seem to be united by an internal and external bond with the other members but still they are not united except by an external bond. For if they were not really inside in any way but only seemed to be, for equal reasoning they would not truly go out when they clearly betray themselves, but would only seem to go out.

Moreover, Augustine says they go out after they have found opportunities, and he adds they were separated even before they went out, but from the invisible bond of charity, not from the external communion of the Church. What Augustine says later in the same work[9] ought to be understood in the same way. There, he says that secret heretics are separated so that they may be judged, even if they do not go out. He speaks on the internal separation, not on the external, and this is not proper in Augustine to secret heretics but to all sinners, whom Augustine affirms are not in the body of the Church, as is clear from the chapters we cited above. Augustine continues in this place: "Wherefore, when John said they went out from us but they were not from us, he did not say they became foreigners by going out, but that they were foreigners on account of this: they declared they left." The Apostle Paul also speaks on certain men who erred concerning faith, they were in one great house, I believe that they had not yet gone out.

Augustine continues, "Even if those onl are to be alled cockle who remain in perverse error to the end, there are many grains of wheat outside, and much cockle within."[10] The sense of such words seems to be that we understand outside the Church there are many

[8] *de Baptismo*, lib. 3, cap. 18.

[9] Lib.4, cap.16

[10] Lib. 4, cap. 10.

manifest heretics who at length will be converted to the true faith, and inside in the Church herself there are many secret heretics who never converted. He has the same thing in *City of God*, where he says, "He rightly called to mind that those who were going to be citizens lurked among his very enemies, just as the city of God would hold itself from their number connected in communion of the Sacraments."[11] Here it must be observed on enemies, who are outside the Church, Augustine said they are future citizens because they are merely not citizens but will be in their time. But on enemies who lurk within the Church, he does not say they are going to be enemies, but they are presently in the Church itself although, they nevertheless pertain to the number of enemies.

Again, when Augustine is treating on John 13, where we read Christ was present while Judas was leaving, he says, "For us, the Lord deigned to signify with his disturbance that it is necessary to tolerate false brethren even as the cockle of the Lord's field amidst the grain even to the time of the harvest, that when some pressing reason compels a separation from them before the harvest, this cannot be done without a disturbance to the Church. This disturbance of its saints by future schismatics and heretics in just the manner the Lord foretold, prefigured himself when Judas, the wicked man, made his exit, and by his departure put an end to his mixture with the wheat which had been so long tolerated; he was disturbed but not in the flesh, rather in the spirit."[12] Further on, in the same tract, he declares that Judas was one of the Lord's disciples and nevertheless bore the type of the heretic, "One from the number, but not rightly; one in species but not in virtue; by a corporal mixture but not by a spiritual bond, joined in a unity of the flesh but not a friend of the heart; ... Both are true, both from us and not from us, according to one from us, according to another not from us, according to the communion of the Sacraments from us, according to the propriety of his crimes not from us." He speaks likewise in

[11] *De Civitate Dei*, lib. 1, cap. 35.

[12] Tract. 61 in Ioan.

another work, "Some men are still placed in heart on the side of the Donatists but show themselves to be with us corporally; in regard to the flesh they are inside, but in regard to the spirit outside."[13]

Next, in his work *On Catechizing the Unlearned*, he distinguished three kinds of Christians, secret heretics, bad Catholics and good Catholics: "There are those who wish to be Christians, to either be brought into the view of men from whom they hope for agreeable temporal assistance or because they do not want to offend some that they fear. But if they are reprobate, the Church bears them, albeit for a time, just as the sand bears the chaff for a time. If they do not correct themselves and begin to be Christians on account of the coming eternal rest, then in the end they will be separated. They cannot flatter themselves that they can be in the sand with the wheat of God, because they will not be in the barn with it, rather, they will be destined for the fated fire. There are also others with better hope, but still not with lesser danger, who now fear God and do not mock the Christian name, nor enter the Church of God with a feigned heart, but hope for happiness in this life."[14] You can clearly see there, from the discussion of these two kinds of men, the first is of those who do not fear God but mock the Christian name and enter the Church with a feigned heart, and still they are in it and remain and make up the number [of Christians] and will not be separated until that clear exodus.

St. Gregory the Great, while explaining the words of Job 16:9, *My wrinkles bear witness against me*, says: "What, except the duplicitous are meant by 'wrinkles'? The wrinkles are all those who live two-faced in this life, who shout the faith of the holy Church loudly but deny it with their works. Without a doubt, they lie that they are faithful in a time of peace because they see the same faith honored by the powers of the world; but when the holy Church is disturbed by the gales of sudden adversity, they show themselves on the spot to be soft in a treacherous mind.... But because the Church holds

[13] *de gestis cum Emerito*, cap.1.

[14] de Catechizandis Rudibus, cap. 17.

even many reprobates within the fold of faith, when a time of persecution rages, she suffers these enemies whom she seemed to nourish with the words of preaching. Let it be said, therefore, 'my wrinkles bear testimony against me,' *i.e.* they rebuke me in declaration who now place themselves in the body by their duplicity and do not amend their malice. ... Even in a time of peace the holy Church suffers false brethren while there are many in her who despair of the promise of eternity and still lie that they are faithful, but when the time of malice breaks out the mendacious man lays aside what must be gainsaid, he comes before the face because he resisted the words of the true faith with a loud voice."

4) It is proven from reason and the similitude of the human body argues for that which we seek. The Church is like the human body, as the Apostle teaches in Romans 12 and 1 Cor. 12. Moreover, in the human body we see there are many different kinds of parts to the extent that some are live and feel, some are alive and do not feel, some are neither alive nor feel, which is obvious. Therefore, nothing prevents that in the Church there will be some men who have the faith and charity, as well as some who have only faith, and some who do not even have the faith at all but merely an external union.

Next, if those who lack internal faith are not, nor can be, in the Church, there will be no further question between us and the heretics on the visibility of the Church, proportionally, (which I make much of), so many disputations of the most erudite men, which to this point have been published will be redundant. All who have written to this point object to the Lutherans and Calvinists because they make the Church invisible. I will now prove it beyond question.

The Lutherans and Calvinists establish certain visible and external signs, namely, the preaching of the word of God and the administration of the Sacraments, and they constantly teach that wherever these signs are seen there is also the true Church of Christ. Nevertheless, because they mean only the just and the pious pertain to the true Church (and no man can say for certain who might be truly just and pious among so many that outwardly wear justice and piety before them, although it is certain that in every place there are many hypocrites and false brethren), then our writers correctly conclude that the former make the Church invisible. Since, for the Lutherans and Calvinists, justice consists only in faith and the same thing is said by those who say the Church is the body of the just and the pious and the body of true believers, then who does not see that we would plainly agree with them if we were to exclude all those from the Church who do not have true faith in their heart?

For this purpose, it is necessary that it should be constituted for us—with infallible certitude—what body of men make-up the true Church of Christ, since the traditions of Scripture and clearly all dogmas depend upon the testimony of the Church; unless we were absolutely certain what is the true Church, everything will be altogether uncertain. But one cannot constitute what the true Church might be with infallible certainty if internal faith in every member or part of the Church is required. Who knows for certain in whom there is such faith? Consequently, faith (whether it is something invisible or secret) is required for someone to pertain to the Church in some way.

Some respond to this argument in two ways. Firstly, it is certain enough that the body of faithful men can be recognized, so that it could be said if the effect of faith is discerned, then the type of protestation and confession of faith is of some sort; we even say that we truly and properly see a man even though we do not see the soul except in its effects. Secondly, they add that it is not necessary for it to be easy for us to see distinctly who these men are that make the Church, rather it is enough to assign a certain body of men within which we would know for certain or at least could believe that they all pertain to the Church. Accordingly, if the universal Roman people were shown to someone in the forum or in the theater, even though some outsiders might ultimately be mixed in, truly it would be said that he saw the Roman people even if he could not discern Romans from foreigners.

But neither answer seems to satisfy, and the first is easily refuted: The recognition from the effects is not certain, rahter, conjectural.

Furthermore, the example of man does not convince, for in the first place, the effects of life in man are natural and necessary, but the effects of faith are free and voluntary, hence much less certain. We could never know for sure just by looking at someone that he whom we see is a man; accordingly it can happen that when we believe we see a man we might see an Angel or a demon in human form. Certainly, Abraham, Lot, Tobit and others in the Old Testament often believed some to be men who were angels. We, however, want to have infallible certitude concerning the Church, such as we have not from man himself, but from the form and exterior colors, as well as features of the human body, by which we cannot be deceived when we look upon it.

The second answer does not satisfy for many reasons. a) Because it can happen that the number of hypocrites would so increase that there might be more secret heretics than true and perfect Catholics and no one could truly say this body is the Church of Christ, seeing that in the body which he points out, a greater part does not pertain to the Church, nor would he himself know who might be those few who make up the Church. Although, it would have to be hoped that a greater part of those who profess the faith are sincere, still that is not certain.

b) Because the whole Church would not come together in one place so that we could say for certain that in this body is the Church; rather, it has been dispersed through various places, and we might be certain on no part, or that whole part might be without the true faith; wherever we go we will always be in doubt whether we communicate with the true Church of Christ. Now, this is not opposed to what we said elsewhere, that the particular Roman Church cannot defect from the true faith,[15] for the whole Roman Church itself comes together in some place at the same time, but is gathered while spread out in different churches, which are in the city of Rome, nor do we know for certain with infallible certitude in

[15] *On the Roman Pontiff*, book IV, ch. 6.

that body, to which we by chance have approached, that all are not without true faith in heart.

c) Because it can also happen that a whole general Council might be outside the Church. How great would it be if, among so many thousands professing faith in Christ, three hundred or four hundred men, who come together in a Council, might lack the true faith? Evidently matters that are otherwise so well known, and which it is necessary that they be certain, will be called into doubt. Certainly Brenz, as we remarked in the disputation on Councils, elevates the authority of Councils for this reason, because we are not certain whether any of the Fathers had true faith in heart, and therefore were in the Church of God, for a false Church is not a column and firmament of truth, rather, only a true Church.

d) Because if we do not distinctly know who might constitute the Church, then we will be ignorant, not only as to what the Church is but where it is, or rather more where the Church hides, which is insufficient to save the visibility of the Church, which we will take up in the following chapter; but now let us see what some object.

Firstly, they object that faith is a foundation like the form of the Church, when we read, "Just as a good architect placed a foundation and no man can place another foundation apart from that which has been placed, which is Christ Jesus;"[16] and, "You are built upon the foundation of Apostles and Prophets in Christ Jesus the chief cornerstone."[17] "One God, one faith, one baptism."[18]

I respond: The form of the Church is not internal faith (unless we mean to have an invisible Church) but external faith, *i.e.* the confession of faith. St. Augustine teaches this very clearly,[19] and experience witnesses it. For they are admitted to the Church who profess the faith. Moreover, in those passages, faith is not said to be the form or the foundation of the Church, but the foundation of

[16]1 Corinth. 3:10.

[17]Ephes. 2:20.

[18]Ephesians 4:5.

[19]*contra Faustum*, lib. 19, cap. 11.

justice, or the doctrine which is in the Church. Add that the Scriptures, just as they place faith in the Church, so also do they place charity and every gift of the Holy Spirit, but no Catholic teaches that those who do not have charity and the gifts of the Holy Spirit are not in the Church.

Secondly, they object that in the definition of the Lateran Council, which is contained in the chapter *Firmiter, de summa Trinitate et fide Catholica,* there is one universal Church of the faithful, outside of which no man is saved; to which there is a similar definition of Pope Nicholas which is contained in *de consecrat.* dist. 1, can. *Ecclesia,* the Church is a gathering of Catholics, but none are faithful and Catholic who do not have faith in their heart, even if they profess it in mouth.

I respond: These are not definitions of the Church. The Lateran Council only meant to assert that there is one Church, not to accurately describe what it might be. Moreover it addresses the Church of the faithful, because by this name the baptized Christians are distinguished both from those who are manifestly infidels and also from catechumens who are not called faithful, as we showed above. Thus, it is the same as if the Council would have said the Church of Christians is one, not many. Secondly, the name of faithful can be received for one who publicly professes the faith, and we will speak soon in the same way about the name Catholic. Thirdly, it could truly be said that the Church of the faithful, *i.e.*, of those who have true faith in heart, is one; for chiefly, the Church only gathers those who are intentionally faithful, but when some false men are mixed in who do not truly believe, that happens apart from the intention of the Church. For if she could refuse then she would never admit them, or immediately exclude those just admitted after their fall.

Thus we come to those words of Pope Nicholas, "The Church is a gathering of Catholics." We are necessarily compelled to say that they are called Catholics who profess the Catholic faith, irrespective of their internal faith; for Nicholas bids that Churches not be made, *i.e.* as he explains it, gatherings of Catholics, without the nod of the

Apostolic See. Moreover it is plain that gatherings of Catholics cannot otherwise happen than by calling into one place all of those that are said to be Catholic, *i.e.* those who publicly profess that they are Catholics.

Thirdly, they object with the testimony of the Fathers, who said that heretics are not truly Christians, such as Tertullian,[20] Cyprian,[21] Athanasius,[22] and Augustine,[23] but the Church of Christ cannot be made of any but Christians, consequently, those who do not have true faith do not pertain to the Church.

I respond: Those fathers speak on manifest heretics who have the faith of Christ neither in their heart nor in their mouth. The Christian name is of profession, and they are called Christians who preserve and follow the law and faith of Christ publicly.

Fourthly, they object that before the coming of Christ, not only the Synagogue of the Jews pertained to the Church of God, but all the Gentiles as well who, though dispersed throughout the world, truly worshiped one God. From that it seems to follow that faith might be a bond of the Church and hence, he who does not have faith does not pertain to the Church.

I respond: all those, and only those, constituted the Church of God, in all ages, who had been gathered at the same time in confession and assertion of one faith in one God, the creator of heaven and earth, whether these were made by sacrifices, or in another mode.

The last objection. The principle reason why secret heretics are included among the members of the Church, is that it seems that it is constituted for us with infallible certitude what body of men might be the Church; but this certitude cannot be had, even if secret heretics pertain to the Church, which is confirmed by the following arguments.

---

[20]lib. *de Pudicitia.*

[21]lib. 4, epist. 2.

[22]serm. 2 *contra Arianos.*

[23]lib. *de gratia Christi,* cap. 11.

a) Those who are not baptized are not members of the Church, but no man knows for certain who might be truly baptized, both because the character of Baptism is invisible, and because even when exterior Baptism is furnished, few are present to see, and consequently the rest ought to be content with human faith.

b) The Church cannot exist without Bishops and priests, as Jerome teaches.[24] But who knows for certain who might be true Bishops and priests since that depends upon the intention of the one ordaining and upon an invisible character.

c) The excommunicated are not in the Church, as we taught above, but many are secretly excommunicated, namely, excommunicated *ipso facto* by law, and not promulgated in the presence of the people, for that reason will we not be compelled to doubt when we see someone whether they may be in the Church or not?

d) It often happens, or certainly can happen in some places, that manifest heretics feign themselves to be Catholics, and also Jews, Turks and pagans mix themselves with the faithful, and still, either they will not be of the Church, or we will say that the Church is the body of heretics, pagans and hypocrites.

I respond to these arguments: *resp. a*) That someone might be in the body of the Church does not require the character of Baptism, but external Baptism; nor is external Baptism required to reckon someone might be in the Church, but only that he might be admitted since, if anyone asks to be admitted to the Church, it will not happen without Baptism. Nevertheless, if someone says he has been baptized, and the contrary is not certain, he shall be admitted to the other sacraments, and through this he will be of the body of the Church. Now, the sign of this that if afterward it were to become know that he was not baptized, then, if he deceived them he will be expelled from the congregation and not received again unless, after doing penance, he will be baptized. On the other hand, if it is not his fault, he would not be cast out, rather what he lacked will be

---

[24] *Contra Luciferianos.*

perfected in him. It would not be judged that he was not in the Church, but will be judged to have entered through another way than the ordinary power. For this very reason, Innocent III,[25] judged that a priest who was not baptized was truly in the Church, and commanded sacrifice to be offered for his soul just as for the faithful. Dionysius of Alexandria, as we have it in church history,[26] judged that a certain man was truly in the Church whom it was certain was not truly baptized but only secured the other Sacraments as one of the baptized.

Resp. b) Two things can be considered on Bishops: Firstly, that they hold the place of Christ so for that reason we owe obedience to them, and because they cannot deceive us in those things necessary for salvation. Secondly, that they might have the power of Order and Jurisdiction. If it is considered in the first mode, we are certain with an infallible certitude that these, whom we see, are our true Bishops and Pastors. For this, neither faith, nor the character of order, nor even legitimate election is required, but only that they be held for such by the Church. Since they are Bishops on account of the Church, they are not against it; God assists those who are held for such lest they would err in teaching the Church. Now, if this is considered in the second manner, we do not have any but a moral certitude that these will truly be Bishops, although it is certain, with infallible certitude, that at least some are true, otherwise God will have deserted the Church. For this purpose, to hold the Church is certain and clearly visible in so far as the heads and members, the first consideration suffices.

Resp. c) The secret excommunicates are in the Church by number but not by merit, *de facto* not *de jure*.

Resp. d) In the first place, I say the difficulty is that men of this sort are not detected on the spot, but nevertheless delude the Church for a long time, still nothing detrimental can happen from that. The Church does not number those among her own except by reason of

---

[25] cap. Apostolicam, de Presbytero non Baptizato.

[26] *Hist. Eccles.*, lib. 7, cap. 8.

external profession (they do not judge men regarding their internal life). Moreover, that external profession is very holy, although badly usurped by men such as these. Therefore, they are in the body of the Church while they are joined to the faithful in the bond of profession and obedience, because it binds the universal Church, and renders it into one body. Nevertheless, it does not follow that the Church on that account is the body of heretics, pagans and hypocrites, since even if a few men such as these are in the Church, nevertheless, we are certain with the certitude of divine faith that in the same Church, there are truly many faithful, pious and elect; just as in the human body nail and hair are discovered which do not live, and still no man thence gathers that the human body is nothing but nails and hair.

CHAPTER XI

Another Controversy is Proposed: Whether the Church is Always Visible, or Whether it can Err and Defect

WE HAVE explained what the Church is. Now we must speak about what kind of thing it is. There is conflict between us and the heretics on three matters. 1) They say the true Church is invisible and known only to God. Thus it is noted by Frederick Staphilus[1] that, in the beginning the Lutherans made the Church invisible, then at length, when they saw the absurdity which followed thence, by a secret counsel, they established that the Church may be said to be visible, but still by this name of visible they mean really invisible.

First of all, we take Luther in his work on *The Slave Will.* When Erasmus objected to him that it was not credible that God would desert the Church for so long a time, Luther responded that God never deserted the true Church, but that which is commonly called the Church is not the Church of Christ, *i.e.* the Pope, Bishops, clergy, monks and the remaining multitude of Catholics, rather it is a certain pious few whom, like a remnant, God preserves. And this was always in the world, that the Church that men said was the Church was not rather the certain pious and few. In another place he says the Church is spiritual and only perceptible by faith.[2] In another work he says the same thing, "Who will show us the Church since it is hidden in the spirit and only believed? In the same way as it is said, I believe in the holy Church?"[3]

---

[1]*Prima Apologia*, part. 3.

[2]lib. *contra Catharinum.*

[3]*De abroganda Missa privata*, pars 1.

Now the Centuriators of Magdeburg define the Church as a visible body,[4] nevertheless they distinguish two Churches, and say the true Church is for the most part scanty, while the false one is very numerous,[5] because only they pertain to the true Church who enter through the narrow gate, *i.e.* the truly pious, hence the true Church is invisible. They add that in the time of Christ, truly the Shepherds as well as the Magi, Zacharia, Simeon, Mary, and Anna, were in the Church but not the Priests and the Sadducees, because the former were pious, the latter were impious.[6]

Philip Melanchthon repeats as often as he can that the Church is visible.[7] Nevertheless, he says in the same place that the word of God must be followed in controversies according to the confession of the true Church. Moreover, this true Church he says cannot be Bishops and priests, nor a greater part of a Council, but certain pious and elect illuminated by God. Moreover, he says in the time of Elijah, the true Church was Elijah, Elisha, and the others that adhered to them, but not the remaining multitude of the Jews. Lastly, that in the time of Christ, the Church was Zachariah, Simeon, Mary and the shepherds because they were pious.

Brenz says in the Württemberg Confession[8] that the Church of God has the promise, still one must not stand before the judgment of Councils because few of the elect are there, and because often the greater part conquers the better part. And in his prolegomena he says: "You see that he [Pedro de Soto] makes the Church visible and perceptible in its corporeal senses. Therefore that article of the Creed will have to be blotted out, 'I believe in the holy Catholic Church,' and must be replaced with, *I see and perceive the holy Catholic Church.*'" In like manner, Calvin says, "Scripture speaks on the Church in two ways, on the one hand when it gives the name to

---

[4]Cent. 1, lib. 1, ca. 4, col. 170.

[5]*Ibid.*, col. 178.

[6]*Ibid*, col. 181.

[7]*in locis*, locus 12.

[8]cap. *de Conciliis.*

the Church, it understands that which is really in the presence of God. ... It is necessary for us to believe the Church is invisible and visible only to the eyes of God."[9] and again, "Moreover, to embrace the unity of the Church in that way, there is no need to pick out the Church herself with the eyes, or to touch it with the hands."[10]

2) They teach that the visible Church so erred in faith and morals that it defected inwardly. Calvin says this in his preface to *The Institutes*: "But it is no small thing that they erred from the truth, while they did not recognize the Church except that which they discerned with their physical eye.... They groan unless the Church is always shown with a finger.... Why don't we rather more permit God that, since he alone knows who are his own, he will, now and again, take the exterior notice of his Church from the sight of men."

3) They teach that the true Church, that is the invisible one, cannot indeed defect, nor err, in those matters which necessarily pertain to salvation; nevertheless it can err in other things. Calvin argues thus.[11] We assert the contrary and we will confirm each point with its own arguments.

---

[9] *Institut.* lib. 4, cap. 1, §7.

[10] *Ibid.*, §3.

[11] *Instit.* lib. 4, cap. 8, §13, and other places.

CHAPTER XII
The Church is Visible

FIRST, that the true Church is visible can be proved from all the Scriptures where the term Church is discovered. A visible congregation is always meant by the term Church. Calvin could not, and did not, advance even one passage where the term is attributed to an invisible congregation. Certainly, when it is said in Numbers, "Why did you lead the Church of the Lord into the wilderness?"[1] the Church is called that people who had gone out from Egypt. Thus in Kings, Scripture manifestly speaks on the visible Church, when it says, "The king turned his face and blessed every Church of Israel; for every Church of Israel stood."[2] In Matthew 16:18, "Upon this rock I will build my Church," by the name of rock one either understands Christ, or the confession of faith as the heretics do, or Peter as we believe, the foundation of the Church is always something perceptible, as is clear, and consequently, the Church herself is perceptible, or visible. Even if now we see neither Christ nor Peter, still both had been put forth to be seen by corporeal senses, and now both are seen not in themselves but in a vicar, or in their successor, just as the King of Naples is not invisible when the king is away since he is seen in his viceroy. "Speak to the Church, if he will not hear the Church, etc."[3]

Certainly neither [foundation] can be saved if the Church were invisible, as Acts relates, "Attend to the whole flock over which the Holy Spirit has placed you as Bishops to rule the Church of God."[4] How could they rule a Church that they did not know? "These being

---

[1]Numbers 20:4.

[2]3 Kings [1 Kings] 8:14.

[3]Matth. 18:17.

[4]Acts 20:28.

removed from the Church passed into Phoenicia,"[5] and in the same chapter, "When they came to Jerusalem, they were received by the Church." "Paul went up and greeted the Church."[6] How do these agree with an invisible Church? Paul says that he persecuted the Church of God;[7] but it is known whom he persecuted from Acts 9:2. Next, he says, "I write these things to you, son Timothy, that you know how you ought to live in the house of God, which is the Church of the living God, etc."[8] But rightly he could not live in it unless he know what it might be.

Secondly, it is proven from other Scriptures where the Church is not named, but is clearly described. "He placed his tent in the sun."[9] St. Augustine explains that he placed his Church in the open, just as the sun which cannot be completely hidden, so neither can the Church be hidden.[10] Likewise in Isaiah 2:2, Daniel 2:35, and Micah 4:1, the Church is compared to a great and conspicuous mountain which can be in no wise hidden, according to the common exposition of Jerome on these citations, as well as Augustine.[11] Likewise in Matthew, "A city placed on a hill cannot be hidden."[12] Augustine explains that this is about the Church. Therefore, the gospel parables on the sand, the net and the sheepfold, the dinner party etc. all show that the true Church, which is the kingdom of heaven, is visible.[13]

Thirdly, it is proved from the very beginning and progress of the Church. So as to pass over the Old Testament we note that the

---

[5]Acts 15:3.

[6]Acts 18:22.

[7]1 Corin. 15:9, Galat. 1:31, Philip. 3:6.

[8]1 Tim. 3:14-15.

[9]Psalm 18[19]:6.

[10]tract. 2 in epistola Ioannis.

[11]Tract 1 in epist. Ioannis.

[12]Matt. 5:14.

[13]*de Unitate Ecclesiae*, cap. 14, and other places.

Church was so visible that they carried the visible sign of circumcision in their flesh. In the New Testament the Christian Church was whole in the beginning in the Apostles and disciples of Christ, who were so visible that the Holy Spirit visibly descended over them on the day of Pentecost. Next, on one day three thousand men were added to them, and again five thousand by the confession of faith and Baptism, as is clear from Acts.[14] Thereafter, all these and only these were held to be in the Church of Christ, who had united themselves to those first through Baptism and Confession of faith, and thence they did not receive through heresy or schism, or were expelled through excommunication.

Fourthly, it is proven from the very plan of the Church. The Church is a certain society, not of Angels, nor of souls, but of men. For a society of men cannot be spoken of unless it consists of external and visible signs, for it is not a society unless the members of that society recognize each other, *i.e.*, unless the bonds of society are external and visible. It is also confirmed from the custom of all human societies, for in the army, in a city, in a kingdom, and like things, men are ascribed to them in no other manner than with visible signs. For this reason St. Augustine says, " There can be no religious society, whether the religion be true or false, without some sacrament or visible symbol to serve as a bond of union."[15]

Fifthly, in the time of Christ, as Melanchthon and Illyricus would have it, the Church was only in Zacharia, Simeon, Anne, Mary and a few other pious persons, but not in the priests and the remaining multitude of the Jews. But it is certain that Zacharias, Simeon and the others communicated with the Priests in the temple, the sacrifices, etc. Zacharias was sacrificing in the same temple; Anna did not leave the temple; Mary went yearly to the temple; Christ himself sent lepers to the priests and said, "Do what they tell you." Therefore, the Lutherans actually act wrongly by not communicating with us and by not obeying the Pope.

---

[14]Acts 1-4.

[15]*Contra Faustum*, lib. 19, cap. 11.

Sixthly, it is proven from necessity; for we are all held to unite ourselves to the true Church and persevere in it under the danger of eternal death, *i.e.* to obey its head and communicate with the other members, as is clear from St. Cyprian,[16] Jerome,[17] and Augustine.[18] But this cannot be done if the Church is invisible.

Seventhly, from the aforesaid in the previous question, if the Church is a gathering of men using the same Sacraments and professing the faith of Christ, under the rule of legitimate pastors, as it was proved there, it necessarily follows that it is visible.

Finally, by the testimony of the Fathers, such as Origen, "The Church is full of brilliance from East to West, etc."[19] Cyprian, "The Church, imbued with the light of the Lord, sprinkles its rays throughout the whole world."[20] Chrysostom says, "It is easier for the sun to be extinguished than the Church hidden."[21] Augustine says, "There is no safety in unity except from the promises of God that were declared to the Church, that, being set up on a mountain (as it was said), cannot be hidden,"[22] and again, "Can we not show the Church with our finger, brethren? Is it not clear?"[23] "What more is there to say than that they who do not see so great a mountain are blind? Who close their eyes to the lamp placed upon a lamp stand?"[24]

---

[16] *de Simplicitate Praelatorum.*

[17] in epist. 1 ad Damasum de nomine Hypostasis.

[18] *de Baptismo*, lib. 4, cap. 1.

[19] Homil. 30 in Matthaeum.

[20] *de Unitate Ecclesiae.*

[21] Homil. IV, in cap. 6 Isaiae.

[22] *Contra epist. Parmeniani*, lib. 3, cap. 5.

[23] Tract. 1 epistola Ioannis.

[24] *Ibid.*, Tract. 2.

CHAPTER XIII
The Visible Church Cannot Defect

NOW it can be easily proven that this true and visible Church cannot defect. Moreover it must be observed that many waste their time when they try to show that the Church cannot defect absolutely, for Calvin and the other heretics concede that, but they say it ought to be understood about the invisible Church. Therefore, we mean to show the visible Church cannot defect, and by the name Church, we do not understand one thing or another, but the multitude gathered together, in which there are Prelates and subjects.

1) It is shown from the Scriptures where the Church is clearly named, "Upon this rock I will build my Church, and the gates of hell will not prevail against it."[1] What is said in 1 Timothy is similar to this, "That you might know how you ought to live in the house of God which is the Church of the living God, the pillar and firmament of truth."[2] In both it is a question of the visible Church, as we see and still hear the very truth asserted that the gates of hell are not going to prevail against that Church.

2) The promise is clear from other passages without the name *Church*, such as in the last chapter of Matthew: "Behold I am with you even to the consummation of the age." Such words were spoken to a visible Church, evidently to the Apostles and the remaining disciples, whom the Lord spoke to on the day of his ascension. And since these men were not going to remain in the body even to the end of the world, it was necessary to say this promise pertained to

[1]Matt. 16:18.

[2]I Tim. 3:15.

their successors. Therefore St. Leo I[3] and Leo II[4] understand this on the perpetual duration of the Church.

Moreover, in Ephesians we read, "And he gave some as Apostles, others Prophets, other Evangelists, others Pastors and Teachers to the consummation of the Saints in the work of ministry, in the building of the body of Christ until we all run in the unity of faith, and the recognition of the Son of God, in the completion of strength and the measure of the age of the fullness of Christ."[5] There the Apostle teaches that the ministry of pastors and teachers is going to remain in that Church for the continual building of the body of Christ, and hence the visible Church, even to the day of Judgment. Were there only an invisible Church in the world, that ministry could not be found which cannot be exercised unless shepherds and sheep recognize it. It must be noted that although the Fathers understand this passage on the spiritual measure of the mystical body, more recent authors understand it on the corporal measure of the body of the blessed which they say is going to be of such a magnitude, as things were or had been in its perfect state of age. Nevertheless, all understand this passage on the last days, when the number of the elect will be filled.[6]

Besides, the Psalmist says, "God founded her in eternity,"[7] *i.e.* his Church, which is his city, as Augustine explains, and the matter speaks for itself, for the whole Psalm is on the foundation of the Christian Church, just as of a new and visible city. It begins, "The Lord is great and exceedingly praiseworthy, in the city of our God on his holy mountain: the whole world is founded in exaltation, etc." Likewise in Isaiah, "The Spirit of the Lord is upon me, ... and I will strike a perpetual covenant with them, and their seed will be known

[3]in epist. 31 *ad Pulcheriam Augustam.*

[4]in epistola *ad Constantinum Augustum.*

[5]Eph. 4:11.

[6]See Augustine, *de Civitate Dei*, lib. 22, cap. 15, 17 et 18 where he touches on each explanation.

[7]Psalm 47[48]:9.

among the Nations, and their seed in the midst of the people. All who see them recognize them, because they are the seed which the Lord has blessed."[8] That this chapter is understood on the Church of the New Testament, Christ taught in Luke IV when he recited it in the Synagogue and explained it on his coming. Certainly this passage is so clear that it does not require exposition. How will that body be invisible if it is said, "All who saw them knew them because they are the seed which the Lord has blessed."

3) Next come the testimonies from parables in which the Church is meant by the consensus of all, for the sand in which there are grains and chaff; the net in which there are good fish and bad; the field in which there is the grain and cockle; the dinner party in which there are the good and evil reclining; the sheepfold in which there are sheep and goats mean the visible Church, as even the heretics affirm. For an invisible Church does not have wicked and good, but only the good, according to their opinion. But the same parables teach that the Church visible Church is never going to perish even to the Day of Judgment. In Matthew it is said, "He will clean his field, and he will gather the wheat into his barn, but the chaff he will burn in the inextinguishable fire,"[9] which certainly will happen before the day of judgment. And again, "Permit each to rise even to the harvest. The harvest will be the end of the world ... Thus the angels will go out in the consummation of the age, and will separate the wicked from the midst of the just, etc."[10]

Fourthly, it is proven from the Scriptures, which speak on the reign of Christ. The Psalmist says, "His throne is as the sun in my sight, and just as the moon completed forever, and a faithful witness in the sky . . . and I will place his seed in age upon age and his thrown as a day of heaven."[11] "In the days of those kingdoms God will raise the kingdom of heaven which will never be destroyed: and

---

[8]Isaiah 61:8-9.

[9]Matt. 3:12.

[10]Matt. 13:30.

[11]Psal. 88[89]:38.

his kingdom will be handed to another people."[12] "And for his kingdom there will be no end."[13] These passages cannot be understood except about the fact that the true and visible Church of Christ is not going perish. For the Kingdom of Christ, without a doubt, is his true Church. One cannot call a few secret men dispersed and separated from each other a kingdom, where one does not know the other such as the invisible Church of the Lutherans. For the kingdom is a multitude of men gathered who know one another.

Besides, in Psalm 88 [89] where the eternal kingdom of Christ is spoken of, it also says that in it there will be the good and the evil, and hence that the Church is visible, "But if its sons forsake my law and do not keep my justice, ... I will visit their iniquity with the rod and their sins with beatings, but I will not dispense my mercy from it, etc." St. Cyprian beautifully explains such a passage in *de Lapsis*. In the other verse in Daniel where it says the kingdom of Christ is perpetual, we also read that the kingdom is a great mountain filling all the earth, which Isaiah[14] and Micah[15] call a conspicuous mountain according to the Septuagint.

5) It is proven from the testimonies of thc Fathers. Origen and Chrysostom affirm it in the places we cited, but Augustine and Bernard express it more clearly. St. Augustine, disputing on Psal. 101 against the Donatists, (who said the whole visible Church had perished and only remained among the just in Africa) said, "But that Church, which was of all nations, no longer exists, it perished, yet those who are not in it say this. O impudent voice, just because you are not in it does not make it so. See to it lest you might were to be

[12]Daniel 2:35.

[13]Luke I.

[14]ὅτι ἔσται ἐν ταῖς ἐσχάταις ἡμέραις ἐμφανὲς τὸ ὄρος κυρίου καὶ ὁ οἶκος τοῦ θεοῦ ἐπ' ἄκρων τῶν ὀρέων καὶ ὑψωθήσεται ὑπεράνω τῶν βουνῶν καὶ ἥξουσιν ἐπ αὐτὸ πάντα τὰ ἔθνη. Isaiah 2:2

[15]Micah 4.

no more, since it will continue to be, even if you do not."[16] Further on, he introduces the Church speaking in this way: "How long will I be in this world? Tell me, on account of those who say the Church did exist but does so no longer, that it apostatized and perished from all nations; yea it announced and that voice was not empty. Who announced it to me, unless it was on the road? When did he announce it? Behold, I am with you even to the end of the age." He says similar things on Psalm 147 and in his work *On the Unity of the Church*, chapter 13, 20, and in other places.

The response cannot be made that Augustine speaks about the invisible Church since that does not perish nor is it going to, as the Donatists admitted, when they tried to apply the verse "I am with you even to the end of the age," to themselves, as Augustine related above.

On that verse in the Canticles, "I held him, nor will I let him go until I lead him into the house of my mother," St. Bernard explains, "Then and thereafter, the Christian race is not going to defect, not faith from the earth nor charity from the Church; the rivers came, the winds blew and dashed against her, and she did not fall, to the extent that she was founded upon the rock, and the rock was Christ. Therefore, neither the verbosity of the philosophers nor the jeering of heretics nor the swords of persecutors could or will be able to separate her from the love of God."[17] These cannot be understood on the invisible Church, for the swords of tyrants will not pursue her, nor the verbosity of Philosophers or the jeering of heretics; therefore, the visible Church does not defect. Vincent of Lérin agrees, who rebukes the opinion of Nestorius as a grave error which taught the whole Church erred in the mystery of the Incarnation, to the extent that it followed blind teachers.[18]

Lastly, it is proved by natural reason. Firstly, if at some time only an invisible Church remained in the world, then at some point

[16]In Psal. 101, sermon 2.

[17]Serm. 79 in Cant.

[18]Commonitorium.

salvation would be impossible for those who are outside the Church. They cannot be saved unless they enter the Church, just as in the time of Noah they perished who were not added to the ark. Yet, they could not enter a Church which they were ignorant of, therefore they have no remedy.

Besides that, it is also shown from the plan of the one true Church that it is visible, therefore if the visible Church were to perish then no true Church would remain.

Next, either those hidden men who constituted an invisible Church openly profess their faith and abstain from the worship of idols or not; if they profess it, then the Church is not invisible, but particularly visible just as it was in the time of the Martyrs; if they do not profess it, then there is no Church since the Church is not the true Church if there are no good men in it who are saved. Moreover they are neither good nor saved who do not confess the faith, but instead, after they restrain it in their heart, profess treachery and idolatry outwardly, since in Romans the Apostle says, "For the man who believes in heart to justice, let confession be made by his mouth unto salvation,"[19] and again, "Everyone who denies me before men, I will deny him before my Father."[20] Consequently, it involves a contradiction for there to be a Church that altogether lacks a visible form, unless one were to place it outside the world where it will never be necessary to confess the faith.

---

[19] Romans 10.

[20] Matthew 10.

CHAPTER XIV
The Church Cannot Err

IT remains that we prove the Church cannot err in any way, not even by apostatizing from God. Still, first place must be given to a little more careful explanation of our adversaries teachings and our own.

Calvin says that the famous proposition, "The Church cannot err," is true with a two-fold restriction. 1) If the Church does not propose doctrines outside of Scripture, *i.e.* if it rejects traditions not written and only faithfully proposes what is contained in the Scriptures. Moreover, if you ask whether we might be certain that the Church always faithfully proposes those things that are in the Scriptures, Calvin responds by applying a second restriction, the Church always proposes faithfully what is contained in the Scriptures in matters necessary to salvation, still not in other matters and consequently some blemishes of error always remain in the Church.

The second restriction is that "The Church cannot err," is understood on the universal Church alone, it is not extended to the Bishops who are representatives of the Church, as it is said on the Catholic side. Every Bishop manages the person of his particular Church and therefore all Bishops manage the person of the whole Church. So Calvin holds of the greater institution,[1] while in the lesser institution,[2] he fraudulently and mendaciously explains our opinion, saying we advance that the Church cannot err whether it uses the Word of God or not, since still he does not know we do not speak on the word of God absolutely, but only on the written word,

---

[1] *Instit.* lib. 4, cap. 8, §11, 12, 14, 15.

[2] *ibid.*, cap.8, §146, 148, 149 et 150.

and to say the Church cannot err whether it proposes that which is contained in the Scriptures, or doctrines outside of the Scriptures.

Next, our teaching is that the Church absolutely cannot err, neither in matters absolutely necessary, nor in others which must be believed or proposed that we must do, whether they are expressly held in the Scriptures or not, and when we say the Church cannot err, we understand that both on the universality of the faithful and on the universality of the Bishops, so that the sense might be of this proposition that the Church cannot err, *i.e.* that which all faithful hold as *de fide* is necessarily true and *de fide*, and likewise that which all Bishops teach as pertaining to the faith necessarily is true and *de fide*.

Since these have been explained this truth must be proved. 1) From the universal Church as it contains all the faithful and especially from that we read in 1 Timothy 3:15, "The Church of God is a pillar and firmament of truth." Calvin responds that the Church is called a pillar and firmament of truth because, like a most trusty guardian, it preserves the preaching of the written word of God, not because it cannot err in any matter.

On the other hand, in this manner the offices of copyists were the pillars of truth because they very carefully safeguard all Scriptures, then the Apostle mentions Scriptures here, but he simply says the Church is the pillar and firmament of truth. Besides, how much more is a pillar than a simple guard? For the house rests upon the pillar and without that it falls. Thus when the Apostle calls the Church the pillar of truth, he means the truth of faith, in regard to us, rests upon the authority of the Church and the Church sanctions whatever is true and rejects whatever is false. Add that the Church was a pillar when there were no Scriptures, from which it follows that it is not called a pillar on account of protection of the Scriptures. Next, if it were a question of protection, then it would be better if Paul had compared the Church to a strong-box than to a pillar, for strong-boxes preserve books.

2) Besides, the Church is governed by Christ just as a spouse by her head, and by the Holy Spirit just as by the soul, which is clear

from Ephesians, "He gave it a head over every Church, which is his body,"[3] and, "One body, one Spirit,"[4] and "A man is the head of a woman just as Christ is the head of the Church."[5] Therefore, if the Church could err in doctrines of faith or morals, error would be attributed to Christ and the Holy Spirit. For that reason, the Lord said, "The Spirit of truth will teach you all truth."[6]

Calvin responds that Christ and the Holy Spirit teach the Church all the truth that is simply necessary, but still some blemish is always left behind. It doesn't follow that error would be attributed to Christ or the Holy Spirit, just as ignorance, which is beyond doubt in the Church, is not attributed to them.

I respond: Just as a man who is head of a woman is not held to remove all ignorance from his wife, still he is held to remove all error from which some great evil might arise, although the wife may be excused by ignorance; so also Christ is held to remove all error from the Church, from which great evil arises, such is all error in regard to faith. For it is a great evil because the Church would worship God with a false faith, since divine worship consists in Faith, Hope and Charity, as Augustine teaches.[7]

3) We are obliged under the penalty of anathema to believe the Church in everything, as is clear from Scripture, "But if he will not listen to the Church, let him be to you as a heathen and a tax-collector."[8] Councils impose every anathema on those not assenting to the decrees of the Church, but it would be wicked to oblige under so grave a penalty to assent to uncertain and false matters.

Calvin responds: Christ commanded that we listen to the Church because he knew the Church was going to teach nothing outside of the written word of God. On the other hand, so as to omit a great

---

[3]Ephes. 1.

[4]Ephes. 4.

[5]Ephes.5.

[6]John 16.

[7]*Enchridium*, cap. 3.

[8]Matt. 18.

many things which we said in the disputation on traditions, the true Church teaches that the epistle to the Romans is the word of God, but the epistle to the Laodiceans is not, and likewise the about the Gospel of Mark and that of Nicodemus and other things that can be said, which were never written, consequently, it is not true that the Church teaches nothing outside the written word of God.

4) The Apostles' Creed teaches that the Church is holy and this holiness properly consists in the profession of doctrines, therefore, Christian profession contains nothing but what is holy, *i.e.* what is true in regard to a doctrine of faith and just in regard to precepts of morals, and in this it really excels all the professions of the Philosophers, Heathen, Jews and heretics. For all have some false doctrines mixed with true ones.

5) If Calvin's opinion were true, then a great part of dogmas of faith could be called into doubt, for there are many *de fide* teachings which are not absolutely necessary to salvation. Duly, to believe in the histories of the Old Testament, or that the Gospels of Mark and Luke are canonical writings, nay more any of the Scriptures, is not altogether necessary for salvation, since without this faith many were saved before the Scriptures were read; afterward, in the time of the New Testament, many barbarian nations were saved without them, as Irenaeus writes.[9] But this is most absurd, nor would Calvin admit there can be any doubt about Scripture, therefore it is not true that the Church cannot err only in those matters necessary for salvation.

Lastly it is proven from the Fathers who, as we noted in the *Controversy on the Word of God*, on the question on the judge of controversies, all call upon the Church in whatever question of faith. Certainly they would not do this if they thought the Church could be deceived in some way. Tertullian says, "Well then, all Churches erred and the Holy Spirit looks to no one."[10] Augustine said, "We hold to the truth of the Scriptures since we do that which has

---

[9]lib. 3, cap. 4.

[10]*de Praescript.*

already pleased the universal Church, which the authority of Scriptures itself commends, that because the Holy Scripture cannot be deceived, whoever fears to be deceived by the obscurity of this question, let him consult the Church about it, as Sacred Scripture points out without any ambiguity."[11] And again, "He speaks of the most insolent madness to dispute against that which the universal Church senses."[12]

Now that the Church also can not err representatively is proven first from the fact that if all Bishops would err, the whole Church would also err, because the people are held to follow their own pastors, by what the Lord says in Luke, "He who hears you, hears me,"[13] and "Whatsoever they say, do."[14] Secondly, from the epistle of the Council of Ephesus to Nestorius, where Nestorius is compelled if he would satisfy the Church he could swear an oath to attest that he believes just as the Bishops of the East and West do. Likewise we see that St. Augustine calls the decree of a general Council the consensus of the universal Church,[15] and rightly so since the Church does not teach that it does not discern anything except through her pastors, just as any body you like through its head. For that reason, in Scripture a congregation of Priests and elders is called the assembly (*ecclesia*) of all Israel.[16] Chrysostom explains what verse of Matthew XVIII, "Speak to the Church," that is, to a Prelate. But this has more to do with the tract on Councils.

---

[11]*Contra Cresconium*, lib. 1, cap. 33.

[12]Epist. 118.

[13]Luke 10.

[14]Matth. 23.

[15]*de Baptismo*, lib. 1, cap. 18.

[16]3 Kings 8.

CHAPTER XV
The Arguments with Which they Set up an Invisible Church are Refuted

IT remains that we rebut the arguments of our adversaries. And the first is where they try to show that the Church is invisible by these testimonies. 1) "I will give my law in their hearts, and I will be their God, and they will be my people."[1] There, God distinguishes the Church of the New Testament from the Church of the Old Testament, which was an external body and for that reason had a written law on external tablets, e.g. stone; the Church of the New Testament, however is a people that has an interior law and for that reason it is written on their hearts. The same thing is contained in Luke, "The kingdom of God does not come with observation and they will not say, "look her, or look there. Behold, the kingdom of God is within you."[2] And in John, "The hour comes and now is when true worshipers will adore the Father in spirit and truth."[3] Therefore the Church of the New Testament does not consist in some exterior sign, nor is it bound to places and corporal ceremonies, just as we see in Hebrews, "For you have not come to an easy mountain or an accessible fire, but to Mount Zion, the city of the living God," etc.[4] There he compares the Synagogue to Mount Sinai, as well as the visible and tangible Church to the spiritual Mountain of Zion. Likewise in first Peter, "And you yourselves are built just as living stones of a spiritual house, a holy priesthood, offering spiritual sacrifices to God;"[5] But this house is the Church. At length that the

---

[1]Jeremiah 31:33.

[2]Luke 17:20.

[3]John 4:23.

[4]Hebrews 12:18-22.

[5]1 Peter 2:5.

Church exists is an article of faith, consequently the Church is not seen, but believed."

I respond: In the first passage from Jeremiah, it does not compare the Church with the Synagogue but the New Testament with the Old, which is clear in that passage. And although the New testament is properly charity, which is the law written on our hearts, the Old Testament is properly external doctrine, or the law written on stones, still it does not follow that the Church of the New Testament is invisible; just as the body of any animal you like is visible, still it has many internal parts which are not seen, such as the heart, the liver, the vitals of life, and like things; so also the visible Church has many invisible things, Faith, Hope and Charity, etc. and although these gifts are invisible, they are necessary in the Church and in the Church alone; still not in all its parts, just as a sense is necessarily in an animal and only in an animal, and nevertheless not in all its parts.

To the second I say the kingdom of God is understood in Luke by grace, through which God now reigns in the hearts of men, as Theophylactus explains it, or Christ himself as Bede explains it. For Christ speaks on both comings. The Pharisees asked, "When will the kingdom of God come," *i.e.*, the kingdom of thc Mcssiah? But the Lord responded that the Messiah came and is going to come again on the Day of Judgment. Therefore, on the first coming he said, "The kingdom of God will not come with observation; behold the kingdom of God is within you," *i.e.* the Messiah has come and is present now. On the second he adds, "And they will say to you, behold he is here, or behold there, do not go out, just as lightening strikes under heaven, etc., so will be the coming of the son of man."

To the third I say, it is taught in that passage that the particular worship of God in the Church is going to be internal, but for that reason it does not follow that the Church herself is invisible, as we said above, nor does it follow that all external worship must be rejected and external temples be destroyed. The Lord does not treat on the place of prayer in that verse, but on the manner and rite. For if he meant to say that true worshipers are no longer going to worship God in Jerusalem or on Mount Gerizim, what he said would have been false. It is certain that Peter and John, after they received the Holy Spirit went up to the temple in Jerusalem at the ninth hour for prayer.[6] It is also certain that afterward there always were in Palestine Christians who worshiped God in Jerusalem and on mount Gerizim, and everywhere that bordered those places. He speaks on the rite of worship, or of prayer, in other words, you will adore the Father neither on this mountain nor in Jerusalem, *i.e.* neither the rite of the Samaritans nor that of the Jews, but you will worship in the rite of Christians which is a rite worshiping in spirit and truth, but that is explained in two ways.

Chrysostom, Cyril, Euthymius oppose "in the spirit" in this passage to the ceremonies of the Jews, insofar as they were corporal, that "in truth", to the same ceremonies in so far as they were a figure and shadow of things to come. Theophylactus, St. Thomas and Cajetan oppose "in the Spirit" to the ritual of the Jews, which was especially external and corporal, but that, "In truth," to the ritual of the Samaritans, which was false and erroneous, for these worshiped the true God as well as false gods. Consequently, the Lord says that the rite of the Christian people will be particularly spiritual and at the same time true and pure from all error, although the spiritual rite will not exclude corporal ceremonies, in so far as they promote spiritual worship.

I answer the fourth with Chrysostom and Theophylictus, St. Thomas and others. Through the spiritual mountain of Zion and the city of the living God the Apostle does not understand the Church militant, but the Church triumphant, which is constituted from blessed souls. Accordingly, he compares the Synagogue with the Church and says the men of the Old Testament came to a physical mount Zion that they would see God there in some manner through corporeal images, but the men of the new Testament came not in fact but in hope, to the spiritual mount Zion, *i.e.* to the glory of the blessed, where God is seen face to face, and it is added for this

---

[6] Acts 3:1.

reason, "And the abundance of many thousands of Angels, and the spirits of the perfect just, etc."

I respond to the fifth that something can be said to be spiritual in two ways. In one way, according to substance, which is why in Ephesians they are called, "Spiritual wickedness in the heavens."[7] In the other way, according to the ordination to the Spirit, because something is ordered to the spirit or the spirit is dominated in it. This is why in 1 Corinthians 2:15 a man is called spiritual, and in 1 Cor. 15:44 the spiritual body, and in 1 Peter 2:5 all good works are called spiritual offerings, such as almsgiving and fasting. Therefore, St. Peter, when he says the Church is a spiritual house, he understands this in the second way, for he means the Church is not a house made from wood and stones, but built from men consecrated to God.

To the sixth it can be said that in the Creed it is not merely I believe in the Church, but, I believe in the holy Church. Consequently the holiness of the Church is without any doubt invisible. But it is better to say that in the Church something is seen and something is believed. For we see that body of men which is the Church, yet we do not see the fact that this body is the true Church of Christ, rather we believe it. For the true Church is that which professes the faith of Christ. Who clearly knows our faith is of Christ? We indeed believe it is firm and certain, but it is one thing to believe and another to see, nay more to believe is the very thing defined by the Apostle, the argument is not of appearances.

What must be noted so as to understand it better, is that every teaching that is *de fide* is born from two propositions on faith and then the whole conclusion is not apparent; or one is on faith and the other is from what is apparent and then the conclusion is partly apparent, partly not apparent. Such is this conclusion, these men who now profess the faith under the Roman Pontiff are in the Church of Christ; for it arises from a syllogism: the Church of Christ is a body of men professing the faith of Christ, under the rule of the

---

[7]Ephes. 6:12.

legitimate pastors; but these who are under the Roman Pontiff today are of such a body; therefore they are the Church of Christ. In such a syllogism, the major is on faith, and consequently is not apparent whereas the minor is evident, for we place nothing in the minor that is not perceived with the eyes or the ears. Therefore the conclusion is properly advanced as partly evident and partly non-apparent.

Next, the very matter, or (that we might speak logically) that *incomplexity*, concerning which the plan and definition of the Church is preached, is a certain visible thing; whereas the *complexity*, or the connection of what has been preached with the subject is preserved only by faith. The examples whereby this is illustrated are not lacking. Accordingly, that man who is Christ the son of God, the Apostles saw and at length that he was Christ the son of God they did not see, but they believed. For this reason in John 20:29, it was said to Thomas, "You have believed Thomas because you have seen me." And in the creed we say, "I believe in one Baptism," although we might see and perceive Baptism, *i.e.* the aspersion of water and the conferral of the words. Therefore we do not see, but we believe that the sprinkling of the water and the conferral of the words is the Baptism of Christ, that is a specific sacrament.

CHAPTER XVI
The Arguments Whereby our Adversaries try to Show the Church can Defect are Answered

NOW, our adversaries attempt to show that the Church can defect and at some time did defect with these arguments. 1) In the beginning of the world Adam and Eve alone constituted the whole Church at least in power; but each lost the faith and apostatized from God, as is clear from Genesis III and from the Fathers.[1]

2) In the time of Moses the whole Church apostatized from God. For Aaron, the High priest, proposed to worship the calf, and the whole people shouted, "These are the gods of Israel."[2]

3) In the time of Elijah the whole visible Church had defected. For in 3 Kings Elijah says, "I alone am left. And the Lord said to him, 'I have reserved to myself seven thousand men in Israel who have not bent the knee to Baal'," [3] but these were secret not doubtful, since not even Elijah knew them.

4) It is said in Isaiah, "The ox knows its owner and the ass the trough of its lord, but Israel does not know me. From the soul of the foot even to the crown of the head there is no health in it."[4] And in Jeremiah, "The houses of Israel have been confounded and their kings and princes, even the priests and prophets speaking in the wood; you are my Father, why do you contend with me in judgment? All have forsaken me, says the Lord."[5] And in Chronicles,

---

[1]Ambrose, lib. de Paradiso, cap. 6; Augustine, *Echirid.*, cap. 45 and Prosper, *lib. de gratia Dei*, contra collatorem.

[2]Exodus 32:4.

[3]3 [1] Kings 19:10.

[4]Isaiah 1:3.

[5]Jeremiah 2:26.

"Many days will pass in Israel without the true God, without a priest or teacher, and without the law."[6]

5) It was foretold that the Church would be in visible inactivity. "The hosts will cease, and the sacrifice."[7] "When the son of man will come, do you think he will find faith on earth?"[8] "Unless the great dispersal will happen first, and the man of sin will have been revealed."[9] Therefore, Calvin thinks that what we read in Jeremiah has been said to us, "Do not trust in the words of the a lie, saying the Temple of the Lord, the temple of the Lord,"[10] namely these ancient Jews did not believe the prophets' warnings about the desolation because they saw the had the temple of the Lord, and external ceremonies; so Calvin thinks we boast that we have the ancient Churches, the successions of Bishops, the Apostolic See and meanwhile we do not attend to the Scriptures, which clearly foretell desolation to us.

6) The General Council of Basel deposed Eugene as a heretic and all those adhering to him and chose Felix, thereupon after the Council was concluded and dispersed, again Eugene crept into the See without any canonical election and from him were born as many as were Popes, Cardinal and Bishops afterward, therefore at least from that time the Church adhering to the Roman Pontiff was not the true Church and since there was no other visible body, the visible Church perished. Calvin places this argument in the preface of his *Institutes* and again in the last place as though it were his strongest argument, adding, "This is discovered that it is necessary for them to adhere or to define the Church otherwise, or else we hold all to be schismatics."

7) They advance the testimony of the Fathers and first of all Hilary. "The love of walls gave you a beginning; you venerate the

---

[6]2 Chron. 15:3.

[7]Daniel 9:27.

[8]Luke 18:8.

[9]2 Thess. 2:3.

[10]Jeremiah 7:4.

Church of God badly in buildings, you badly heaped under them the name of peace; to me mountains, lakes, prisons and deep holes are safer."[11] There he says the true Church was so obscured in his time that it could only be found in catacombs and caverns. Then Jerome, speaking in the same time, says, "The whole world groaned and marveled that it was Arian."[12] St. Basil says the same thing,[13] and St. Bernard,[14] so deplore the vices of the prelates of their times that they sufficiently show everyone had gone their own way and there was no visible Church. Then, Chrysostom teaches that sometimes there is no visible sign by which the true Church could be recognized, and therefore the only recourse is to return to the Scriptures.[15]

I respond, *ad* 1) If that our first parents sinned was for the Church to defect then not only the visible but even the invisible Church defected which is against our adversaries' point. Secondly I say there was no Church then, nor only two human beings in the Church, rather it was only the beginning of the Church and the beginning was both material and formal. Adam was the material beginning of the Church because he was the first of all in the Church; he was also the formal principle because he was the head or teacher and ruler of the people of God so long as he lived. Consequently the head of the Church cannot err by teaching false doctrine, nevertheless he can err by living badly and even by thinking badly as a private man. We see this happened in Adam since at one time he lived badly and perhaps even thought badly about God, nevertheless he did not teach badly.

ad 2) In regard to Aaron and the people that worshiped the golden calf, I say in that time there was neither a head nor a body of the Church to have defected since only Moses was the head whom it is certain did not err. Accordingly, Aaron was not yet the high priest

---

[11] *Contra Auxentium.*

[12] *Contra Luciferianos.*

[13] epist. 69 et 70.

[14] Serm.33 *in Cantica.*

[15] Hom. 49.

since that happened later, as is clear from Exodus 40:12. Moreover the body did not fail, for all the Levites were immune from that sin, which is clear from the same chapter, where Moses said, "'If anyone is of the Lord let him join with me,' and all the sons of Levi gathered around him."[16]

ad 3) Concerning the time of Elijah, both the consequent and the antecedent of this argument are denied. The consequent because the plan for the Jewish people and the Christian people are not the same. The people of the Jews were not a universal Church as the Christian people are, but a particular one and on that account faithful and just men were found outside of that people, such as Melchisedech, Job and later Cornelius, the Centurion and the Eunuch of Queen Candice, as well as several others. Therefore, even if the whole Synagogue of the Jews defected all the Church of God on earth would not have defected on the spot. But the antecedent is also denied since it cannot be shown that the Synagogue of the Jews altogether defected even to the coming of Christ. After that it did not as much defect as it was changed into something better.

Now to that about Elijah I say that he did not speak on every people of the Jews, but only about thc part that had been subjected to the king of Samaria. It is certain from the same book of Kings that in the time of Elijah Asa ruled in Jerusalem and after him Josaphat, the best kings, and under them the people and the priests very clearly persisted in true religion. Next, when the Lord said, "I have reserved to myself seven thousand men," he added, "in Israel." Then those who were under the king of Samaria were said to be of Israel, while those who were under the king of Jerusalem were said to be of Judah. Thus Philip Melanchthon was evidently deceived, since in his work he says that in the time of Elijah the Church was only in Elijah, Elisha and a few priests.[17] Calvin followed him in this error in the preface of his *Institutes*, which especially rests upon this argument on Elijah.

---

[16]Exodus 32.

[17]*in Locis communibus,* cap. de Ecclesia.

ad 4) Augustine responds to this when he taught that Prophets and Apostles sometimes rebuke the whole people as though not one of them were good, although there still might be many good and on the contrary sometimes they console all as if all were good when it is certain there are many wicked. Ezekiel says, "All the house of Israel is contrite on their forehead, and hard of heart."[18] Yet he also says, "The sign of the Thau is upon the foreheads of all that groan and weep, over all abominations that are done in its midst."[19] In Galatians the Apostle says, "O irrational Galatians, who bewitched you to not obey the truth?"[20] Yet he says later, "Brethren, and if a man be overtaken in any fault, you, who are spiritual, instruct such a one in the spirit of meekness."[21]

To the verse from Chronicles I respond that in the first place it is only understood on the kingdom of Israel, not the kingdom of Judah. Next, perhaps the Scripture speaks on the time that was going to be after the coming of the Messiah, for now many days have passed in Israel without God, without Priest and without the Law.

ad 5) I say that we do not boast in temples and the succession of Bishops and the Apostolic See in themselves, but on account of the promise of Christ who said, "You are Peter and upon this rock, ... and the gates of hell will not prevail." The Jews never had such a promise. Nor is it true that the ruin of the Church was foretold in the Scriptures, rather the opposite is true everywhere. Hence, to that passage of Daniel, even if Hilary, as well as even Hypolitus and Apollinarius who are cited by Jerome[22] understand that prophecy on the time of Antichrist, still it is beyond doubt that they were deceived. For Daniel speaks on the overturning of Jerusalem and the end of the sacrifice of the Jews. This is how Chrysostom and

---

[18]Ezek. 3:7.

[19]*ibid.*, 9:14.

[20]Galat. 3:1.

[21]Galat. 6:1.

[22]in cap. 9 Danielis.

Theophylactus, and Jerome,[23] Augustine,[24] as well as Eusebius,[25] Clement of Alexandria,[26] Tertullian,[27] and the common opinion of the Jews as we also see cited by Jerome in his commentary on Daniel 9.

And the heretics are compelled to admit this answer; for they say that now is the times of Antichrist and has been for many centuries, and nevertheless the sacrifices and the sacrifice has not ceased, therefore they ought to understand this passage of Daniel not on the time of Antichrist but on the overturning of Jerusalem, which is evidently gathered from the Gospel. "When you will see the abomination of desolation which was spoken of by the Prophet Daniel, standing in the holy place, he who reads shall understand, then those who are in Judea should flee to the mountains.[28] Likewise he explained the same thing in Luke, "When you see Jerusalem surrounded by an army, then know that its destruction approaches, then those who are in Judea, let them flee to the mountains."[29]

Now, to that which we find later in Luke, "Do you think he will find faith on earth?"[30] I say that the Lord does not speak on faith simply, but on the outstanding faith that is found in only a few, and in the last days among very few. This is how Jerome explains it,[31] and Augustine,[32] or we could say with Theophylactus that the Lord speaks on faith absolutely and means few faithful are going to be left

---

[23]in cap. 24, Matth.

[24]epist. 80 ad Esichium

[25]lib. 8 Evangel. demonstr. cap. 2.

[26]*Stromata*, lib. 2.

[27]*Contra Judaeos*, cap. 5.

[28]Matt. 24:15.

[29]Luke 21:20.

[30]Luke 20:8.

[31]*contra Luciferianos*

[32]*de Unitate Ecclesiae*, cap. 13.

in the time of Antichrist, but still not be none, nor so few that they could not make the Church.

Now to that of Paul I say that by the name of dispersal either Antichrist himself is understood, as Chrysostom, Theodoret, Oecumenius, Theophylactus and Augustine[33] explain. They argue it should be called a dispersal as a metonym, because it will cause many to leave Christ; or it means the defection from the Roman Empire, as Ambrose, Sedulius and Primasius explain, which is a very probable opinion, or at length it will mean a going out from the Church that is not general but particular, *i.e.* not of all but of many, or at least of all secret heretics, as some of the Fathers beautifully explain it.[34] In the same way that many who were in the Church for a long time with a feigned spirit, at length clearly leave through the profession of manifest heresy, so when Antichrist comes nearly every secret heretic who then will be discovered in the Church will leave it, and join themselves to Antichrist.

ad 6) I say that the Council of Basel was at first legitimate, for even the legate of the Roman Pontiff was present, as well as a great number of Bishops, but in the time that it "deposed" Eugene and elected Felix, it was not a Council of the Church but a schismatic Council, seditious and of altogether no authority. Thus it is called in the last Lateran Council, sess. 11, and hence Eugene was always a true Pope and this clearly another lie of Calvin when he says that this Council preserved its authority and dignity even to the end.

In the first place, at the time the Council dared to pronounce sentence, there was no legate of the Pope present and all the Bishops had left, but a certain Cardinal from Arles usurped the office of president and because the Bishops were very few, they introduced into the Council a multitude of priests so that it became contrary to the form of ancient Councils, being composed not of Bishops but of priests.

---

[33] *de Civitate Dei*, lib. 20, cap. 19.

[34] with Augustine, *de Civitate Dei*, lib. 20, cap. 19.

Next, in the same time another Council was held in Florence in which the Supreme Pontiff presided and since the Latin and Greek Bishops who sat there without comparison many more than were at Basel, and together with the Bishops the Greek Emperor and the legate of the Latin Emperor were present, so that it could not be doubted which of the two was a true general Council of the Church.

Thirdly, God willed to show what he thought by afflicting Basel with a plague so horrible that a greater part of the Fathers who were there either were killed or were compelled to withdraw. Aeneas Sylvius (the future Pius II) related all of this in his history of the Council of Basel as well as what the heretics there had recently published as if favoring them on account of the condemnation of Eugene, when really he did them a great deal of harm. Add that the Council of Basel was continued at Lausanne and it subjected itself to Pope Nicholas V, as is clear from his epistle.

ad 7) Now we come to the citations of the Fathers. To the one from Hilary, firstly I respond in the way Augustine once did to the Donatists,[35] who objected with the same testimony, that the Church was at one time obscured by a multitude of scandals, still it stood out in its most loyal members, just as it did in the time which Hilary spoke. The Church stood out in Pope Julius I, Athanasius, Hilary, Eusebius Vercellensis, and then in Pope Damasus, Ambrose, Basil, Gregory Nazanzien and many others who were steadfast pillars of the Church.

Secondly, I say that Hilary spoke in that citation on the Church at Milan, in which many simple people venerated Auxentius as a Catholic even though he was still an Arian, since Auxentius behaved with such a wonderful subtly the Arians knew them as one of their own yet he was believed to be Catholic by man simple men. Hilary meant that no trust should be put in Auxentius even if he seemed to be a Bishop and preached in the Church and that it would be better to remain in prisons and caves with right faith than to be in the Church of God with heretics.

---

[35]Epist. 48.

Nevertheless, what he said about one city, one Church and one Bishop cannot be applied to the universal Church. It can happen that one Bishop in one city and in one temple should teach heresy but still that all the Bishops in other cities and churches of the whole world would not do the same thing.

To that passage of Jerome I respond, there are two figures in his words, one of understanding, when he says, "The world groaned," for he calls the world a great part of the world, but not the whole world, the second of abuse, when he says, "and marveled to find itself Arian," for he calls the Arians improperly those who subscribe to heresy through ignorance. He speaks on that multitude of Bishops who throughout the world agreed with Ariminus and being deceived by the Arians decreed that the term ὁμοουσιος (*homoousios, i.e.* consubstantial) must be abolished, even though they did not know what it meant. Certainly they were not heretics, nor did they err at least materially, just as if some Catholic might advance a blasphemous opinion externally with the tongue thinking it is a pious prayer, such a man would not properly be a blasphemer. For that reason the same Bishops, as they were admonished and recognized the fallacy, immediately corrected their error and with tears did penance for the blasphemy, even though it was only advanced by the tongue, and it seemed the whole world marveled and groaned to find itself Arian.

To Basil I say that in those epistles he did not deplore the vices of Catholics but the misery of the Church on account of the infestation of heretics. What was said in that citation are against Bishops, not against Catholic Bishops as Brenzthought, but against Arian Bishops.

It is perfectly credible that Brenz erred from malice rather than ignorance. In the same place that he teaches that Catholic Bishops are not the true Church he relates from the history of Ruffinus about the holy monk Moses, who refused in any way to be ordained by the

Bishop of Alexandria, who was the primary Patriarch of Alexandria after the Roman Pontiff.[36]

But in the same book and chapter, Ruffinus says that the Bishop of Alexandria was an Arian and savagely persecuted Catholics and for this reason Moses refused to be ordained by him in preference to a Catholic Bishop, thus there is no reason with which one could excuse or cover-up the fraud and impudence of Brenz.

To the quote from Bernard I say that he rebukes the vices of morals, but not of doctrine, and for that reason believed that those wicked Bishops were not truly Bishops. He himself refuted the heretics who said that bad Bishops were not really Bishops from the Apostolic Institution.[37]

To the quote from Chrysostom the response is above, those words were taken from an incomplete work which either has an Arian heretic for an author or was corrupted by heretics.

---

[36]Ruffinus, *hist. Ecclesiast.* cap. 6.

[37]Serm. 66.

CHAPTER XVII

The Arguments Whereby our Adversaries try to show that all Shepherds of the Church can Err at the Same Time.

OUR adversaries try to show that the Church, or at least all the shepherds of the Church could err at the same time. 1) Because in the time of the prophet Micah, all the Prophets (about 400 with the exception of him) erred, as is clear from the Kings,[1] hence the Church, which they followed as they ought, was deceived. Secondly, in Isaiah it says, "His watchmen are all blind, they know nothing."[2] Thirdly, in the Lord's passion the High priest along with all the priests and elders of the people condemned Christ to the penalty of death. In Mark 14:64 the whole people, seduced by the priests, cried out to Pilate, "Crucify him!" In Mark 15:13 we see that at the same time all the Apostles lost the faith, since the Lord, "Reproached them for their unbelief and hardness of heart, etc."[3] And in Matthew, "You will all be scandalized on my account."[4]

Add that there are also Catholics that say during in the Lord's passion the true faith only remained in the Blessed Virgin Mary, consequently they believe this is signified by the one candle that is kept alight in the Night Office[5] during the Triduum such as

[1]3 Kings 22:23.

[2]Isaiah 56:10.

[3]Mark 16:14.

[4]Matthew 26:31.

[5]This refers to *Tenebrae*, which was celebrated with mostly the same ceremonies from ancient times until 1962, and today in all Churches attached to the liturgical books of that year. In that office there are 15 candles, which are extinguished as the Psalms are changed until there is one left. –Translator's note.

Alexander Alensis,[6] and Juan Torquemada.[7] But these are light enough and will be refuted with little labor.

To the first I say, those four hundred prophets clearly were pseudoprophets, and it is not unknown that they were even counseled by Achab himself. For in the same book when King Josaphat said, "Is there not any prophet of the Lord by whom we might ask the Lord?" Achab responded, "One remains, but I hate him because he prophecies nothing but evil." Certainly if anyone now in the midst of Saxony would counsel four hundred Lutheran ministers about justifying faith, and afterwards one Catholic, it would be no wonder if the greater part would err. Still, besides the Lutheran ministers, because apart from Saxony and neighboring places, there are many others where the true faith is preached, so it does not follow that all the Jewish teachers in the time of Achab erred, even if the four hundred erred. The Prophets who were in Samaria erred, but besides these there were in Judaea many other Prophets and (what is foremost) there were priests in Jerusalem, by whom they duly apply to respond to consult from the law of the Lord.

To the second I say the those words of thc Prophets are figurative, and directed to all, but really they ought to be understood not on all, but on many, as we said above.

To the third I say the priests and the High Priests did not have the privilege to not err when teaching the people, even to the times of Christ, but with Christ present and teaching us their error was a little nuisance. Nay more, this seems to have been foretold by Jeremiah when he said, "The law will perish from the priest, the word from the profit and counsel from the wise."[8] However, on account of the honor of the priesthood God provided that the judgment of the high priest Caiaphas in some sense (though not

[6] 3 parte q. ult. artic. 2.

[7] lib. 1 *de Ecclesia*, cap. 30, et lib. 3, cap. 61.

[8] Jeremiah 18.

from his intent) was true and just. It is said in John 11:51 that he was the priest for that year and he prophesied.

What attains to the people, who cried out, "Crucify him," I say that people was not all of the Jews, but only some and perhaps a lesser part, for in the city of Jerusalem there was also Nicodemus and Joseph of Arimathea, and many others who disapproved of this, and outside of Jerusalem in the rest of all Judaea, and there were many Jews dispersed throughout the world who knew nothing about the death of Christ, hence they remained in the true faith and religion.

Now I will speak to what the what was said to the Apostles: First, it is clear the Apostles were not Bishops except by designation, rather they were only material parts of the Church which could err, nor did the Church consist in them alone, for the status of the Christian Church with the obligation to enter it began on the day of Pentecost, when after all the mysteries of the redemption were carried out the Apostles began to publically promulgate faith in Christ as well as Baptism in Jerusalem. Therefore, even if all the Apostles erred in the time of Christ's passion in regard to faith, their error caused no harm to the universal Church.

Secondly I say, it is not probable that the Apostles lost the faith, since we do not read that they were rebuked except on the faith of the resurrection, but they could not lose that when they did not have it, unless after the Lord rose, were Christ often to have preached to them beforehand that he was going to rise; nevertheless they thought he spoke figuratively and they did not understand, nor did they believe. Accordingly, when he said in Luke, "They will kill him and he will rise on the third day," Luke adds, "and they understood none of this, and the word was hidden from them and they did not understand what was said."[9] We also read in John 20:2 that Peter and John, after they heard from Mary Magdalene that the Lord's body was taken from the tomb, right away they ran to the tomb and after they saw the garments and the shroud they believed that the body of

[9]Luke 18:33.

Christ was taken by someone, "For they did not yet know the Scriptures that it was fitting or him to rise again from the dead," *i.e.* they believed he was taken by someone because they did not know he ought to rise again. Besides, in Luke it was said to Peter, "I have prayed for thee that thy faith shall not fail."[10] How believable will it be that on the same night the faith of Peter failed so that it would not remain in faith, since what did not remain in his mouth is certain. Next, Mary Magdalene burned with the greatest charity in that three day period, as is clear from John 19:25 and 20:1, but without faith there can be no charity, therefore the Magdalene did not lose faith in Christ, which she had beforehand, therefore it is not the case that faith only remained in the Blessed Virgin.

Now, to what is said in the last chapter in Mark, "He rebuked their unbelief," this does not mean they lost the faith that they had, but they were late to believe what they did not yet believe, which at least would have been some kind of sin, but not properly infidelity. Moreover, that of Matthew 26:31, "You will all suffer scandal on my account this night," means the sin the Apostles would commit in flight, fear and staggering, even in regard to the faith, due to the fact of the Lord's passion; still not every staggering is infidelity, but only deliberate staggering.

But I marvel at Juan Torquemada, who, on account of this very weak argument based on the candle, says it is against the faith of the universal Church to assert that faith did not remain only in the Blessed Virgin on the day of the Lord's passion. Rupert says,[11] that the last candle is also customarily extinguished at that time, and he adds that on those three nights after all the lights are extinguished, a new fire is customarily lit from a stone, and through it all the lights which beforehand were extinguished are lit, which signifies the Prophets whom the Jews killed in different centuries, and brought darkness to the minds of those killing them. Through the last Christ is signified, whom they killed, giving birth to the worst darkness in

[10]Luke 22:32.

[11]lib. 5 *de divin. offic.*, cap. 26.

themselves, but through the new light, which is struck from the stone after those three days the new light of Christians is signified, which arose from Christ the stone struck by the Jews in our minds.

But if custom were neglected, the ancient Churches shall bring the force into that use which we have now, the last candle is not extinguished; then the response can be made with Abulensis[12] that through that candle the Blessed Virgin is meant, in whom alone, it is piously believed, there was explicit faith in the resurrection in those three days. Still, it does not follow that there was error in others or infidelity, because they were not held to explicitly believe in the resurrection until after its legitimate promulgation and approval, and especially for those who were out of Jerusalem and had heard nothing about Christ, and there it seems dangerous to say that true faith only remained in the Blessed Virgin; both because if the Church would have perished then not one person could be said to be the Church, since the Church is the people and the kingdom of God; and because then they who were away from Jerusalem even to that time that they had the true faith, would soon have lost it without fault.

END BOOK III

[12] *quest. 14 prologi in Matthaeum.*

Book IV

On the Marks of the Church

CHAPTER I
A Treatise on the Marks of the Church is of Great Profit

WE turn to the Controversy on the Marks of the true Church, which is a very useful controversy. For, everyone affirms that the true faith, the true remission of sins, the true hope of eternal salvation, can be found in the true Church alone. It is so clear that St. Cyprian said: "They cannot remain with God, who refuse to remain as one in the Church of God. Although they may burn with a flame, indeed they have been handed over to the fire, or being cast out they place their souls before wild beasts; for them there will be no crown of faith, rather the punishment of the faithless: such can be killed, but not crowned."[13]

All the Fathers teach alike, and even the heretics do not deny this. Therefore on that account, every heresy treats itself alone as the true Church, and all others it places outside the Church, as Lactantius teaches in these words: "It is only the Catholic Church which retains true worship. Further, this is the font of truth, this is the household of faith, the temple of God, whereby, if anyone will not have entered, or if one would have gone out from it, he is a stranger to the hope of life and eternal salvation. Nevertheless, five individual sects of heretics reckon that they are the true Christians, and that their Church is Catholic."[14] Therefore, if we should agree on this controversy, all the rest might be settled easily. Two things must be dealt with. In the first place, the opinion of today's heretics on the marks of the Church must be refuted. Secondly, the Catholic teaching on them must be explained and defended.

---

[13] Cyprian, *De simplicitate praelatorum.*

[14] Lactantius, Lib 4, cap. Ult. divinarum institutionum.

CHAPTER II
The Teachings of the Heretics are refuted.

THUS unto the first. Luther, in the book *On Councils and the Church*, in the last part of the book proposes these seven marks. Firstly, the true and incorrupt preaching of the Gospel. Second, the administration of baptism. Third, the legitimate use of the Eucharist. Fourth, the legitimate use of the keys. Fifth, the legitimate election of ministers, in order that they should teach and administer the sacraments. Sixth, public preaching, and psalmody, as well as catechism, but in a language which can be understood by all. Seventh, and lastly, the mystery of the cross, that is, the tribulations within and without, so that inwardly there might be sorrow, pusillanimity, and terror; outside poverty, contempt and that they might be held by all men as heretics, servants of demons, and Cathars.

It must be noted that Luther is exceedingly careful lest he might take any of those marks which are in the creed of Constantinople; since all the ancient councils wished to distinguish themselves from all other sects by those marks, especially through "Apostolic Church." Next, the remainder usually propose only two, which embrace the first five marks of Luther, that is, the sincere preaching of the word of God, and sincere use of the sacraments; and from these two each sect "proves" itself to be the true Church. The Augsburg confession teaches thus, in article 6 and in the defense of the same. Likewise, Brenz in the Wittenberg Confession, on the chapter on the Church, as well as John Calvin in the Institutes,[15] and the Centurators of Magdeburg[16] add two others to these two, which can be reduced to the fifth and seventh of Luther. That is, constancy

[15] *Instit.*, Bk 4, ch. 1 §9, 10 and 11.

[16] *Cent. 1*, lib. 1, ch. 4, col. 137 and 174; *Cent. 1* lib. 2, ch. 4, column 379, 380 and 381.

in the confession of faith (or perseverance), and obedience toward the ministers of the word, in so far as they administer the word.

These notes are not in any way sufficient. In the first place, they do not declare what the true Church might be according to the heretics, rather what it probably might be; consequently we cannot know who the elect might be, or the just, and chiefly we learn where the Church might hide, rather than where it might be. Besides, nor does this sufficiently reveal it. It can easily be proved from individuals.

To the first, it is so for three reasons. First of all, the marks ought to be proper and not common. If I should wish to describe a certain man for you, whom you have never seen, so that when you will see him you may pick him out from a crowd, I ought *not* to say that there is a fellow who has two eyes, two hands, etc., for these are common to all. Nor even ought I to designate him through marks which, although they might be proper according to an individual, they are not proper in the opinion of others, since many usually claim these for themselves. Thus, he who is sought would never be discovered.

To be sure, sincere preaching of truth is a mark common to all sects, at least in their own opinion. For, either preaching ought to be pure from all error, or only made from essentials and fundamentals.

If the first should be given, we can gather from this very mark that the Church is among none of the Lutherans; for it is they themselves who affirm their Churches are not without blemish. Luther, in his book on the Church, clearly says that the word of God is a mark, although it is preached more in some places and in others less, and Calvin affirms the same thing.[17] If the second, already it will be a mark common to many sects.

Certainly the Lutherans and Zwinglians do not disagree on a particular fundamental of faith, as on the Trinity or the Incarnation. Nay more, even the Pelagians thought they had a "true Church," who in their primary articles did not disagree, before they gave birth

---

[17] *Inst.*, Bk 4 ch. 1 § 12.

to Nestorians. Even Coelestinus (as we learn from St. Augustine)[18] tried to show that he was not outside the Church, and yet, the Lutherans and Calvinists detest nothing more than the Pelagians; rather, they set us outside the Church before all, because they reckon us Pelagians.

In addition to this second mode, in the very matter there are some who do not agree with this mark, like the Anabaptists; nevertheless it is asserted by all in one opinion. What sect was there ever which did not say that it held the true preaching of truth? Certainly St. Augustine says that the Catholic Church is recognized easily by many marks, but the heretics have nothing except the promise of truth, that is, what might be among them the truth, and sincere preaching.[19]

Secondly, the marks ought to be more familiar in that matter whose marks they are, otherwise they are not known at all, rather unknown. Now, our adversaries do not only want external preaching to be a mark of the Church, but preaching and reception. There indeed the true Church is, they say, where the word is preached, heard and believed. But who can know where the word is truly believed? Wherefore, the same holds concerning external preaching. Without a doubt what the true Church may be is more knowable than what the true preaching of the word might be; for we learn this from the Church, as Irenaeus, Tertullian, Augustine and all the Fathers teach.

Irenaeus said: "Why, truly even if on some modest question dispute were to arise, wouldn't it be fitting to hasten to the oldest Churches, and to take up the question at hand from them, which is in the matter certain and pure?"[20] Tertullian likewise: "The apostles preached what Christ had revealed to them, and here I put forth that nothing ought to be proved otherwise, than through these same Churches, which the apostles themselves built: if these are so, it is

[18] *De peccato originali*, Bk 2 ch. 22.

[19] Augustine, *Contra epistolam fundamenti*, ch. 4.

[20] Irenaeus, bk. 3, ch. 4.

certain hence that every doctrine found with those apostolic Churches agrees with the root and origins of faith, it must be reckoned true, the rest that does not ought to be written off as lies."[21] It is shown by the same reason; for true preaching is preaching, and interpretation of the true divine scriptures; what might be the true scriptures, however, and what might be their true sense, we cannot know, except from the testimony of the true Church, as Augustine teaches.[22] Even Brenz himself, in the Wittenberg confession, affirms that the Church has the right of testimony on true scripture, and even of interpreting the true scripture. Furthermore, Calvin wishes the Church to be the faithful watchman of the word of God,[23] and Philip Melanchthon in *Locis capite de Ecclesia* requires the testimony of the true Church to impose a decision on lawsuits. But first, the guardian of the treasure ought to be known, rather than the treasure; and the teacher more than the doctrine, although doctrine is sought from a teacher, not the other way around. Therefore, the Church is a mark of true preaching, rather than true preaching a mark of the Church.

Third, the true marks are inseparable from the true Church, but the Churches of the Corinthians and Galatians, to whom Paul wrote, were true Churches, and nevertheless there was not in those Churches true preaching at a certain time, as can be understood from the apostle, who says he is writing to the Churches of God, which are at Corinth, or in Galatia, where he complains that at Corinth, because some taught there would not be a resurrection, and at Galatia nearly the whole epistle scolds them, because they taught that they must keep the law of Moses with the gospel.

But you say, how were these true Churches, when they taught heresy? I respond: It is one thing to err, and be prepared to learn, and when you will learn, to obey; it is another to wish not to learn, and when you will have learned the truth, to refuse to acquiesce.

---

[21] Tertullian, *De praescript contra hereticos.*

[22] Augustine, *Contra epist. Fundamenti*, ch. 5; *de utilitate credendi*, ch. 14.

[23] Bk. 4, ch. 1 § 5.

Neither of these can be in the universal Church; in a particular Church, however, there can be the first, in neither the universal Church nor a particular Church the second, rather only in the synagogue of Satan, and in Churches of the wicked. Again, there can be a doctrine pure from all other error in a false Church; for schismatics, such as the Luciferians and Donatists, from the beginning held the whole doctrine, and nevertheless were outside the Church. If they should say they do not have the whole doctrine, because true doctrine teaches one must remain in the unity of the true Church, or the converse, since schismatics believe and teach that it behooves one to be in the true Church and to obey the true head, although they do not do it; and hence they do not err in faith, rather they fail in charity. Yet, schism, if it should endure for long, will at length sink into heresy.

Still, Brenz, Philip Melanchthon and Calvin object on behalf of this mark, making use of certain places of Scripture: "My sheep will hear my voice."[24] Therefore, there is a Church, where the word of God is heard. Likewise, they appeal to Ephesians V: "Cleansing her by the washing in the word of life."[25] The Church is cleansed in the word, therefore wherever the cleansing word is, there is the Church. So Melanchthon argues in his *apologia*. Calvin, however, concentrates on Matthew 18: "Where there are two or three, etc."[26]

Brenz produces that from John 10:35: "He called them gods, to whom the word of God was spoken." And in the next chapter, "You are clean, on account of the word, which I spoke to you." [John 15:3]. That, indeed, is the Church, which is clean in the presence of God. And that of Romans: "The gospel is the power of God for the salvation of all believers." [Romans 1:16]. Chrysostom adds: "Whoever therefore wishes to recognize which Church may be the true Church of Christ, from where shall he do so, unless only

---

[24] John 10: 27.

[25] Ephes. 5: 26.

[26] *Instit.*, bk. 4, ch. 1 § 9.

through the Scriptures?"[27] And Augustine: "We learn of Christ in the Scriptures, we learn of the Church in the scriptures," etc. In like manner, we also find from Augustine: "The question turns about among us, where the Church might be; what, therefore, are we going to do in our words intending to seek that, or in the words of its chapters? I reckon what chiefly in those words we ought to seek, which is truth, and knows its body best." Lastly, from the same: "Let us not hear: I say these things, you say these things, but let us hear: thus says the Lord ... I refuse the documents of men, rather that the holy Church be proved from the divine precepts."[28]

I respond. The first citation does not teach where the Church might be, but teaches who might be the elect, without a doubt those who steadfastly hear from the heart, and retain the word, as St. Augustine shows; although, since it cannot be known who it is in fact that hears with their heart, this cannot be a visible mark of the Church, but is a mark of each individually, that conjecturally one might recognize his election.

The second citation proves nothing; for that cleansing is invisible, nor does Paul wish to teach in that place, what may be or where may be the Church, but what good God will have conferred to the Church.

The third citation does not show where the Church might be, but where Christ may be. Where, indeed, is the true Church, there is Christ. Besides, if it were a mark of the Church to be gathered in the name of Christ, then certainly it will not be to be gathered in just any way in the name of Christ, for even all heretics and schismatics are gathered in the name of Christ. Rather, it will be gathered by those who exercise the authority of Christ, such as are legitimately ordained bishops, and those succeeding them, and so on and so forth back to the apostles, whom Christ at first left behind in His place. Thus in that way such a mark would coincide with ours, which we will take up later on.

---

[27] *In Matth.*, Hom. 49.

[28] *Epist. 166*; *De Utilitate Credendi*; *de unitate Ecclesiae*, ch. 2; *ibid* ch. 3.

The fourth citation proves nothing. Firstly, because there, only princes are called gods, to whom God consigned something; therefore, that word of God is to be made to some purpose. Secondly, because the word of God does not make gods, if it is merely preached, but if it should be received and believed: but this is invisible, as is obvious.

The fifth place is like unto the second, wherein the same Brenz says the Church is clean in the sight of God, that is not in the sight of men; and he does not notice from this mark follows, that it becomes manifest to God, not to us.

The sixth place proves nothing; for the effect of the Gospel is invisible.

Yet Calvin presses on. The word of God is fruitful, and wherever it is preached, it increases, therefore wherever it is preached, there is some Church.

I respond. If this reasoning proves something, it merely proves that where it is preached, there are some good men; but we do not know them. Morever, it doesn't prove this; for the word of God always increases when legitimately preached; it is by the ordinary power from those preachers who were sent. Besides, we see it preached among heretics in various sects where it does not increase unless by mistake. As to the citation from St. John Chrysostom, we have already responded to it often. Rather I will concentrate on the citations from St. Augustine. It is proven from Scripture where the Church may be, not from a mark of the Church as it were, but because Scripture teaches what might be known as long as it teaches, what kind it might be, where it began, and how it increased.

You will say, "at least Scripture is more known than the Church, seeing that therein the Church is proved."

I respond. Considered simply, the Church is earlier and more known than the Scripture is. For the Church was before Scripture, and the Scripture was given to it by God, She hands it down to others, and explains it: nevertheless, at some time hypothetically the Scripture was better known when obviously Scripture was received, and speaks clearly and a question arises on the Church itself. As now and then on the other side the Church was received, and known, and a question arises on Scripture: and thus one is proved from the other. When the grace of the word was disputed on the baptism of heretics, because Scripture speaks obscurely, and the Church was known, Augustine proved, according to the Scriptures, that the baptism of heretics was valid, because the Church held it as valid. On the other hand, when it was disputed on the Church, whether the Church was in Africa alone, because the Scriptures were received and clear, Augustine proved from them; and we do the same thing when we deduce the marks of the Church from the Scripture, but it is not for the reason that they are simply more known than the Church.

The second mark is refuted by the same arguments. For all claim the same for themselves: apart from Catholics, Calvinists are separated from the Lutherans, because they both think that they alone have the true sacrament of the Eucharist. The Anabaptists, however, are separated from both, because they think they alone have the true use of baptism. On that account the Pelagians held all the sacraments, and likewise all the schismatics. Secondly, the legitimate use of the sacraments is less known than the Church might be. For this is the legitimate use of the sacraments, which is in conformity with Scripture, as they teach themselves. Yet the Scriptures depend on the Church, not the other way around, as we have often said. Thirdly, the Church at Corinth was a true Church, and nevertheless they are scolded, because they did not treat certain sacraments purely,[29] as were likewise the African Churches, which were under Cyprian, and under those eighty six bishops, whose teachings he says were of the true Church, as St. Augustine and St. Jerome also teach.[30] They did not purely treat the sacrament of baptism as the same Jerome and Augustine teach.

[29] 1 Corinthians XI.

[30] Augustine, *De Baptismo*, bk. 6, ch. 7; Jerome, *Contra Luciferianos.*

The third mark must be refuted, that is prayer and psalmody, which is the sixth Lutheran mark. It is refuted, because if one should speak on invocation, which proceeds from the heart, it is an invisible mark. Moreover, if one speaks on an external invocation and psalmody, it is a very common mark. For all sects at this time, even the Anabaptists, say the Lord's prayer, and sing the psalms in the vernacular, even the Arians long ago did the same thing, as Socrates relates,[31] as well as Ambrose.[32] Nay more, it can almost be said, that at this time to sing the psalms in Latin is a mark of the true Church, because this seems to be a relic of antiquity alone, and of the universal Church, which is not changed daily as the sects of heretics.

The fourth mark is refuted, which is the seventh Lutheran mark, without a doubt; internal sorrow, pusillanimity, external persecutions and to be called heretics. With respect to being internal, as a mark it is very false, since if they are internal, they are obscure. Likewise, pusillanimity is a vice, and Paul everywhere exhorts to internal joy, and says the kingdom of God is joyful in the Holy Spirit.[33] With respect to externals, it is not a perpetual mark, for the Church in the beginning and in the end suffered great difficulties: but in the midst it was in bloom, and everything was predicted.[34]

The fifth mark is of the Centuriators of Magdeburg, that it would be the true Church in which they are found who persevere in the confession of faith even to death. Such is refuted firstly, because confession of the true faith is no more a mark than the true preaching of the Scriptures, and the legitimate use of the sacraments.

Secondly, because a true Church could not be gathered in any way by the Lutherans. These say that for many centuries before the coming of Luther, the confession of true faith ceased, and the

---

[31] Lib. 6, c. 8.

[32] *De Tradendis basilicis.*

[33] See Romans 14, Coloss. 3, Philipp. 4, Ephes. 5.

[34] See St. Augustine, *Epist. 50.*

Church was preserved in hiding, and was altogether invisible, therefore the Church of the Lutherans is new, and hence false.

Thirdly, because we see this mark in all sects, and no less than in the body of Lutherans; for in the first years our Church has innumerable martyrs, who persevered steadfastly in the confession of faith; thereupon the Montanists exceedingly boasted of their martyrs, as can be seen both from Eusebius[35] and Tertulian[36], the latter who wrote while he was a Montanist against Catholics, objecting against them that they had acted wickedly by fleeing persecution.

Likewise, Massalians with Epiphanius,[37] who says they also had martyrs, for they boasted much in their number. The same is certain of the Donatists, as St. Augustine says: "Those who lived as thieves, they honored as martyrs."[38] On the Anabaptists who lived at the time of St. Bernard, he writes: "Some marvel that not only patiently, but even happily they were lead to death."[39] Aeneas Sylvius [later Pope Pius II] wrote about the Adamites, "men joined with women, happy and usually singing to be rushed to the fire.[40] "In our time, no one is ignorant that in this obstinacy of dying for faithlessness, the Anabaptists hold first place, second the Calvinists, and well-nigh no pure Lutherans, who, nevertheless, propose this as a mark of the true Church.

---

[35] *Hist.* Bk 5, ch. 18.

[36] *De fuga in persequutione.*

[37] *Haeres.* 80.

[38] *Epist.* 68.

[39] *in Cantica,* Serm. 66.

[40] *De hist. Boemorum,* ch. 41.

CHAPTER III
The True Marks of the Church are Proposed

SINCE we have briefly refuted these "marks," it remains that we should propose the true marks. It must be observed from the beginning, however, that the Catholic Church is as a sun, which diffuses its most beautiful rays of light from every side, that it can be recognized very easily through them. Indeed, it has many marks, or testimonies, and signs, which discern her from every false religion of the Pagans, of Jews, and Heretics. Indeed, they do not evidently cause truth: she is the true Church of God, but nevertheless they cause it to be evidently believable, for it is not the same thing to be evidently true and evidently believable. For something to be called evidently true, it must appear to be either in itself, or in its principles. For something to be called evidently believable, it does not need to appear so in itself, or in its principles, nevertheless it has so many and such serious testimonies, that any wise man you like rightly ought to believe it. It is as though a judge should see a man to be killed by a thief, or lethally wounded and dies afterward, he has the evidence of truth, that the thief is a murderer; if however, he might not have seen the killing done, but might have twenty serious men as witnesses, who say they saw it, he has evidence of believability.

Therefore, we say the marks of the Church, which we produce, do not simply make the evidence of truth, because if that were so, no one could be found who would be able to deny it, just as you could find no one who would deny the teachings which the mathematicians prove; but, nevertheless, they cause the evidence of believability, according to the Psalm: "Your testimonies are exceedingly believable."[41] But among those who admit the Scriptures are divine, as well as the histories and the ancient writings of the

---

[41] Psalm XCII.

Fathers, they even make evidence of truth. Even if the truth of articles of faith cannot be evident to us absolutely, nevertheless that truth can be evident hypothetically, that is, by supposing the truth of the Scriptures. The Scriptures being supposed, what is evidently deduced from the Scripture, is evidently true.

Next, these marks are called by various names, and St. Augustine places six marks,[42] St. Jerome two,[43] St. Vincent of Lérin in his *Commonitorium*, three. From more recent writers, Driedo and Pedro de Soto[44] three others. Cardinal Hosius four.[45] Nicholas Sanders, six.[46] Miguel de Medina, eleven.[47] Gunter of Peter places twelve.[48]

We propose fifteen marks, which if anyone might wish, could be recalled to those four, which commonly and by more recent authors are assigned to the Constantinoplan creed, One, Holy, Catholic and Apostolic.

---

[42] *Contra epist. Fundamenti*, ch. 4.

[43] *Contra Luciferianos*, in fine.

[44] Driedo bk 4, ch. 2, part 2 *de Eccles. Dogmat.*; Pedro de Soto *Prima parte defensionis*, ch. 44 and following.

[45] *In explicatione symboli.*

[46] Bk 8 *de visibili monarchia*, ch. 50.

[47] Bk 2 *de recta fide.*

[48] *De notis Ecclesiae.*

CHAPTER IV
The First Mark is Explained.

THE FIRST MARK, is the very name of the Catholic and Christian Church; for, as St. Augustine teaches, even if every heresy should wish to appear and be called the Catholic Church, nevertheless, when the heretics are asked by the pagans where one would go to come together at a Catholic Church, none of them dares to show his house.[49] St. Cyril teaches, "If you will go out into some city, you do not ask where the Church might be, or the house of God, for even the heretics say theirs is the house of God, and the Church. Rather you ask, where might the Catholic Church be; that indeed is the proper name of this holy Church, the mother of us all; as if one might say, if you ask this, no heretic will show you his Church."[50]

Pacianus says, in his letter to Sympronianus, which is on the catholic name: "Certainly, that which has endured through so many centuries was not borrowed from men. That which you refer to as Catholic, does not denote Marcion, nor Apelles, nor Montanus, just as it does not suppose heretics as authors ...My name is Christian, Catholic is my cognomen; that addresses me, that shows who I am." He says the same thing most beautifully, that the Catholic name agrees with the principle head and the trunk of that tree, from where many branches are cut off from different times: the heretical sects are the branches, that is, certain parts cut off from the tree of the Church: it is the very tree, which rests upon its root, as well as always remains the same, and Catholic is what the whole tree is called. Likewise, there is no heresy which would not take the name from some man as its author, and the Christian name should be abandoned by those who it leaves. Thus, in 1 Corinthians 3, some of

---

[49] Augustine, *Contra epist. Fundamenti*, ch. 4.

[50] *Cateches.* 18.

the schismatics were saying: "I am of Paul, others, I am of Apollo, others, but I am of Cephas."

St. Justin Martyr says: "And they are distinct with respect to their cognomens, designated from certain men, since each one was the author of some new doctrine. Among them, some are called Marcionists, others Valentinians, others Basilidinians, other Saturinists, and others still by another word, whatever it may be coming from the first inventor of their teaching."[51] Irenaeus adds: "They even have words, from Simon, the prince of the most impious teachings, which are called *Simony*."[52] Lactantius says: "Although the Marcionists or the Arians are called Christians, those who have lost the name of Christ and clothed themselves in a human and external name, have ceased to be Christian."[53] St. Athanasius says against the Arians: "The people have never received a name from their bishops, but from the Lord, in whom they believed. Certainly we did not inherit names from the blessed apostles, but we are named after Christ because we are Christians. But they who deduce the origin of their faith from somewhere else rightly bear the names of their authors. For which reason, since we are all Christians and are called such, Marcion the inventor of his heresy is cast out. The rest who remain retain the title of Christians: those who followed Marcion were no longer Christians, but called Marcionists. Such is also the case with Valentinus, Basilides and Manes, and the others who bestowed names upon their sects."[54]

Chrysostom confirms this: "They have certain men after whom they are called: according to the name of the heresiarch, so also the sect is called, for us however, no man gave a name, rather the faith itself."[55]

---

[51] St. Justin Martyr, *Dialogue with Trypho.*

[52] Irenaeus, bk 1, ch. 20.

[53] Lactantius, lib. 4, ch. 30.

[54] Athanasius, *contra Arianos*, serm. 2.

[55] *In Acta Apostolorum*, Homil. 33.

Jerome says at the end of his work against the Luciferians: "If you will hear, in any place, those who are called Christians not by the Lord Jesus Christ but named after someone else, such as Marcionists or Valentinians; know that it is not the Church of Christ, but the synagogue of Antichrist." Today, therefore, if some are called "Martinists," or Lutherans, some Zwinglians, others Calvinists, etc., yet no one ever called us after some man, it is certain that ours is the true Church.

Wait a minute, they will say, you are everywhere called Papists, Romans, or Romanists. I respond: formerly Catholics were called "*homousians*," but that word attested to truth. For these are not the names of some new author and heresiarch, as their names are: but *homousians* means one who believes the Son is consubstantial with the Father, which is a true dogma. Papist is deduced from Pope [Papa], such was even Peter, and Christ himself, as is known. Roman, however, and Romanist, even before 1100 years was the same, which is Catholic, as is clear from St. Ambrose.[56] Add what Chyrostom said in the same sermon quoted above, that it is not bad to be called Catholics by those who govern the Church in the name of Christ, as long as we are not to be called after some man, as the heretics are. It seems as though he foresaw we would be called Papists at some time. Add that we are not called Papists, except by the Lutherans in Germany, and in neighboring regions; we are not however called that in Greece, Asia, Africa, India, and at length, there is no need to mention Italy and Spain.

---

[56] *In oratione de obitu Satyri.*

CHAPTER V
The Second Mark

THE SECOND MARK is Antiquity; for without a doubt the true Church is more ancient than a false one, just as God existed before the devil. We read in the Gospel that the first sowing was good seed, afterwards came the cockle.[57] Also, the Church is called Catholic, because it was in every time, and likewise is called apostolic, because it was founded by the apostles, and hence is the most ancient. That our Church is older than all the associations of pagans, nay more, that our Scripture is older than the gods of the nations, Tertullian proves in his *Apologeticus.*[58]

In every manifest change of religion, these six signs of it are always able to be shown. Firstly, the author of the change. Secondly, some new doctrine. Thirdly, the time in which it began. Fourthly, the place where it began. Fifthly, who opposed it. Sixthly, that some scanty body little by little began to grow when others entered into it. On the other hand, we find all these things in the very Church of Christ, which, nevertheless, was not a new Church, but only a type of change of the status of the Church according to the predictions of the prophets.

First, we know the author was Christ, whereby we are called Christians. Secondly, the new doctrines of the Trinity and Incarnation began to be believed explicitly. Thirdly, this was preached in the 15th year of the Emperor Tiberius Caesar. Fourthly, it began in Judea. Fifthly, this religion was soon assaulted by the scribes and pharisees, and thereafter by the nations with great force. Sixthly we know, in the beginning there were many fewer Christians than there were Jews, even when the separation was

---

[57] Matthew 13.

[58] *Apologeticus*, ch. 19 and 20. Cf. St. Augustine, *de Civitate Dei*, bk 18, ch. 37 and 38.

made. If, therefore, in this change of the state of the same Church those six things can be shown, the same things can be shown much more in any perfect change. We have already shown all those in the individual sects of heretics. But our adversaries could not show anything like this ever happened in our Church after apostolic times.

We will illustrate the matter with some examples. We know that the author of the Arians was a certain priest from Alexandria named Arius. Likewise, Nestorius, the bishop of Constantinople, was the author of the Nestorians, and moreover, Martin Luther, a priest and Augustinian monk, was the author of the Lutherans.

Secondly, we know what doctrines they invented. Arius taught the Son of God was a mere creature. Nestorius, that in Christ there were two persons. Luther, that men are justified through individual faith alone, that is, men should hold that they are justified through this alone. In like manner, he also denied the Eucharist to be a sacrifice.

Thirdly, we know the times in which they began. The Arian heresy began in the year 324, the Nestorian heresy in 431, and that of the Lutherans in 1517.

Fourthly, we know the places. Arianism began in Egypt, Nestorianism began in Thrace and Lutheranism in Saxony.

Fifthly, we know that right away the Arians were attacked by Pope Sylvester, by the Council of Nicaea, by Sts. Athanasius and Hilary, and others. The Nestorian heresy was attacked by Pope Celestine, the Council of Ephesus, St. Cyril, and many others. The Lutheran heresy was attacked by Pope Leo X, by the Council of Trent, by all Catholic universities and many Theologians.

Sixthly, we know that at the beginnings of these heresies their followers were very few, and from the beginning of their separation there were many more Catholics diffused throughout the world than there were Arians, Nestorians, or even Lutherans, which not even they can deny.

On the other hand, they are unable to show any of these characteristics on our side. For in the first place, they never object to us that there is an author of our sect, nor do they call us by any particular man's name, because if that were the case they would do so with great pleasure.

Secondly, they have never shown the first origin of any of our teachings; in fact, the Centuriators recorded who the authors were that defended our teachings, which they now oppose, but they did not discover the origin, unless it was in the time of the apostles.[59] They even number Justin and Irenaeus among our supporters, whom it is certain followed right after the times of the apostles. In the next chapter of the same citation, they enumerate all the heresies of every age as well as who resisted them, yet, they never record that some heresy was devised by Roman Pontiffs, rather that all heresies were condemned by them. Today, they object to many heresies on our side. Tilman Hesch wrote a book on six hundred heresies of the Popes, but these heresies, apart from the falsehoods of Tilman, are very ancient dogmas, which actually can be proved by the Centuriators rather easily. For example, Illyricus discovered our doctrines in every book of the Fathers; but among the Fathers he calls them blemishes, among us, heresies. This is clever on the part of our adversaries: in order to show that we are outside the Church, they call our doctrines heresies, but lest they might appear to be separated from the Church of the Fathers, they call the same doctrine merely "blemishes" when it is found amongst them.

Thirdly, they have never been able to trace out a clear point of our supposed defection from the Church. They simply say that after the first five hundred years this sect began to strengthen, yet when it began, they have absolutely never said.

Fourthly, they never showed, in what place it began, for after the first five hundred years, Pope St. Gregory flourished, with whom the whole world communicated, as can be seen from the epistles which he sent to every land. Likewise, after the death of Gregory the sixth Ecumenical Council was celebrated, wherein one may clearly see, that the whole east and west were joined at that time with the Roman Pontiff as members with their head.

[59] *In singulis Centuriis,* ch. 4, about the end.

Fifthly, they never showed who attacked it, as though it recently arose, and what councils were convened against it. Indeed, they do object that the Council of Constantinople under Copronymus (which seemed to them to be a general council), condemned images, something that Rome defended. But that was not a general council, since it did not have any true Patriarch. Moreover, that council did **not** condemn a dogma which arose at that time, but an ancient dogma, and one received in the whole Church. It did not establish that the veneration of images should not be received, but rather that it should be abolished, and that images should be stripped from the Basilica. See the works of Cedrenus, Zonaras, and Paul the Deacon.

Sixthly, it cannot in any way be shown that our Church ever separated itself from some greater part, so that those adhering to the Roman See were very few, and the remaining Christians many more; for, from the epistles of St. Gregory, which he wrote to the bishops of the East, as well as to the bishops of Africa, Spain, Gaul, and Italy, it is certain that nearly all Christians communicated with him.

The older Fathers always used this argument from antiquity against heretics to show the true Church. Tertullian says to them: "Who arc you, and where do you come from? Where have you been hiding for so long?"[60] Optatus says: "Show the origin of your seat, you who wish to claim you are the holy Church."[61] St. Hilary in his work on the Trinity: "It seems to me these latest times bring propagators of blasphemy. It is too late for these unheard of teachings to correct my faith, which I received from you and in which I have put my trust, O Lord."[62] St. Jerome says: "Whoever you are that assert new doctrines, I ask you, that you spare Roman ears, that you spare the faith, which has been praised by the apostolic mouth. Why after four hundred years do you strive to teach what we did not know before? Even to this day, the Christian was clean

---

[60] *De prescript. Contra haereticos.*

[61] Optatus, lib. 2 *contra Parmenianum.*

[62] Hilary, *De Trinitate*, bk 6.

without that doctrine of yours."[63] He adds at the end of his work against the Luciferians: "In this very matter, because they were established later, they show themselves to be of the sort that the Apostle predicted were going to come about." Thereupon, St. Augustine, places antiquity among the marks of the Church.[64]

Our adversaries bring four arguments to these answers. Firstly, Calvin responds that no unconquerable argument can be produced from antiquity. For Ishmael was older than Isaac, and nevertheless it was said: "Cast out the maidservant, and her son." But Ishmael was not a figure of a false religion, but only that the Old Testament was good and from God. Also, since the state of men in that Covenant was of servants who are spoken of with respect to fear, a new and more perfect Covenant ought to succeed it, which pertains to the free, who are lead by love. The Apostle writes in Galatians: "It has been written, that Abraham had two sons ...who are spoken of in allegory: these are the two Testaments, etc.[65]

Secondly they say our Church can not be shown to have begun in some time or through some author, etc., because it is not really new, but because it happened together with that change and little by little error crept in and was not averted and while the shepherds were sleeping. Whereas, while certainly some changes did not happen all together, but little by little, as is clear from Luther, who in the beginning did not deny indulgences, etc., nevertheless, we do know about individuals, when and how they arose. On that account, the Gospel of Matthew does not say the cockle arose while the men were sleeping, but was sown *while* they were sleeping; it soon appeared, however, and was recognized. How then were our "heresies" not detected for a thousand years? Certainly, not only the shepherds, but even God would have slept too long, if through so many ages he never roused anyone, who would resist these errors.

[63] Jerome, *in Epistol. Ad Pammachium et Oceanum.*

[64] *Contra epist. Fundamenti*, ch. 4.

[65] *Instit.*, Bk 4, ch. 2 § 3.

And it would have made a lie of what we read in the Gospel: "I am with you always, even to the consummation of the age."

Thirdly they say that although it cannot be shown when the beginning of this depravity occurred, that it can be shown when the eminent change occurred. For in the beginning of the year 600, the Pope obviously was changed into Antichrist, when the Roman pontiff obtained from Phocas the emperor, that he should be called head of bishops, and when he opened the temple of the Pantheon of all the gods. The Centuriators of Magdeburg teach this, and many of our adversaries agree. Theodore Bibliander also, in the tablets of his Chronology in the beginning of the year 600, placed the appearance of Antichrist, that is of the Pope, and Luther, by a computation of time, preferred St. Gregory as the last pope; and here and there the Calvinists and Lutherans extend the purity of the Church to the first 500 or 600 years.

But in the first place, after the year 670, long after the times of Phocas, the sixth Ecumenical Council was celebrated (which our adversaries receive as sacrosanct as is clear both from the confession of Zurich, and the Centuriators, as well as others). In that very Council the party of the Roman Pope Agatho was preeminent, for his teaching was explicated through legates and through his epistles, and everyone followed them, as even the Centuriators amply relate.[66] Either the Pope was not yet Antichrist, or the whole Church, and a holy general council both venerated and followed Antichrist.

On that account, it is false that Phocas first gave the name of head of the Church to the Roman Pontiff, because Justinian the elder, who was almost a hundred years before Phocas, in his epistle to Pope John II, calls that Pope head of all Churches with eloquent words. And this same thing is found in an epistle of the same John II responding to Justinian, where the Pope repeats a summary of the letter of the Emperor, and it is found on each side of the Epistle.[67] The Centuriators are not ignorant of this, for they recall the fourth

---

[66] *Cent. 7*, ch. 9.

[67] *In codice*, bk. 1, titul 1, leg. 4, and 6.

law of the Codex, which was taken up from the letter of Pope John.[68] Therefore they lie against their own joint knowledge.

Also, before the times of Justinian, the Council of Chalcedon calls Pope Leo the head of all Churches. Even Leo himself thus addresses Rome: "Through the holy seat of Blessed Peter, made head of the world and more extensively, a guardian in divine religion rather than earthly dominion."[69] And further down: "It is no small thing that, what bellicose labor supplied to you, is what Christian peace has placed under you." Therefore, Phocas was *not* the first who gave this name to the Roman Pontiff, but the first to restrain the pride of the bishop of Constantinople, who wanted to be made equal with the Roman Pontiff.

Now, concerning the Church, which is called the Pantheon: I say firstly that it is an argument against our adversaries. For, we read in Daniel, that Antichrist will fight against all gods, and alone in secret would adore the god Maozim, and in 2 Thessalonians it is said he will be elevated above every other, which is called God. Therefore, if the Pope opened a temple to all the gods, in such a matter he would not be Antichrist. Besides, long before the temple of the Pantheon was consecrated to God in memory of all the saints, there already were temples in Rome were consecrated to St. Peter, Paul, Lawrence and Sebastian, etc.

But Melanchthon objects that the invocation of the saints did not exist before the times of St. Gregory,[70] therefore it began then. I respond: it is a lie. For many Fathers, and among them Ambrose, called to mind the invocation of the saints.[71] On Antichrist, however and the invocation of the saints we have already treated upon it in many other places.[72]

---

[68] *Cent. 6*, ch. 10, col. 670.

[69] Leo, *Serm. 1 de sanctis Petro et Paulo.*

[70] *In Confesione et Apolog.* Art. 21.

[71] Lib. *De viduis.*

[72] See *De Romano Pontifice*, bk 5.

Fourthly, Calvin responds in the preface of the Institutes, that his Church is not new, but very ancient; more so, it is the very Church which Christ founded, however, it was not seen through many ages, and now at length has appeared. But St. Augustine makes an argument against this same opinion which previously was held by the Donatists;[73] either that [his] Church, which appears today, perished before and now has been resurrected; or it did not perish but had only been hidden, and now has raised its head. The first proposition cannot be, for it could not then be reborn if the mother had perished. If it perished, St. Augustine asks, "Therefore from where did the Donatists appear? From what soil did it blossom? From what sea did it emerge? From what heaven did it fall?" Besides, the promises of Christ would be false: "The gates of hell will not prevail against it." And in the last chapter of Matthew: "I am with you, even to the consummation of the age."[74] The second proposition cannot be, because then either that hidden Church professed its faith, or it did not profess it; if it professed, therefore it was not hidden, but manifest: and if manifest, how could nobody notice it? Why wasn't it taken and coerced by inquisitors, who already arose in the Church a long time before Luther? Why is there no vestige, no memory of them? If they did not profess the faith, but truly and properly hid (which the other side is compelled to defend), therefore that was not the Church, and hence there was no true Church in the world. For, as they say, the confession of faith is a mark of the true Church: and "Confession by mouth is made unto salvation."[75]

For that reason, if that were the case, how, when Luther and Calvin appeared, was there nobody who would have united themselves to them, except for those who were deceived by them? If many Lutherans and Calvinists were so hidden, wouldn't many have soon recognized in the preaching of Luther and Calvin their friends, and even though they were not called, run to them? It was not so;

---

[73] Augustine, *against the Donatists*, bk 3; *De Baptismo*, ch. 2.

[74] Matthew 16: 19; 28.

[75] Romans 10.

for nearly everybody who is a Lutheran or Calvinist, affirms themselves to have been Catholic beforehand, and did not think that Catholicism was a new doctrine. Moreover, Luther himself affirms that he at some point was not Lutheran, but a Catholic monk, and celebrated masses for 15 years seriously and devoutly.[76]

In the end, if the Church was so hidden as Calvin says, then it would follow that the Church of Christ was worse and more miserable than every heretical sect, and in that even worse off than the Jewish people after the destruction of Jerusalem, which certainly is a blasphemy, although God everywhere predicted the glory of the Church through the prophets, and promised that he would be with it always. What follows then, is obvious; for every heretical sect has its temples, its bishops, its sacraments. And in like manner, the Jews after the destruction of Jerusalem always had some synagogues, where they freely exercised their ceremonies, as can be seen in the times of Pope St. Gregory,[77] and they were never compelled to worship false gods. Yet, the Church which Calvin imagines was hiding for nearly a thousand years, had no temples, no sacred rites, no bishops, it did not even have a corner of earth where it could freely exercise acts of its religion, and what is worse, was compelled to be in servitude to false gods, to adore idols, to communicate in sacrileges, which is an even more horrible and longer captivity, than there ever was among the Jews; moreover, that Church of his would be even more deformed than the ruins of the synagogue.

---

[76] See the book, *De Missa angulari,* or Joannes Cochlaeus, *in actis Lutheri* for the year 1534. Likewise, bk 2 of Luther against Zwingli, or *Septicipitem* of John Cochlaeus, ch. 24.

[77] Bk 7, epist. 5.

CHAPTER VI
The Third Mark

THE THIRD MARK is Long Duration, without interruption. Truly the Church is called Catholic, not only because it always was, but even because it always will be, according to Daniel IX: "The kingdom which will not be destroyed in eternity." Also Acts V: "If this is a work or council of men, it will come to nothing; but if it is from God, you cannot destroy it." Concerning the heretics, however, St. Paul says: "They will proceed no further."[78] St. Cyprian says that schismatics always swarm in the beginning, but cannot have increase, rather immediately fade out due to their deprave rivalry.[79] St. Augustine, commenting on Psalm 57, where it is read "they come to nothing, as water flowing down," says: "Let them not terrify you, brethren, as certain rivers which are spoken of as running streams. They are filled with the waters of winter. Do not fear: after a while it passes, the water runs down, it resounds for a time, soon it will cease. They cannot stand for a long time. Many difficulties have already died off, they ran in their streams as much as they could, they flowed down: they are dry streams, scarcely a memory of them is found to show that they ever were."

Now it is certain that our Church has endured to this point from the beginning of the world. Or, if we speak from the status of the New Testament, it has endured from Christ to this point for 1577 years, in vain have all attacked her, first the Jews, then the pagans, lastly the heretics. Not only has it endured, but even has increased from persecutions. As the waters of floods rush over the palaces of kings, and also overthrow them, so have persecutions destroyed temporal kingdoms, but the kingdom of Christ, which is the Church, not only did they not destroy, but made even more glorious.

---

[78] 2 Tim. III: 9.

[79] Cyprian, *Epistol. 2.*

Therefore St. Justin Martyr says in his Dialogue with Trypho, that persecution is to the Church, like pruning is to vineyards, as indeed by the pruning of vineyards they are called to fruitfulness, so also the Church rises in persecutions. Tertullian elegantly calls the blood of the martyrs the seed of Christians[80], which Pope Leo seems to have expressed when he said: "The Church by persecutions is not decreased, but increased, and the Lord's field is always clothed with the richest grain, while from a grain which falls individually, many more are born."[81]

However much the heretics of this time do not concede that our Church has endured for 1577 years, yet they concede it to have endured without any interruption from St. Gregory the great to this time; that is nearly a thousand years. Such a time even by itself, would still be longer than the life of any heresy; certainly they cannot show through any history or ancient writing that a change of religion came to pass in the Roman Church in the time of St. Gregory.

Thereupon, it can be proven that our Church is the true Church even by this argument; for before the times of Luther, there were no other religions in the world but these; Paganism, Judaism, Islam, Greek Orthodoxy, Nestorianism, the heresy of the Hussites and the Roman Church. Now it is certain that the true Church of Christ was not with any of the aforementioned sects, as even the Lutherans will affirm, therefore it was the Roman Church, what follows from their opinion is that every true and visible Church perished from the world—which cannot be, as we taught above. But on the other hand, all heretical sects fail after a time, apart from those which have recently arisen.

Theodoret relates that seventy six different heresies which had arisen were present even in his time, and witnesses that they all had been extinguished, with the exception of a very few.[82] St. Augustine

---

[80] *Apologeticus*, last chapter.

[81] *Serm. 1* de Petro et Paulo.

[82] Theodoret, *de haereticis fabulis*, bk 3.

counts eighty eight heresies, wherein he witnesses that many perished.[83] We count even to the time of Luther two hundred diverse families of heretics: but from these none survive, except a certain relic of the Nestorians and Monophysites in the east as well as the Hussites in Bohemia; all the rest have utterly perished. And the providence of God is exceedingly wonderful in this matter, because hitherto even to the times of Luther, there were at least two hundred heresiarchs, of which many had several bishops, Churches, and powerful patrons, even emperors and kings. They wrote so many numerous books, that it appeared they would never die out; and nevertheless they did, so that none of them survived, not even their books, nor dogmas, nor names, or any vestige, except in the books of Catholics. Therefore, if Catholics had not written their names in their books, we would not know that they ever existed.

How strong did the roots upon which the Arian heresy rested appear to be in the times of St. Athanasius and Hilary? But now, I ask, where is it? It vanished as dust, which is scattered by the winds of the earth. Two hundred years ago the Albigensian heresy reigned in France, which apart from force of doctrine, abounded more in soldiers and power than the heresy of the Calvinists now, as can be recognized from Paulus Aemilius:[84] and nevertheless, where are the Albigensians now? How few are they who have heard or named them?

Next, the Lutherans were scarcely born when they began to wither, the reign of Luther began in 1517, but he reigned for scarcely seven years, for in 1525 Zwingli arose, and two years later the Anabaptists rose, who drew the greater part of the Lutherans away from Luther and to themselves. Yet the Lutherans who remain so changed the doctrine of Luther, that hardly any pure Lutherans can be found. Illyricus seriously complains about that in the prefaces of all the Centuries.

---

[83] *De haeresibus*;; *Expositiones in psalmos*, 57.

[84] *De rebus Gallorum*, bk 6.

But Zwingli did not reign long, for in 1538 Calvin arose, who strengthened in such a short time, that scarcely a few towns in Switzerland remained Zwinglian. In the same manner the Calvinists were reduced by the Libertines in France, the Trinitarians in Poland, and the Samosatens in Transylvania, daily they are made fewer and fewer.

Calvin, as he was perceptive, foresaw that his reign would not last long, and predicted in the preface of the Geneva Catechism, which he sent to his ministers in eastern Frisia: "I am anxious about posterity, that still I can hardly dare to think about it. Unless God should miraculously bring aid from heaven, I myself see the worst barbarism to threaten the world. And would that our sons would understand, that this is more a true prophecy than conjecture." Such anxiety of Calvin sufficiently declares his sect to be plainly a human affair, not devised by the Spirit of God, but by a certain industry and human plan, and therefore by far is missing that spirit, which said: "Upon this rock I will build my Church, and the gates of hell will not prevail against it."

The Centuriators also prophesy the same thing in the preface of the second century concerning their Lutheranism: "Especially variations in doctrine and inclinations seem to threaten it; and thus the sins of men earn such atrocities which happen day after day. And indeed, the times of the German prophet Martin Luther, by whose voice and ministry the light of the Gospel was recalled as from Egyptian darkness, just about corresponded to the age of the apostles. Now, however, it has been taken away, as we enter another age of the gospel, where many fanatics begin to sprout, and rule little by little." Later, in the preface to the fifth Century, after they showed the particular articles on free will, on justifying faith, and on good works, they declare that they are not fully defended by many Lutherans, but subjected to Papism: "That truth recently made so clear has perished. Philosophy, Papism and other sects far and wide occupy the first seat in the temple of God."

Therefore we conclude with St. Jerome, in the last dialogue against the Luciferians: "I advance the brief and open opinion of my mind, that I must remain in that Church, which was founded by the apostles, and endures even to this day." And with St. Augustine: "Will we hesitate to submit to the bosom of that Church, which obtained the summit of authority by the apostolic seat through successions of bishops, while the heretics roared around in vain?"[85]

[85] *De Utilitate Credendi*, ch. 17.

CHAPTER VII
The Fourth Mark

THE FOURTH mark is the Extent, or the Multitude and Diversity of Believers. Indeed, a Church that is truly Catholic ought not only to embrace all times but all places, all nations and all races of men. Therefore, St. Vincent of Lérin explains what a Catholic might be in his *Commonitorium*, where he says that they are properly Catholics, who hold to that which has been believed always, everywhere and by all. And thus it was preached in the Psalms: "I will give to you the nations as your inheritance, and as your possession the ends of the earth,"[86] and, "Your dominion will be from sea to sea."[87] And the Lord himself in both the last chapter of Luke and the first of Acts of the apostles, says that the Gospel must be preached in all nations, which was begun in Jerusalem.

However, some things must be observed before we shall draw out the argument on this Mark. The first is from St. Augustine and St. Bede, namely, that for the Church to be Catholic, first it is required that it should not exclude any times, places, or races of men; whereby it is distinguished from the Synagogue, which was a particular Church, not a catholic one, because it was bound to one time, that is, even to the coming of the Messiah; likewise, in one place, that is the temple of Solomon, outside of which they could not sacrifice, and to one family, that is the sons of Jacob.[88]

Secondly, as noted by St. Augustine,[89] that the Church might be catholic, it is not required that it must be in every place of the world, but merely that it becomes conspicuous in all provinces, and bears fruit in them, so that in all provinces someone should be from the

---

[86] Psalm II.

[87] Psalm LXXI.

[88] Augustine, *de unitate Ecclesiae,* ch. 6; Bede *in Cant.*, ch. 6.

[89] *Epistol. 80 ad Hesychium.*

Church; until this should happen, the day of the Lord will not come, as obviously is predicted in Matthew 24.

Thirdly from Driedo,[90] it is not required that in this it happens together so that in one time there ought to necessarily be some faithful in all lands; it is sufficient enough if it happens successively. Whereby it follows that if only one land should retain the true faith, still truly and properly it could be called the Catholic Church, provided that it should be clearly shown that it was one and the same with that which was in some time or at different times in the whole world, in so far as now whichever diocese you like is called Catholic, because it has continued with others, which make the one Church catholic.

But you will say, "this is to fall into the error of Petilianus and the Donatists, who said the Church was in the whole world, but afterward perished from all provinces, and remained only in Africa, whom St. Augustine condemned."[91] I respond, the Donatists erred in two things. First, they wanted the Church to only be in Africa while at the same time it manifestly still bore fruit in the whole world. Secondly, because their African Church would not continue with those which were in the whole world because in those were always found the good and the wicked, as St. Augustine proves, and the Donatists wanted only the good.

Lastly, with respect to this mark, although the Church ought not necessarily be in all places at the same time, nevertheless in this time it ought necessarily be, or have been, in a greater part of the world. For, everyone agrees, even the heretics, that the Church is already old; if therefore it would not have increased in its adolescence and youth, how could it rise now in old age? It would behoove it, therefore, to have already increased, and also if not occupied the whole world, at least a great part of it.

Now, that our Church occupies a great part of the world, and is truly Catholic is so proved. For in the time of the apostles it began to

---

[90] Driedo, *de Ecclesia dogmat.* Nota, bk 4, ch. 2, par. 2.

[91] *Sermon 2 on Psalm 101.*

bear fruit in the whole world, as Paul says.[92] Likewise, in the time of Irenaeus, it was scattered through the whole world, that is, through all provinces then known, which he relates.[93] Tertullian reports the same thing later in his time,[94] as does St. Cyprian.[95] St. Athanasius says the same thing in his book on the humanity of the word, and a little after, Sts. John Chrysostom and Jerome,[96] St. Augustine as well as Theodoret,[97] and Pope St. Leo the Great.[98] Moreover, St. Prosper of Aquitaine sings thus:

> Rome the seat of Peter, for pastoral honor,
> Made head for the world, whatever it does not possess by arms,
> It holds by religion.[99]

Perhaps, in fact, our adversaries do not deny these things. We will show the same thing from later times. It is plain that in the time of St. Gregory, our Church was spread throughout the whole world as we recorded above from the same letter of St. Gregory to the Churches of the east, as well as of Africa, Spain, France, England and Sicily. Likewise, from Bede, and indeed St. Bernard who, disputing in the presence of King Roger of Sicily, asserted in his time that the whole east and west obeyed the Roman Pontiff, and in like manner France, Germany, England, Iberia, and many barbarian nations.[100]

Thereafter, in our time, the Roman Church apart from Italy and all of Spain, apart from nearly all of France, Germany, England, Poland, Bohemia, Hungary, Greece, Syria, Ethiopia and Egypt, in

[92] Colossians I.

[93] Irenaeus, bk 1, ch. 3.

[94] *Contra Judaeos*, ch. 3.

[95] *De unitate Ecclesiae.*

[96] In Matt. Ch. 24.

[97] Augustine, *Epist. 78 and 80 ad Hesychium*; Theodoret, *De Legibus.*

[98] *Serm. 1 de sanctis Petro et Paulo.*

[99] Lib. *De ingratis.*

[100] See *The life of St. Barnard*, bk 2, ch. 7.

which many Catholics are found, in the new world itself, we have Churches without the mingling of heretics, in all four parts of the world; to the east, in the Indies, to the west, in America; to the north in Japan; to the south in Brazil, and in the further part of Africa. But the sects of the heretics have never occupied the new world, or at least, only a scanty part of it.[101]

The sects of Islam, along with the heresies of Nestorius and the Monophysites, which still flourish in the east, never passed over to the west. The Lutheran Heretics have never crossed the sea, nor seen Asia, Africa, Egypt or Greece. Wherein we understand that what is found in the beginning of the preface on the Concord of the Lutherans, published in 1580, is a lie, where they say that the Augsburg confession has spread throughout the whole world, and has begun to be in the mouth and speech of all. But from three parts of the world, two greater ones, Asia and Africa, the name of this Confession has never been heard. In Europe there are many lands, such as all of Greece, Italy, Spain, who in fact know nothing of the Augsburg confession, let alone exercise it. France, Switzerland and England do not accept it, unless it is in name only; nay more, it is a rare city which is possessed of only one heretical sect. And although it appears at this time that the heretics obtained a great part of the north, nevertheless, all those places are not held by one sect, but many, which fight among themselves no less than with us.

St. Augustine teaches beautifully that, as the Church is everywhere, so also heresy is everywhere. But the Church is one and the same everywhere; heresy, however, is not the same, but very different, which does not know one from the other, and hence none of them can be Catholic. While the Church, meanwhile, as a living vine, extends its palms everywhere.[102]

---

[101] –Translator's note: In 1590, the English alone had small settlements in America, which paled in comparison to the Spanish and Portugese. The first large colony of Protestants would not appear until the 17th century, consisting only of the English and the Dutch.

[102] *De pastor.* Ch. 8; *Contra epist. Fundamenti*, ch. 4; *De utilitate credendi*, ch. 14, 17 and other places.

The heretics cannot hope that their sect should at some time in the future occupy the whole world: for the Church ought not to begin to rise when it has already grown old, as we said above. And if St. Augustine found it most absurd, that the heresy of the Donatists should be propagated after the year 300 into the whole world,[103] how much more absurd will it be now after the year 1577? Will the Lutheran or Calvinist heresy really be diffused from Wittenberg into the whole world?

---

[103] *De unitate Ecclesiae*, ch. 14 and 15.

CHAPTER VIII
The Fifth Mark

THE FIFTH Mark is the Succession of Bishops in the Roman Church deduced from the apostles even to us; hence it is called Apostolic. Besides, all the Fathers used this succession as a most clear argument to show the true Church. Irenaeus enumerates the roman bishops from Peter, even to Eleutherius, who sat in his times. And he says that, through this succession all heretics are confounded.[104] Tertullian says: "Let the heretics start from the origins of their Churches, let them unfold the order of their bishops, so through the succession running down from the beginning, their first bishop had someone from the apostles, or apostolic men as his author and predecessor. In this manner, the Church of the Romans relates that Clement was ordained by Peter."[105]

The heretics sometimes fabricated such a thing. Eusebius in his history and in the Chronicle, as well as Jerome and Prosper who continued the Chronicle of Eusebius, diligently recorded the succession of roman bishops, so that the continuation of the Church would be manifest. Epiphanius enumerates in order the roman bishops, and adds: "Nobody should marvel that we have reviewed individuals so exactly. Through this, indeed, clarity is shown."[106]

Optatus enumerates all the roman bishops from Peter even to Syricius, who sat in the seat of Peter at that time, in order that he might show that the Donatists did not have a Church who could not embark on a like succession back to the apostles: "You, show the

---

[104] Irenaeus bk 3. ch. 3.

[105] *De praescript.*

[106] Epiphanius, *Haeres..*, 27.

origin of your seat, who would claim the holy Church for yourselves."[107]

Next, St. Augustine enumerates for the same purpose, the roman pontiffs from Peter even to Anastasius, who sat at that time. And against the position of Donatus he says: "Count the priests, or, from the seat of Peter itself, and in that order, of the Fathers who succeeded him. Look to it, he is the rock, which the proud gates of hell shall not conquer."[108] And again: "Keep me in the Church which is from that seat of Peter the Apostle, whom the Lord entrusted with the task of feeding his sheep, in a succession of priests even to the present episcopacy."[109]

If, therefore, so many Fathers took pains to show that the Church is true by the continuation of 12, or 20, or 40 Popes, how much more should we mark an uninterrupted continuation of 200 or more Popes? Especially when we shall see that other apostolic sees fell away, such as Antioch, Alexandria, and Jerusalem, whereby, after these places were stolen from the [eastern] Romans by the Persians or Saracens, which happened nine hundred years ago, there succession either ceased, or was very obscure. And in regard to the city of Rome, whose ownership has so often changed between rulers, at one time in the hands of the emperors, then the Gothic kings, then Greek Exarchs, then even consuls, whether justly or unjustly in their power, and as often as this city has been turned over, nevertheless the seat of Peter has never failed, never been overturned, but has always remained immovable.

In the event you should wish to better understand this argument, some things must be noted. First, in no way can the Church exist without shepherds and bishops, as St. Cyprian rightly teaches, the Church is the people united to the bishop, and the bishop is in the Church, and the Church in the bishop.[110] For that reason St. Jerome

---

[107] *Contra Parmenianum*, bk 2.

[108] In epist. 165 *ad Generosum.*

[109] *Contra epist. Fundamenti*, ch. 4.

[110] In epist. 9, bk 4.

says: "If it does not have priests it is not a Church."[111] This is certainly proved from St. Paul: "And he gave some as apostles, some, however, as prophets, others shepherds and teachers to the consummation of the saints, to build up the body of Christ, until we might all meet, etc."[112] Where he teaches apostles, he means the pastors who were going to exist in the Church even to the day of judgment. Then indeed, we will meet the Lord in the unity of faith, in the perfect man, in the measure of the age of plenitude of Christ. The same apostle teaches that bishops are the shepherds of the flock, in Acts 20: "Attend to your own and the whole flock, in which the Holy Spirit has placed you as bishops to rule the Church of God." Furthermore, even Luther does not deny it, in fact he preferably places among the marks of the Church to have true shepherds.[113] From which it follows, it is not a true Church that has either no shepherds, or at least no true ones.

The second note; only those who are within the Church have always been held to be true bishops. That is, those who were shown to descend from the apostles through a legitimate succession and ordination. All others were thieves and robbers, obviously who did not enter through the gate, but went in from another place. For it is certain that Christ, by whom the Church of the new Testament began, only chose twelve apostles as bishops and priests, and entrusted to them all authority of shepherding and governing the Church; but the apostles afterwards chose and ordained other bishops, and handed to them the same power, who thereupon ordained others. This is shown, not only by ancient historians like Eusebius and others, but even by the Centuriators of Magdeburg. Hence, because Paul, who was made an apostle outside of that order by Christ after his ascension into heaven, was not recognized in the Church for such, unless first he would have been baptized into the Church and was received in friendship by the apostles; nay more, he

[111] *Contra Luciferianos.*

[112] Ephesians IV: 11.

[113] Luther, *de Ecclesia et Conciliis.*

was ordained by them, as is clear from the Scripture.[114] Thus, among the people of the Old Testament, who were propagated by carnal generation, none could be counted as among that people of God, unless he descended from the twelve sons of Jacob; moreover none were priests, unless they descended from Levi through Aaron. Therefore, they very diligently conserved genealogies, as is seen in the entire Old Testament. In the same way, among the people of the New Testament, they are multiplied by spiritual generation, so that none are Christians, except converted through the apostles, or their successors, or those sent by them; none are bishops, unless they succeed legitimately to the same, and therefore we so diligently record the successions of bishops.

The third note requires two things; that some bishop should rightly be said to descend from the apostles, and hence be a legitimate bishop. One is succession, the other is ordination. As to succession, it requires that he who desires to be counted as a true bishop should succeed some apostle, in the way that Clement succeeded Peter, and Polycarp succeeded John. Certainly he should succeed someone whom an apostle made a bishop, as Ignatius succeeded Evodius and Anianus, Mark whom Peter had made bishops, or at length, if the episcopacy is new, that he becomes a bishop by one who has apostolic authority, which is the Roman Pontiff alone. St. Augustine writes that in the Roman Church the supremacy of the apostolic seat always flourishes.[115]

The reasoning behind this, is that the establishment of new episcopacies cannot pertain to anyone who might have a defined region, such as particular bishops, but to he who is over the whole Church, and to whom properly falls the care of propagating the Church, such as were all the apostles. Indeed, Peter did so by his office, and the rest by delegation, and whoever enters otherwise is not of the apostolic Church, since he cannot show his origin from the apostles. Nevertheless, we do not deny whether even patriarchs

---

[114] Acts 9 and 13; Galatians I.

[115] *Epist. 162.*

and metropolitans could at sometime erect new episcopacies, which St. Athanasius certainly did in the east, and St. Boniface had done in Germany; yet they had the faculty from the apostolic seat.

As far as ordination, it is required that for one to be a bishop, he was ordained by three bishops, who even themselves were ordained by others, and these by others, until one should arrive at the apostles. This is clearly held in canon 1 of the Apostolic Canons, where it is commanded that a bishop should be ordained by two or three bishops, that is by two assisting the metropolitan, or by many.[116] Likewise, Anacletus teaches that James was ordained a bishop at Jerusalem by Peter, James and John, and in the same manner by three at the least, all others ought to be ordained."[117] The same is held in the Council of Nicaea and Carthage.[118] Nay more, the Apostle indicates this very thing when he writes: "Do not forget the grace which is in you, which was given to you with the imposition of hands of the priests."[119] Accordingly, by the name of priests [πρεσβυτεροι] he understands the body of bishops, who together with the ordinand placed their hands above the head of the one to be ordained, as St. John Chrysostom, Theopylactus and Oecumenius express. And it is no wonder that the body of bishops is called a body "of priests", for the noun *presbyterus* formerly was synonymous with bishops [επισκοπος] as is certain from the epistle of Irenaeus to Pope Victor, which is found in Eusebius.[120]In that epistle, Irenaeus addresses popes as roman priests [*presbyteros*], namely Victor, Anicetus, Pius, Telesphorus, and Xystus. Therefore, there can be no doubt whether it was ordinary for at least three

---

[116]–Translator's note: The Apostolic Canons are decrees found in the Eighth book of the *Apostolic Constitutions*, which date from the early Church, although modern scholarship questions whether it was written by the Apostles.

[117] *Epist. 2.*

[118] *Nicaea, I.*, ch. 4; *Carthage* IV, ch. 2.

[119] 1 Timothy IV.

[120] Hist. Bk 5, ch. 24.

bishops to be required to ordain a new bishop, unless perhaps by some dispensation with one bishop ordaining while abbots were invested with episcopal insignia, who in turn functioned in the place of bishops, as was usually done at some time due to the lack of bishops.

The fourth note: it was the custom of the ancient heretics to imitate many Churches in the ordination of bishops, as we see from St. Cyprian and Augustine. Therefore, the holy Fathers did not reprove them for that reason, rather they did so because there was a defect of succession, and from that alone proved that they were not true bishops, seeing that they did not pertain to the apostolic Church, since they did not have their origin through succession from the apostles. Now, the heretics of our times have neither, that is, neither ordination, nor succession, and on that account are by far more shameless than any other heretics ever were, who usurped for themselves the name and office of bishop.

From that the unanswerable argument is taken up in this way: The Church cannot be without bishops, as we have shown. There are not bishops among the Lutherans, for they do not have ordination, nor succession from the apostles: therefore, the Church is not among them. And indeed, neither Luther, who is held as the Bishop of Wittenberg, nor Zwingli, who is held as the Bishop of Zurich, nor Oecolampadius, who, on an epitaph on his tomb, is called the first bishop of Basel, nor Calvin who is called the bishop of Geneva, none of them would deny this, since none of them were ordained by three bishops, nor by one with a dispensation with assisting abbots, as has been noted. At any rate, by the Nicene Fathers and the Fathers of the Council of Carthage, nay more, even by the apostles themselves, those who had stated that a bishop ought to be ordained by three other bishops, the aforementioned are not true bishops, and what Cyprian says agrees: "These assume for themselves the name of bishop who put themselves in charge, beyond what one would expect from the rash, putting themselves forward so as to constitute themselves without any law of ordination, being given the episcopacy by no man."[121]

Now, Brenz responds: "We are legitimately called thus by the people and the government, and received the episcopacy from them." Now, we do not dispute on the election of a bishop, which we know was celebrated differently during different times. Indeed, it is certain that the apostles and the old roman bishops sent bishops to different cities without any requisite agreement of the people. It is also certain that at some time the people, together with the clergy, chose the bishop, and at other times, only the clergy. For the rest, no matter how the election happened, ordination was always necessary, which *not* the people, but the bishops alone (and at that at least three) regularly conferred, which no one is ignorant of, except a man who reads nothing. Let Luther say by which bishops he was ordained that he should be made the bishop of Wittenberg. Let the rest say by whom they were ordained, but they do not because they cannot.

Thereupon, because they did not succeed in the episcopacy of ancient bishops, it is absolutely certain that in all cities, where these have made themselves bishops, there were already beforehand, and still are even in many other places, Catholic bishops that had legitimately succeeded older ones; and one does not succeed, unless the bishops have died, or been legitimately deposed. They even claim that they are the first bishops of these cities. Certainly there still exists in Basel, the epitaph on the tomb of Oecolampadius, where it says, as I noted a little before, and I myself have read it, not without a laugh, that Oecolampadius was the first bishop of this city. Concerning these things, therefore, the same thing as what St. Cyprian said in his epistle to Magnus may be recalled: "Novatian is not in the Church, nor can he be counted a bishop, who with contempt for apostolic tradition, succeeded no one and was ordained by himself ...How can one be considered a shepherd, who as a profane stranger succeeded no one and began from himself while the

---

[121] *De simplicitate praelatorum.*

true shepherd remains, and has succession by ordination in the Church of God, while presiding in that office?"[122] He also adds, in his epistle to Antoninus: "Cornelius was made a bishop when the place of Fabian, that is, the place of Peter, the place of the sacerdotal chair, was empty, in which it had been occupied by the will of God, and also by all of our firm agreement. Therefore, whoever now would wish to be made the bishop, it is necessary that he become a bishop on the outside."[123] Similar things to this were cited above on legitimate succession, from Irenaeus, Tertullian, Epiphanius, Optatus and Augustine.

Yet, they object, that Papist bishops have left the true faith, therefore, they are no longer bishops, thus pious ministers can rightly take up their places.

I respond to this argument of Brenz (after which he admits that there may be a doubt where the true faith might be, although with us it is very certain): we cannot depose catholic bishops who have possessed their seats for so many centuries peacefully, unless they are legitimately judged and condemned; for in every controversy the condition of the one possessing it is better. Moreover, it is certain that catholic bishops were not condemned by any legitimate judgment. For who condemned them, apart from the Lutherans? But these are accusers, not judges. Who indeed made them our judges? On that account, even if our bishops were already condemned, they would not immediately succeed them, when no one had made them bishops, that is, those who had the authority of establishing bishops: nor would they be true bishops since no one ordained them, who had the right to ordain as we showed above.

Secondly, the same objection of Brenz, which is in his prolegomena against Pedro de Soto: Caiaphas legitimately succeeded the older priests, and could even deduce his elders from Aaron, and nevertheless the apostles did not seek that they should be ordained by Caiaphas; rather they legitimately succeeded Caiaphas and all

[122] Bk 1, *Epist. 6 ad Magnum.*

[123] Bk 4, *Epist. 2 ad Antonianum.*

those bishops against the will of the latter, and were made bishops and priests without any succession, therefore even the ordinary bishops might imitate Caiaphas, although without their ordination and succession they govern the episcopacy.

I respond: The priesthood of Aaron was temporal, and only endured until the beginning of the New Testament; thereupon, the priesthood according to the order of Melchisedech began, which was established by Christ. Since the apostles were the first fruits of that priesthood, they did not need to succeed Caiaphas, but are the beginning of the new priesthood, as is clear from Psalm CIX: "You are a priest forever;" and from chapter 7 of the Hebrews. Therefore, as there were not true priests from Aaron even to Christ, unless they had succeeded Aaron, so from the apostles even to the end of the world there will not be true priests, except for those who succeed the apostles. Nevertheless, it is true that the priests of the Aaronic priesthood should be held in honor unto burial; the apostles honored that, as is clear from St. Cyprian,[124] where he adduces the fact from Acts: "I didn't know brethren, that he is the chief priest."[125]

Thirdly: Calvin objects, asking for what reason should we also enumerate the successions of the bishops of Africa, Egypt and all of Asia, and he himself responds by insulting us, because that most holy succession perished there.[126]

I respond: Calvin either wishes to conclude from this that because the succession perished in those places, there is not a Church, or there is a Church. If the first, he argues for us: For if there is not a Church there, because there is no succession, therefore here there is a Church, because here there is a succession. If the second, we respond, those who pertained to the true Church in those places indeed could not show a continual succession of bishops of their particular place, but could show the continual succession of all bishops, who are Roman bishops, to whom these affirmed

[124] Bk 1 *Epist. 3 ad Cornelium*; bk 4, *Epist. 9 ad Florentium Pupianum.*

[125] Acts 23: 5.

[126] *Instit.* Bk 4, ch. 2 § 2 and 3.

themselves to be subject. This is the reason why the old bishops were more solicitous about the succession of the Roman Pontiff than they were of their own. Irenaeus was the Bishop of Lyons in Gaul, Optatus and Augustine were bishops in Africa, Epiphanius of Salamis in Cypris, Eusebius of Caesarea in Palestine, and nevertheless, none of them wanted to elaborate the succession of their Church, but only of the Roman Church. Indeed, it appeared sufficient for them to show the continual succession in the principle Church, of which they themselves rejoiced to be members.

Fourthly, Calvin also objects: "In the Greek Church the unbroken succession of bishops is still preserved, nevertheless, that is not, according to the Roman Church, a true Church, therefore succession is not a Mark of the true Church.

First I respond: The Greek Church cannot show a certain succession; for in the first place, Calvin affirms, in Asia and Egypt, and hence at Antioch, Jerusalem and Alexandria the succession was broken; only the Church of Constantinople remains among the patriarchal seats, which did not appear to lack a proper patriarch. Yet, the Church of Constantinople is not apostolic, nor does it show a certain origin from the apostles, although Nicephorus the patriarch tried to deduce in a Chronology a succession of bishops from Andrew the apostle at Byzantium. Nevertheless, none of the Fathers hand that down, nor was the byzantine Church called apostolic by the Fathers, and the Fathers of the First Council of Constantinople openly affirm that Church in that city is new.[127] Therefore, certainly the Church of Constantinople has some kind of succession from Constantine to the present, but not from the times of the apostles, which is the essence of the question.

I say secondly, the argument we advance from legitimate succession is to particularly prove it is not a Church where there is no succession, which is evident; but it doesn't necessarily follow, that there is a Church where there is a succession. Therefore, by this argument we evidently prove that there is no Church among the

---

[127] *Epist. Ad Damasum romanum pontificem.*

Lutherans. On the other hand, that there is no Church among the Greeks, we prove in another way, for without a doubt they were convicted of schism and heresy in three plenary councils, of the Lateran, Lyons and Florence, particularly their heresy denying the procession of the Holy Spirit from the Son, which is a manifest heresy, and Lutherans and Calvinists also affirm that.

Lastly, add that all those patriarchal Churches had manifest heretics for bishops for a long time, and hence the succession of the old shepherds was interrupted.[128]

Fifthly, Calvin objects in the same place that the ancient Fathers, who show the Church from the succession of roman pontiffs, did this because in those times it was certain the faith and religion had not changed in the roman Church; and now the contrary is certain.

I respond: Either Calvin understands that, in those times, the Church was composed of Catholics only, or Catholics together with heretics, because in the Roman Church there was no change in religion. If he assumes the first, he says nothing, for even in this time it is composed of Catholics, but religion has not been changed in the Roman Church. If he asserts the second, he lies. There were not heretics, if all always thought that true faith was in the Roman Church. On that account the Donatists attacked the Roman Church, as now the Lutherans and Calvinists do.

Optatus says: "From where is it, that you contend to usurp the keys of the kingdom for yourselves, O Donatists, who fight against the seat of Peter with your presumptions and bold sacrilege?"[129] St. Augustine adds: "Did you make the seat of the roman Church, in which Peter sat, and in which now Anastasius sits? Why do you call

---

[128]–Translator's note: To couch this in modern terms, Bellarmine is making the distinction between material and formal succession, the former meaning ordaining new bishops, the latter their jurisdiction in the Church. Bellarmine's use of "succession" here refers primarily to formal succession, whereby he says the Greeks have material and not formal succession, and the Protestants have neither.

[129] Bk 2 *cont. Parmenianum.*

the apostolic seat the chair of pestilence?"[130] And nevertheless, Optatus and Augustine argued from this succession against the Donatists, as we showed above.

[130] Bk 2 *contra literas Petil.*, ch. 51.

CHAPTER IX
The Sixth Mark

THE SIXTH MARK is the Agreement in Doctrine with the ancient Church. Indeed, the true Church is called apostolic, as Tertullian witnesses, not only on account of the succession of bishops from the apostles, but even on account of the kinship of doctrine, as he says, which is that it retains the doctrine which the apostles handed down. Moreover, it is certain that the ancient Church was the true Church for the first five hundred years, and hence retained apostolic doctrine whereby Theodosius the emperor is praised by Sozomen because by this method he restrained the heretics of his time. He bid the leaders of the sects to come together, thereupon he asked whether they thought the ancient Fathers, who ruled the Church before their separation, which then had arisen from religion, to have thought rightly and truly that the apostles were saints, and when they conceded this, enjoined them: "Then let us examine your doctrine against their writings, and if should agree with them, it may be retained, but if not, let it be thrown out."[131]

Now we can prove in two ways from this Mark that ours is the true Church, and not that of our adversaries. Firstly, by advancing the teachings of the Fathers, whereby we should confirm each of our doctrines. In fact this manner is very lengthy, and more liable to many calumnies and objections. The second way is shorter and more certain, without a doubt by showing first from the confession of our adversaries, that our doctrine is indeed the doctrine of all the ancients. Then showing whether the dogmas of our adversaries were held in the ancient Church by exploring the heresies. Then it will be certain, our doctrine agrees with the doctrine of the ancient catholics, but their doctrine agrees with the doctrine of the ancient heretics.

---

[131] Sozemen, *Hist.*, bk 7, ch. 12.

Thus we proceed to the first. Calvin in his *Institutes* opposed our teaching, and everywhere affirms himself to be against all antiquity. Wherein it follows, that our doctrine is altogether consistent with antiquity. Moreover, he says: "The term 'free will' [*liberum arbitrium*] has always appeared among the Latins, the term with the Greeks, ἀυτεξούσιος, is much more presumptuous."[132] And below that: "I myself should not wish to usurp an expression of this sort, and should others consult me, I would that they abstain from using it."[133] He says the same thing about all the Fathers, with the exception of Augustine, to have brought out human strength, and on free will either to have differed or tottered, that nothing certain could be taken up from their writings.

He so professes that he follows no Father with the exception of Augustine; and a little after, he even deserts Augustine.[134] For he condemns that opinion of Augustine, from his 106th epistle, that our will cooperates with grace, not leading the way, as it were, but following behind, and yet Calvin says it does not cooperate as one who follows behind, but simply everything is done by grace. "And certainly, the opinion of Augustine should not be received in all things, which assigns grace to sanctification, because in the newness of life we are regenerated through the Spirit." Therefore, in the point on grace and free will, Calvin affirms that he is opposed to all antiquity. Likewise, he says: "The error of the Fathers cannot be excused, for they do not attend to the person of the mediator, nearly of the whole doctrine, which is read in the gospel of John, they observe that fasting must be practiced, and intertwine themselves in much speaking."[135] Calvin teaches in this place, that the Son of God was subjected to the Father even with respect to his divinity; and that all the Fathers teach the contrary. He himself says, they all erred, and their error is not excusable.

---

[132] *Instit.*, bk 2, ch. 2 § 4.

[133] *Ibid.*, § 8.

[134] *Ibid.*, ch. 3. § 7.

[135] *Ibid.*, ch. 14. § 3.

Likewise, he says: "That which is called 'limbo' is a fable from some subterranean place, although it indeed has great authors, nevertheless it is nothing but a fable."[136] He calls the ancient Fathers the great authors, for he does not usually name the scholastic doctors, unless he uses the term "sophists."

He continues: "Let readers take one thing from Augustine, if they wish to have something on the sense of antiquity. Next, between him and us, this can appear to be the dividing line, what he teaches on the plague of concupiscence, then at length it becomes sin, the will falls with the appetite; but we have that itself for sin, which altogether by some cupidity against the law of God, a man is tickled, nay more, depravity itself, which generates lusts of this sort in us, we assert to be sin."[137] Here, he openly declares himself contrary to all the Fathers, and also even to Augustine himself, in the question on concupiscence, which is an extraordinary question. For from this foundation they deduce that true justice is not in us, but merely imputed, and there are no good merits, nay more that all works are sin.

Likewise he adds: "Nearly all the Fathers whose books are extant either fell on this side, where it is treated on satisfaction, or spoke exceedingly roughly and inflexibly."[138] Moreover: "Thirteen hundred years ago it was received in use, that there should be prayers for the dead. But I declare, all the Fathers were snatched into error."[139] He says in the same vein: "I affirm, everywhere the old doctors used the name of merit ...antiquity sinned ...antiquity sinned beyond measure in severity, because it required more from a bishop than Paul required and especially celibacy through a succession of time... The austerity of the Fathers was beyond measure and can in no way be excused, which both was utterly at variance with the precept of the Lord, and was wondrous in a dangerous way, since they appointed a

---

[136] *Ibid.*, bk 2, ch. 16., § 9.

[137] *Ibid*, bk 3, ch. 3. § 10.

[138] *Ibid*, bk 3. Ch. 4. § 38.

[139] *Ibid*, bk 3, ch. 15. § 2.

penance for the sinner in one case seven years, in another for four, and three, and for another for his whole life."[140]

Note, this appears so bitter to Calvin that he himself reckons through faith a man is so justified, that almost nothing remains to be repaid. But if this were true, then he most rightly accuses all the Fathers; hence it follows, that in Calvin's judgment, our teaching on punishment remaining after the remission of the fault was the teaching of all the Fathers.

Nevertheless, Calvin continues to show his break with antiquity: "I do not dare to excuse the Fathers in everything, and they sowed certain seeds of superstition and gave occasion to the tyranny which afterward arose, and then prevailed everywhere with the superstitious observation of lent, wherein every common man thought he must furnish some special obedience to God by those practices, and his pastors commended for holy imitation ... Therefore, it was pure κακοζηλὶα[141] and full of superstition, which ordained fasting under the title and color of the imitation of Christ ... That marriage was forbidden to the priests, was impious and tyrannical."[142] But when it was forbidden, he notes in the margin: Syricius in an epistle to the bishops of Spain. Yet, Syricius sat almost 1200 years ago. And below he adds on this law: "These things which appear to cause reverence in the priesthood, I confess, were received with great applause even in antiquity."

Again: "I see many centuries ago, even nearly at the beginning of the Church that the custom was received, that in danger of death the laity should baptize if the minister was not present at that time, I do not see how it can be defended by firm reasoning ... I do not believe the Fathers can be excused, since they sinned by manner of action; they imitated the Judaic custom of sacrificing more than either

[140] *Ibid*, bk 4, ch. 4 §10; bk 4 ch. 12 § 8.

[141] –Translator's note: κακοζηλια (kakozēlia) means a pathetic imitation.

[142] *Ibid*, bk 4, ch. 12 § 20; § 23.

Christ ordained or the reasoning of the Gospel would permit."[143] So much for Calvin.

Now the Centuriators of Magdeburg at the end of the chapters *On Individual Centuries*, record nearly all the teachers of those periods taught those dogmas, which we defend today, but that they merely call blemishes of the holy Fathers. And because it would be too long to speak on everything, I will mark only a few things, from the *Centuries*, 2, 3, 4 and 5.

Therefore in the second *Century*, on free will, they say that it was conceded by all the Fathers of this century: "In the same way, Clement asserted everywhere free will, as it appears in the darkness of this sort, not only to have been all the teachers of this century, but even repeatedly to have risen in the following centuries and even to have increased."

It must be noted, that the Lutherans have this point on free will for the foundation of their whole doctrine. Luther says that this point is most rightfully the summation of his affairs, to the extent that the articles on the papacy, on councils and similar things can be called trifles.[144] Therefore, in this particular controversy, and in the very summation of the matter all the Fathers (as the Centuriators themselves witness) favor us. Thereupon they say: "The doctrine on justification was more negligently and obscurely handed down by these teachers, and they do not teach that we are justified by faith alone."[145] Moreover, they say: "You shall see in the writings of the teachers of this century, no obscure vestige of the invocation of the saints; ... All the teachers of this age exalted the martyrs without measure."[146] The Lutherans deny that there is a certain type of baptism of martyrdom, or that sins are expiated in any way through martyrdom.

---

[143] *Ibid*, bk 4, ch. 15, § 20; ch. 18, §21.

[144] Luther, *in assert.* Arctic. 36.

[145] *Centur 2.* Col. 60.

[146] *Centur. 3*, ch. 4, col. 83; col. 85.

Continuing, they cite the testimony of nearly all the Fathers of the fourth century, such as Athanasius, Basil, Nazanzien, Epiphanius, Ephrem, Ambrose, and Prudentius on the invocation of the saints, which nevertheless the Centuriators call idolatry.[147]

For the fifth century, they say: "As in the first several ages, the distorted doctrine on free will was invented, so even in this age ... Although at times they seem to speak well and correctly, nevertheless, they establish at length that there is free will in matters, even spiritual ones by their overturning of reason ... Without a doubt this age added good works of men, that which emanates from a contorted doctrine of justification."[148] And immediately they cite much testimony of all the Fathers of that age, even Augustine, that works are meritorious, which they hold as a great error.

Now, against those who say that all the ancients erred, Tertullian elegantly speaks: "All right, now [let us say] every Church would have erred; even the Apostle would have been deceived from his testimony given on certain matters. The Holy Spirit would have regarded no Church, so as to lead it into truth, the purpose for which He was sent by Christ, who asked this from the Father, that he should be the teacher of truth. The overseer, Christ the vicar, would have neglected the service of God, permitting the Church to understand otherwise, believe otherwise than he himself preached through the apostles. And what is like unto it, that so many and so great a number should err in one faith? Therefore, who would dare to say that they might have erred, those who handed down [doctrine]? In whatever manner error came, it reigned of course only as long as there was an absence of heresies! The truth waited for some Marcionists and Valentinians to be freed. Meanwhile the Gospel was incorrectly promulgated. To many thousands upon thousands have been imbued wrongly, etc."[149]

---

[147] *Centur. 4*, col. 295.

[148] *Centur.* 5, col. 500; 506.

[149] *De praescriptionibus.*

Now as we come to the second part it must be set forth, that in the ancient Church those [opinions] which were held as errors were commonly placed in a catalogue of heresies, after being investigated and condemned, by such Fathers as Irenaeus, Jerome, Epiphanius, Philastrus, Augustine, Theodoret, Damascene and by other approved authors: for since these holy and learned men had never dared to simply relate any doctrines in a catalogue of heresies, if they knew there could be some doubt about them in the Church. And on that account we read that there was no one who ever contradicted those Fathers, as it were, whom they did not justly ascribe as a heretic. With this prefaced, we proceed to the catalog.

I. The Simonians taught men were saved according to the grace of Simon, whom they made God, and *not according to just works*, as Irenaeus says.[150] The Eunomians taught in like manner, that sins could not harm any man, if only he had faith, as St. Augustine witnesses. The same Augustine says that this heresy on the sufficiency of faith alone to salvation without works arose in the time of the apostles, from something not properly understood from Paul, and for that reason, the other apostles directed their pen against this heresy in their epistles, that is Peter, John, James and Jude.[151] But this same is the opinion of all the sects of this time.

Luther said: "A man can be pleasing to God in no other way, nor do anything, other than faith; for God cares nothing for works." And again: "A Christian is so rich, that he could not perish even if he wished, no matter how badly he might live, unless he refuses to believe."[152] Albeit Calvin, Brenz and certain others tried to some degree to temper this opinion, when they say that good works are necessary; as an effect of faith, nevertheless they still adhere in the same error; for even with that necessity being posited, they teach that works do not merit eternal life in any way, although God requires these as testimonies of faith. This was, however, the very

---

[150] Irenaeus lib. 1., ch. 20.

[151] *De Haeres.*, ch. 54; *De fide et operibus*, ch. 14.

[152] Lib. *De Captivitate Babylonica*, ch. De Eucharistia.

heresy of Simon, who was teaching men to be saved through grace, not through just works. On that account, with that necessity of works being posited, all sects teach that if anyone after committing all crimes should have an act of faith, no sin is imputed to him, which is nothing other than what Eunomius and Luther teach.

II. Thereafter was the heresy of Florinus, that God is the cause of sins, which Irenaeus said is more than a heresy, and even Vincent of Lérin attributed it to Simon Magus in his *Commontorium.* Calvin shamelessly teaches the same thing: "Men sin, not only by the permission, but even by the will of God, so that they pursue nothing by deliberation, unless God would have decreed something among them, and established it by some arcane direction."[153] He also says that Adam fell into sin not only with God's foreknowledge and permission, but even according to his will. A little below that he adds: "Some men scorn to hear the word of God, they are depraved, but into this depravity, they are led by God, that he might show his power and severity among them."[154]

Luther openly taught the same thing: "That wish, in which Judas willed to betray Christ, was a work of God, it was not in the hand of Judas, or of any creature, to change that will."[155] Peter Martyr taught likewise,[156] and Philip Melanchthon in his commentary on Romans, where he says the betrayal of Judas, as well as the conversion of Paul, were the work of God;[157] which commentaries are said to have so pleased Luther, that he said Philip was a second Paul. Nevertheless, Melanchthon retracted the error, both in his work *In Locis* and in his *Apologia* article 19 of the Augsburg Confession.

III. There was a heresy of Origen that the image of God perished in Adam, to which he had been created, as Epiphanius says, who was

---

[153] *Instit.*, bk 1, ch. 18. § 2.

[154] *Ibid*, ch. 24, § 14.

[155] *De servo arbitrio.*

[156] *Commentarius*, ch. 2, bk 1 Reg.

[157] *Commentarius* , ch. 8 ad Romanos.

a witness to this.[158] Calvin teaches the same thing: "Through sin, the heavenly image was obliterated in the first man."[159] Likewise, an error of Origen was that there is no hell, unless it were a horror of conscience, as Jerome tells us in an epistle.[160] Calvin teaches the same thing.[161]

IV. The Peputiani Heretics, as Augustine says, not only gave power to women, but also honored them with the dignity of priesthood.[162] Luther says in those articles, which Pope Leo X condemned, that women can equally absolve in the sacrament of penance, or children, just as a bishop or Pope.[163] And now in this very matter, in England a certain woman is supreme pontiff of the Protestants.[164]

V. The Heretic Proclus said that sin always lives in the reborn; concupiscence is true sin, nor can it be abolished through baptism, but is rendered unconscious as it were by faith;[165] after him, the Messalian Heretics taught the same thing.[166] This is the very opinion of Luther, and likewise Melanchthon and Calvin.[167]

A particular error of the Novatians was that there was not in the Church the power to reconcile men to God, unless through baptism. Afterward they added, that the baptized ought not to bc anointed

---

[158] Epiphanius, *Haeres.*, 64.

[159] *Instit.*, Book 2, ch. 2 § 5.

[160] *Ad Avitum.*

[161] *Instit.*, Bk 3, last chapter, § ultimo.

[162] *De Haeres.*, ch. 27.

[163] Article 13.

[164] –Translator's note: Here Bellarmine means Queen Elizabeth I, who by the Act of Royal Supremacy of 1558, was the supreme head of the English Church, possessing all the powers which the Pope formerly held and thus, in effect, was a bishop and head of every priest and bishop of the English Church.

[165] Epiphanius, *Haeres.*, 64.

[166] Theodoret, bk 4, *De hereticis fabulis.*

[167] Luther, *Arctic.* 2 and 31 and in the assertions of the same; Phillipus, *in locis communibus*, ch. De peccato originis; Calvin, *Instit.*, bk 4, ch. 15 § 10.

with chrism by the bishop.[168] Such an opinion in the first part is expressly of the Calvinists. For Calvin says there is no sacrament of penance apart from baptism: "But what Jerome said: 'Penance is the second lifeline after the shipwreck,' is obviously impious, and can not be excused."[169] On the other side, it is an error of all the Lutherans. Luther recognized only three sacraments, Baptism, penance and bread. Nevertheless, a little further in the same book, he rejects penance.[170] The Augsburg confession eloquently rejects confirmation, while Calvin says that our Chrism is the oil of the devil and polluted by lies, and on that account the Calvinists anoint their greaves[171] with it, when they can.

VII. Sabellius taught there was one person in God, not three, as Epiphanius witnesses.[172] In our times, Michael Servetus taught the same thing, without any ambiguity, and now this opinion rules in many places.[173]

VIII. St. Jerome says of the Manichees, in his preface of the dialogues against the Pelagians, "It is the mark of these men to condemn nature and remove free will." And St. Augustine adds: "The Manichees do not attribute the origin of sin to free will."[174] All sects openly teach the same thing. Luther says in article 36 that free will is a thing in name only. But in the assertions of the same article, he says it is a name without a substance, and all things happen by absolute necessity. And besides, in the book which he wrote against free will to Erasmus, he placed the title "On the slave will." Calvin

---

[168] Theodoret, bk 3, *De haeret. fabul*; Pope St. Cornelius in Eusebius, *hist.*, bk 6, ch. 33.

[169] Calvin, bk 4, *Inst.*, ch. 19,§ 17.

[170] Luther, *De captivitate babylonica*, ch. De Eucharistia; *ibid*, de extrema unctione.

[171] –Translator's note: A Greave is a piece of armor that protects the tibia, or extends from the tibia to the knee.

[172] Epiphanius, *Haeres.*, 57.

[173] Bk. 1, *de Trinitate.*

[174] *De Haeres.*, ch. 46.

did not permit man choice in any matter, so much so that he could not even tolerate the name. Nevertheless, in this, Calvin is more impious than a Manichean, because a Manichean attributed to a wicked god the origin of sin, but Calvin to a good God.

Besides, the Manichees everywhere attacked the Fathers of the old Testament, as Abraham, Sampson, Sarah, Rebecca and the like, as Augustine witnesses. Calvin did the same thing. He says: "Sarah sinned in many ways, when she placed her handmaiden under her husband. But Rebecca, by various frauds and impostures, corrupted the truth of God, since she procured the blessing of the son by a wicked plan, she deceived her husband, and compelled her son to lie ... The deed of Judas Machabeus, wherein he offered sacrifice for the dead in Jerusalem, was not without superstition and preposterous zeal."[175] He says that Abraham was an idolater, and "In Sampson, the vicious lust of revenge is in control when he says: 'Fortify me O Lord,' etc." Likewise, Calvin taught that a woman is never allowed to baptize, and adds: "it ought not be dragged out as an example, that Sephora the foolish woman circumcised her son, whereby she gravely sinned in many ways."[176]

IX. The Donatists wanted the Church to consist of the just alone, and also therein deduced that the visible Church had perished in the whole world, but had remained in Africa alone. St. Augustine, who witnessed this, relates that they cruelly cut down Catholics, and especially hated monks and bishops, whom they called Pharisees, and in the first place the Bishop of Rome, whose seat they called the chair of pestilence. Moreover they broke altars, despoiled Churches, sold sacred chalices, gave the Eucharist to dogs, and threw away the sacred chrism.[177]

It is certain that the doctrine and life of the Calvinists is the same, for Calvin teaches that the Church consists of the good

---

[175] *Instit.*, bk; *Ibid*, ch. 5, § 8.

[176] *Instit.*, bk 3, ch. 14, § 11; ibid ch. 20 § 15; Ibid bk 4 ch. 15 § 22.

[177] *De Unit. Ecclesiae*, ch. 12; bk 2 *contra Petilian*, ch. 51 and 61; bk 3 ch. 40; epist. 163 and elsewhere. Cf Optatus, bk 2 and 6 *contra Parmenian.*

alone,[178] as does the Augsburg Confession in article 7. They all teach that the visible Church has perished for many ages, and is now only in northern parts, where they themselves live, particularly Calvin.[179] Next, the Calvinists have left out none of those things which the Donatists blasphemously, or cruelly, or sacrilegiously said or did against Catholics, their sacraments and the altars, etc., but obviously they have done and said many and worse things, which can be seen in the history of Suri and from the book that he recently published, by the title of *De furoribus gallicis*, and from other worthy authors.

X. The Arians taught that the son of God is a lesser being than the Father, as we see in the same citation in Epiphanius. Thereafter, the same Arians did not receive any unwritten traditions in any manner, as Maximinus, the Arian bishop taught.[180] Afterwards, many others imitated them, such as Nestorius, Dioscurus and Eutyches, as mentioned in act 1 of the Seventh Ecumenical Council. Therefore, the same Arians committed many and more terrible sacrileges against the sacraments, altars, priests, monks and nuns than the Donatists had, as is clear in the writings of the Fathers of that time.[181]

Many of those who today openly teach the first error of the Arians are called Tritheitae, as can be recognized from the *Prothesibus Valentini gentilis.* And although Luther, Melanchthon, Calvin and others like them hold Arius as a heretic, nevertheless they cannot deny that in their own writings they have sown the seeds of this error, from where these new Arians arose, whom they fight against, as we showed in another work.[182] Moreover, all the heretics of this age teach the second error. The sects of this time

---

[178] *Instit.*, Bk 4, ch. 1 § 7.

[179] *Instit.*, bk 4, ch. 2 § 2.

[180] Quoted by St. Augustine, bk 1, ch. 2 and the last Contra Maximinum.

[181] Athanasius, *Apologia pro fuga sua.*; Ruffinus, bk. 11, *hist.*, ch. 3; Theodoret, bk 4, *hist.*, ch. 19 and 20; Victor of Utica, bk 2 and 3 *de Wandalica persecutione.*

[182] In the Praeface to the books *De Christo.*

reject all traditions, as is clear from their own writings.[183] Next, those cruel and sacrilegious deeds of the Arians, if only the names might be changed, are the ones which the Calvinists everywhere commit.

XI. The Aerian Heretics[184] taught three errors, as witnessed by Epiphanius and Augustine. Augustine noted that he taught: "That it is not fitting to pray or to offer sacrifice for the dead, nor should fasting be established or solemnly celebrated, but rather fasting was to be done when each wished, lest it might appear they were under the law."[185] Thereafter, that no difference ought to be discerned in a priest from a bishop. Epiphanius adds, that they preserved a contrary custom on Friday, even in Lent, and especially ate meat even in Holy Week, and if ever they wished to fast, they usually did so on Sunday and not another day.[186]

Nearly all the Calvinists and Lutherans teach and do the same things. Calvin avowedly disputes against praying for the dead. He condemns fasting in Lent and calls it superstitious. Thereupon he says: "The Bishops, priests, pastors and ministers have the same function and duty."[187] The Centuriators of Madgeburg, although they usually number the errors of other heretics, omit those which they recognize to be their own errors. For, when they come to Aerius, because they saw only these three errors were recorded as proper to Aerius, by Epiphanius and Augustine, they could not omit them: Therefore they placed those, but soon added, if there might be nothing else, that these were not errors, but simply contrary positions. Therefore, they affirm these three opinions are common among them which Aerius held to, and they don't deny that in the ancient Church these were held as condemned heresies. From which

---

[183] Brenz in his prolegomena; Calvin, *Institut.*, bk 4, ch. 8 § 8.

[184] –Translator's note: Aerius (not Arius) was a priest of Sebaste in what is now Turkey.

[185] Augustine, *De haeres.*, ch. 33.

[186] Epiphanius, *Haeres.*, 75.

[187] *Institut.*, Bk 3. Ch. 5 § 6; *Ibid*, bk 4, ch. 12. § 20; *Ibid*, ch. 3. § 8.

it follows that the Centuriators, although then not yet born, were heretics of the ancient Church.

XII. Jovinian asserted that man could not sin after baptism, if he had been truly baptized, that is if in reality he had received faith and the grace of God, thereupon abstinence and fasting were not meritorious: on that account, there is equal dignity and merit with virginity and the married life. Wherefore, they even married several nuns with their urging. They also taught all the rewards of the blessed are equal, and what is more, that the Blessed Virgin lost virginity of the flesh by giving birth.[188]

Calvin also holds the first of these errors, since he teaches true faith, which is separated from grace (grace in his understanding), once held, can never be lost, and therefore is nothing except a sign of the elect.[189]

Calvin teaches the second one, when he complains of all of the Fathers because they praised fasting as though it were meritorious.[190]

The third error is of Martin Luther in *Epithalamio*, where commenting on ch. 7 of the first epistle to the Corinthians, he makes four comparisons. The first comparison is with chastity as an idea, and there he affirms chastity to be a more noble gift. The second comparison of chastity with matrimony in the presence of God, he says to be equal. The Third comparison is with married women and maidens, and he says: "It behooves us to admit that a married woman excels a maiden in the sight of God." The fourth comparison, is of the state of spouses with the state of religious and ecclesiastics professing celibacy; and he says the state of the married, from its nature, is spiritual, divine, heavenly, and as gold, the state of celibacy is secular, earthly and as a punishment. Similar things are taught by the Augsburg Confession and Calvin.[191]

---

[188] Jerome, bk 1 and 2 *contra Jovinian*; Augustine, bk. *De haeres.*, ch. 82.

[189] *Instit.*, bk 2, ch. 2 § 11 and 12.

[190] *Ibid*, bk 4, ch. 12 § 19. The same error is found in the Augsburg Confession, art. 24, and in citations of Philip Melanchthon, ch. De Mortificatione.

[191] Art. 23; Calvin, *Inst.*, bk 4, ch. 13, § 3.

The Fourth error is of Bucer and Molinaeus. Bucer being the author, affirms in the third part of *Evangelical Union*, that Jesus when he was born, opened the womb of the Blessed Virgin Mary.[192]

The Fifth error is of Luther in a sermon on the birth of the Blessed Virgin Mary, and in the commentary of the first epistle of Peter, where he says that all Christians are holy and just in a measure equal to the Mother of God, from where without a doubt it follows, nearly all are equally blessed.

XIII. Vigilantius also taught many things. First, that the relics of the saints must not be venerated. Secondly, the prayers for the dead from others were not heard, wherein it follows the saints are invoked in vain. Thirdly: that Ecclesiastics ought to be married. Fourthly: it is not expedient to leave behind all things and give to the poor, and, with the world being left behind, to hasten to a state of religion.[193]

Today all the sects teach this. Luther, in his sermon on the Holy Cross, says the relics of the saints are a seduction of the faithful, and therefore they ought to be shut in under the earth; and in his book on the necessity of abrogating the Mass, he affirms that: "God has no greater care of the holy tomb of the Lord than of cattle, for which reason the Apostle says: 'Does God care for cattle?'"[194] He also says that the invocation of the saints is stupid and pernicious.[195] He says the same thing in *Epithalamio:* "Matrimony is a precept of divine law for all, even for ecclesiastics and monks, who do not realize they have the gift of continence." But he calls the gift of continence, not a grace, by which we do not consent to carnal temptations, but one by which we are not tempted, no one has such a gift. Thereupon he dissuades openly from monastic vows and from religion, and only

---

[192] –Translator's note: That is, they denied the virginity of Mary *in partu,* (during birth). See St. Peter Canisius, *De Incomparibili Virgini Maria, Dei Genitrix*, book 2.

[193] Jerome, *Contra Vigilantium.*

[194] *De Abroganda Missa,* parte 3.

[195] *De Eucharistia ad Waldenses.*

permits that women 60 years old or more, as well as 80 or 100 year old men should remain in monasteries. The Augsburg confession teaches the same thing, for it treats against the articles of the saints, and against the continence of clerics and monks.[196]

Likewise, Calvin treats against the invocation of the saints when he says: "The Papists in their Litanies, Hymns and Sequences, wherein they render something for dead saints, make no mention of Christ,"[197] which is a very crass lie. Calvin continues, however, against the visitation of relics.[198] And in fact the Calvinists burned and cast into the flames the bodies of St. Irenaeus, Martin, Hilary, Bonaventure, etc. Against celibacy of clerics and the profession of monks, Calvin also disputes.[199] Moreover, the Centuriators did not wish to count Vigilantius among the heretics, but they write in that Century, where they say there was contention among two holy priests, that is Vigilantius and Jerome, on relics and invocation of the saints, but treated it as though Jerome debated by shouting, but Vigilantius by solid arguments.[200] In that place they also attribute a certain judgment of Erasmus on the book of Jerome against Vigilantius to Gregory, as if Gregory desired to restrain Jerome. But these issues are taken up in other places.

XIV. The Pelagians taught two things, among others. First, that among men there is no original sin, and especially among the sons of the faithful.[201] Secondly, through whichever sin you like, although it be the lightest, justice perishes and hence every sin is mortal.[202] The first of these Zwingli eloquently teaches, as well as Bucer and

---

[196] Article 21; art. 23.

[197] *Instit.*, bk 3, ch. 20 § 21.

[198] *Ibid.*, bk 4, ch. 13, § 7; *Admonitionem de reliquiis.*

[199] *Ibid.*, bk 4, ch. 12 and 13, whole chapters.

[200] *Centur. 4*, ch. 8, col. 602.

[201] Augustine, *Contra Julianum*, bk 6, ch. 2 and 3; *ad Bonifacium*, bk 4, ch. 2 and 4.

[202] Jerome, *contra Pelagionaos*, bk 2.

Calvin;[203] except that Zwingli simply denies original sin in any man, and merely teaches that we contracted certain miseries through Adam. On the other hand Bucer and Calvin only deny original sin in the sons of the faithful, whom they say are born saints, and even can be saved without baptism. Every sect teaches the second error.[204] All the rest wish every sin to be mortal by its nature.

XV. The Nestorians taught that in Christ there are two persons and two natures.[205] All the same Fathers condemn this, as Vincent of Lérin witnesses, yet it is the very teaching which Luther, Calvin and all the others furnish remarkably well. The chief error of Nestorius, however, is taught by Theodore Beza, whether from ignorance or from malice, namely in that he places two hypostatic unions in Christ, one of the soul with the flesh, and the other of divinity with humanity.[206]

XVI. In the same time there were also some, I don't know whether they might have been Nestorians also, who taught that the body of Christ does not remain in the Eucharist, if it is preserved on a second day, which St. Cyril calls an insanity.[207] Bucer again devised this error, teaching that in the Eucharist, the body of Christ is not present, except when it is consumed.[208]

XVII. The Monophysites taught that there is one nature in Christ, as one person; so this has been restored in our time. Gaspar Wenckfeld asserts that after the ascension of Christ his human nature was converted into divine, and now is true God, not creature.[209] It appears the same thing, or at some time something

---

[203] Zwingli, *de baptismo*; Bucerus, *ch. 3 Matthaei*; Calvin, *Inst.*, bk 4 ch. 15, § 20.

[204] Luther, *assert.* Art. 32; Philippus, *in locis*, ch. De discrimine peccati mortais et venialis; Calvin, *Instit.*, bk 2, ch. 8 § 58; bk 3 ch. 4 § 28.

[205] Theodoret, bk 4, *de haeret. Fabulis.*

[206] *De Hypostatica duarum in Christo naturarum unione.*

[207] *Epistola ad Calosirium episcopum.*

[208] See also Conclaeum, tract 8, bk. 3, *Miscellaneorum.* Melanchthon, *in locis*, ch. De coena Domini; Calvin, *Instit.*, bk 4, ch. 17, §39.

[209] *De divina majestate humanitatis Christi.*

worse, was taught by Brenz, who in a sermon on the Ascension of the Lord teaches: "The humanity of Christ was everywhere, always, by his very incarnation." Jacob Smidelinus teaches the same thing.[210]

XVIII. Xenajas I of Persia openly asserted that the images of Christ must not be venerated, as Nicephorus witnesses.[211] Calvin now asserts the same thing, and he does not wish that the sign of the cross should be raised in any way: wherein he shows himself the brother of the devil, unless he could conquer the devil himself with impiety. For the devil detests the cross because he fears it, and honors it by fear; Calvin detests it, because he despises and also mocks it.[212] He also says that for the first five hundred years there were no images in the temples of the Christians, which is a remarkable lie, since even Calvin himself witnesses the contrary! In the preface to the Institutes, he says that Epiphanius wrote in his epistle to John of Jerusalem, that he saw the image of Christ in the temple, or an image hanging of I don't know which saint. Besides, Lactantius witnesses it in his poem to the crucifix, as does St. Basil in his prayer *in Barlaam*, around the end; Gregory of Nyssa in his oration against Theodore, not far from the beginning, Paulinus on the birth of St. Felicity, Prudentius on S. Cassian, Evodius on miracles of St. Stephen, and St. Athanasius, or whoever is the author of the questions to Antiochus, q. 16, etc. They all teach in their time that images of the saints were in the temples, all of these lived 1100 years ago, as is well known. Add what Nicephorus says, the image of the Blessed Virgin painted by St. Luke, was placed in the temple, which Pulcheria, the sister of Theodosius, set up at Constantinople in honor of the Blessed Virign.

XIX. The Lampetiani taught that monasteries ought to be free, that is, without perpetual vows.[213] In our time Luther teaches the same thing about monastic vows; they cannot be vowed piously in

---

[210] *In disputatione Tubingensi*, ch. 34, de Christo.

[211] Bk 16, ch. 27.

[212] *Instit.*, bk 1, ch. 11, § 7; ibid §13.

[213] Damascene, bk. *de centum haeres.*, near the end.

monasteries, unless by this form: "I vow chastity, poverty and obedience even to death freely, that is that I might be able to change my mind, when I wish."[214]

XX. Of certain ones, who denied that the Eucharist is the true body of Christ, and wish it only be a figure or image of the body of Christ; they are related in the VII general Council.[215] Theodoret relates the same thing in a dialogue, long before Ignatius, which is called *Impatibilis.* Zwingli and Calvin teach this heresy in our time.[216]

We have to this point twenty heresies of the heresiarchs, which were condemned by the Church during the first seven hundred years. What we hold as heresies, our adversaries hold as articles of faith; it follows that our doctrine agrees with the doctrine of the ancient Church, but of our adversaries with the ancient heresies.

---

[214] *De votis monasticis.*

[215] Act 6, tom. 3.

[216] Zwingli, *De verbis coenae Domini*; Calvin, *Instit.*, bk 4, ch. 17 §12.

CHAPTER X
The Seventh Mark

THE SEVENTH MARK is the Union of Members among themselves and with the head; for the Church is one body, one spouse, one flock, as scripture teaches everywhere,[217] as well as in the creed of the Council of Constantinople, where we say "one Church." Moreover, the particular union of the body consists in the union of the members with the head, and among themselves. We must speak on each union, even in the first place on the foremost, that of the Roman Pontiff. However, since we have already given a treatise in another place[218] on the Head of the Church, here we merely bring a few testimonies of the Fathers to the fore, whereby we will show that union with the Roman Pontiff was always held as a mark of the true Church among the ancient Fathers.

Irenaeus clearly says, "It is necessary for every Church (that is, those who are, in all respects, faithful) to agree with the Roman Church on account of a mightier pre-eminence."[219] St. Cyprian says: "After those things, still in addition to having constituted for themselves a pseudo-bishop from heretics, they dared to sail to the chair of Peter and the principle Church, from where priestly unity arose, to bring letters from the schismatic and profane, nor did they think they were romans, to whom faithlessness could not have admittance."[220] Speaking on the chair of the Roman Pontiff, he says: "We know we are exhorted, that we should acknowledge the Catholic Church as tree and root and hold fast to them."[221] St.

[217] Romans 12; Cantic. VI; John X.

[218] –Translator's note: See *On the Roman Pontiff*, in 5 books by St. Robert Bellarmine, Mediatrix Press, 2015.

[219] Bk. 3, ch. 3

[220] Bk 3, ch. 3.

[221] Bk 4, epistol. 8.

Ambrose, in his oration on the death of Satryrus, says: "He asked if he agreed with Catholic bishops, that is, if he agreed with the Roman Church."

St. Jerome, on the noun *hypostasis*, says: "Here, in three parts, the Church is torn, and each is eager to seize me for its own. Meanwhile, I declare: if anyone is joined to the chair of Peter, he is for my part. Meletius, Vitalis, and also Paulinus say they adhere to you. I can believe it if it were asserted by one of them only; as it is, either two are lying or all three."[222] He says also, in an earlier letter (epistle 15): "I unite myself to your beatitude, that is, in communion with the chair of Peter: I know upon that chair the Church was built. Whoever shall eat the lamb outside this house, is profane: if anyone was not in the arc of Noah, he perished while the flood was master. I don't know Vitalem, I spurn Melatius, I have nothing to do with Paulinus. Whoever does not gather with you, scatters, that is, who is not of Christ is of Antichrist." Jerome also adds in an epitaph to Marcellus: "St. Athanasius and his successor, Peter, Alexandrian bishops, dodging the persecutions of the Arian heresy, fled to Rome, as to the safest port of their communion."

Optatus, for some pages from the beginning says, that the first dowry of the true Church is even the especial chair of Peter, which is at Rome, and thereupon it proves that the Donatists do not pertain to the true Church, because they are not joined with Syricius, who was then sitting in the seat of Peter.

St. Augustine, speaking about bishop Cecilianus: "Why wasn't he able to attend to the plotting multitude of enemies, since he saw he was of the Roman Church, in which the preeminence of the apostolic seat always flourished, joined through letters of communication?"[223] He also says: "Come brethren, if you wish, that you might be inserted into the vine. It is painful, when we might see you so cut off: Count the priests, or from the very seat of Peter, in that order of the Fathers who succeeded him: He is the rock, which

---

[222] *Epistola ad Damasum* on the term "hypostasis" (Epistola 16).

[223] *Epistola 162.*

the gates of hell will not conquer."[224] Pope Leo the Great in his epistle to the bishops of Vienna: "The Lord so wished the oath of preaching the gospel to pertain to the duty of all apostles, that he principally placed it in the most blessed Peter, chief of all the apostles, that his gifts might defuse from that head, as into every head, so that I would exhort anyone who had dared to recede from the solidity of Peter, to understand this is itself a divine mystery."[225]

Add to these testimonies experience; we see indeed all those Churches, which divided themselves from that head, just as branches cut away from the root, immediately wither. Certainly the Asiatic and African Church, which so flourished at one time that they had celebrated numerous councils and always held many men, either with respect to doctrine, or sanctity, or very famous, each fortified by God, from that time in which they had made a schism from the Roman Church, they have celebrated no councils, they have had no men with the odor of sanctity, or known for doctrine throughout the whole world, and now they walk in supreme ignorance.

Let us now come to the agreement of the members among themselves. It is certain, concord is a sign of the kingdom of God, which ought to stand in eternity. Discord, however, is of the kingdom of the devil, because, at length, it ought to come to ruin. "Every kingdom divided against itself, will be despoiled."[226] "God is not of dissension, but of peace."[227] And St. Augustine says: "The devil desired to effect through heretics that in the Church of Christ there might be free dissensions, just as there were in the academies of philosophers: that as these through many divisions at length died out, and were consumed by each other, so it will be in the Church."[228]

---

[224] Psal. Cont. Partem Donati.

[225] Leo, epist. 87.

[226] Matt. 12.

[227] 1 Corinth. XIV.

[228] *De Civitate Dei*, bk 18, ch. 32.

Now it is very clear from this mark, our Church alone is the true Church of God: Accordingly, in the first place, all the holy writers in our Church wonderfully agreed among themselves, although there were different men in different places, times and languages who wrote, which St. Augustine observes on the matter.[229] Thereupon all decrees of legitimate councils and popes agreed among themselves, even in all dogmas, although they were promulgated by different men, in different places, times, occasions and against very different, nay more, contrary heresies. This is an obvious sign of one and the same Holy Spirit, governing this Church. The diligence of heretics shows this is true, that although they laboriously pursue all things, nevertheless, they have not discovered anything of any importance which they could condemn; as we showed in the disputation on Councils.

Thereupon, now all Catholics, dispersed throughout the whole world believe the same things on all dogmas of faith. Nor can they think otherwise, since all subject their sense to the sense of one and of the same supreme pastor from the chair of Peter with the counsel of other pastors directing the Church.

There was never any sect of heathen, or of heretics, in which there was such a consensus, and this can easily be shown. First, on the pagan sects, Augustine teaches that both Juno and Hercules, and other gods disagreeing with themselves belonged to the same religion, and even waged war among each other.[230] Concerning all philosophers it was known, as St. Basil says, "It is not fitting that we should fight against the philosophers, since these suffice in their mutual dissensions to overturn the other's doctrine."[231]

The same was the custom of all the heretics, which is most certain. For Irenaeus teaches that the heresy of Simon, the first heresiarch, soon divided, and thereupon were born the sects of

---

[229] *Ibid.*, ch. 41.

[230] *Serm. 11, de verbis Domini.*

[231] Basil, orat. 1, *de opere sex dierum*. Cf. Theodoret, bk. *De Fide*; Augustine, *De Civitate Dei*, bk. 18, ch. 41.

Menandrians, Basilidians, Saturinians, etc. In the same place, he writes on the Valentinians, that when they seemed many, there were hardly two, or three who could agree among themselves in every dogma.[232] St. Augustine writes on the heresy of the Donatists that it was cut up into many minute scraps in his time.[233]

The Marcionists were soon divided, and thereupon the Lucianists were born, then the Appellians and Severians, as Epiphanius teaches.[234] The Montinists were divided among Peputians, Artotyritas, Phyrgastas, etc., as Epiphanius writes. The Manicheas also divided into diverse sects, as St. Augustine witnesses. The Messalians, however, were divided into Martyrians, Sathanians and Entusiasts.[235] The Arians were soon divided into Acacianos, Macedonians and Eunomians, as can be seen from Ruffinus. The same Arians also changed the faith almost every year, as Hilary writes in each book to Constantine. For equal reason, the Monophysites were so divided that nearly all sects which had existed in the east are children of Eutychus, the author of that heresy, as is certain from Evagrius and Damascene.[236]

In our time, it is certain from a little book on the *Concord of the Students of Luther*, by Fredrick Saphylus. Lutherans were hardly born before they began to be divided into Anabaptists, Confessionists and Sacramentarians; and again, individual sects in some and others even to 34 different ones, and this was in the time of Staphylus. Now, however, they number nearly 100 very different sects advancing one Luther. Yet this happened by the providence of God; for in this way heresies consume themselves; indeed their division is not mathematic, which proceeds into infinity. Wherefore the Prophet

---

[232] Irenaeus, bk 1, ch. 21; bk 1 ch. 5.

[233] *De Baptismo*, bk 1, ch. 6.

[234] Bk. 1, tom. 3, *contra haereses.*

[235] Epiphanius, bk. 1, tom. 3, *contra haereses*; bk. 2 tom. 1; *haeres.*, 80.; Augustine, *de haeres.*, ch. 46.; Theodoret, bk. 4, *de haeretic. Fabul.*; Ruffinus, bk. 10, *hist.*, ch. 25.

[236] Evagrius, bk. 3 and 4, *histor.*; Damascene, bk. *de centum haeresibus.*

Isaiah says: "I will make the Egyptians to attack the Egyptians."[237] And St. Hilary adds: "War for the heretics is peace for the Church."[238]

Add to that, even the same heretical authors do not agree with themselves, which is most certainly a mark of a false doctrine, as Luther himself says: "Lies, you cannot more certainly show except when they are contrary to themselves. It has indeed been ordained by God, that the impious shall always confound themselves, because lies do not agree, but always witness against themselves."[239] Next, John Cochlaeus collects the innumerable contradictions of Luther in *Septicipite*, where he throws out at the end, 36 different opinions of the same Luther on one article, that is, on communion under both kinds. The Augsburg Confession also, which they all hold to be sacred, they so changed and edited differently, that they themselves do not know which might be the true Augsburg Confession, on which matter you can consult Harmoniam of Andrew Fabritio Leodi, where you will see apart from the remaining edition of 30 years, there is even an edition of 40 years which is double the size of the other.

Yet our adversaries respond to this argument as they can. Firstly, Calvin, in the preface of the *Institutes*, says that it is no wonder if from their religion soon divisions should rise, as well as contrary sects, for it also happened to the Church of the apostles; indeed, Simon came from these, and Nicolaitae, etc. The Devil is truly always present where he sees good seed is sown and he comes and sows over it cockle. Thereupon, the same Calvin says, from this mark can be gathered, that the Catholic Church is not the true Church since there are as many assemblies of schismatics and divisions as there are monasteries. Formerly, indeed monks lived separated from others, but they did not partake of the sacraments separately; nay more they ran to the Churches of the ordinary

---

[237] Isaiah 19.

[238] *De Trinitate*, bk 7.

[239] *De Votis Monasticis.*

ministers, and there with the rest of the people entered into sacred things. But now, each monastery has erected a private altar for itself, and they partake of the sacraments separate from the Christian people, which they witness by their names, since some are called Benedictines, other Franciscans, still others Dominicans. Thirdly, some add more sects, Thomists, Scotists and the like, which are among us.[240]

I respond to the first: This is the distinction between the division of heretics from the Church, and the division from some heresy, because in the Catholic Church, a certain rule is discovered of settling controversies, that is the opinion of the supreme pastor, or of a general council, and therefore dissension does not arise from the doctrine of the Church, but from the malice of the devil alone. On that account, in every respect wherein they arise, they are soon condemned, and after the heretic has been thrown out, the fissure is restored, it makes no more progress in the Church herself. But with the heretics, there is not any rule of ending the controversy. Indeed, each wants to be put in charge of others and to be the judge of others, and thereupon it happens, as that ordinarily each new heresy you like soon after gives birth to others, and others, until through many divisions it is consumed, so that it would seem a miracle if some heresy should endure for a long time. Therefore the doctrine of the Church in itself gives birth to union and association of souls: but heresy in itself, and from its own nature, blossoms forth into divisions and schisms. Since we shall look at the manner of other heresies, the Lutheran sect was soon divided into so many other sects, and daily more and more it is divided, nor is it hoped by them that there will be any end to the division, we rightly judge them heretics, and at length, the name of Lutheran will utterly perish.

I speak to the second argument: in the first place, it is a lie of Calvin that the ancient monks did not have their own altar, but received the sacraments in the Churches of ordinary parishes. For Epiphanius, in his letter to John of Jerusalem witnesses that they

[240] *Instit.*, bk 4, ch. 13., § 14.

ordained Paulinianus a priest in the monastery of St. Jerome, who confected the sacraments in that very monastery with the rest of the monks, because St. Jerome, because of humility, did not dare to offer the sacrifice of the altar too often. Likewise, Cassian tells that in the desert itself, monks had their own priests, there were even monks who ministered the sacraments to the others.[241] St. Augustine teaches that not only in solitude, but even in cities, such as Milan and Rome, monks had put a priest in charge of their monasteries; without a doubt it was a priest, since was to confect the sacraments in the monastery, so that the monks would not be compelled to go out from the monasteries in order to go to the Churches.[242] Thereafter, St. John Damascene wrote in his history on Barlaam and Josaphat, that Barlaam celebrated the sacrifice of the Mass in his cell, while Josephat alone was present as his minister.

I say in the second place, a schismatic can not materially become anything else on account of a different altar, rather formally; otherwise all parish priests would be schismatics, because they have different altars in the same city. And all bishops would be schismatics, because they have different altars in different cities. Therefore, they alone are schismatics, who erect a proper altar, so as to esteem the altar of others as profane. Thereupon it is evident that the monks of this time are not schismatics by this very fact, because they obey the one supreme pontiff, are ordained priests by ordinary bishops, and thus are frequented by the people. Next, the names of the orders, Benedictine, Franciscan, Dominican, etc., are not taken up from the author of some doctrine, but from the one who established a more severe discipline, as has been noted.

I say to the third objection, Thomists and Scotists do not disagree, unless it is in those matters which do not pertain to faith, as St. Augustine says on the dissensions of teachers in his time;[243] and on that account they and every Catholic always subject

---

[241] Cassianus, *collat. 18*, which is of the abbot of Pyamon, ch. 15.

[242] *De moribus Ecclesiae*, bk 1, ch. 31.

[243] *Contra Julianum*, bk. 1.

themselves to the Church's definition. Hence, although they seem to oppose each other with words, nevertheless in the business itself they all agree in matters of faith; since all profess themselves to believe that one doctrine, which has been judged to be something which must be believed in the Roman Catholic Church.

But heretics disagree on particular matters of faith, and one holds the other as a heretic, and nevertheless they recognize the same Luther as a father.[244] Moreover, our adversaries cannot deny it by any reasoning: Accordingly, the Anabaptists would not deny that they are heretics to the Lutherans and Zwinglians, and the other way around; and nevertheless they all proceeded from the same Luther. The Zwinglians are heretics to the remaining Lutherans, as is certain from the testament of Brenz, and in many books of Luther. Zwinglians and Calvinists, however, do not dare to detest Luther, but in very serious matters they disagree with him, as is clear from the books of Calvin, Beza, and Peter Martyr, on the Lord's super, and on the place of Christ's body.

Again among the Confessionist Lutherans, rigid and lax seriously contend with each other. It appears so from the books of Johan Wigand and Illyricus against George the elder and Philip Melanchthon, and of the latter against the former. The Centuriators in the preface to the 5th century speak thus about themselves: "Although some are still teachers of the Church of God dispersed in different places, nevertheless they are not only by the children of this age, but even by their own fellow laborers and confreres, mocked, molested, afflicted, beaten down and broken, while they proclaim them stoic and seditious: even as the crimes of sedition and heresy dash against them."

John Wigand says in his book on the error of George the elder: "You, O George, are that man, who disturbs Israel, not we, who warn you on the foul errors opposed to the word of God. For you have brought forth cockle and foul errors into the Church of God with books, and disseminated them far and wide, and propagated them.

---

[244] Cf., Cardinal Hosius, *contra Brentium*, bk. 1; St. Peter Canisius, in his preface to the books of Vega printed at Cologne.

But we exhort the Church of God, as in truth, and once recognized and accepted with purity of doctrine by God for salvation the organ of Luther shall stand firm." And below, after a fourth error: "George glories in great boldness, lest he would cut one hair from the doctrine of Luther, and meanwhile the whole doctrine of Luther on free will, he attributes to a base mind and the devil in the chair of Luther." Even further, after a seventh error, he says: "The man of God, Luther, destroyed and publicly refuted those pernicious errors of [George] the Elder both in his writings and disputations."[245]

In addition, a very serious question amongst the rigid arose on original sin. For Illyricus contends the sin of origin was a substance, and he calls the contrary opinion a Pelagian specter. Conversely, Johan Wigand, Tilman Hesch, and others write against Illyricus, as if he were a manifest Manichean. Certainly Hesch, from the beginning of the *Remedy Against Illyricus*, teaches that this question pertains to the foundations of faith.

Thereupon, from the same province of Saxony, within ten years contradictory opinions went out, published under public names, on the most serious matter of all. For in the synod of Dresden, around 1571, while celebrating common consensus they rejected the teaching of Brenz, Illyricus and others on the person of Christ, and nevertheless, that very opinion was condemned by them in 1580 in the *Book of Concord*, which they had publicly received; and as the synod and the Concord of Wittenberg were published, they bore before themselves the authority of the same prince.

CHAPTER XI
The Eighth Mark.

THE EIGHTH MARK is Holiness of Doctrine. Indeed, the true Church is not only Catholic, Apostolic and one, but also Holy, as the creed of the first council of Constantinople holds. It is certain that the Church is called "holy," because her profession is holy,

[245] Wigand, *De errore Georgii Majoris.*

containing nothing false with respect to doctrine, and nothing unjust with respect to a doctrine of morals. Wherefore, in Psalm 18, the law of the Lord is called immaculate, faithful testimony, a clear precept of the Lord. Evidently from this mark is shown no Church is true but ours. Indeed, there is no sect of the Pagans, or of the Philosophers, or of the Jews or Turks, or Heretics, which will not contain some errors, tried and manifestly contrary to right reason.

Concerning the pagans, it shows the worship of many gods is absurd and foul, as many of the Fathers understood,[246] and there is not anyone that doubt this matter today.

On the ancient philosophers Theodoret teaches the same thing in his book on the Laws, which is the ninth to the Greeks, where he teaches Lycurgus permitted adultery to be legal: in the laws of the Persians, incestuous marriages were permitted between mothers, sons and sisters. In the laws of the Massagetae, those who were going to die or were old could be eaten by their neighbors. In the laws of Tibareni, the old were thrown from high towers, in the laws of the Armenians, dead bodies of men were thrown to dogs: in the laws of the Scythians, the living who had offended them were buried with the dead. In the Laws of Plato, which appeared to be the best of all, the most outrageous vices were prescribed or praised, as the sharing of wives, wicked lust, abortion, infanticide and like things.

As to the Muslims, the same is clear from the Qur'an. For it teaches that all are saved by their laws, if they should keep them, be they Jews, Christians or Turks.[247] It also teaches everywhere that the beatitude of the future life consists in food and drink, and a multitude of wives, while no mention is ever made in the whole Qur'an of the vision of spiritual actions, or the love of God. In chapter 43 it says that God and the angels pray for Muhammad. Similar very absurd things are everywhere read in the Qur'an.

---

[246] Minucius Felix, in Octavio; Arnobius, bk 4, 5, 6, and 7 contra gentes; Augustine, de Civitate Dei, bk 7.

[247] Ch. 2, c. 5, 28, 47, 48.

From the Jews that wrote after the coming of Christ, it is manifest from their books. For in the first place, in the doctrine of the Talmud, which is their written word, not God's, innumerable errors are discovered.[248] Rabbi Solomon, whom the Jews reckon to be the greatest, teaches in his commentary on Genesis on that verse: "This now is bone from my bones," that Adam had sexual intercourse with all the beasts and wild animals, and he could not satisfy his lust until he at last embraced Eve.[249] The same rabbi, in his commentary on Numbers, in that verse *On the first day offering holocausts to the Lord*, he selects "the holocaust of the Lord," and says it is a precept to offer a holocaust on the day of a new moon for the sin of God, which he committed when he diminished the light of the moon.[250] The same Rabbi Solomon tells such a fable in chapter 1 of Genesis, on that verse "Two great lights;" and the same in chapter 4 of Deuteronomy, in that: God created man," he says Adam was so grown, that he could touch heaven with his head, while he was on earth. Similar things occur everywhere in the books of the Jews.

Concerning the ancient Heretics the same thing can be shown. Indeed, there was almost no heresy which did not have manifest errors. The Gnostics taught, among other things, that they ought to practice orgies, and that every lust should be exercised, nevertheless they shunned conception. If by chance conception should follow, they would extract from the womb of the pregnant woman, and grind it in a mortar, and devour it as a condiment like honey and pepper; and in this way they said they celebrated the great Pasch.[251]

The Carpocratiani taught that everyone was held to perpetrate every kind of wickedness, and if or when they died, they had not perpetrated everything, they said their souls would be sent back to

[248] See Sixtus Senensem, bk 2, *Bibliothecae Sanctae.*

[249]–Translator's note: *Comment. Cap. 2 Gen. In illud Hoc nunc os ex ossibus meis; dicit Adamum cum omnibus bestiis, et feris carnaliter congressum, nec potuisse libidinem explere quousque ad Evae amplexus pervenit.* This is Bellarmine's summary of that line in the Talmud.

[250] In ch. 28, *Numeri.*

[251] Epiphanius, *de Haeresi*, 26.

their bodies, and this as often as it took to fill the measure of crimes, and in this way they explained that part of the Gospel: "You will not go from there, until you will have paid the last farthing."[252]

The Montanists made sacrifice from the blood of year old infants, whom they wounded with small copper pins, the whole of which they squeezed out with incredible cruelty.[253]

The Manicheans taught it was just as much a sin to pluck a leaf from a tree and murder a man. The same asserted parts of the divine essence were held captive by the princes of darkness, and from them some are liberated, the others are condemned for eternity.[254]

The Donatists made martyrs for themselves, by casting themselves headlong off a mountain, or suffocating themselves or throwing themselves into the fire, or threatening death and killing those who refused to kill themselves.[255] Infinite things of this kind can be added.

The sects of our time teach that every man is justified by means of individual faith alone, whereby each believes for certain that he is just in the sight of God on account of Christ, which can be compared with any paradox you like. For it is plainly not above reason, or apart from reason, but entirely contrary to it. I ask, therefore, were I to begin to believe that I am justified, whether I am or not; if I am justified, therefore, I am not justified through the faith by which I believe I am justified, because that faith comes after my justice; if I am not justified, therefore, that faith is false and it is not divine justifying faith, unless we might say, men are justified through a lie.

Besides, every Lutheran particularly extolls the spirit of prayers and invocation, and yet this faith abolishes the Lord's prayer. For if I believe for certain, that I have no sin, I would be a liar were I to say with this faith: "Forgive us our trespasses." On that account, Calvinists altogether condemn the Anabaptists, for they do not think

---

[252] *Ibid.*, 26.

[253] Augustine, *De Haeres.*, 26.

[254] *Ibid.*, 46.

[255] Augustine, *Epist. 50*; Theodoret, *De Haeret. Fabulis.*, bk. 4.

they are justified, or saved, unless they turn from their errors, and nevertheless they know the Anabaptists believe for certain that they are just, therefore they are compelled to say they are just and not just at the same time.

Besides this common dogma, each holds their own doctrines, full of manifest absurdity. The Anabaptists, more than any other, have many night assemblies wherein they marry dogs, as is collected from their articles, which John Cochlaeus refuted, and they even took their own sisters openly as wives. Article 11 of the Anabaptists is: "No man ought to publicly preach;" and article 17: "prayer should be done after the sermon, in order that they might be fruitful and multiply." Article 19: "it is permitted for a brother to take his true sister as a wife."

The Lutherans hold that very manifest error as their own, namely, that infants, while baptized, use reason, so that they hear the word of God, believe, and love, which is in the Wittenberg synod of 1536. Nevertheless, that is opposed to truth, as St. Augustine writes, those who say this do injury to the human senses. How credible is it that an infant who weeps and struggles as much as it can while it is washed, understands what is going on? Next, the Calvinists have as their own teaching that is not only opposed to piety, but also to reason, that everything which happens does so by absolute necessity, even so much that God is the cause of all sin, wherein nearly all Lutherans disagree with them.

But our Church, the Catholic Church, teaches no error, no foul thing, nothing contrary to reason, although many things are above reason. Hence, it alone is absolutely holy, and to her alone corresponds what we say in the Creed: *I believe in the holy Church.* This matter the Fathers showed against not only the pagans,[256] but also the heretics, as St. Thomas most accurately shows in the *Summa Contra Gentiles.*

---

[256] Justin Martyr in both apologies; Tertulian, *Apologeticus*, ch. 36,sqq.; Arnobius, bk. 1, 2, and 3, *contra Gentes*; Minutius Felix, *Octavius*; Augustine, *de Civitate Dei contra Paganos.*

Therefore, we conclude with St. Augustine: "Nothing filthy and wicked is set forth to be gazed at or imitated in christian Churches; but either precepts of the true God are recommended, his miracles narrated, his gifts praised, or his benefits implored... Truth was seen to be not contradictory to reason, but only different from custom."[257]

---

[257] *De Civitate Dei*, bk. 2, ch. 28; bk. 22, ch. 7.

CHAPTER XII
The Ninth Mark

THE NINTH MARK is the Efficacy of Doctrine. Only the true Church has doctrine that is not only immaculate, but even converts souls, as is said in Palm 18, a living sermon penetrating even to the division of the soul and spirit (Hebrews 4). Although the ancient philosophers displayed great wisdom, and persuaded people of their laws with supreme eloquence, nevertheless they never could even draw a nearby town to their laws, as Athanasius and Theodoret teach.[258] Because their words were not living words, but dead, not of the spirit of God, but of the spirit of men. On the other hand, the Muslims dragged many but by the terror of arms, not by force and efficacy of doctrine, for indeed Muhammad himself teaches in the Qur'an that men must be compelled to the faith by war.[259] Next, the heretics are never read to have converted any heathens or Jews to the faith, but only to have perverted Christians, which even Tertulian recorded: "Why should I speak on the cheat of their ministry? Since it is their business not to convert the heathen, but overturn us, they undermine our [side], and build up their own."[260]

But you might say with Freculph in his Chronicle,[261] that in the time of the emperor Valens the whole race of the Goths was converted from paganism to Arianism.

I respond: The Goths, were not converted by the Arians, but wretchedly deceived. Indeed, the Goths who already for a long time had gone out from their borders and fought under the auspices of the Roman Empire, and heard many excellent things about Christians, from their own will, with no one impelling them, asked

---

[258] Bk *de Humanitate veri*; Thedoret *de legibus.*

[259] Chapter 18 and 19.

[260] *De Praescript. Haeret.*

[261] Bk. 4, ch. 20.

for bishops from the emperor, by whom they should be taught, and it is said they were prepared to believe anything from them. But the Emperor, since he was an Arian, sent Arian bishops, and thus the Goths were miserably deceived, since they wished to be made Christians, but were made Arians, nevertheless not by any virtue or miracles of the Arians. For, how difficult is it to pour poison drop by drop into a man who is prepared to receive it? Moreover, Freculph does not relate this history in full: it is certain from Socrates, Sozomen and Theodoret,[262] that the greater part of the Goths were Christian and Catholic, but were afterward deceived by Arians. Therefore, heretics do not convert men to the faith, nor can they. For heretics indeed have the Scripture, but they do not have the true sense of the Scriptures, which properly is the sword of the spirit. Indeed the words are not a sword, but a scabbard, wherein the sword of the spirit is contained. Therefore, since these do not fight with a sword, but only with a scabbard, it is little wonder, if they do not strike the hearts of infidels? Neither should it be a wonder that they pervert Catholics, for men are prone to going down to the wide and easy road, which these open up for them. And God permits this to happen on account of the ingratitude of those who were once enlightened, and who did not respond to the light they had received with good works.

Whereas, truly the holy and apostolic Church once, in a short time and through contemptible men, drew the whole world by means of an external splendor, without arms and pomps. The whole world, that is great men as well as the small, the learned and unlearned, young, old, men and women. And it drew them not to the delights of this world, but to things which must be believed beyond all reason, and to the cross, the narrow and most perfect way, which is repugnant to flesh and blood, and all these things on account of no reward in this life, but only in the future life. And it so persuaded

[262] Socrates, bk. 4, ch. 27; Sozomen, bk. 6 ch. 37; Theodoret, bk. 4, last chapter.

this, that many preferred more to lose all riches, honors, friends, relations and even their own life, than the faith of Christ.[263]

Thereupon, from the time of St. Gregory even to our times, even from the testimony of our adversaries, many can be proved to be converted by the Catholic Church. For, in the Sixth Century, at the bidding of St. Gregory, not the heretics (who even then were not lacking), but monks and bishops converted the pagan English to the faith of Christ, as the Centuriators of Magdeburg attest.[264]

Thereafter, in the time of Pope Conon, St. Kilian was sent by the Pope to convert the Franks, as the Centuriators themselves say.[265]

After that, in the times of Gregory II and Gregory III, and Zachary, a great part of Germany was converted to the faith, not by the Iconoclast heretics, who then abounded in the world, but through St. Boniface, a bishop and martyr, whom Pope Gregory II had sent, as the Centuriators affirm: "In this century, after the time had dawned, which the Lord in his mercy had determined, the matter succeeded with greater fruit. For the Lord raised Vinofridus, whom the Romans call Boniface, who, with his colleagues, propagated their Churches in Germany, and he governed and advanced the work of their hands."[266]

In the preface of the same Century, they blasphemously and with the greatest ingratitude speak thus about St. Boniface, their own apostle: "The pope had at hand his hand picked galley slaves, very skilled in this sort of bird-catching, bold and rash, who enticed and entangled in rewards and honors, did their best with zeal in all nations and kingdoms ... Such a galley slave was Boniface, called the apostle of the Germans, who so brooded over this supreme study of skill and force that all Germany was reduced to the power of the

---

[263] Athanasius and Theodoret, loc. Cit.; Augustine, *de Civitate Dei*, ch. 5, where he places among the greatest miracles, that a few apostles by means of only the efficacy of the divine Word, conquered the whole world without eloquence or arms.

[264] Centuriators, *Cent. 6*, ch. 2, col. 37.

[265] *Cent. 7*, ch. 2, col. 31.

[266] *Cent. 8*, ch. 2, col. 20.

roman pope. Although in several places it is told that he abolished pagan idolatry, nevertheless he did not sow the seed of pure and incorrupt christian religion ... That pseudoapostle, inflated with such insolence that not only did he despise all counsels from on high, but he even maliciously brought in that roman tyranny just as heretics and disturbers of the Church." Here, the Centuriators seem to have forgotten that St. Boniface was a papist since they speak so well of him! Behold how they treat the apostle of Germany, whom every historian of that time speaks about with the greatest honor.

Thereafter, the Centuriators affirm that the monks of Morbejen converted the Vandals, and that the Bulgarians, Slavs, Poles, Danes and Moravians were converted in that century, but subjected to the Roman Pontiffs, wherein they prove these nations were converted by Papists. Likewise, they record that many kings and peoples were converted by the work of the Emperor Henry I, Bohemia by Adalbert, and Moravia by Methodius, whom nobody can deny to have been Papists, since it is certain that they were subject to the Roman Pontiffs.[267]

The Centuriators continue on, and teach that in the 11th century a great part of the Hungarians were converted, and were given bishops and confirmed by the Roman Pontiff, this confirmation at the request of King St. Stephen of Hungary who had recently converted.[268]

After those times, similar conversions were not lacking in the Catholic Church. Accordingly Pope Adrian IV, before his pontificate, was sent by Pope Eugene to convert Norway to the faith, as Platina and others attest; and unless I am mistaken, the Centuriators themselves attest to this in their 12th or 13th edition, at least I hear, I have not seen it yet. It is also certain in this century that St. Vincent, a Dominican, converted twenty thousand to the faith, both Jews and also Saracens, as St. Antoninus, who was a contemporary, writes.[269]

---

[267] *Cent. 9*. Ch. 2, col. 15; Cent. 10, ch. 2, col. 18 and 19.

[268] Centur. 11, ch. 2, col. 27.

[269] 3 pars hist. Tit. 23, ch. 8 § 4.

Lastly, in our own time many thousands of nations have converted to the Catholic faith. Some of the Jews also in individual years were converted and baptized at Rome by Catholics devoted to the Roman Pontiff, and even the Turks have not been lacking, who were converted both at Rome and at other places. On the other hand, the Lutherans have scarcely converted one or the other, although they compare themselves with the apostles and the evangelists, and they have many Jews in Germany, and in Poland, and in Hungary there are many Turks nearby. St. Augustine then, most properly, compares heretics with partridges, who gather the young which they have not produced, while on the contrary the Church is like a most fertile dove, which daily brings forth new young.

CHAPTER XIII
The Tenth Mark

THE TENTH Mark is the Holiness of the Authors, that is, of the first Fathers of our religion. Indeed, the true Church does not only have holy and efficacious doctrine, but even holy teachers, and famous with respect to the glory of their deeds. Now we will speak on uprightness, and afterward on miracles.

Now if one were to consider the great teachers of the Catholic Church, first the patriarchs and prophets, thereafter the apostles, then the doctors, who struck against individual heresies, and at length the establishers of the religious orders, he will discover they were all so holy, chaste, pious and sober, that our adversaries shall have nothing which they might condemn them for, except an excess of holiness. St. Augustine says the same things about the monks of his time, and on Catholic teachers: "These are learned bishops and shepherds, deep in holiness, keen defenders of truth, who took in the Catholic faith in their milk and ate it in their food, of which milk and bread they administered to small and great alike. With such, after the apostles, the Holy Church increased by means of such planters, irrigators, builders, shepherds and nourishers."[270] Add to this, that Luther himself affirmed Bernard, Dominic and Francis to have been saints, as well as Philip Melanchthon and others from our adversaries.[271]

But the teachers of the heathen were either light poets, or proud philosophers, and impure on each side. For the particular wise men of the Greeks were impure beyond measure, to such an extent, that they were even infamous among their own rites, particularly on account of their vices against nature, as Athenaeus witnesses,[272] and

[270] *De moribus Ecclesiae*, ch. 31; *in Julianum*, bk. 2.

[271] Luther, *De Captivitate Babylonica*, ch. 2; Melanchthon, *Apolog.*, Art. 5, and 27.

[272] Bk. 13, ch. 27.

on our side Theodoret in his book on the Laws, and clearly even St. Paul himself.[273] Muhammad however, could contrive nothing more incontinently, for he himself in the Qur'an, says that he has received the privilege from God to marry every woman which he might have loved, even if they were kin.[274]

On the heresiarchs many things can be said, but one is the common vice of all; pride. St. Augustine says: "In different places, there are different heresies, but pride, as one proud mother, begot them all, just as our one Catholic mother has begotten all faithful christians diffused throughout the whole world."[275] Certainly no heresy is discovered from intention, devised in itself, but *per accidens* from some wicked occasion, as monsters are usually generated.

Egesippus, as quoted by Eusebius, says this on Theobute, the first of all heretics: "Then, the Church was called maiden, because she had not yet been corrupted by the deceit of an adulterous word, but then a certain Theobutes, because he merited the rebuff of the episcopacy, began from the beginning to disturb and corrupt all things.[276]

After this rose Simon Magus, who, it is certain from Acts chapter 8, had canvassed for episcopal authority, and wished to give money so as to buy it. After he was excluded, he devised a new heresy, that one who could not be in the Church, at least could rule it on the outside.

A little after Simon Magus, Valentinus came, about whom we learn from Tertulian. In his book, *contra Valentinianos*, he said: "Valentinus had hoped for an episcopate, since he was possessed of genius and eloquence, but being unworthy, another was put in charge of the place from the prior right of testimony, he broke from the Church of the authentic rule (as those with a mind for rule usually do, excited with the presumption of enkindling revenge), etc.

---

[273] Romans I: 25.

[274] *Qur'an*, ch. 43.

[275] *De pastoribus*, ch. 8.

[276] Eusebius, *hist.*, bk. 4, ch. 22.

Thereafter arose Marcion, of whose beginning St. Epiphanius tells us: "Marcion was raised up by ambition, after he did not receive the presidency he went into the Church, and devised counsel for himself... with emulation therefore, he was both moved to great indignation and filled with pride he planned to make a divide, raising a heresy after himself and saying: 'I will cleave your church and I shall leave it broken forever.' Really, he did cause no small division, but he did not break the Church, which is truth itself no those who obey her."[277]

On Montanus, Theodoret writes: "He, by ambition, was moved with the lust of obtaining the first place, and called himself the Paraclete."[278] On Novation he writes the same thing according to Cornelius in his epistle: "He relates that with lust of the episcopacy, which he conceived secretly within himself, he fell into ruin in all these matters."[279] Epiphanius says on Sabellius: "He was brought to greater arrogance and madness, he said he was Moses, and his brother Aaron."[280] Theodoret says that Arius, "Since he was related to a great number of the priests of the Alexandrian Church, and he saw a great Alexander sitting in the pontifical seat, was struck with envy; and when he pursued the matter battles against him commenced, thus he discovered the occasion for impious dogmas."[281]

Epiphanius speaks on the heresy of the Semi-Arians: "Therefore, they came to contention, again the same with their companions, on account of a certain hatred and human rivalry, quarrels broke out among themselves, arguing about the primacy."[282] The same author adds on Aerius: "When Eustachius came to the episcopacy, Aerius desired it more, but did not attain it. Hence arose their rivalry."[283]

---

[277] *De Haeres.*, 42.

[278] Bk. 3, *de haereticis fabulis.*

[279] *In epist. Ad Fabium*, bk. 6; *hist.*, ch. 35.

[280] *Haeres.*, 57.

[281] Theodoret, *de hereticis fabulis*, in the beginning, bk 4.

[282] Epiphanius, *haeres.*, 73.

[283] *Ibid.*, 75.

Theodoret writes that: "Nestorius spent a great part of his life capturing the favor of the people with a swarthy vestment, faking paleness, composed with words, until at length he attained to the episcopacy." Likewise, Socrates writes on the heresiarch Sabbatius: "Moreover he burned with the desire of attaining the papacy."[284] John Wycliff, because he could not be a bishop, became a heresiarch, as Thomas Walden writes.[285]

In the same way, our adversaries certainly cannot deny that the sects of this time rose from ambition, pride, envy and hatred. For first, the beginning of all the heresies of this time was certainly the envy and ambition of Luther, as he was angry when the office of promulgating indulgences was transferred from his order of monks to the Dominicans, as John Cochlaeus writes in the acts of Luther in the year 1517. Wherefore (as the same relates a little after in the acts of the year 1519), in the first disputation that was held in Lisius between Luther and Eck, Luther exclaimed: "This case neither began on account of God, nor will it be ended on account of God." He says the same thing in his epistle to Argentienses, that he would gladly deny the body of Christ to be in the Eucharist, if the Scriptures were not so clear, because by this reasoning it seemed that he could be more of a hindrance to the papacy.

Luther boasts such pride in his book against the king of England,[286] that he said kings, princes and popes were not worthy to answer his correction of their blindness. He willed that he be held as a holy man, whether men wished or no, and made his teaching greater than that of a thousand Cyprians and a thousand Augustines. And in the book *De Missa Angulari*, so as to prove that he has for his own Father, he who is the king of all the sons of pride, as he says he was taught by the devil, that the Mass might be a wicked thing, and

---

[284] Socrates, *Hist.* Bk. 5, ch. 20.

[285] Bk 2, *Doct. Fid.*, ch. 60.

[286]–Translator's note: That is, Luther's 1522 reply to Henry VIII after the latter wrote the *Assertio septem sacramentorum adversus Martinum Lutherum*, in 1521, 12 years before Henry himself would leave the Church.

convinced by the reasoning of the devil to abolish the Mass. Thus, such was the wickedness of Luther, that even his own could not tolerate him. For Conrad Genserus writes on this, that in all his collections of books: "That point must not be concealed, that Luther was an impatient man of a forceful genius, even that he should be unwilling to consider anything unless it agreed in all things with himself." And further on: "The Lord saw to it, lest he should be a nuisance to his Church by contention and effrontery of the mouth, whose rattling he formerly so happily advanced."

The Protestant Ministers of Zurich, in response to a book which Luther had written against Zwingli, say: "Prophets and Apostles are zealous for the glory of God, not private honor, nor pertinaciousness and pride. Yet Luther seeks his own, he is pertinacious, he conducts himself with excessive insolence, and in all his corruptions he is for the most part discovered to be of a malignant spirit, which scarcely is found in a friend or a paternal mind." All the disciples of Luther are the same, and if from their books all the boasting, lies, taunting, curses and insults were taken up, they could scarcely be small books, rather they would be great volumes.

As for what pertains to the people, however, there are indeed many bad men in the Catholic Church, but from the heretics none are good. And although this matter is well known to them, who knew the manners on each side, nevertheless they cannot bring themselves to condemn the testimony of Luther, twisted from truth itself. Afterwards, in a commentary on the Gospel for the first Sunday of Advent, he says: "The world becomes more degenerate, there are now men more desirous of vengeance, greedier, more removed from all mercy, more immodest and undisciplined, and more wicked than there were under the papacy." Thus Luther. This testimony is true, wherein there is little dissimilarity from the witness of Jacob Andrew Smideliwi, whose sermon on St. Luke[287] you may find partly in St. Peter Canisius' work, *De Corruptelis Verbi Dei.* Among other things, Smidelwi says about his own Lutherans:

---

[287] *Sermon 4* on ch. 24 of Luke.

"So that the whole world will not recognize them to be Papists, they do not trust in good works, even inwardly they nearly exercise nothing of works. In place of fasting there are feasts, and they are idle in drinking feats of drinking night and day. Where it would behoove one to treat the poor kindly, they strip and flay them. They turn prayers into oaths, blasphemies, and curses of the divine name, and that so desperately, that Christ is not even so blasphemed by the Turks today. At length, in place of humility, pride rules everywhere, as well as wickedness, glorification, and all of this sort of life they say was instituted by the Gospel."[288]

I add even a third witness, that of Erasmus, who both knew their affairs well, and appeared to not altogether abhor their doctrine. In an epistle to Gerardus Geldenhouwer, which he wrote in 1529, he said: "Look around, this evangelical people, and observe whether they indulge less in luxury, lust and money than those do whom you condemn. Bring me the man that this gospel of yours should render from a reveler to a sober man, from cruelty to kindness, from rapaciousness to liberality, from curse to blessing, from unchastity to modesty. I will show you men who have become far worse." See also John Cochlacus in his preface to the book of the deeds and writings of Martin Luther.

---

[288] Peter Canisius, *De Corruptelis Verbi Dei,* bk. 1, ch. 4.

CHAPTER XIV
The Eleventh Mark

THE ELEVENTH Mark is the Glory of Miracles. There are two foundations which must be put forward. One, that miracles are necessary to new faith, or to persuade of an extraordinary mission. Two, that they are efficacious and sufficient, for we shall deduce from the first that there is no true Church with our adversaries, and from the second that it is with us.

Therefore, that miracles are necessary is proved in the first place from the testimony of Scripture. Moses was sent by God to the people, and said: "They will not believe me, and they will not hear my voice."[289] God did not respond that they ought to believe, whether they wish to or not, but he gave him the power of making miracles, and said: "That they might believe that the Lord had appeared to you." etc. And in the New Testament, "Going, preach, saying: 'The kingdom of heaven is at hand. Heal the sick, raise the dead, cleanse the lepers, cast out devils.'"[290] In John we read: "If I had not done works among them, which no other man could do, they would not have sin."[291]

Besides, one who is sent, ought to show testimony of the one who sent him, his authority, otherwise no one is compelled to receive him. However, everyone who is sent to preach, or is sent by God through ordinary prelates, or extraordinarily by God alone, and indeed, the one who is sent through an ordinary prelate, ought to show the testimony of the ordinary prelate, without a doubt, by letters fortified with his seal. One who is sent by God alone, ought to show the seal of God, which is nothing other than miracles. Thus it is said at the end of St. Mark: "These departed and preached

---

[289] Exodus 4.

[290] Matt. 10: 7-8.

[291] John 15: 24.

everywhere with the Lord's help, confirming the sermon and following with signs." Also in Hebrews 2: "Contest God with signs and virtues."

As a sign that this is true, not only does St. Augustine say[292] that miracles were necessary that the world should believe, but even Philip Melanchthon concedes it, for he says that when there is a great darkness, new teachers are called, and miracles are always added by God, that we might know for certain that they were sent by God.[293]

Now what pertains to the second point, that a miracle should be a sufficient testimony, and where there is a miracle, there the true faith is, can be easily shown. Accordingly, true miracles cannot happen, unless by the power of God. Indeed a miracle is so called because it is above the strength of every creature, and therefore is miraculous to all creatures, and besides they are even called the testimonies of God in the Scriptures, as we saw above. Whereby, if something is confirmed by a miracle, it is confirmed by the testimony of God. God however, cannot be a witness to a lie, therefore what is confirmed by a miracle must be true. Moreover, it is not opposed that true miracles do not always happen to confirm faith, but merely to glorify the life of saints. For when miracles happen to show the glory of some saint, those miracles show that such a man was truly holy, although no man may be truly holy without true faith: "Because the just man lives by faith."[294] The same miracles show and confirm true faith.

With these foundations being placed, it will be easy to gather that the true faith is not found among the heathen, Turks, Jews and heretics, for they have no true miracles, and nevertheless, all these preach a new doctrine, and are not sent by ordinary prelates.

On the Pagans, it is known, for only trivial things are read, which can easily be done by a trick or by the demons, such as

---

[292] *De Civitate Dei*, bk 22, ch. 8.

[293] Ch. 3 on Matthew.

[294] Hebrews X.

Valerius Maximus relates,[295] on statues and brutes speaking, or on a Vestal virgin drawing water with a sieve. Cicero reports of an augur who sliced a stone with a razor.[296] Tertulian in his Apologeticus, and St. Augustine in the City of God show how all these things were easily done by demons.[297]

On the Jews after the coming of Christ, it is known that they do not have any miracles, and that one from the pool, which endured while Christ was preaching, afterward was lost.

On the Muslims, St. John Damascene says that Muhammad could prove his law by no testimony. The Qur'an itself confesses the miracles of Christ, but gives for itself a sword: nevertheless in ch. 64, it says once about the moon that it did some miracle, I do not know what since it was not expressed clearly. The expositors, however, say at some time the moon was divided into two parts, then Muhammad received it in his hands and renewed it, then returned it to the sky, but no one saw this miracle, except the author, that is, Muhammad.

Concerning false prophets and heretics, it is no less certain, that they often tried to do miracles, and were always frustrated in their hope. The history of the prophets of Baal is known, who wanted to call down fire from heaven through the invocation of Baal: nevertheless they could not, because the true prophet Elijah effected through the invocation of the true God in that business.[298]

Egesippus wrote that Simon Magus was deluded with equal reasoning, for he tried to rouse a dead man, and fly through the air, but succeeded in nothing.[299] The Manichees tried in vain to heal the sick son of a king, as Epiphanius writes.[300] Cyrol the patriarch of the

---

[295] Valerius Maximus, bk 8.

[296] *De Divinatione*, bk 1.

[297] Tertulian, *Apologeticus*, ch. 22 and 23; St. Augustine, *de Civitate Dei*, bk 10, ch. 16.

[298] 3 Kings, (1 Kings) 18.

[299] Egesippus, *de excidio Hierosol.* Ch. 2.

[300] *De haeresi*, 66.

Arians publicly blinded a certain man, who made himself to look blind and implored aid from him.[301] A certain Eunomianus was conquered by St. Macharius in a contest to raise a dead man.[302] The Monothelite, Polychronius, sweated in vain in the raising of another dead man, as the sixth ecumenical council attests in its public acts, no 15.

The Donatists performed miracles against themselves, as when they threw a vessel of chrism against a rock, which was held up by an angelic hand and could not be broken. On another occasion, they commanded the Eucharist be given to dogs, and they were torn to pieces by the same dogs.[303]

Theodore of Mopsuestia writes on Timothy Aeluro Eutychianus, that many nights he dashed about clothed in a black habit through the cells of the monks, saying that he was an angel sent from God, that he might signify for them, lest they might communicate with Proterius (who was the holy and Catholic bishop of Alexandria), and instead might designate him a bishop in place of Proterius.

Paul the Deacon writes on a certain Iconoclast that was enclosed in a certain tomb, then from there Constantine the Iconoclast began to convey praises upon him in heaven to which he responded, so that, without a doubt, it would be as though their heresies were confirmed.

The same thing is altogether certain on the heretics of our age. For, in the first place, Luther twice tried to perform a miracle: he wished at some time to cast the devil from one of his disciples, but he was in danger lest he be killed by the demon.[304]

Again (as John Cochlaeus writes in his acts of Luther for 1523), Nesenus miserably drowned in the Elba, with the hope of a miracle, Luther tried in vain to recall him to life with empty muttering. On the other hand, although Luther had not succeeded in miracles for

---

[301] Gregory of Tours, *histor., Francorum*, bk. 2 ch. 3.

[302] John Cassian, *Collatione* 15, ch. 3.

[303] Optatus, *contra Parmenianum*, bk. 2.

[304] See Staphylus, who was present for a complete response.

the living, nevertheless after his death he showed a characteristic miracle. For when his dead body was carried in the middle of winter, in such a time when dead bodies are usually preserved for many days, he was closed in the best tin coffin so that he might be buried at Wittenberg. Yet, so foul an odor began to breath, that no one could carry him. Hence they were compelled to leave the body behind on the journey. See the little history on the death of Luther, which is usually joined to Cochlaeus' book on his life and acts.

Felicianus Ninguarda relates another miracle, in his book against Anne of Burgundy, and Lindanus in *Dubitantio*, as well as Alan Copus of a certain minister who, on the borders of Poland and Hungary in the year 1558 willed to raise a man by the name of Matthew, whom he had persuaded to contrive as though he were dead, and in reality he accomplished death.[305] The same story is told concerning Calvin by the same authors, but more completely by Jerome Bolsecus in his life of Calvin, ch. 13, from which we will place a few quotes.

"I ought not pass over his crafty and subtle plot, which he used at that time, when he intended to recall to life a certain man named Bruleus, from the country of Ostunum. For he undertook that he would obtain fame and a name for himself as a holy and glorious prophet of God, and an accomplisher of miracles. This is that history. That man, whom I said was named Bruleus from Ostunum, emigrated to Geneva, and since he and his wife were poor, they sought the favor of Calvin, that being commended to him, they might be made partakers of some savings for the poor. Calvin kindly promised them a subsidy for life if they would not deny a work which he wished to be performed in a certain matter through them. It would be beneficial for the faith, and required great secrecy. In turn they offered themselves to that which he requested of them.

Calvin had instructed that this wretched Bruleus should feign sickness. Then the ministers should commend them to the people in a sermon, that they might assist with prayers and almsgiving that

---

[305] Alan Copus, bk. 6, *Dialogi.*

they might succor their poverty. Not long afterward he put on the face of death and feigned that he was dead. Hence, Calvin being advised secretly, went out for a stroll as if he were ignorant of all these matters; furthermore, accompanied by a great throng of friends, at length he came to Bruleus' house, where he heard the shouts and wailing of the wife, who expressed how miserable and exceedingly desolate she was. He inquired what in the world might be the matter, entered, and suddenly fell on one knee, and the rest of the throng followed. Then Calvin implored with profuse prayers in a deep voice that God would show his power and restore this dead man to life, and that he would will to, so as to declare his glory to all the people, and together make himself (Calvin) manifest in particular, as his grateful servant, and to show that he was truly appointed to the reformation of the ministry of the gospel as well as of the Church. After such prayers, he approached the dead man, and while taking hold of the of the poor man with his hand, he commanded in the name of God that he would rise. Again he repeated, and more frequently the same words even with a deeper elevated voice. What happened? He [Bruleus] neither heard nor spoke, nor roused himself, for he was dead. By the Just judgment of God, therefore, who detests shams and lies, he who feigned death was found truly dead. The wife stirred him in every way, and struck him by every means, and she neither wrenched out a sound nor could effect that he move himself; rather he was all cold, wholly stiff. After this was recognized, she gave forth wailing in earnest and began from the depth of her spirit to attack Calvin, saying he was an imposter, a murderer, a thief, who killed her husband, calling from the order of the matter, in which she exposed the death with clear and loud voice ... However much the servants of Calvin might wish to deny this, it was investigated and sufficiently recognized, and the truth of the matter was proved, nay more, confirmed through the wife herself."[306]

---

[306] Bolseco, *in vita Calvini,* ch. 13.

We can oppose to these what Tertulian says: "If they preach another God, why do they use things and letters of the same, against what they preach? If he is the same, how is he different? Otherwise, let them prove that they are new apostles: let them say Christ descended again, and gave to them the power of displaying the same signs. Therefore, why would I want to advance their virtues, except that which I recognize to be their chief virtue, which is a perverse imitation of the apostles? They raised men from the dead, these newcomers make dead men from the living."[307]

Calvin responds in the preface of the *Institutes* and in other places, that we injure him, because we are demanding miracles from them, while they merely preach the ancient doctrine, and innumerable miracles confirmed by the apostles and martyrs.

On the contrary: for we showed above that their doctrine is new, and opposed to antiquity. Thereupon it is certain that they at least teach something else than ordinary pastors of the Church teach. It is even certain that they are not sent by ordinary pastors, therefore we are not held to receive them, nor can we do so safely, unless they would prove their mission and apostolate with divine testimony.

Calvin responds: John the Baptist was also sent extraordinarily, and nevertheless he made no sign.[308]

But although John himself performed no miracles, nevertheless in that very matter, many and great ones were performed by God. First, that he was born from an old and sterile woman: thereafter, his father became mute, and after his tongue was freed in the birth of his son, which leapt in the womb, which from boyhood lived in desert places. From Luke's gospel, we learn that John was the son of a priest, and hence a priest and an ordinary minister. Besides, he taught nothing against the common doctrine, and did not separate himself from the rest of the priests and people. And although the princes and pharisees hated him, because he preached Christ, nevertheless, when interrogated by Christ, on what they thought

---

[307] *De praescript.*

[308] John 10.

about John the Baptist, they did not dare to reject him.[309] Thereafter, Josephus witnesses that John was held by the Jews to be among the best of men, in view of his justice and righteousness.[310] Wherefore, the Centuriators lie when they say that John was held by the priests and the pharisees as a heretic.[311]

We come now to the second part, and we will show that our Church is the true Church of God from miracles, for there are many well documented ones in each age.

And first, from the eleven centuries, it is from the eleventh volume of the Ecclesiastical History of the Centuriators of Magdeburg; They record all of the miracles from the authors of those times, and in individual centuries they discover the many miracles in confirmation of our dogmas, such as sacramental confession, relics, images, the Eucharist, the Papacy, monasteries, invocation of the saints, etc., and they cite these titles.[312] And although they add on afterward that all of those were illusions of demons, or false stories, nevertheless they assert nothing, which is to say that they prove these miracles are opposed to the gospel of Luther.

It will be beneficial, nevertheless, to briefly record how the Church has been illuminated with miracles in all ages, so that even now we might understand that she is the true Church which is most like antiquity, that is, in which endures this gift. We have in the first century the miracles of Christ and the apostles, which are recorded in the Gospels and Acts.

---

[309] Matthew 21.

[310] Josephus, *Antiquities*, bk. 18, ch. 10.

[311] *Cent. 1*, bk 1, ch. 10, col. 363.

[312] Tomus XI, *Historicae Ecclesiasticae Magdeburgensium*, c. 13.

In the second century we have the miracles of Christian soldiers in the army of Marcus Antoninus, about which you can read in Tertulian, Eusebius and other Fathers.[313]

In the third century, we have the miracles of Gregory Thaumaturgi, which are recorded by St. Basil, St. Gregory, Jerome and Eusebius.[314]

In the fourth century, we have the miracles of Anthony, Hilary, Martin, Nicolas, and others, written by St. Athanasius, Jerome, Sulpitius and others.

In the fifth century, we have many miracles, which Augustine writes down that happened in his time.[315]

In the sixth century, we have miracles, which St. Gregory relates in the dialogue, where he relates the deeds of two Roman Pontiffs, John and Agapetus.[316]

In the seventh century, miracles were done in England by St. Augustine and his companions, on which Gregory relates.[317] Likewise we read about King Oswald through the wood of the cross.[318]

In the eighth century, there are the miracles of St. Cuthbert and John in England, as Bede witnesses in his Ecclesiastical History.

In the ninth century, the miracles of Tharasius, written by Ignatius of Nicaea. Likewise there were other innumerable miracles of every kind done in the city of Soissons in the translation of the relics of St. Sebastian the martyr, which happened in the year 826.

---

[313] Tertulian *ad Scapulum, Apologeticus* , ch. 5; Eusebius *Hist.*, bk 5 ch. 5; Oros, *hist.* Bk 7, ch. 15; the epistle of the emperor, which is joined to the works of Justin Martyr.

[314] St. Basil the Great, *de Spiritu sancto*, ch. 29; Gregory of Nyssa, *Vita*; Jerome, *de Viris Illustribus*; Eusebius, from the version of Ruffinus, bk. 7, ch. 25.

[315] Augustine, *de Civitate Dei*, bk. 22, ch. 8.

[316] Gregory, *Dialogus*, bk. 2, ch. 2 and 3.

[317] Bk. 9, epist., 58; Bede *hist.*, bk. 1, ch. 31.

[318] Bede, *Ibid.*, bk. 3 ch. 2.

These were written in the annals of the Franks with supreme faith by the author, who flourished in that very time.

In the tenth century, the miracles of St. Romauld, written by St. Peter Damian. Also, of King Wenceslaus the king of Bohemia, and Udalrici and Dunstanus, the details of which can be read in Surius.

In the eleventh century, the miracles of king St. Edward who was a virgin, St. Anselm, Pope Gregory VII and others. Thus for the first eleven centuries.

In the twelfth century, St. Malachi and St. Bernard illumined the Catholic Church with miracles. St. Bernard wrote in the life of Malachi, bishop and papal legate, after he had related many of his miracles: "In what kind of the ancient miracles was Malachi not resplendent? If we will look at just a few things, which have been said, he lacked not prophecy, nor revelation, nor the grace of healing, nor the changing of minds, not even, at length, the raising of the dead."

Moreover, St. Bernard, a monk and father of monks, as well as being most devoted to the Roman Pontiffs, shined with many miracles, more than any of the saints whose written lives are extant. For in one day in the Diocese of Constance, it is certain that they gave sight to eleven blind men, cured ten crippled and eighteen lame, as Godfrey writes, who lived with him.[319] Besides all five of these books are so full of miracles, that it would be difficult to begin to count them.

In the thirteenth century, there were many famous Catholics in the Church, particularly St. Francis, whose life was full of miracles, as recorded by St. Bonaventure. Likewise, St. Dominic, whose life, although it was written more carelessly, nevertheless shows for certain that he raised three men from the dead. Others who were famous in the same century with miracles were St. Peter Martyr, and St. Thomas from the order of Preachers and St. Anthony and St. Bonaventure from the Friars minor, whose lives can be read in

---

[319] Gotfridus, *vita Bernardi*, bk. 4, ch. 4.

Antoninus' history.[320] At the end of the century, many famous miracles were done by St. Celestine V, both before and after he was Pope, as Cardinal Cameracensis writes in his life.

In the fourteenth century, there were also many famous for miracles, but especially St. Catharine of Siena, and St. Nicolas of Toledo, whose lives are also recorded by Antoninus in the aforementioned work.

In the fifteenth century, St. Bernadine of Siena and likewise St. Vincent, both living and dead were famous for many miracles, which can be seen from the same Antoninus, even that it is certain that men were raised from the dead through them.[321] The same St. Antoninus was famous for miracles in the same century, and his life is extant with Surius.[322]

In our own century St. Francis of Paul was famous for many miracles, as in the bull of canonization Pope Leo X wrote, which is extant in Surius. Our Blessed Father St. Francis Xavier, a priest from the Society of Jesus, was famous in India for every kind of miracle. It is certain from his Indian letters, which they, who lived with him, were sent to this place, and paralytics, deaf, mute, blind were all cured, the dead were recalled to life, and when he died he was conveyed to the island of Goa from Malacca, and he calmed the sea. Thereupon his body, after 15 months was untouched by death, and found to smell sweetly, although he was covered with lime for many months.[323] There is no doubt that even to this day [1590] he is preserved whole and incorrupt.

These are compared with the life and death of Luther. Luther left a monastery, married after a vow of continence, made war on the Pope; Francis entered a religious order, most diligently kept his vow of continence: obliged himself to the pope by a peculiar vow of obedience, and being sent by him, set out for the farthest shores of

---

[320] *Hist.*, 3 part, tit. 23 and 24.

[321] *Ibid.*, tit. 23, and 38.

[322] Surius (Lorenz Sauer), *de Probatis Sanctorum Historiis.*

[323] –Translator's note: Lime hastens a body's decay.

the world. Certainly these contrary journeys advance, that one or the other of them strayed from the right road. Who can be a better judge than God, who searches the depths and hearts of men? How could God openly express his opinion, by granting to one the singular gift of miracles and by preserving his body apart from the order of nature perpetually incorrupt, while at the same time another that could not raise a fly, and whose body began to rot immediately even apart from the order of nature, and at that in the middle of winter, when all things are stiff with ice, and so rotted that the stench could not be contained within the tin coffin?

Rightly, therefore, does St. Augustine say that he is maintained in the Church by the bonds of miracles.[324] Even Richard of St. Victor dares to say: "O Lord, if we believe something that is an error, we are deceived by you; for these have been confirmed among us by signs and miracles, which could not be done except by you."[325]

Yet, Calvin responds in the preface of the Institutes, and the Centuriators of Magdeburg in each of the Centuries, that the miracles of our saints are either made up or imaginary, or that they do not happen and are falsely told by historians, or if they indeed happened, they were tricks of the devil. Wherefore the Centuriators say, if those matters are true, which Sulpitius writes about the miracles of St. Martin, then no doubt Martin was a necromancer.[326] And indeed, they do not prove the miracles are false, they merely say so.

Moreover, they endeavor to prove they were the deceits of devils from the fact that, true miracles confirm the gospel, as is certain from the last chapter of Mark; these, so they say, overturn the gospel and confirm idolatry, that is, the cult of relics and images, the invocation of the saints, the Mass, and other things of that kind. They add secondly, that from the miracles there is no supreme

---

[324] *De Utilitate Credendi*, ch. 17; *Contra epistolam fundamenti*, ch. 4.

[325] *De Trinitate*, bk. 1, ch. 2.

[326] *Cent. 5*, c. 10, col. 1393.

argument to prove truth faith, which they try to prove by four arguments.

First, because even Antichrist will perform signs and great wonders.[327]

Second, because Augustine says the Donatists were not to be believed even though they did miracles, where they called them in contempt "wonder workers."[328] Moreover, after he taught the miracles of the Donatists were not to be believed, he adds not even the miracles of the Catholics: "Such miracles, whatever they are, happen in the Catholic Church, therefore they must be approved, because they are done in the Catholic Church: The Church itself, however is not manifested, because these happen in it."[329]

Thirdly, that formerly at the tomb of Jeremiah miracles were performed, which were the works of demons. There it is clear, because they were done for the advantage of those who were worshiping Jeremiah for a God, with sacrifices and divine honors.

Fourth, because it is certain from Suetonius that the Emperor Vespasian gave sight to a blind man, and at one time healed a lame man. Likewise from Socrates,[330] the Centuriators advance the miracle of Paul the Novation Bishop,[331] although what they collected was not true religion, in which Vespasian or Novatian worshiped.

But we shall respond to each point. To the first, since they deny miracles to happen, which are related by our historians, I respond: They deny it shamelessly. It is foolish to believe Calvin and Illyricus more when they write on the ancient histories, when they were not there, than Bernard, Bonaventure or Anthony, who were there. Besides, as St. Augustine responded to the pagans who denied the histories of our miracles, "If it is allowed to deny former miraculous deeds without any reason, then not only shall our faith in all books

[327] Matt. 24; Apocalypsus 13; 2 Thess. 2.

[328] *Tractatus in* Joann, no 13.

[329] *De Unitate Ecclesiae*, ch. 16.

[330] Hist. Bk 7.

[331] Cent. 5, ch. 13, col. 1463.

perish and be abolished, but even of every other religion. Indeed, some gods are held, with works and wonders, written by learned men, they persuade the world of their divinity, whether true or false."[332]

To the second, when they say they are tricks of the demons, I respond: In the first place this is an old calumny, for in the same way the scribes and pharisees spoke about the miracles of Christ, and the pagans on the miracles of the martyrs, as they usually called them magicians and necromancers. Even the Arians, Eunomians and Vigilantians spoke thus about the miracles of Catholics, as Ambrose, Jerome and St. Victor attest.[333] Thereupon, it has no probability that St. Martin, Francis and certain others, who were very simple men, might have used magical arts.

But they say these miracles overturn the gospel. I respond: Indeed they do, the gospel of Calvin, that is not of Christ; furthermore they prove what these so boldly affirm. Nor is it less easy to prove the last argument, by which they prove miracles do not make certain faith.

To the first I respond. The miracles of Antichrist will be lies, as the Apostle says,[334] they are not true and solid, but appearances and wonders of men, nevertheless, not absolutely miracles, such as can be done through a craft of the demon. It is clear from the Apocolypse 13, where for the greatest miracles of Antichrist it is proposed that he will make fire come down from heaven, and that an image of a beast might talk. This is easy for the devil, however, as is obvious. But the miracles of the saints are giving sight to the blind, curing the lame, raising the dead: which they cannot do except by the power of the one whom we sing of in Psalm 135, "Who alone does great wonders."

---

[332] *De Civitate Dei*, bk. 10, ch. 18.

[333] Ambrose, *Serm. De ss. Gervasio et Prothasio*; Jerome, *cont. Vigilantium*; Victor, *de persequut. Wandalica*, bk. 2.

[334] 2 Thessalonians 2.

To the second, I say: The miracles of the Donatists which Augustine condemned, were not such miracles such as are of the saints, but certain secret visions only, which they boasted that they had seen without any witness; such was the vision of Zwingli, who in the book titled, *A subsidy on the Eucharist*, he says he saw a spirit, but could not discern whether it was white or black; such was even the vision which is related in a book titled *Querela*, or *somnium Lutheri*, where Luther is related to have appeared to certain Lutherans, complained of them with sad countenance, because they were his disciples but were meaning to desert his doctrine in short order. Therefore, not without reason does St. Augustine call these sort of miracles fables.

On the other hand, Augustine makes the most of true miracles, as is clear from the City of God, where he brings in great miracles against the pagans, made by relics of the saints, especially of Stephen the first martyr.[335]

To that, which Augustine says, the Church is not shown from miracles but from the Scriptures, I respond. St. Augustine says the contrary in another place,[336] where he says "The Church can be shown from miracles, not from the Scriptures, rather, the Scriptures are shown from the Church." Lest, therefore, he might be opposed to himself, it must be said in each place he speaks hypothetically. Because, indeed, the Manichees admitted miracles, and denied the Scriptures (for they said the Old Testament was from the devil, and the new to be corrupted by falsifications), accordingly Augustine proved the Church from miracles, thus Augustine proceeds in another fashion against the Donatists, and from the Scriptures proves the Church, thereupon through the Church wishes miracles to be judged.

However, it must be observed that the Church is shown by miracles, and miracles from the Church, but in a different kind of proof; just as a cause is shown from its effect, and from the cause the

---

[335] *De Civitate Dei*, bk. 22, ch. 8.

[336] *Contra Epist. Fundamenti*, ch. 4 and 5.

effect. For from miracles the Church is proved, not with respect to evidence, or certitude of the thing, but in so far as to the evidence, or certitude of credibility. The reason of which is, because before the approval of the Church, it is not evident or certain concerning any miracle with the certitude of faith, it may be a true miracle; nevertheless it is such that evidently it should make an affair credible. And indeed, because it might not be evident, certainly because then the faith should be evident. That it might not be certain with the certitude of faith, is obvious, because it is not certain with certitude for us, to which it cannot be the basis of falsity, that it was not the illusion of a demon. Indeed, although the demon cannot make true miracles, nevertheless it can apparently do even the greatest.

Why, therefore (you ask) are they held to believe in the preaching of Christ, those who say his miracles? I respond: Because a man cannot be saved without the faith of Christ: and therefore he is held to receive that faith as a necessary means to his salvation. However, God refused to force men to believe unbelievable things, but only when through miracles, and similar motives was faith made credible: but from the Church the miracle is proved, in so far as it provides certitude of the thing, because when the Church declares a miracle happened, it is a true miracle, and we are certain that it is thus.

To the third, I say: it is a lie of Calvin that the people worshiped Jeremiah with sacrifices and divine honors. For he brings no witness of this affair, except what he places in the margin (Jerome in the preface to Jeremiah). Besides, neither in the preface of Jerome for Jeremiah, translated by him, nor in the preface of the commentary of Jerome, is any mention made of this history. Besides that, it is recorded in certain other prefaces in the bibles of Benedict, prefixed to Jeremiah to what appears Calvin looked at. But this is not from Jerome, nor is any mention made therein of sacrifices or divine honors; but only that some miracles happened at his tomb. At length, Epiphanius and Isidore, in the life of Jeremiah, say that miracles happened, but they say nothing on sacrifices and divine honors.

I respond to the fourth: Neither a truly blind man, nor a lame one were cured by Vespasian. For as Tacitus writes, the doctors asked whether the plague was curable: they responded it was curable. He said: "The doctors disagreed in different ways, this man's power of sight was not wholly consumed, and if they could drive out the obstruction, if a healthy force might be applied upon the crook in the fallen limbs, he can be made whole."[337] Therefore it is no miracle, if the sickness is naturally curable, the works of the devil were cured. Add what Tertulian teaches in the *Apologeticus*, that it is believable that every plague was from the devil, who causing trouble in one man's eye, and another's shin, would impede the use of the members, and in the end, it would appear to be the healed when in fact they had ceased to harm them.[338]

To the last, I offer a response concerning the miracle of Novatian: the miracle was not in confirmation of Novatian's faith, but of Catholic baptism. Truly, Socrates writes on the miracle, that when a certain Jewish impostor came to the Novatian bishop, Paul, for the purpose of being baptized by him, so as to mock his own baptism, immediately all the water of the holy font vanished. But this was not a miracle of the error of Novation, but is clearly of the true baptism, wherein the same Socrates adds that it was recognized shortly after, that he was a Jew who had already been baptized in a catholic rite by Atticus, the bishop of Constantinople. Therefore, since God refused baptism to be so mocked, which is rightly maintained in the Church, he did not permit the Jewish impostor to be baptized again by the heretical bishop.

---

[337] Tacitus, *Hist.*, bk. 4.

[338] *Apologeticus*, ch. 22.

CHAPTER XV
The Twelfth Mark

THE TWELFTH Mark is the Light of Prophecy. Just as Christ promised in the last chapter of Mark the gift of miracles, so also does he promise the gift of prophecy, by means of Peter, in Acts 2 explaining the second chapter of Joel, which certainly is the greatest. Since it is certain, that no man can know the contingencies of things to come except for God: "Announce what is coming in the future, and we will know that you are gods."[339] And on the other hand, it was placed as a mark of false doctrine that a prophet would predict something, and it would not happen.[340]

Now among the heathen and the heretics, there were no true prophecies, but many false ones, unless by chance it came about in testimony of our faith, as were the prophecies of the Sybills and Balam. Albeit the heathen had many oracles of Apollo, nevertheless these were either ambiguous when Apollo in reality didn't know what might happen, or they preached what the demons were about to do; or those things which were beginning to come about they announced to the ignorant as things to come; or at length they preached those things which happen from natural causes unknown to us; that is by those things according to a greater subtlety of nature.[341]

The heretics also, as often as they wished to predict something were deceived. Clearly that is the case with the false prophets of the Old Testament.[342] In the New Testament period, at one time there was a man named Montanus, who wanted to be viewed as a prophet

[339] Isaiah XLI.

[340] Deuteronomy 18.

[341] See St. Athanasius, *Vita S. Antonii*; St. Augustine, *de divinatione daemonum*; and Theodoret, *de Oraculis.*

[342] 3 Kings (1 Kings) 22.

with two prophetesses Prisca and Maximilla, and they preached wars, and I do not know what other things to come; but the contrary happened, as Eusebius records.[343]

In our times, Luther, whom the Lutherans resolutely call the Apostle of Germany, predicted it would come to pass that if he preached his doctrine for another two years, the Pope, Cardinals, Bishops, monks, nuns, towers, bell towers, the Mass, etc. would all vanish, and nevertheless he preached after that not two, but nearly twenty two years; he died in the year 1546, and nevertheless the Pope, Cardinals, Bishops, monks, etc. did not vanish.[344] Cochlaeus related on Thomas of Munster, who called himself Gideon, and armed numberless peasants against the princes of Germany: he predicted that certain victory was theirs, and moreover, in the morning they would remove all the throng of war-like tormentors. Instead, a little after they were slaughtered, and Thomas was taken and struck with an axe. Cochleaus relates further, that Lutheran prophets constantly asserted, that in a year the day of the last judgment was coming, and so marked the very day that they did not wish to seed or plow.[345] Nevertheless these were discovered to be lies.

But in the Catholic Church, besides the prophets of the old Testament, and those who were in the first five centuries from the coming of Christ, there were even true prophets and monks attached to the Roman Pontiff in later ages when, according to the Lutherans, the Church had perished. St. Gregory writes thus about St. Benedict: "Benedict reproved the king for his conduct, and he also foretold in a few words all the things which were going to happen: 'You do many wicked things, you have done many wicked things, now you rest for a time from iniquity. Indeed you will go to Rome, going across the sea, reigning for nine years, you will die in the tenth.'"[346]

---

[343] Eusebius, *Hist.* Bk 5, ch. 16 and 18.

[344] Cochleus, *in actis Lutheri anni 1525.*

[345] *Ibid.*, anni 1533.

[346] *Dialog.* Bk 2, ch. 15.

On St. Bernard, it is written in his life, that he predicted to four men conversion, three thinking nothing of this, the fourth even less about the matter; all the things, as he had predicted, happened. But it is altogether wondrous, that the same thing is told about a certain nobleman; one of his sons asked St. Bernard that he would pray for his conversion, and the saint responded: "Fear not, I will bury him a real monk here in Clairvaux." How many prophecies are in this one statement? For both that he would at some time become a monk, and that he would persevere in the monastic order until death, and piously and uprightly was going to finish his last day before Bernard himself, and in Clairvaux, as well as that he would be buried by the hands of Bernard himself. There are six different prophecies among themselves, and nevertheless, all things were fulfilled with the singular providence of God. Thus indeed the author continues: "And he became a perfect monk, and was buried by his holy Father (as he had predicted) in Clairvaux: just as indeed he could not die with him away, he was sick for five months, and very quickly, rather immediately having the next response of death in himself, he held fast until his holy Father returned, who, as he once had promised, handed him over to burial.

St. Bonaventure writes on the life of St. Francis, that when the Christian army was going to join battle with the Saracens on a certain day, he warned the generals not to fight on that day, for it had been revealed to him by God, that the victory of the enemy was going to befall them on that day. But when the generals condemned the warnings of St. Francis, the Christians were cut down and scattered in an unheard of slaughter. Many other things of this sort can be added; indeed there are almost no holy men honored in the Church who were not glorified with this gift, together with miracles. But these few places will suffice.

CHAPTER XVI
The Thirteenth Mark

THE THIRTEENTH Mark is the Confession of our Adversaries. Truly, the force of truth is so great, that it even compels our adversaries to give testimony to it now and again, according to that which is read in Deuteronomy: "The Lord our God is not ours as their gods, and our enemies are judges."[347] Now, no Catholics have ever been found to have praised, or approved the doctrine, or the life of any of the heathen, or the heretics. Indeed we know there is only one true faith, and without it, there is no true justice. Therefore we firmly assert, that all err who do not follow our doctrine. The Pagans, however, or the Jews, Turks and heretics do not always speak thus about us.

From the Pagans there are many testimonies. Pliny the Younger wrote to the Emperor Trajan, that Christians detest every vice, and live in a most holy manner, and he could only reprove them in this alone, that they too easily poured out their life for their God, and because they rise in the hours before dawn to sing praises to Christ.[348] Tertulian witnesses, the Pagans refused to examine a case of Christians, but condemned them without discussion, for they knew that no evil would be found in them. Moreover, he affirms that those emperors who are reckoned to have been the best, favored Christians such as Marcus Aurelius, Vespasian, Antoninus Pius, etc., while those who were moved to persecute them are held to have been the worst emperors, even by the heathen themselves, as Nero and Domitian.[349]

There also exists a letter of the emperor Marcus Aurelius, wherein he witnesses when his army labored in Germany with great

---

[347] Deut. 32.

[348] Pliny the Younger, epist. Ad Trajanum, bk 10.

[349] Apologetics, ch. 1 and 2; ch. 5 and 6.

thirst for five days, and the Romans were surrounded by such a multitude of Germans, that it was impossible to escape by human strength. Then he had recourse to his ancestral gods, but in vain; thereafter some Christian soldiers, who were in the army, asked that they might pray to their God also. Next, they had scarcely gotten on their knee to pray when immediately a most joyful rain descended from heaven upon the Romans; but upon their enemies fire and hail were mixed. Tertulian calls this epistle to mind in the *Apologeticus*, and it has recently been discovered and printed in the works of Justin.

Thereupon, St. Anthony, St. Hilary and St. Martin were held in honor and reverence even by the Pagans, as Athanasius, Jerome and Sulpitius write in their lives.

We have from the Jews, in the first place testimony from Josephus, who affirms Christ was more than a man, and truly the Messiah.[350] Philo wrote a distinguished book on the praises of those Christians, who were living in Egypt under Mark the Evangelist. The aforementioned book was written on the praise of Christians, not on some Jewish sect, as the Centuriators reckon.[351] Many other writers reference this work.[352]

Muhammad in the Qur'an, chapter 2, teaches that Christians are saved, and in chapter 4 calls Christ the greatest of the prophets, and had the very soul of God. St. Bonaventure also records, that the Sultan of Egypt, although a Muslim, held St. Francis in the highest honor and reverence, although he knew that he was Christian and Catholic.

The same can be said concerning the heretics. For St. Gregory writes that St. Benedict, a Catholic, was held in such great honor by Totila, an Arian king, that he called him a true servant of God and a

---

[350] *Antiquities*, bk. 18, ch. 6. –Translator's note: Modern scholarship has seriously questioned whether this particular passage of Josephus is authentic, but no such doubt existed in the 16th century.

[351] *Cent. 1* bk 2, ch. 3, col. 18.

[352] Eusebius, *Histor.*, bk. 1, ch. 16; Epiphanius, *Haeres.*, 29; Jerome, *de viris illustribus* on Philo,; Sozomen, bk. 1 ch. 12; Bede in the preface on Mark.

prophet.[353] Even Luther when he had already become a heretic, wrote thus against the Anabaptists, who rejected in hatred of the Pope the baptism of infants: "We affirm, that there are many good Christians under the papacy, nay more that every good Christian even from there comes down to us. By all means we affirm in the papacy there are the true holy Scripture, true baptism, the true sacrament of the altar, true keys for the remission of sins, the true office of preaching, true catechesis, as are the Lord's prayer, the Ten Commandments and articles of faith. I say, moreover, there is true christianity under the papacy, the true center of christianity."[354] Where if he grants the center to us, certainly he preserves nothing for himself, except for the skin or the shell.

Calvin calls St. Bernard a pious writer.[355] But certainly Bernard was a papist, and no pious man is without true faith. Melanchthon, in his defense of the Augsburg confession, calls Bernard, Dominic and Francis saints, which Luther also did in his book on the need to abrogate the Mass, near the end. Likewise, as Cochlaeus writes in the acts of Luther for the year 1531, when peace was settled, after many battles amongst Catholics and heretics in Switzerland, the heretics wrote that they wished to forgive their confederates for having remained in their true, unshakeable, and Catholic faith; but the Catholics wrote, that they wished to forgive their confederates for remaining in their faith, they added nothing about true unshakeable and catholic.[356]

---

[353] *Dialogue*, bk. 2, ch. 15.

[354] *Contra Anabaptistas.*

[355] *Institut.*, ch. 10 § 17.

[356] *Concordiae*,, art. 1.

CHAPTER XVII
The Fourteenth Mark

THE FOURTEENTH Mark is the Unhappy Exit, or End, of those who oppose the Church. Although God punishes them and scourges them, nevertheless at length he casts the chaff into the fire. "All ye nations praise His people, for he avenges the blood of his servants, and brings retribution upon their enemies."[357]

On the miserable end of Pharaoh, the first persecutor of the Church, we read in Exodus XIV. On Dathan and Abiron the first schismatics, we read about in Numbers 16; on Jezebel, in 4 (2) Kings IX; on Antiochus, 2 Machabees 9; on Pilate, that he had killed himself as Eusebius writes.[358] He also relates the slaughter of the Jews which Josephus more broadly relates in his work *On the Jewish War*. Concerning Herod the Great, Josephus writes that he died gushing out worms since he had first killed his wife, and then his sons, and thereupon wished he had killed himself.[359] On Herod the Tetrarch, Josephus adds that hc lost his kingdom and was relegated to perpetual exile where he lived most miserably.[360] On his daughter Herodias, see Nicephorus.[361] On Herod Agrippa see Acts 12. As for Nero, Domitian and the other emperors who persecuted Christians, all were cruelly killed, either by themselves or by others, or certainly perished miserably, as is certain from all the chronicles and histories. For Trajan was struck with a dreadful paralysis, and together with that died from dropsy. Diocletian gave up his empire on account of resentment, that he could not destroy Christians. Maximianus and Maximinus were struck with such dreadful sufferings that even the

[357] Deut. 32.

[358] Eusebius, *Hist.*, bk. 2, ch. 7.

[359] Josephus, *Antiquitat.*, bk. 17, ch. 9.

[360] *Ibid*,, bk. 18, ch. 14.

[361] Bk. 1 ch. 20.

heathen doctors said it was a divine plague.[362] Maxentius perished in a river and left behind a bloodless victory to Constantine.[363]

We come to the Heresiarchs and Apostates. Simon Magus, when he wished to fly, was knocked down by the prayers of St. Peter, broke his legs, and shortly after died with supreme ignominy.[364]

Manes was flayed alive by the king of Persia, not on account of faith, but because while trying to heal the son of the king he killed him.[365]

Montanus, Theodotus and their prophetesses killed themselves by their own snares.[366] The Donatists indeed threw the Eucharist to dogs, and were torn to pieces by the same dogs, as we quoted previously.

Arius wished to enter into a Church, but after a sudden movement of his stomach he went to the public toilets, and together with excrement all his intestines and his soul poured out.[367]

Julian the Apostate was killed by divine retribution, and lacked even a common burial; for the earth was opened of its own will, and he was swallowed, as St. Gregory Nazianzen writes in an oration that is found with Athanasius.

The Arian, Valens, who succeeded in the persecution of Julian, was burned alive by the Goths who were also Arians.[368]

Nestorius miserably died with his impious tongue consumed by worms. [369] Hunericus the king of the Vandals, an Arian and

---

[362] See Eusebius in his Chronicle, and bk. 9 *histor.*, last chapter.

[363] Eusebius bk. 9, c. 9 from the version of Ruffinus.

[364] Egesippus, *de exicidio hierosolymitano*, bk. 3, ch. 2; Arnobius, bk. 2 *contra gentes.*

[365] Epiphanius, *haeres.*, 66.

[366] Eusebius, *Hist.,* bk 5, ch. 16.

[367] Athanasius, *orat.1 contra Arianos*; Ruffinus, *Hist.,* bk 10, ch. 13.

[368] Ruffinus, *histor.*, bk. 11, ch. 13.

[369] Evagrius, bk 1 hist. Ch. 7.

persecutor of the Church, was consumed with worms gushing through his whole body.[370]

The Emperor Anastasius, the patron of the Monophysite Heretics, was struck by lightning and died, as Cedrenus, Zonaras and Paul the Deacon write on his life. In the time of the Emperor Leo the Iconoclast, pestilence followed the burning of images in the forum of Constantinople, which killed three hundred thousand people.[371]

Luther was taken up by a sudden death. For though he was happy and healthy and took up a splendid and rich supper in the evening, challenging all to a laugh with his jokes, nevertheless he died the same night. See Cochlaeus in the life of Luther.

Zwingli was cut down in war against Catholics, and a little after, his spiritual brother Oecolampadius of Basel, although he had gone to bed healthy in the evening, was discovered dead in his bed in the morning by his wife.[372] Andre Carolstadt was infected by a demon, as the ministers of Basel wrote in an epistle, which they published on the death of Carolstadt.

John Calvin was consumed by worms, and expired just as Antiochus, Herod, Maximinus and Hunericus, as Jerome Bolsecus witnesses in his life. Bolsecus[373] adds, that he died invoking demons, blaspheming and cursing.

---

[370] Victor bk 3.

[371] Mattheus Palmerius, *Chronica*, year 1241.

[372] Cochlaeus in *actis Lutheri*, anno 1531.

[373] It should be noted that Bolsecus (Bolsec), from whom St. Robert get's his information on these points, is prone to exaggeration. Bellarmine was a wise enough scholar to leave out the less savory accusations of Bolsecus. Moreover, modern scholars question some of his accusations. Nevertheless, the biographers of Calvin do not record this episode. -Translator

CHAPTER XVIII
The Fifteenth Mark

THE LAST Mark is the Temporal Happiness, divinely conferred upon those who defend the Church. Catholic princes have never so adhered to God from the heart as when they easily triumph over the enemy. In the first place, the victories in the Old Testament of Abraham, Moses, Joshua, Gideon, Samuel, David, Hezechiah, Josiah, and the Machabees are known. In the New Testament, Constantine, who was the first among the emperors to defend the Church, in that he conquered Maxentius in almost the same way as Moses did Pharaoh.[374] Augustine adds: "The Emperor Constantine was filled with so many earthly rewards, that no one is heard to desire the like, not by praying to demons, but worshiping the true God. One Augustus held and defended the whole Roman world. He was most victorious in administration and waging war. He succeeded above all in overthrowing tyrants. Old, he died from sickness and age, leaving behind sons as emperors."[375]

On Theodosius the Elder, St. Augustine also wrote that he was truly Catholic and pious, so much so that he fortuitously succeeded in everything, even in battle, the weapons of the enemies would fall back upon their authors, with God's aid.[376] Theodoret adds that the apostles, Sts. John and Philip, appeared on white horses in the same battle fighting for the emperor Theodosius.[377]

On Honorious, it is certain he was very attached to the Roman Pontiff, as is clear from his letters to Pope Boniface. St. Augustine writes that God so fought for him, that in one battle more than 100,000 Goths were laid low, and king Radagasius himself was

---

[374] Eusebius, *Hist.*, bk. 9, ch. 9.

[375] Augustine, *De Civit. Dei*, bk. 5, ch. 25.

[376] *Ibid.*, ch. 26.

[377] Theodoret, bk. 5, *Hist.*, ch. 24.

captured with his sons and killed, while hardly a man was wounded or killed from the Romans.[378]

On Theodosius, the younger Socrates writes, that while his army was fighting with barbarians, meanwhile he was absent in the city in prayer with God, and around 100,000 Saracens were led by angels into the Euphrates, and perished miserably.

Justinian the Elder, while he was Catholic, most happily conquered, so that Italy, Africa and many other provinces were restored to the Roman Empire, as is clear from Evagrius.[379] But after he became a heretic, and wished to propose an edict that his heresy must be accepted, soon he was taken up by a sudden death, and freed the Church from a great fear, as the same Evagrius writes.[380]

Heraclius also, as can be recognized from John Zonara and other historians, while he was Catholic, carried back victory over the Persians, and recovered the cross of the Lord, when Roman affairs looked exceedingly desperate. But when he fell into the Monothelite heresy, all those things turned out unhappily, and he was cut down by an unheard of plague.

Likewise, it is certain from the histories of the Greeks, that the emperors of the east from that time, wherein on account of the tearing apart of images, separated themselves from the Roman Church, and day by day deteriorated more and more, until at length they nearly lost their empire. But in the west, it is manifestly gathered from the histories of the Latins, that their emperors flourished more and more, or less as they were more or less attached to the Roman Church.

In the time of Urban II, about the year of our Lord 1098, Christians, who were in a holy war decreed by the Pope for the recovery of Jerusalem, were in extreme desperation at Antioch, in that a numberless army of Turks and Persians were present, whilst they were too few, and daily exhausted by hunger, so that even very

---

[378] *De Civitate Dei*, bk. 5, ch. 23.

[379] *Histor.*, bk. 4, ch. 16.

[380] *Ibid.*, bk. 4, last chapter.

strong men leaned upon their staffs, and had but a few horses. It was so bad, that the general Godfrey, used a borrowed horse, and many princes were compelled to fight on donkeys. At length God revealed where the holy lance might be, and this being born before them, gave them victory in battle, so that they killed 100,000 Turks, and from their ranks hardly four thousand fell. Even a light rain divinely fell upon them, which added strength to their souls and bodies. At length three holy men appeared from heaven fighting for them.[381]

In the time of Innocent III, 100,000 Albigensian Heretics were slaughtered in battle by 8,000 Catholics, as Aemilius Paulus records.[382]

In our own times, in the year 1531, five battles began for the Catholic faith in Switzerland with Swiss Heretics, and the Catholics always conquered, although they were inferior in number and arms.[383]

Charles V reported victory by a divine miracle over the Lutherans in the year 1547.

In France and the Netherlands Catholics brought back many victories over the Heretics, and not without a miracle. Nay more, the heretics were hardly ever superior when fought in battle. Moreover, these on the marks of the Church, and on all this disputation, have been said for the sake of brevity.

LAUS DEO, VIRGINIQUE MATRI MARIAE.

---

[381] See Paul Aemilius, bk. 4; William of Tyre, bk. 6, near the end; and Dodechinus, the continuator of Marianus Scotus.

[382] Aemilius Paulus, *Historiae Francorum*, bk. 6.

[383] See John Cochlaeus in the acts of Luther, for the year 1531.

Made in United States
Orlando, FL
23 December 2024

56480808R00293